Australian Music and Modernism, 1960–1975

Australian Music and Modernism, 1960–1975

Michael Hooper

BLOOMSBURY ACADEMIC
NEW YORK • LONDON • OXFORD • NEW DELHI • SYDNEY

BLOOMSBURY ACADEMIC
Bloomsbury Publishing Inc
1385 Broadway, New York, NY 10018, USA
50 Bedford Square, London, WC1B 3DP, UK
29 Earlsfort Terrace, Dublin 2, Ireland

BLOOMSBURY, BLOOMSBURY ACADEMIC and the Diana logo are
trademarks of Bloomsbury Publishing Plc

First published in Great Britain 2019
Paperback edition first published 2021

Copyright © Michael Hooper, 2019

For legal purposes the Acknowledgments on p. xiv constitute
an extension of this copyright page.

Cover design: Louise Dugdale
Cover image © Echuca Landscape II (1966) by Fred Williams.
Courtesy of Lyn Williams and the Art Gallery of New South Wales

All rights reserved. No part of this publication may be reproduced or
transmitted in any form or by any means, electronic or mechanical,
including photocopying, recording, or any information storage or retrieval
system, without prior permission in writing from the publishers.

Bloomsbury Publishing Inc does not have any control over, or responsibility for,
any third-party websites referred to or in this book. All internet addresses given
in this book were correct at the time of going to press. The author and publisher
regret any inconvenience caused if addresses have changed or sites have
ceased to exist, but can accept no responsibility for any such changes.

A catalog record for this work is available from the Library of Congress.

ISBN: HB: 978-1-5013-4818-1
PB: 978-1-5013-8146-1
ePDF: 978-1-5013-4820-4
eBook: 978-1-5013-4819-8

Typeset by Integra Software Services Pvt. Ltd.

To find out more about our authors and books visit
www.bloomsbury.com and sign up for our newsletters.

For Ellen

Contents

List of Examples viii
List of Figures xi
List of Tables xii
Permissions xiii
Acknowledgements xiv

Introduction: Australian Music Now 1
1 The Formation of an Academic Discourse of Australian Music 11
2 Infrastructure for New Music, Serial Technique and Don Banks's *String Quartet* (1975) 31
3 Richard Meale I: Sydney 61
4 Nigel Butterley: Australian Music and Britain 93
5 Peter Sculthorpe: Australian Music and Nationalism 133
6 Richard Meale II: Adelaide 163
7 Landscapes in Painting and Literature: Lumsdaine and Sculthorpe 205

Notes 240
Bibliography 288
Index 301

Examples

2.1	Banks's row forms for *String Quartet*	48
2.2	Banks, *String Quartet*, bars 1–6	50
2.3	Banks, *String Quartet*, bars 15–19, annotated with the serial structure	51
2.4	Banks, *String Quartet*, bars 164–7	52
2.5	Banks, *String Quartet*, bars 76–88, annotated with the serial structure	54
2.6	Banks, *String Quartet*, bars 31–41, showing the first durationally serial section	57
2.7	Banks, *String Quartet*, bars 255–62, the beginning of the work's second section	59
3.1	Meale, *Homage to Garcia Lorca*, bars 1–4	76
3.2	The opening of the 'Postlude', bars 1–4	78
3.3	The second section of the 'Postlude', bars 26–9	79
3.4	Meale, *Clouds Now and Then*, bars 1–5	83
3.5	Meale, *Clouds Now and Then*, bars 29–34	86
3.6	A condensed version of the organ's pitch material in Meale's *Very High Kings*, bars 1–16	87
3.7	Meale, *Clouds Now and Then*, bars 49–59, 'Section C', annotated with three possible structures	88
4.1	Butterley, *Laudes*, 'I', bars 1–8	99
4.2	Butterley, *Laudes*, 'II', bars 1–12, annotated with serial structures	101
4.3	The connections between long-held pitches in the bars after the section that begins in bar 8 of *Laudes*' second movement	104
4.4	Butterley, *Laudes*, beginning of 'III'	104
4.5	Butterley, String Quartet, bars 1–14	111
4.6	The unfolding of register, measured in semitones, in the chords from one bar before Figure F	114
4.7	Butterley, String Quartet, 'II', final 8 bars	114
4.8	Butterley, String Quartet, 'II', opening section	116
4.9	Butterley, *Fire in the heavens*, bars 104–7, the lyrical music	130
5.1	Sculthorpe, *Irkanda IV*, bars 1–5	136
5.2	'Ketjak' in Sculthorpe's String Quartet No. 8, 'II', bars 1–12	139
6.1	The derivation of the pitch material for Meale's *Coruscations*	167

6.2	An early sketch for Meale's *Coruscations*	168
6.3	Meale, *Coruscations*, p. 1	169
6.4	Webern's Op. 27/ii, bar 21, used by Boulez as example 6 in *Boulez on Music Today*	170
6.5	Meale, *Coruscations*, p. 6	171
6.6	Meale's sketch for *Coruscations*, showing his early stages of working with the sonorities	172
6.7	Meale, *Coruscations*, p. 10, the reprise of the opening	174
6.8	A typeset version of the sketch for the ending of Meale's *Coruscations*, and the final score, with the different pitches annotated	175
6.9	A sketch for Meale's *Coruscations*, and the final score, with the different clefs annotated	176
6.10	A sketch for the beginning of Meale's *Coruscations*, and the final score	177
6.11	Meale, *Incredible Floridas*, 'I', bars 1–8	184
6.12	Meale, *Incredible Floridas*, 'I', bars 21–5, melody	185
6.13	Meale, *Incredible Floridas*, 'I', bars 26–31, violin and cello	185
6.14	Showing D in relation to the midpoint of the cluster	186
6.15	Meale, *Incredible Floridas*, 'II', bars 1–10	187
6.16	Meale, *Incredible Floridas*, 'II', bars 28–33	187
6.17	Meale, *Incredible Floridas*, 'III', bars 1–3, with the pitch relationships annotated	189
6.18	Meale, *Incredible Floridas*, 'IV', bars 1–6, with the pitch structures annotated	190
6.19	Meale's sketch of the matrix for *Incredible Floridas*	191
6.20	Meale's sketch showing his serial workings for *Incredible Floridas*	193
6.21	Meale, *Incredible Floridas*, 'IV', bars 23–31, showing the interface of triadic and serial music	194
6.22	Meale, *Incredible Floridas*, 'IV', bars 48–52, with the pitch structures annotated	195
6.23	Meale, *Incredible Floridas*, 'IV', bars 53–8, with the serial structures annotated	195
6.24	Meale, *Incredible Floridas*, 'IV', bars 65–70, with the pitch structures annotated	196
6.25	Meale, String Quartet No. 1, pp. 1–2	200
6.26	Meale, String Quartet No. 1, 'II', showing the cloud of harmonics through which a single line is played	203
7.1	Lumsdaine, *Aria for Edward John Eyre*, bars 191–203	210

7.2	Sculthorpe, *Red Landscape*, bars 1–18	229
7.3	Sculthorpe, *Landscape II*, bars 1–12	231
7.4	Sculthorpe, *Music for Japan*, p. 1	234
7.5	The pitch content of the twelve chords from Figure 2 of Sculthorpe's *Music for Japan*	235
7.6	*Music for Japan*, from Figure 8, showing an instance of Sculthorpe's use of Nono's 'all-interval wedge'	236

Figures

6.1	A P/I matrix for Meale's *Incredible Floridas*	192
6.2	The conjunction of ic1/5 and 'major thirds' (ic4) at bar 50 of *Incredible Floridas*	194
7.1	The matrix for Lumsdaine's *Aria for Edward John Eyre*, annotated to show possible paths used to generate the pitch material for the harp	214
7.2	Frederick McCubbin's *The Pioneer*	218
7.3	Fred Williams's *Echuca Landscape II*	219

Tables

2.1	The Order of Dyads within Banks's Matrix	48
3.1	List of First Australian Performances Given by Richard Meale	69
3.2	The Lengths of Cycles in the 'Postlude'	78
3.3	Different Schemes for the Structure of Meale's *Clouds Now and Then*	85
4.1	Peter Watters-Cowan's Summary of the Connection between Row Forms Used in Butterley's String Quartet	112
4.2	Instances of the Unfolding Motif in the First Movement of Butterley's String Quartet	113
4.3	Instances of the Unfolding Motifs in the Second Movement of Butterley's String Quartet	113

Permissions

Fred Williams *Echuca Landscape II* 1966 oil on canvas © Estate of Fred Williams Used with permission. Image courtesy of the Rex Irwin archive at the National Art Archive, Art Gallery of NSW, Sydney.

Frederick McCubbin *The Pioneer* 1904 oil on canvas 225.0 x 295.7 cm National Gallery of Victoria, Melbourne Felton Bequest, 1906 (253-2)

Nigel Butterley interviewed by Hazel de Berg for the Hazel de Berg collection, 24 October 1967. TRC 1/303-305.

Richard Meale interviewed by Hazel de Berg in the Hazel de Berg collection, 1965. TRC 1/174.

Peter Sculthorpe interviewed by Belinda Webster in the Esso Performing Arts collection, 15-16 June 1989. TRC 2466.

Felix Werder interviewed by Hazel de Berg in the Hazel de Berg collection, 18 November 1969. TRC 1/409-410.

'Caliban v. Prospero' by Peter Porter. Published by ARC Publications, 2003. Copyright © Peter Porter. Reproduced with permission of the author c/o Rogers, Coleridge & White Ltd., 20 Powis Mews, London W11 1JN.

Richard Meale *Clouds Now and Then*|für Orchester © Copyright 1980 by Universal Edition (Australia) Pty Ltd/UE29023.

Richard Meale *Coruscations*|für Klavier © Copyright 1974 by Universal Edition (Australia) Pty Ltd/UE29033.

Richard Meale *Incredible Floridas*|für Kammerensemble © Copyright 1980 by Universal Edition (Australia) Pty Ltd/UE29027.

Richard Meale 1. Streichquartett|für 2 Violinen, Viola and Violoncello © Copyright by University Edition (Australia) Pty Ltd/UE29095.

Aria for Edward John Eyre by David Lumsdaine © Copyright University of York Music Press Limited. Print Rights administered in Australia and New Zealand by Hal Leonard Australia Pty Ltd ABN 13 085 333 713 www.halleonard.com.au Used By Permission. All Rights Reserved. Unauthorised Reproduction is Illegal.

Homage to Garcia Lorca by Richard Meale © Copyright Boosey and Hawkes Music Publishers Ltd Print Rights administered in Australia and New Zealand by Hal Leonard Australia Pty Ltd ABN 13 085 333 713 www.halleonard.com.au Used By Permission. All Rights Reserved. Unauthorised Reproduction is Illegal.

The musical examples were typeset by Peggy Polias.

Acknowledgements

This book began in 2012 as an Australian Research Council Discovery Early Career Researcher Award (project DE120101192) at the University of New South Wales, funded by the Australian government. The University of New South Wales supported my research in many ways, not least through the stability of permanent employment. My project was associated with the Centre for Modernism Studies in Australia.

I have many people to thank for making this book possible, including: Stephen Adams, Anne Boyd, Nigel Butterley, Rachel Campbell, Sarah Collins, Barry Conyngham, Donald Hazelwood, Miranda Jackson, Rob Keeley, Tom Kennedy, David Larkin, Nicola LeFanu, David Lumsdaine, Donald MacLeod, Elizabeth McMahon, Jon Milford, Alistair Noble, John Peterson, Anna Reid, Nicole Saintilan, Andrew Schultz, Peter Sculthorpe, Shane Simpson, Richard Toop, Frances Tye, Arnold Whittall, Lyn Williams, David Worrall, Raymond Yiu, the estate of Richard Meale and several anonymous readers. The family of Don Banks have generously given me permission to make use of his correspondence and music. My particular thanks to Andrew Robbie for the endless discussions about drafts of the manuscript over the life of the project.

My thanks, too, to the staff of the manuscripts collection at the National Library of Australia. Spending time in the Special Collections Reading Room is one of the unequivocal joys of undertaking research in Australia. Catriona Anderson and Kate Boesen were especially helpful.

Working with Leah Babb-Rosenfeld and Amy Martin has been a pleasure.

The book is for Ellen Hooper for countless reasons, including: the conversations that we had about every aspect of every part of this book; the daily work that she undertook in London leading up to the funding of this project, which made it possible for me to spend time writing the initial applications; her proofreading and copyediting; and her endless patience with me working long hours.

Introduction

Australian Music Now

The West is a very long way away.[1]

The composer Roger Smalley began his contribution to a debate in Sydney about the meaning of Australian Music by positioning himself as an outsider, as both an 'Englishman', and an Englishman living in Perth. 'The West' of which he speaks in the epigraph above is Australia's west coast, and his comment is a reminder that distance still mattered, even in 1988, which is the year that the debate took place, and that Perth felt like a long way from Sydney. The year 1988 was the bicentenary of Australia's colonization, which made it a year of significant nationalist fervour, and it produced a series of discussions about Australian Music. The principal strands of these discussions were: whether Australian Music exists; whether it ought to exist; if it does exist, how it can be defined; if it were to come into existence, how it would be recognized. Possible connections between Australian Music and Australian nationalism were also the cause of much debate. Whatever the disagreement that these debates produced, their arguments have remained relatively stable for a long period, from the late 1970s until the present. Smalley argued that there was in fact a distinctively Australian music, which he defined through a series of musical attributes: the sounds of animals (principally birds and insects), modal melodies, 'simple repetitive rhythms', formal simplicity and a lack of counterpoint. Smalley polemically associated the list's attributes with the music that Peter Sculthorpe and Ross Edwards were writing at the time, which indicates that he considered their work as central to Australian Music.

The attributes that Smalley lists do not well describe the music that was being composed in the years before he arrived in Australia in 1976, which is a period that the composer Barry Conyngham raised in response to Smalley's argument. Conyngham did so through Sculthorpe, who, though not present at the debate, had sent Conyngham his thoughts in advance:

> Peter's [Sculthorpe] idea was that, in this day and age, maybe Australian composers can transcend their natural, existing environment in some sort of world music.[2] I thought this was terrific, but I suddenly remembered that I had heard that saying somewhere else. I had heard it in 1963 from Richard Meale. Now it is interesting that these two opposing planets of Australian music seemed to have flipped over,

and I'm afraid that while to Marshall McLuhan[3] world society seemed attractive in 1963, given our present culture I am not sure that world culture is an aim I would join in pursuing.[4]

Something approaching a 'world music' was also advocated by the critic-academic Roger Covell in his 1967 book *Australia's Music: Themes of a New Society*. Covell ended his book with a vision of the future in which regional boundaries are transcended in favour of a common music throughout Asia and the Pacific. By 1988 his position had significantly changed:

> I was a little dismayed when I heard Peter Sculthorpe's proposition [in Conyngham's response to Smalley] to the effect that Australian composers could transcend regional limitations. Frankly the [national] government is not interested in that. It is not interested in having composers become universal or internationally famous. It wishes only to construct a program of Australian composition which will be approximately equivalent to the international popularity of the wombat and the koala. Anything more than that is not desirable.[5]

Recent explanations of music in Australia continue to support the 'wombats and koalas' version of Australian Music. In 2016 a broadcast of Australian Music by the BBC began with Tom McKinney quoting Bill Bryson (for whom life in Australia involves sunbathing, drinking coffee, and dangerous wildlife), and it continued with Brett Dean introducing Meale's *Clouds Now and Then* (1969):

> Richard Meale together with Peter Sculthorpe really brought Australian Music and especially Australian orchestral music into the twentieth century. They both went about it in very different ways. Sculthorpe's scores are very extrovert, and very colourful and very much about place, I mean they're very vivid; Richard Meale on the other hand is a much more inward-looking composer and there was something about having his music to open this concert which was a sort of 'statement of intent' [...] The first four pieces are very much music of a very inward nature and perhaps not that that you normally attribute to the Australian psyche or persona I guess. It's [Meale's music] very contemplative, and certainly *Clouds now and then* is very much that. It's a ravishing score but it's also very quiet and very intimate.[6]

Dean is one of today's best-known Australian composers, and he is influential enough to have programmed and conducted a recording by the BBC Symphony Orchestra. It is therefore striking that his introduction departed from the more nuanced way that Sculthorpe and Meale were understood in the 1960s. At that time Australian Music was not uniformly conceived, and the modernist music that was being written also produced significant differences between composers, and between works from the same composer. Sculthorpe composed a mix of 'inward-looking' works – the chamber music in particular, such as *Irkanda IV* and the sixth String Quartet, earned Sculthorpe a reputation for writing music that was 'lonely' and sorrowful – and more colourful orchestral works, such as the *Sun Music* series (1965–9),[7] which do contain the 'extrovert' materials that Dean mentions. Although Dean describes Meale's music as 'inward-looking', his orchestral music in the 1960s was actually often very 'extrovert', especially *Very High Kings* (1968), but also *Homage to Garcia Lorca* (1964) (the London performance of which was reviewed in 1965 by *The Times* with the headline 'Extrovert Performance of Sydney Orchestra'[8]), and *Nocturnes* (1967). Meale's music at that time may have been abstract, but it was rarely introspective. In the case of *Clouds Now and Then*, Meale himself described it as 'lyrical',[9] which suggests outward expression, and although some of the piece is quiet, some of it is also *fff*. The title comes from a haiku, which reads: 'Clouds now and then, giving men relief from moon viewing', and in his initial programme note Meale wrote that 'the poem transcends [a] very refined contemplation of natural beauty by drawing us back into the reality of life'.[10] This suggests that we should specifically not hear *Clouds Now and Then* as introspective contemplation, but as the drama of being distracted from contemplation by the world around us. In other words, it is a composition written against introspection. It is simply not the case that Sculthorpe and Meale were neatly opposed in the way that Dean suggests, though the exuberance of the *Sun Music* series, and of Sculthorpe's subsequent successes (including 'extrovert' later works such as *Kakadu* (1988), for example), has come to be how Sculthorpe is best known. The result of Dean's introduction is to position Sculthorpe as the composer most like the caricature of Australia offered by Bryson,[11] and to define Australian Music through those of Sculthorpe's works that come closest to the stereotype. Dean does so at the expense of a form of Australian Music that suits Meale's *Clouds Now and Then*, which, considering Dean's programme included no music by Sculthorpe and did include Meale's piece, shows the pervasive dominance of Sculthorpe within the current conception of a particular consideration of Australian Music. His comments are also an example of how even significant works from the 1960s – such as Meale's *Clouds Now and Then* – are currently explained through ideas far removed from the era of their composition.

Sculthorpe was not always so dominant, and the differences in conceptions of Australian Music between 1969 and 1988 are not reconcilable through the adjustment of defining elements (a little more counterpoint, a little more formal complexity, a lot less rhythmic repetition). Indeed, my argument in this book is that in the period from 1960 to 1975 a fundamentally different conception of Australian Music held sway. In the 1960s and early 1970s composers working in Australia defined a form of Australian Music that was built on difference, difficulty, and argument (quite unlike the debates that took place in 1988, which did so against the backdrop of stable questions and fixed positions). This conception has been overshadowed by two forces: the more recent discourses that have had little time for historicizing the term 'Australian Music', and which have obfuscated its history rather than critiqued its manifestations; and the composers themselves, many of whom shifted their musical priorities markedly in the late 1970s, embracing neo-tonal aesthetics, and supporting a form of Australian Music based on personal identity.

The 'celebratory model' of Australian Music, which focusses on a handful of individual composers, emerged to overcome the apparent aesthetic volte-face that was made in a short space of time in the late 1970s. The nuances of this model are beyond the scope of this book, but two examples should give a sense of how it operates. My first example of the 'celebratory model' is an article by Roger Covell – 'Richard Meale: Intuitions of a Solitary Modernist', written in 1988 – in which he tries to reconcile the success of Meale's (then) recent opera *Voss* (1985) with his earlier music. Covell's first sentence clearly sets out his method: 'This is an attempt to contribute to the reception history, not of a work, but of a composer.'[12] The gesture is generous, seeking to recuperate Meale's earlier music for a late 1980s audience. The recuperation was needed, since 'In [*Incredible Floridas*] the composer reached one of the furthest points in his creative career from easy comprehension'.[13] With Covell uninterested in the reception of the music, the music is marginalized as having been written according to the fashions of the time, with Meale's modernism an instrument of the establishment:

> There is no reason to suppose that Meale himself would be sorry that this period [of modernism] is over, except perhaps in the sense that he would not wish to cut himself off completely from his own past. As the standard-bearer of the new in music in this country for the best part of a generation he was expected to remain in an intransigent, unappeased posture, impervious to the blandishments of the musical establishment while becoming inevitably better known and more influential within that establishment[.][14]

Such an 'establishment' only properly began to be formed during the 1960s (with the expansion of Australian universities,[15] and the more open attitude of the Sydney Symphony Orchestra, for example) and then more quickly in the early 1970s (with rapid increases in funding for the arts and the founding of an Australia Music Centre), all of which was as important for Covell's prestige as it was for Meale's. In the mid-1960s Meale could not have acted according to an 'establishment' that was yet to be established. Additionally, the establishment of infrastructure during this time was not guided by those with an ear for 'easy comprehension'; for example, the increased funding was led by the composer Don Banks, and it resulted in substantial support by the Federal government for a wide range of music, modernist and otherwise (as I will explain in Chapters 1 and 2). Covell's comment therefore says more about the political-economic landscape of the late 1980s, and the acceptance of the neoliberalism (as it was later called) that had begun to guide arts policy, of which the 'celebratory model' is exemplary, than it does about Meale's modernism. Covell's article is also an example of the way that the modernist works of the 1960s and early 1970s were viewed with some embarrassment because of a disconnection between the music and listener comprehension. Nonetheless, in Covell's argument, modernism is justified as a necessary phase in a progression towards more understandable music.

In an article from 2015, Joel Crotty made a similar argument for Sculthorpe, in which he considered Sculthorpe's *Music for Japan* (1970) and its later revision (1996), which added didjeridu. Crotty worked harder to historicize the piece than Covell did for any of Meale's music, but Crotty nevertheless emphasized a sense of continuity through Sculthorpe-the-person even when that was at odds with the composition: 'If the work [*Music for Japan*, 1970] is in some way autobiographical, then a revision to reflect the composer's mid-1990s aspirations appears still to be keeping with the score's original intention. The didjeridu, not used in his work since 1963's *The Fifth Continent*, could very well be there [in *Music for Japan*] to perpetuate the composer's Australian-ness, somehow possibly lacking in the original score.' In arguing against 'the work', Crotty creates a person–work continuity through the consideration of *Music for Japan* as autobiographical, only to reinstate the most problematic aspect of 'the work concept' – composer intentionality. Even if we speculate about such intentions, Sculthorpe had used the didjeridu in 1963, as Crotty argued, and we ought therefore to consider the non-use of didjeridu in 1970 as an active decision rather than a deficiency that needed revision. Although both works were written by Peter Sculthorpe, *Music for Japan* (1970) is not the same as *Music for Japan* (1996). Crotty and Covell are exemplary of the desire, which emerges strongly in the 1980s, to explain the modernist phase of Australian Music as secondary to the greater continuity offered by the composers who formed the movement in the 1960s and early 1970s, and to downplay the significance of their earlier music except where it can be rehabilitated for present purposes.

The second example of the way that Australian Music came to be discussed in terms of 'celebration' is exemplified in the following comment made by Conyngham in 2000:

> So I think the challenge we have to confront in terms of Australian composition and presentation is what I call the confidence issue. I think we need to have a more authoritative and strong assertion of what we do, and the value of what we do.[16]

A lack of 'confidence' is the problem at the centre of Conyngham's address, and his solution is:

> to celebrate each other and build that sort of confidence, because I really do believe that in that confidence will come confidence in the other partners in this relationship. Not the least of which [are] funding authorities and government, but also critics, and of course the most important people of all: the people who actually listen and experience our music.
>
> If WE aren't confident about it, if WE aren't assertive about the value of what we do, then why should we ask anyone else to be?[17]

What is pressing here are the capital letters 'WE', and the centrality of 'celebration'. A book about Australian Music from 1988 until the present would focus on those two ideas, for they are the pillars of the discourses by which Australian Music is now known. But this is not a book about that time, and Australian Music in its earlier phase, from 1960 until 1975, was less clear about 'WE' and was little concerned with celebration. Although confidence is also a concept that is important to that period – I historicize it in Chapter 2 – none of the era's composers spoke about celebration, and the 'WE' to which Conyngham refers was a concept that was subject to significant disagreement.

Conyngham's comments came at the end of a long decade of academic reconsiderations of Australian Music. Scholarship from the 1990s demonstrates recourse to a handful of touchstones, and the new musicological inquiries in Australia at that time came with a new form of Australian Music, as scholars sought better social explanations for artistic practices, principally in the wake of the new musicology. This took place in the work of, for example, Kay Dreyfus, who in 1995 argued for a wider range of critical perspectives than Australian Music had previously seen. Her work countered the existing compositional canon of Australian composers, principally by discussing composers before 1960, and Grainger's rehabilitation after 1975.[18] What happened between 1960 and 1975 was seen implicitly as needing no new historical re-evaluation, since for Dreyfus the 1990s were the new 1960s: 'if the 60s saw Australian composers and compositions establish themselves, the decade of the 1990s will, I have no doubt, be seen as the time when the study of Australia's music history was legitimised'.[19] That new musicological legitimation took place alongside very little study of the music of the 1960s and early 1970s, partly because those years were seen as one of the few periods in Australia's musical history that already had a substantial scholarly history, although – as Dreyfus's argument about the establishment of musicological study in the 1990s suggests – this was not the case.

A similar broadening of the topic of Australian Music took place in 1994, with Crotty as guest editor for the Australian Music Centre's journal *Sounds Australian*. In the autumn issue he assembled a variety of scholars to revise 'the 1960's [sic] view of Australia's Music History'.[20] In undertaking this revision, the articles focus on music *before* the 1960s, and so, as in Dreyfus's essay, Crotty's criticism of the dominance of the 1960s neglects the 1960s itself. The exception to this avoidance was his own introduction; he began by describing the issue as 'a celebration and a reflection of our musical heritage'.[21] Crotty argued that the 'confidence' that came with the 1960s cast the previous years as 'un-Australian', since the specific 'confidence' here is the confidence of being Australian rather than British. The issue's focus on earlier composers was designed to reinforce their work as Australian, and in so doing to reform the discourse of Australian Music as historically more continuous. This was an attempt to counterbalance the 'ahistorical' 1960s, to undercut their 'claim on the present and future'.[22] As useful as Crotty's *Sounds Australian* is for reminding readers of the composers that were working in Australia before 1960, it nevertheless avoids the 1960s, which therefore remain 'ahistorical' and beyond scrutiny. The new history that this issue of *Sounds Australian* writes contributed to the 'distinctively Australian' argument, in which earlier composers are understood through a nationalist lens. The broad temporality that the argument supports is a move away from Britain, and the date by which this was accomplished is pushed back from the 1960s to the early twentieth century. Nevertheless, the relationship with Britain was an important one, especially in the 1960s and 1970s, during which time composers worked to form *new* connections between Australia and Britain: for example, many of the compositions from the time were performed in Britain, and many of the composers were published from London. Significant energy was devoted to forming those new relationships, and the new organizations that were founded in Australia in the 1970s demonstrate the ongoing to and fro between Australia and Britain; those organizations, chief among which is the Australian Music Centre, are the very ones that paradoxically later supported a centralized discourse celebrating Australian Music.

Coming right at the end of the decade of the 1990s, and published in 2000, is Bruce Johnson's *The Inaudible Music: Jazz, Gender and Australian Modernity*. Although outside the new musicology, Johnson's book is exemplary of the approach that characterizes that movement. It described jazz as a form of modernity diffused throughout Australian society. Johnson argued against the 'pervasive reluctance on the part of institutional music discourse in Australia to give serious consideration to "music" in terms broader than "art music"',[23] at a time when others were also moving in the same direction. That 'broadening' has been both enlightening and essential, though the field could hardly have contracted, given how few musicologists were working on music in Australia during the period that he criticizes, and which was constituted by a small handful of scholars at best.[24] Nevertheless, Johnson is right to highlight the way that 'Australian cultural discourse deferred to Eurocentric and "top-down" models of cultural influence' and that 'it has been very slow to recognise the arrival of modernist sensibilities except as propagated by high art European sources'.[25] This is especially true of the scholarship in the two decades before the publication of his book. However, Johnson's criticism relies chiefly on James Murdoch and Covell's account of the 1960s.[26] We now need to better understand Johnson's argument about the changing relation with Europe, and to do so by scrutinizing the new connections that were being made in the 1960s and early 1970s, by writing a more detailed history of those decades, and with careful criticism of Murdoch and Covell. This is needed to make better sense of why composers in the 1960s, in a new movement of musical modernism, made new connections with Europe when, as Johnson persuasively writes, the history of Australia's musical modernity had begun long before.

This book is therefore about Australian (art) Music between 1960 and 1975, and the new modernism that was being made at that time. The book considers the movement of modernist composers that emerged in the 1960s as socially significant. Neither the current understanding nor the earlier discourses of Australian Music are well known outside Australia, though they ought to be, both because the music is worth knowing, and because the arguments that shape this book contribute to wider arguments about modernism, nationalism, and compositional aesthetics. Rather than demonstrating the evolution of the current concept of Australian Music, in this book I focus on its earlier formation. What results is a different picture of Australian Music. The period with which I am concerned here coincides with the first self-conscious and sustained interest in musical modernism in Australia, and so the contest for distinctiveness takes place through music formed consciously by the ideas of modernism. Before 1960 there had been composers in Australia who contributed to musical modernism more widely (Percy Grainger, for example), but it is only from 1960 that a movement of art music emerged that one can properly consider as one, beyond the work of individual composers. The complex reasons for this change will emerge throughout the book, but chief among them are the new organizations – and new funding – for new music. My approach to explaining this is historical, and it includes extensive reference to the archives of correspondence that are now available. My approach is also musical, and I pay close attention to the decisions that were being made in the compositions being written. Previous studies of Australian Music have tended to separate composers from their works. My contention is that this is inadequate to understanding what was at stake, and so this book includes the compositional decisions that were being made at the time under study as a core part of Australian Music's history. In writing about modernist art music, my approach creates some uneasy contradictions, but it is important to understand that these contradictions are an essential feature of what was taking place, and they are therefore a necessary part of considering Australian Music as properly modernist. The tendency within recent conceptions of Australian Music has been to use nationalism to provide a coherent narrative, but such coherence scarcely exists. In the 1960s and early 1970s the composers were not working seamlessly towards a central ideal, but this did not prevent the emergence of Australian Music, with its capital letters.[27]

The current understanding of Australian Music therefore differs markedly from its earlier form. One finds in the 1960s and early 1970s both the formation of Australian Music and also the problematization of its form. To be clearer, the 1960s were the first time that a large number of composers living and writing in Australia were also keen to embrace a variety of modernist ideas, and to draw on musical modernism from Britain, and Europe. Since many of those ideas are at odds with nationalism itself, the period is characterized by contradiction and critique. It was also a time before Scultthorpe was definitively Australia's 'leading composer', and when composers such as Meale, Banks and Scultthorpe were working hard to counter what they saw as the parochialism of music in Australia. By the end of the 1970s Scultthorpe had clearly emerged as the country's highest-profile composer, but a decade earlier there were other contenders, and so the conception of Australian Music that I explain does not fit Scultthorpe as well as later definitions do, though it fits him as well as it fits the others about whom I write. The period between 1960 and 1975 is also significant for producing the major ideas of Australian Music, such as the association of music and landscape, and so it informs current debates.

The first chapter explains the academic discourse of Australian Music. Australia's universities expanded rapidly during the 1960s, providing composition posts for many artists, whereas before this time few composers were employed by universities for their compositional expertise. This change came with the foundation of musicology in Australia, and the combination of these events led to the start of a scholarly discourse about Australian Music at the same time that Australian Musical modernism began. This means that the idea of Australian Music and its scholarly form are inseparable, especially since the early musicological journals often described Australian Music through the writing of critics, composers and musicologists, who were all published together. Chapter 1 therefore considers the scholarly argument in terms of the formation of the musicological discipline in Australia, including the 'infrastructure' necessary for its operation.

In the following chapters I consider carefully the history of the 1960s and early 1970s in its own terms, central to which was the music being composed. Scholarship about

Australian Music has often overlooked the particularity of individual compositions, which has resulted in some misunderstandings about the music of the era. Given that these years are interesting precisely because they are years of significant change, they are also a time across which singular narratives are difficult to maintain. The book focusses on a handful of works that contribute to an account of Australian Music that necessarily varies for different composers, for different compositions, and for different ideas. At the time, composers were working with different ideas, in contrasting ways, and in significant disagreement.

The book considers three strands of thought that come together in tension to produce the early arguments about Australian Music. The first strand includes nationalism, and also a reconsideration of what Australia means in musical terms, and I will consider this strand primarily in the chapters about Sculthorpe and Lumsdaine's music. The second strand is the connection between Australia and the UK, which is my focus in the chapter about Butterley's music, though it occurs throughout the book. The third strand is an internationalist stance, which is exemplified by the music of Richard Meale. The chapter on Don Banks includes all these strands in their interconnection, and it also explains the formation of the organizations that have been significant for supporting the evolution of the idea of Australian Music. To be clear, there is much modernist music that the book does not consider, just as there is much nationalist music that will not be found here. The aim of the book is to explain the contest for the idea of Australian Music between 1960 and 1975, and through this history to intervene in the current understanding of Australian Music.

1

The Formation of an Academic Discourse of Australian Music

Australia is said to have no history and to be lucky in this. But, in fact, Australia is embedded in its history like a fly in amber.[1]

The problem with 'Australian Music' today is that the term is almost never contested. The Australian Music Centre, for example, 'fulfills its aims by directly representing Australian composers and sound artists',[2] without openly questioning the word 'Australian'. To be eligible for funding from the Australia Council for the Arts a musician must be an 'Australian citizen or an Australian permanent resident',[3] and the organization's Corporate Plan is to support 'new Australian work',[4] and to invest in 'Australian arts'.[5] Neither the Corporate Plan nor the Australia Council Act (2013)[6] includes serious discussion about what the term 'Australian' means. Secondary-school students have had 'Music of the last 25 years (Australian focus)'[7] as a mandatory topic in one state, and 'analysis of ways in which Australian performers have interpreted a variety of works by Australian composers/songwriters that have been created after 1910' in another.[8] Against such institutional consistency it is difficult for alternative narratives to exist.

The current uniformity was much less the case in the 1960s, partly because few national organizations for the arts in Australia existed, and partly because composers were busy working to forge new international connections. The 1970s was a time when the ties to Britain were supposed to have ended, a delayed reaction to a series of shifts in the relationship between the two nations that had begun with the Federation of Australia in 1901. But the 1960s and 1970s continued to be characterized by a close engagement with Britain by Australian-born and -based composers. This was a time when 'Australian Music' was highly political, and when a small number of high-profile composers were jostling for primacy.

Many of the prominent composers of the 1960s and 1970s who considered themselves 'Australian' had spent at least some time in the UK. Many had studied there, and some were permanently based there (and some remain so). The correspondence from the time is not characterized by an antagonism towards Britain and British music,[9] and instead it reveals productive collaborations, successful enterprise and close friendships. Indeed, looking at the years between 1960 and 1975, one struggles to detect any 'move away' from Britain, and there is little questioning of British compositional practice. Even Richard Meale, for whom the United States, Spain, France and Japan were important places, and on whom the impact of British music is fairly slight, nevertheless had major performances, significant commissions and publishing contracts in London, all of which were crucial for his career. Nigel Butterley remains a proud Anglophile. Peter Scultthorpe's *String Quartet Music*, which made a significant statement about his engagement with Asian music, was premiered at the Wigmore Hall, and is published by Faber Music of London. Don Banks founded a significant portion of Australia's national infrastructure on his experience working with British organizations. Alison Bauld, Anne Boyd, Ross Edwards and Martin Wesley-Smith all studied at the University of York (and did so at the same time).[10] They may have described their time there in terms of 'Australian Music' in a way that would not have applied to either Banks or Lumsdaine in London twenty years earlier, but they all found ways of contributing to the British scene; Bauld still lives in Britain, and Boyd followed her time at York with a lectureship at Sussex before becoming the founding head of the Department of Music at the University of Hong Kong. There was at the time an easy relationship between the prominent composers working in Australia and those working in Britain. Exchanges were readily established. Funding was available to enable the movement of music between locations. Little of the contemporary discourse captures this remarkably fruitful international attitude.

Compared to the UK, Australia's infrastructure for new music in the 1960s was more centralized, revolving around academic institutions and the Australian Broadcasting Commission (ABC). Butterley and Meale both began their compositional careers through the connections and resources that the ABC afforded them as producers. In 1969 Meale joined the faculty in Adelaide, by which time Peter Sculthorpe, Eric Gross, John Exton and Keith Humble held academic positions. This change is crucial for the formation of 'Australian Music'. The rapid expansion in academic positions that took place makes the short period between 1960 and 1975 particularly important.

Australian Music and Musicology

The appointment of composers coincided with the establishment of musicology in Australia,[11] and that establishment would be decisive in terms of the dominant ways in which music in Australia has come to be discussed. In 1948 Donald Peart moved from Britain to take up a position as the founding Professor of Music at the University of Sydney, but it was not until 1963 that the Musicological Society of Australia was established. The society published Australia's first scholarly music journal, *Musicology Australia*, with three issues in the 1960s that contained articles such as: 'The Didjeridu of the Australian Aborigine: A Unique Development of a Common Musical Instrument?', by Trevor Jones; 'Military Music in the Colony of New South Wales, 1788–1850', by Peter Richardson; 'Alfonso Ferrabosco and the Lyra Viol', by Donald Peart; and 'The New Troubadours: Reflections on Pop and Modern Folk Music', by Wilfrid Mellers.

In 1965 Andrew McCredie was appointed Senior Research Fellow in Musicology at Adelaide University and in 1966 he initiated the journal *Miscellanea Musicologica: Adelaide Studies in Musicology*. Its early issues also mix ethnomusicology with canonical (and not so canonical) work. For example, the first issue included: 'The Organ Works of Max Reger', by John Wesley Barker; 'Sources of English Song: A Survey 1620–1660', by Ian Spink (who at the time was deputy head of the Music Department at Sydney University); 'Symbolic and Descriptive Text Settings in the Works of Pierre de la Rue', by Marianne Rosenberg; 'Christoph Graupner as Opera Composer', by McCredie; and 'Peter Maxwell Davies: *The Shepherds' Calendar*', by Peart. Also typical of the time is that the only significant analysis amongst these was that of Aboriginal music, undertaken by Catherine Ellis in 'Aboriginal Songs of South Australia'.

By 1967 musicology had been established in Perth, and the university began producing its *Studies in Music* journal, as well as the *Australian Journal of Music Education*, both edited by Frank Callaway. *Studies in Music*'s first issue published an overview of 'Musical Scholarship in the Twentieth Century' by Gerald Abraham, alongside articles by Basil Deane (on Beethoven), Trevor Jones (on the didjeridu), Peter Platt (on Dering) and David Tunley (on the eighteenth-century French cantata). It also included editions of scores by Dering and Bernier, and a forum including John Exton, who argued, inter alia, for composition as research, and H. E. Hallam, who argued against 'originality'. Its outlook, then, was a similar mix of Aboriginal music and canonical Europeans. None of the members of its advisory panel were Australian, though the editorial board comprised the heads of music departments in Australia. Its stated aim was to 'assist the study of both established and contemporary musical styles', an aim which was borne out in the subsequent volumes.

In 1969 the University of Sydney started *Music Now*, a journal focussed on new music. Peart wrote the introductory editorial, which argued that: 'The cultivation of the music of the past, interesting and valuable as it is, must take second place to the creation of music by composers now alive – and preferably not only alive but "alive and kicking".[12] The journal was also focussed on Australian composition, giving a voice to some of its young composers:

> In Australia we are just beginning. We have a distinct advantage over countries dominated by long tradition. We may respect the past but should not be obsessed by it.[13]

In Peart's argument, composition in Australia was new, young and international. Peart provided a list of the significant events that connect local and international movements:

> The visit to Australia in 1961 of Stravinsky – the legendary figure who seems just about to pass into the Pantheon of great composers – did an enormous amount of good. Here he was, no mere name on a gramophone record label, actually conducting in the Sydney Town Hall! Even more significant was the visit in 1965 and 1966 of Peter Maxwell Davies, the English composer – speaking our language! – and only just over thirty years of age. Also a fine performer, teacher and lecturer,

Maxwell Davies was a tremendous inspiration to us and really started something. One thing we shall be doing in this journal is to follow up his ideas.

The editorial concluded with a benediction:

May music constantly thrive among us, and be renewed, and give refreshment, and food for pleasure and thought!

The contrast between Peart's rejection of the past and his deification of Stravinsky and Davies removes those composers from their particular politics. Free from local histories they are able, by virtue of their recognition of Australia's existence, to bring Australia into modernism's international arena. Peart's article on Meale in *Music Now* was introduced with a sentence that positions Peart as a mediator, whose function was similar to that of to Stravinsky or Davies: 'His [Peart's] work as an activator and catalyst in stimulating and encouraging young and serious native musicians has been a direct influence in the emergence of composers such as Richard Meale, Peter Sculthorpe and Nigel Butterley.'[14] (Davies's second visit to Australia, for a six-month residency teaching composition at Adelaide University in 1966, was more successful both for Davies[15] and for his leadership in Adelaide, which was particularly significant for Ross Edwards, who studied with him there, and later also in London.[16])

Composition and musicology about Australian Music are indissoluble at that time, with much of the musicology about Australian composers being written either by composers, or by scholars keen to see Australian composition flourish. The consequence of the rise in musicology and the appointment of composers as academics is that Australian Music has always been tied to universities. With the academic discourse of Australian Music often written by scholars with little expertise in new music, which was especially the case in the 1960s and 1970s, there was little writing that demonstrated the differences between ideas expressed musically, and those expressed in the programme notes written by composers, even where the two forms of expression disagree. Nevertheless, the academic discourses that were written were also new and exploratory, and the published articles are rarely of conservative academicism. The expansion of academia during the period also brought composers into more stable and influential employment, and by the end of the 1970s their personal narratives were dominating academic discourses about their music.

This chapter therefore argues for the development of the discourse of Australian Music by giving weight to the academic sources published at the time.[17] These sources are more carefully penned than other forms of writing, and they are more likely to tackle specific musical problems when they are relevant. Newspapers such as *The Age* simply did not publish musically analytical writing, and so it remains difficult to assess the relevance of musical details to the writers publishing in its pages. In focussing on the academic scholarship about Australian Music, the chapter avoids the platitudinous writing that was being published in the Australian press at the time. The academic publishers were not against technical detail on principle, and so the quantity of technical writing they produced is indicative of the mode of engagement of their writers, rather than their publishing policy. The academic sources were also more influential to writers after 1975, due to their accessibility on library shelves at a time when accessing old newspaper reviews was difficult and time-consuming.

Australian Music and Modernism

If 'Australian' is one half of the problem, then the other half is 'modernism'. The two make little sense together in 1960, and after 1975 it is clear that their combination is untenable as a description of a mainstream movement. Many of the composers who rose to prominence between those dates did so as progressive, internationally minded, technically exploratory voices. They took advantage of cheaper and quicker travel to diminish the differences that resulted from geographical 'isolation', and they formed organizations to support new music. The term 'modernism' is still, unlike 'Australian', highly contested, which makes it as precarious – and therefore as useful – as ever. It is perhaps here that the most significant disjunctions in scholarship occur. Britain has seen an expansion in scholarship working with the modernist music that has been written since the late nineteenth century, and although some of these studies have focussed on music from a particular period, the conceptual significance of modernism is further reaching. *British Music and Modernism, 1895–1960*, edited by Matthew Riley[18] and Harper-Scott's *Edward Elgar, Modernist*[19] in particular reassess the impact of modernism in music previously considered conservative, and both focus on circumscribed sites in which modernism can be foregrounded. Harper-Scott's *The Quilting Points of Modernism* is more ambitious, arguing from a position where: 'No sane person would claim that Walton is a modernist, so that is of course exactly what I propose to do: he is a privileged coign of vantage from which to view the totality of responses to the Event.'[20] The argument relies on the 'radical contention [...] that the definition of modernism must encompass *all music of the twentieth century*'.[21] His book sets a stage on which Walton is considered as a 'reactive modernist' to revolutionize discourses about modernist music. The argument works for Walton, since 'Every political possibility that presented itself for reflection or action on Walton's part was thus fundamentally determined by the communism-Event,'[22] but it is less clear what this argument would mean for an analysis of a composer living in Australia, in which the communist–capitalist antagonism was much less present, in part due to the earlier dominance of capitalism in Australia. Certainly, Harper-Scott's argument means that we ought to look again at modernism in Australia, since Australian scholarship has tended to view modernism only in aesthetic terms. Since the 1980s, much of this scholarship has dismissed modernism as mere fashion.

For example, in his chapter 'Dreaming of Europe', which is mostly about the mid- to late-twentieth century, Gordon Kerry lumps together 'The various kinds of European modernism, be they twelve-note serialism or wrong-note neoclassicism,'[23] which 'were all being superseded in Europe by the time they made it to Australia'.[24] This repeats the perennial anxiety for Australian consumers, and 'Many shoppers bemoan the fact Australia appears to be a dumping ground for these big international brands – a place to shift out of season or unwanted stock without anyone taking notice.'[25] By the time Kerry gets to the composers Liza Lim and Mary Finsterer, 'European modernism' is reformulated as a 'Modernist Europhile sensibility'.[26] Mark Carroll, in an article about Graeme Koehne, introduces him as 'the Yale-educated, Virgil Thomson-trained Australian composer'.[27] Carroll makes no mention of Meale, with whom Koehne studied in Adelaide, and says nothing of Meale and Koehne's shared interest in Boulez (sufficiently strong for Koehne's Master's thesis to analyze Boulez's third piano sonata). Instead:

> The three works in question likewise celebrate middle-class values – the luxury of travel, ownership of an iPhone, and the indulgence of reflecting on life and prospects for the hereafter. This would itself attract the hostility of those for whom the individual's wants, desires, fears, and pleasures are but narcissist bourgeois indulgences deserving of derision. Those so motivated might be tempted to portray Koehne's music, in both its style and idea, as a product of the global triumph (at least for the time being) of neoliberal capitalism – one that in the West has bathed everything beige, and everywhere else blood red. Koehne, however, insists that the artist must extract him- or herself from the aesthetic ideological battlefields of old, and deal instead with the experiences that arise from life as it is lived.[28]

The very absence of Meale in this article, and the emphasis of Virgil Thompson, obfuscates the ideology that a position against modernism poses, and it presents the ideological battles as long over, since the only challenge that remains is adequately to display one's telephone. Victoria Rogers, writing about Peggy Glanville-Hicks, avoids modernism altogether: 'Her orientation to modality and consonance looks back to the gentle harmonies of the English pastoral school; it also looks forward to the ethos of post-modernism and neo-romanticism at the end of the century.'[29] Modernism in Australian Music has been marginalized, and the reasons (beyond fashion) for working with modernist ideas have been overshadowed by the confrontation of postmodernism (particularly as read by Australia's composers in the pages of *Sounds Australian* and *Ossia*[30] in the 1990s).

To give an example of the problem, it is difficult to discern the extent to which serialism was considered part of an ideology or part of a composer's technical apparatus. The relationship between facets is hard to establish when composers were not able, as Britten did in the 1950s, to have multiple unplanned encounters with Boulez,[31] and it was virtually impossible for a composer in Australia to have encountered Boulez's denunciation of serial composers as reactionaries.[32] Within Australia the ambitious music of the 1960s tends to be discussed without technical details at all, which suggests that serialism was less about prestige in Australia than it may have been for European composers at the same time, and more thoroughly bound up with other problems of modernity, and in particular with 'distance' and 'lateness'. For example, in 1966 Donald Peart declared Australia to have an avant-garde, and he named Meale, Sculthorpe and George Dreyfus as its members (with a mention for Butterley and Sitsky, and a separate discussion of Banks and Malcolm Williamson as non-residents). For Peart the grouping came not through shared technical interests, but from the contrast that their music made against the prevailing condition:[33]

> Never, perhaps, did a country begin in circumstances so unpromising for its musical development as did Australia. To the normal difficulties attendant upon cultural activities in a young country must be added the state of creative music, and especially the attitude of society towards it, in the Motherland during the later eighteenth century and most of the nineteenth. Musical composition was drifting rapidly to a condition of unredeemed bathos; not until the end of the nineteenth century was music being written in England which could provide a point of departure, a basis of any kind for the building-up of an indigenous tradition of composition.[34]

As an academic trained at Oxford and the Royal College of Music, Peart no doubt felt uniquely placed to make such comments, which were published in the *Proceedings of the Royal Musical Association*. His support of the composers for whom he argued was immense. He also gave them academic standing, in part through the journal *Music Now*, which was published from the Music Department at the University of Sydney. Peart had a clear desire for an 'indigenous tradition',[35] and for him this meant a 'non-British' one.

Distance, Travel and Distinctiveness

Peart found in Meale's 1960 Sonata for Flute and Piano – which is dodecaphonic, if not serial – music that indicates that:

> Australian music might not in future lie as close to the British tradition as most of us had casually assumed; that its affinities might lie, not with the Australian aboriginal culture, however brilliantly that might be restated in Western terms (as, notably, it had been re-stated by John Antill in his orchestral piece *Corroboree* of 1946), but rather with the post-Webern European school or with John Cage.[36]

The background to Peart's argument is that the Flute Sonata was the work that enabled Meale to travel to California, where he studied Gagaku, as well as Javanese and Balinese gamelan, at UCLA. That engagement is enough to enable the critique of Britain. It mattered less about the specific ingredients for this 'indigenous tradition', and discerning the differences between the post-Webern school or John Cage was not important, regardless of the significant differences that existed between Cage and Boulez by the time Peart wrote his article in 1966. If, in Australia as in Britain, the 'avant-garde' is 'something imported from abroad', then the problem of Australia's relationship to Britain remains.

Roger Covell began his seminal work *Australia's Music: Themes of a New Society* with what for him is a matter of transplantation – the acclimatization problem:

The subject of this book is specific but not essentially unique. It concerns a European musical culture transplanted by Europeans to a country not in Europe; a theme paralleled in the experience of several other countries: of, for example, South Africa, Canada, New Zealand, the South American countries to a lesser extent, and most strikingly, of the United States of America. Such a musical culture is provincial by definition; and a provincial culture has obvious limitations.[37]

Acclimatization societies were popular in the mid-nineteenth century,[38] and their 'ecological imperialism'[39] was part of a 'biological exchange' between Britain and Australia. Dunlap argues that the 'demand for British productions was strongest in Australia, which looked the least like Britain' and the project therefore aimed to correct Australia's apparent 'deficiencies' with imported flora and fauna. The point at which this makes sense for a discussion of music is in terms of landscape, which for Sculthorpe and the discourse that surrounds him – and in this period, him alone – is enduring. Here, again, is Covell, demonstrating how 'landscape' was vital for the discussion of Sculthorpe's music by the mid-1960s:

> Of all the younger Australian composers, [Sculthorpe] is the one who seems to have taken most seriously the notion of an Australian identity in music. This can be ascertained superficially by a glance at the titles of some of his works [...] [H]e has written a series of works bearing the title of *Irkanda*, an Australian Aboriginal word meaning 'a remote and lonely place'; his 1954 *String Trio* (revised 1960), which makes use of quarter-tone intervals and dates from immediately after the most experimental period of his career, bears the subtitle 'The Loneliness of Bunjil' and carries the following note in the original manuscript score: 'In the very beginning, Bunjil, the Great Spirit, created the world and all things in it, except man ... he became lonely.' It is probably significant that Sculthorpe has done research into the musical traditions of the now extinct [*sic*] Tasmanian Aborigines and certainly significant that his work for speaker, sound-track and orchestra, *The Fifth Continent*, originally commissioned for ABC radio, should take as its text a selection of passages from D. H. Lawrence's *Kangaroo* which seek to evoke some aspects of the character of Australian landscape.[40]

More recently, Skinner connected similarly the landscape topic with Sculthorpe's study of Aboriginal music, arguing that landscape had become a significant idea for Sculthorpe by the beginning of the 1950s.[41] The discourse dominated readings of his music, and its centrality within wider discussions of Australian Music has conditioned readings of other composers that reinforce Sculthorpe as the centre of Australian composition, since the discourse fits him (if not necessarily his music) best.

Covell was the first to write at length about composers under the umbrella term of 'Australia's Music'. He focussed on that term as a useful way of grouping different kinds of music, and his book pushes towards the final chapter, 'Possibilities'. His closing remarks reveal the utopian 'new society' that extends from the nationalist idea, and are worth quoting at length, since they significantly reconfigure Australia within the region:

> It needs to be emphasized that the neighbouring musics with which Australia is evidently going to concern itself are not confined to traditional forms existing in isolated or zealously guarded purity: the exhilarating prospect of a genuine interaction between eastern and western traditions includes the fruitful encounter of western-trained musicians who have become excited by the properties of non-western music and of musicians from non-European races who have eagerly chosen to adopt many of the techniques of the European tradition. Australia's chances of making itself understood among its neighbours and of understanding them may well be helped by an advance guard of musical interchange; and the multi-racial nature of music as it will certainly develop in the Pacific and Asian regions will be – though its dilution of many individual traditions will be regretted sincerely by musicians from all races – of an almost incredible richness. If the opportunity is not ruined by other factors, these areas could see the growth of the most fecund musical culture that has ever existed on earth.[42]

Perhaps it is just as well that 'other factors' arose. Covell's language here was echoed by Sculthorpe: 'A successful blend of music from East and West would be the greatest music ever heard.'[43] The 'advanced garde of musical interchange' refers to Meale and Sculthorpe in particular, as composers in whose music Covell finds a move away from Europe, and both of whom were vocal about their musical responses to Asia.[44] Covell's influence presents a significant problem for understanding Australian Music in the 1960s, as it is often difficult to discern whether Sculthorpe was repeating Covell, or the other way around, or whether they simply shared a very close idea of what Australian Music could be. Covell's vision for Australian Music is a new geography in which Australia is a 'centre' rather than a 'periphery', though his language sounds dangerously neo-imperial.

In 1969, McCredie produced a survey of Musical Composition in Australia for the Commonwealth Assistance to Australian Composers Advisory Board (established 1967 by the federal government) which was published as a set of scores, alongside LPs of composers reading artistic statements and McCredie's introduction.[45] In the latter he outlines the history of the chief problems for music in Australia, which also derive from its colonization:

> The early stages [of musical development in Australia] were [...] marked by several historical disadvantages. Among these was the fact that the years marking the establishment of various seaboard settlements should have inauspiciously coincided with an unusually barren era of English music culture. Equally significant, the establishment of the Australian colonies actually occurred too late to permit the upsurge of a vigorous national tradition capable of withstanding the impact of modern communications in the latter nineteenth century. The absence of a bourgeois element in society was a third factor which impeded musical development.[46]

Conceiving of the development of Australia in terms of English (which here is synonymous with 'British') culture was still, in the 1960s, a commonly held view, about which McCredie, Peart and Covell agreed. The broad mechanism by which the cultural distance between Australia and Britain occurred is summarized by the historian John Hirst. It begins with Britain entering the European Common Market in 1973, which brings 'an abrupt end' to the education of Australians in 'British constitutional liberty'. He continues:

> Very quickly Australia was re-presented as a multicultural society to which all ethnic groups had made and were making their contribution. The British were a suspect ethnic group since they had been the dominant group in the non-multicultural past. They certainly could not be credited with supplying the central institutions of the polity, for that would explode the claim of equal 'contribution'. This left Australia with British institutions but not the history and myth to explain and sustain them. This was the greater loss since they [the Australians] had no political myths of their own, which is an enduring legacy of their experience of empire.[47]

A similar situation would follow the foundation in the early 1970s of Australian musical institutions on British models. This results in a paradoxical situation where the same shift that enables more funding for the arts, and which brings Banks and others back to Australia, for example, also provides the basis for new organizational structures based on the experience and connections wrought by composers who had worked in Britain. Here one glimpses the importance of, for example, Japanese music for Sculthorpe, Meale and others, which was only partly about a struggle to achieve for Australia an identity independent of Britain, for it was also a way of negotiating new relationships with British publishers and performers.

McCredie's second point, about the problems of developing a distinctive culture, is put more positively by Banks, writing from London three years earlier:

> *Australian Idiom*: I doubt if there is one, and whether there should *be* one. [...] Our musical training has for some time been based on a paler version of the English model, and this is not what we need, so what to do? I believe that as a young country unencumbered by the ties of a nationalistic tradition we should use our freedom to range right through the whole international field of music taking what we want from the best and most fruitful developments we can find. We should do this more systematically than we have done in the past and this is going to mean a more determined effort to solve our geographical situation.[48]

For McCredie, modernism in Australia scarcely makes sense with pre-capitalist hierarchies – in McCredie's argument Australia was colonized in the capitalist era – and without a pre-capitalist history Australian culture is defined by trade. The problem for music was that British merchants with significant capital holdings may have been trading with Australians, but they were supporting arts local to them, rather than local to Australian industry. As a result, Australia was defined as a nation in an already-capitalist era, and with little artistic investment. According to this argument, the birth of Australian musical nationalism was constructed from scratch beginning with Federation and the First World War, within a shared economic system. For McCredie, the typical artistic response to Australia's capitalism in the early decades of the twentieth century was that of 'Norman Lindsay in such journals as *Vision* and *Lone Hand*. In *Vision* he had fulminated against the novel and more forward looking ideals of Pound, Eliot and Joyce [...] [H]e was representative of a cultural nationalism, which after two explosive decades before 1914, could settle into a period of complaisant reaction and neo-classicism.'[49] The arts, in other words, play no part in capitalist conflict, because from its beginning Australia's purpose is tied to production.

The myth of progress is modernity's creation, but for McCredie it is unclear how to map changes in Australian Music to the central notion of progress, not because new technologies of communication were absent, but because they had already arrived. This is the crux of what writers at the time were struggling with: when change came it came easily, and with that ease comes the suspicion of superficiality, of 'the easy life' – art without philosophy, urban rather than rural, lucky rather than earned,[50] and in the postwar era the changes that came supported ever more consumerism. Although musical modernism would seem to be distant from such consumerism, there are points of contact. For example, in the June 1966 issue of *Walkabout*, 'Australia's Way of Life Magazine', one learns that 'Richard Meale is an utterly uncompromising young man, the leader of the *avant garde* movement in Australian music, a composer who is totally unconventional and clearly brilliant.' And also that as 'A talented cook, Meale believes in traditional recipes rather than avant-garde experiments.'[51] The article was written to promote Meale's contract with Boosey and Hawkes, and the entry in the contents describes him as a 'composer whose works now have the same contractual footing with a leading London music firm as Stravinsky's, Bartok's and Copland's'. A decade later and his Sacher-commissioned oboe concerto for Heinz Holliger is discussed in *Women's Weekly* alongside a 'New way to slim'.[52] Similarly, earlier in the century the modernist painter Roy de Maistre (who studied at the Sydney Conservatorium of Music) experimented with combining colour and music. His *Colour Music* from 1934 is a striking work, though its recently decoded source as Haydn's Trio in B♭ is not the modernist statement some may have hoped for.[53] His 'colour music wheel' (1917–19) was patented by the department store Grace Bros, and from 1936 the device was sold for interior design, a 'new and scientific tool for producing Colour Schemes without difficulty'.[54] At the same time, the rrrrrreddest rrrrrrreds were chosen for the chairs of the 'Soda Fountain – a popular, American-style eatery that opened in David Jones city store in 1927. Its boldly coloured lacquer modernity held [the painter] Cossington Smith "spellbound" when she first encountered it[.]'[55] Modernism, then, is always in danger of being subsumed by the consumerist culture with which it argues. What makes Australian Music in the 1960s especially significant was that there was wide acknowledgement of what some young composers were trying to achieve, and their sense of ambition aligned with notions of progress, no matter how uneasy the alliance.

Music Now encapsulates the international outlook of Peart's editorial in more than its articles. Its distributing agents were Tarantella Pty Ltd, locally, Fine Music Australia, nationally and Alfred A. Kalmus (Universal Edition), in the 'United Kingdom and

Europe'. The strong sense of celebrity that has become a feature of music in Australia was encouraged through the sale of the 'One hundred copies of MUSIC NOW personally autographed by Australian composers, Richard Meale, Peter Sculthorpe, Nigel Butterley and George Dreyfus',[56] available by mail order at ten times the cover price. Subscriptions cost '$A2.40' for those in 'Australia and the British Commonwealth' with 'Overseas foreign' for an extra 60 cents. The advertisements in *Music Now* demonstrate some of the connections significant at the time. Universal Edition advertised Bernard Rands, George Self and David Bedford. Tarantella advertised Sculthorpe's scores published by Faber, and CBS Records of contemporary music. J. Albert and Son advertises the works by Butterley that it published. There is an advertisement for a concert hosted by the International Society for Contemporary Music (ISCM) (performing Butterley, Meale and Sculthorpe alongside Messiaen, Takemitsu and Yun), and Fine Music Australia marketed its range of contemporary scores.

International/Local

For Banks, being 'unencumbered' by 'nationalistic tradition' meant that, as Susan Stanford Friedman argues, the 'misleading binary that sets up the West as modern and the Rest as traditional'[57] could be avoided. If the musicological descriptions of Australia written in the 1960s/'70s sought to reinstate this opposition, the composers were keen not to, much as they were careful to avoid other related oppositions: of inside/outside, centre/periphery and diffusion/concentration. Against the prevailing conservatism of 1940s Australia, the teenage Meale was reading Proust and Joyce.[58] Andrew Ford asked Meale: 'Were you thinking as you read Proust and Joyce and played Busoni, were you thinking about them as "Modernists"?' and Meale replied, without any sense of nostalgia for tradition:

> No, for one, we didn't have the word then. I mean this was all just perfectly natural, it was all just music, literature, painting etc. We weren't inclined to categorise things much at all in those days. Thank heavens. But I was merely aware of their distinctions, their differences. It all seemed to me to be one great flow the whole of the history of the arts, of music, it seemed to me, a great stream in which we more or less step in during our life.[59]

That sense of a movement is typical of Meale's descriptions of the time, and his sense of a 'great flow' is very different from notions of modernity held by the earlier twentieth-century composers that McCredie discussed. McCredie mentioned the painter Roy de Maistre in passing, and he lingered longer on Grainger, and on the 'free music' in particular, though the difficulties of encapsulating the diversity of Grainger's interests isolates his work from wider movements. McCredie concluded that 'Grainger's wild individualism represented and is likely to remain an historical world of its own',[60] as indeed it has. What separates the music of the 1960s from this earlier era is that by the 1960s more than one or two composers were working with similarly progressive ambitions, and for a time Australian modernism was a thriving movement.

McCredie's characterization of the period between 1955 and 1965 is in terms of social change, 'for it was within this period that Australia experienced some revolutionary changes in her economic and social structure following the discovery of vast mineral resources, an unprecedented technological expansion and mass migration of settlers from Europe'.[61] McCredie usefully emphasized the organizational development in these years, a theme that I will expand in connection with Banks and the 1972 Labor government. The main point to accentuate here is that for McCredie the changes made by composers took hold quickly, with 'an almost overnight international acceptance'.[62] This acceptance changed the situation for Australian composers born after 1945, for whom: 'post-Webern serialism, the theories of Messiaen, Boulez, Nono and Stockhausen, the cult of indeterminacy and cluster techniques, Ligeti and the modern Polish school are not merely accepted as accomplished facts but are assuming an almost classical significance'.[63] From the beginning, then, modernism in Australia hovered between experiment, discovery and stylistic orthodoxy. Throughout McCredie's survey there is little mention of any wider political ambition. The report was commissioned by Australia's federal government, which might account for some of the absence of partisan politics, though the private correspondence between these composers is also remarkably free of such politics. With a disconnection between political and musical spheres it is difficult to translate into an Australian context the opposition between musical expression of political attitude and the changing tastes of musical aesthetics that, for example, informs Rupprecht's reading of Britten's serialism. Similarly, the links upon which Harper-Scott relies to argue for modernism and communism in twentieth-century Britain are more diffuse for those working in Australia. Partly this difference is due to the union movement successfully securing working conditions that far exceeded those in Britain by the time of Australian self-government in 1901. This history provided the environment for an art music driven by aesthetics rather than one that was committed to political change, and this produced a form of modernism that was less about fundamental political confrontation. The exception to this lack of politics is around the infrastructure needed to support new music. Composers were active in working towards a greater significance for their music, and better state funding to support their activities, since Australia's relative economic equality had not resulted in substantial state funding for the arts. The ABC, for example, was not established in its national form until 1932. The postwar economic prosperity consolidated a conservative mindset across Australian politics and the Liberal Party government in 1966 was led by Robert Menzies as it had been at the start of the Second World War. After 1966 the Liberal Party continued to hold office, and McCredie's survey contains a foreword by Prime Minister John Gorton, who had served under Menzies as Minister for the Navy, Minister for Works and Minister for the Interior. He was also (from 1963 until 1968) Minister for Education. In the forward to McCredie's survey, Gorton writes that 'Australian musical composition has seen a marked development in recent times. This growth indicated that Australian composers can now play an important part in the musical life of the world at large [...]. It is hoped that, by focusing attention on this important aspect of the arts in Australia, this Survey will stimulate further growth.'[64] It reads like a foreword to a mining survey.

Although there was little national support for new music at this time, there were several significant local events, such as the festivals in Adelaide and Perth. During the 1971 Festival of Perth a seminar titled 'The Contemporary Australian Composer and Society' took place at the University of Western Australia. A report was subsequently published by its Department of Music. The document records the state of discussion about 'Australian music' (the second word not yet capitalized), and the seminar was one of a number of events that stabilized the discourse. The speakers included composers and academics, as well as André Jurres, President of the ISCM and director of the Donemus Foundation. The problems facing Australian composers emerge clearly in the report, and most of these relate to the low status of composers, including how they were regarded by the ABC, and to the difficulties composers faced when trying to earn enough money to focus on composition. McCredie's contribution was a talk on 'The Preservation of Australian Music'. At the time ABC radio was running a 'Musica Australis' series, which focussed on music from the colonial period, and which had collected nearly 1000 works from that time.[65] McCredie argued that the 'European-American experience supplies the guidelines necessary for the implementation of any systematic programme for the preservation of Australian music.'[66] McCredie also argued that it was time for the systematic and thorough documentation, archiving and collection of the music that had been composed in Australia, from which 'it should be possible to obtain a clearer vision of the necessary steps to be undertaken on behalf of Australian music, if a considerable volume of already composed works is not to be lost to us irreparably'.[67] Alongside new library catalogues of works, and changes to the copyright act to ensure that all published works were deposited in the National Library, McCredie recommended the creation of an 'Australian archive', repeating Covell's call for an internationally connected 'Information Centre' of 'recovery, documentation, edition and publication', 'to embrace all aspects of Australian music history as warrant preservation'.[68] With this in place:

> it should be possible to make a national contribution to international music scholarship on three different counts: firstly we archive our own counterpart of the various national historical *Denkmäler* and *monumenta* editions produced by other countries; secondly we are making a specific contribution to a new area of music scholarship – the systematic investigation of the nineteenth and early twentieth centuries as co-ordinated international team research; and thirdly it will represent a contribution to the study of transplanted music – the basis of any comparative music historiography.[69]

The proposals were endorsed by those present, and the discussion emphasized the need for a 'central Australian music information centre', rather than coordinated centres in the capital cities of each state.[70] The aim in 1971 was therefore for organizations to be set up in Australia that could connect to similar organizations elsewhere, to facilitate two-way communication with musicians internationally. In 1975 such an information centre was established.

Funding Australian Music

The growth in funding for music was rapid in the early years of the 1970s. The Advisory Board[71] began with funding of $10,000. In 1970–1 the Advisory Board's funding had increased to $60,000. In 1973 it was taken over by the Australian Council for the Arts. By the time that Banks was establishing the Australian Music Centre and organizing the many other activities of the Music Board of the Australia Council, he had a budget in the millions.[72] According to Tunley, who was Associate Professor of Music at the University of Western Australia at this time:

> Some idea of the financial support recently enjoyed by Australian composers can be gained by noting that in the twelve-month period 1974–75, the Australian Council provided up to seventy-five per cent of commission fees paid to some forty composers, [which] has made it possible for the author of a work to attend its première performance (in one case sending him to Europe), and has in the same twelve-month period granted generous fellowships to nineteen composers for the purposes of composition, travel, research or further study.[73]

With that prosperity came 'an ebullient spirit of national awareness and independence'.[74] By the time that Tunley wrote this in 1978, the exemplary composer of Australian Music was Sculthorpe: 'For many Australians Peter Sculthorpe suggests the continent's "spaciousness and terrifying sameness"'[.][75] The internal quotation is from Michael Hannan, who assisted Sculthorpe musically from the late 1960s, and who enhanced Sculthorpe's standing through the monograph *Peter Sculthorpe: His Music and Ideas 1929–1979*. No other Australian composer (however defined) had the resources to employ an assistant, nor the good fortune to have an early biographer. But if matters had solidified by the end of the 1970s, they were much less clear five years earlier. In Sculthorpe's first letter to Don Banks, 23 June 1955, he writes: 'I suppose one must class you as an English composer now (more "class" anyway!) + I certainly don't blame you if you're staying right where you are. In fact, I really think that the reason I've never written to you is envy. But now that I've made the ISCM. I feel that I can write to you + not be ashamed! In fact, am I the second Australian after you to have a work accepted?'[76] Faber, Sculthorpe's publisher, still incorrectly lists his Sonatina as 'the first Australian work to be performed at this international clearing-house for contemporary music'.[77] Banks had been in England for fewer than five years; the letter is a rare glimpse of Sculthorpe's attitude – one that is conscious of national identity – and it reveals an early instance of the contest for primacy amongst composers that plays out over the next twenty years.

Sculthorpe's Sonatina was published by the University of Sydney Music Publications, a publisher initiated by Peart, and which issued only a small handful of compositions and editions: Monteverdi's *Crucifixus, Et resurrexit* edited by Eric Gross (1962), Gross's own Two Songs for Female Voices, Op. 8 (published 1962), and then Sculthorpe's Sonatina (published 1964). For the *Sydney Morning Herald*'s 'Music and Drama

Critics', Sculthorpe's piece was published at an important moment, coinciding with Meale's contract with Boosey and Hawkes (which the authors considered 'by far the most important manifestation' of publications amongst the 'Australian composers'). For them, Sculthorpe's piece was 'the work that represented Australia at the 1955 International Society for Contemporary Music Festival in Baden-Baden: virtually the first work by an Australian composer still in firm touch with his birthplace to win an ISCM. performance'.[78] The breathless enthusiasm of the prose suggests Curt and Marea Prerauer as the unacknowledged authors of the article, as does the spinning description of the 'lightweight substance and inconclusive nature of the third movement' as contributing to 'the clarity and economy of the writing'. Nevertheless, the laboured prose also demonstrates the work that was being done to prise apart Banks and Australia, and to downplay the music of Glanville-Hicks, whose Choral Suite had been performed at an ISCM concert in 1938 (with the BBC Singers conducted by Adrian Boult)[79] and who by 1964 was living in Greece. 'Coming first' was important to elevate Sculthorpe's status above Meale, who, by 1964, had also been performed at an ISCM festival.

When, in 1963, Sculthorpe moved from Tasmania to Sydney to take up a lectureship in the Music Department at the University of Sydney, he met Ross Edwards, Anne Boyd and Alison Bauld. He employed Ian Cudgley as his first assistant, an appointment which was necessary to support his busy schedule, including the preparation for *The Fifth Continent* (1963). The latter composition shows many of the themes of travel and distance, from the local – 'Small town' – to the international – 'Pacific' – in its use of Lawrence's text (from *Kangaroo*). By 1964, Edwards was working as Sculthorpe's assistant, undertaking the copying work for the Sonata for Viola and Piano (composed 1960).[80] Covell reviewed the Sonata as breathlessly as the Prerauers might have: 'Sculthorpe's sonata, the dry gasps and desert glare of its percussion encircling the lonely human agony'[.][81] Skinner recounts Sculthorpe's reaction to this review, which goes to the desire at the time for greater acknowledgement of his music, and it also demonstrates the problematic connection between critics and composers:

> It was a virtuoso piece of mythologizing, coded in a manner ('desert', 'static', 'parched') guaranteed to resonate long afterward. Peter told his mother: 'I'm more than usually pleased to have such good crits – more bargaining power with Donald! But perhaps Roger Covell's is a little purple, "the lonely agony of the viola, & so on"; it sounds rather like Max Oldaker!'[82]

Any contest between Sculthorpe and other composers was to change in 1965, when Sculthorpe signed a contract with Faber Music. Faber was actively looking for a range of new composers, including someone from Australia, due to 'Faber's interest in authors (and markets) of the old empire and the looming Commonwealth Arts Festival', which provided an incentive to sign a 'composer from a Commonwealth country with a potential to make an impression in Britain'.[83]

Nationalism and the Individual

In the introduction to *Australian Composition in the Twentieth Century* Tunley wrote that 'From Grainger's *Australian Up-country Song* to Scullthorpe's *Sun Music* and *Irkanda* series, the appearance of works with Australian-inspired titles has lifted the hopes of those who await the creation of a truly national style.'[84] He concluded the introduction by remarking that 'the work of the younger generation of composers here is mostly stamped with that mark of cosmopolitanism which is such a strong feature of today's music in sophisticated societies throughout the world'.[85] He then quoted Gerald Abraham, writing about 'technological man' as 'international', using techniques of 'advanced music' that have no 'national characteristics'.[86] And he closed by dismissing the nationalist question: 'national movements are essentially "popular" movements, and the present upsurge of Australian composition coincides with a time when the gap between the forward-looking composer and the average audience is still wide'. 'Craftsmanship' is the mark of serious work, and that is 'the first consideration'.[87]

The meaning of Australian Music that developed in the 1960s and 1970s did so in an era in which technique meant far more than it would in the 1980s. In the earlier period, technique offered a way of contributing to modernism as a transnational movement (and therefore as a critique of nationalism), whilst in the later period technique merely marked the composer out as old-fashioned. In 1988 the academic Peter McCallum, who was also a critic for the *Sydney Morning Herald*, commented that: 'If I look honestly at my own criticism I would have to say that I probably look more from the points of view of historical development of the musical language, and well-crafted compositions. In other words, I'm stuck in the 1960s.'[88] With this change of emphasis, the 1980s brought much music that repeated ideas from piece to piece – rather than developing technique – and which was more predictably enjoyable. Here too Sculthorpe achieved much, and he came to be the defining composer of Australian Music through the consistency of his presence, from the 1950s throughout the stylistic changes of the 1980s and 1990s. Over this time his music changed, but this served to reinforce his *personal* presence, much as it did for Meale and Edwards, as well-known composers for whom radical musical change took place in the late 1970s that corresponded to the wider return to tonal aesthetics, a return which was as controversial in Australia as it was elsewhere.[89] Meale described this change in personal, rather than aesthetic or philosophical, terms:

[Meale:] […] there was a rupture between my own life experience and what I was doing artistically.
[Ford:] You spoke about changing your identity as a composer, and the fact that some people get used to a composer having a particular identity.
[Meale:] I like it, people like it.
[Ford:] Critics like it of course, critics like to put you in a box[.][90]

The same early period that saw the massive expansion in institutional support for musicology also saw support for composition and performance grow, all of which was of benefit to a new generation of higher-profile composers, who shared an international outlook and a desire to seek new directions for music. With enough composers to support a movement of modernism in Australia, 'Australian' became a convenient term for centring that movement's discourses, and from this a new musical nationalism arose, focussed around Sculthorpe, the composer who also received the lion's share of attention from the mainstream press. For many composers the term 'Australian' was less important, and there is no sense of a centre for their activity, since their impulse is connective and transnational. Those composers – including Keith Humble, Jennifer Fowler, Eric Gross and Graham Hair, for example – received less written attention. Even so, in the 1960s and well into the early 1970s, both the centring and connecting were a work in progress, and for McCredie, writing in the middle of that era, Sculthorpe's 'Australianism' in unusual, setting 'him apart from his contemporaries'.[91]

In the 1960s and 1970s there are signs of the term 'Australian' being a significant problem. The problem is most clearly voiced by David Lumsdaine upon his return to Australia in 1973. This was his first return in twenty years, when he took part in the National Conference of Australian Composers organized by Banks. There was some disagreement between Banks and Lumsdaine about the extent of Lumsdaine's involvement, which prompted a letter by Lumsdaine to Banks, voicing a problem for the 'Australian' that comes before 'composer':

> And that brings me to *compositor australiensis*. This constant prefixing of the words 'music' and 'composer' by the word 'Australian' is more than just a nervous tic. [...] Isn't it something forced on us by a self-conscious social attitude, an attitude which, since it is concerned with *imposing* an identity rather than *discovering* one, can only be suffocating to the development of anybody who lives on this continent and is concerned to explore an infinity of human consciousness. It's an attitude which must be rejected to create any viable native culture which will truly integrate its composers.
>
> When, at the first session here, somebody suggested there should be a certain quota of Australian music performed in Australia (30%!!) I was stunned. But I have now been more worried by the continual and accepted use of the word by the majority of the people here who have spoken. To me, the distinction between 'music *in* Australia' and 'music *of* Australia', 'music *about* or *for* or *from* Australia' seems to have been lost. Most people refer to 'Australian Music' and 'Australian composers' as they would to 'Australian refrigerators' or the 'Australian wool industry'.
>
> All of us here have a community of interest; we're all concerned with creating music now and wherever we may be; and that community of interest is shared with composers throughout the world. It is an interest which refuses to be circumscribed, and where it is, it dies.[92]

For few other composers does *Australia* emerge in its geographical, political and mythical forms with such interrelatedness as it does for Lumsdaine. In this letter, the designation 'Australian composer' is conceived as a political idea with which Lumsdaine disagrees, since it excludes composers who do not fit the nationalist agenda. He also sees it as a protectionist ideology, and therefore equates it with manufacturing tariffs, since quotas are only necessary to protect local interests in a global music market, and he rejects those concepts as a means of describing music. To make his point, Lumsdaine contrasts the music-market model with one built on 'a community of interest', for 'creating music' rather than exchanging musical products, and so contrasts an implicitly capitalist model with a non-capitalist one. What makes this letter so significant is that it gives a concentrated, palpable sense of the change that had taken place between 1953 – the year Lumsdaine moved to Britain – and 1973 – the year he first returned to Australia. The letter presents a sense of exclusion that goes with the idea of 'Australian Music', since the 'community' of which Lumsdaine speaks does not uniformly include everyone at the conference. 'Integration' may have been the reason for hosting the conference, but Lumsdaine finds that 'integration' is about 'imposing an identity', and since that identity is 'Australian', what use will it have for Lumsdaine in Durham?

Lumsdaine's letter was also a reaction to the talk given by J. L. Sturman, who was the managing director of the Australian Performing Right Association (APRA). At the 1973 National Conference of Australian Composers, which had the theme 'The status and role of the Australian Composer', Sturman gave a talk titled 'The Economic Worth of Australian Music', and he began by setting out the argument for considering Australian Music in purely economic terms:

> Any proper evaluation of the role and status of the Australian composer must ultimately include an assessment of the economic worth of the music he creates. Indeed, it is the only criterion that reflects in objective terms the overall public acceptance or otherwise of his music and, while such acceptance may be challenged by succeeding generations, it must surely remain the one readily available measure that is indicative of the composer's ability to communicate effectively with society through this unique medium.[93]

This speech is indicative of the rapid trend towards purely economic arguments for supporting the arts, which continued to strengthen throughout the 1970s, and which by the 1980s had fundamentally changed the idea of Australian Music.

Lumsdaine's criticism of this reductively economic argument is a reminder that the term 'Australian Music' was far from neutral, and that its politics were often associated with those who were as keen to exclude composers as they were to form a new movement. On the eve of Australia Day 1973,[94] Lumsdaine's *Aria for Edward John Eyre* was first performed at a BBC Invitation Concert, and the next day he wrote to Banks:

> Perhaps I better tell you about it, since I doubt if there can be anything happening of greater importance to Australian music – not as you'll realise that I'm being niggardly – it is simply a good and strange work.[95]

Although keenly aware of its problems, Lumsdaine nevertheless used the term 'Australian', and although he had been away from Australia for two decades, he conceived of this composition as 'Australian'. Lumsdaine's letter points to the political aspect of 'Australian Music' that has disappeared from view. It also points to the difficulties of composing against an increasingly centred idea of Australian Music.

Australian Music as an idea gathered prominence in the 1960s, and in 1973 it was consolidated with government funding, as the following chapter explains. By 1975 the modernist movement of Australian Music had ended. It is for this reason that this book focusses on the music of some of the high-profile composers of that time. Through their differences, the idea of Australian Music can again be contested.

2

Infrastructure for New Music, Serial Technique and Don Banks's *String Quartet* (1975)

The relationship between composers based within Australia and those based without changed dramatically with the 1972 election of the Whitlam Labor government. The changes brought new funding for composition, new opportunities for performance, direct support for the publication of scores, a greater sense of two-way movement between Australia and Britain and new fora for composers and performers to discuss music, all of which had a direct impact on the music that was being composed. At the centre of the structural changes was Don Banks, one of the composers who returned to Australia in the early 1970s after a long period of absence. Banks's surviving correspondence is extensive, and it provides a detailed insight into the opportunities and challenges of this time. His 1975 *String Quartet* demonstrates the musical significance of the organizations that he founded as chairman of the Music Board of the Australia Council, since the composition connects the musical work he was undertaking in the 1970s with his experience in London in the years before his return, and with his time as a student of Luigi Dallapiccola in the 1950s. It also provides a musical basis for considering the importance of technique in Australia in the early 1970s.

Since 1949 Australia had been led by a series of conservative governments under Robert Menzies, Harold Holt, John McEwen, John Gorton and William McMahon. The swing to Labor in the 1969 election (an election that it lost, but which set up its win in 1972) brought an increase in 'confidence, optimism and energy'[1] for the Labor party under Whitlam's leadership. 'Confidence, optimism and energy' reflected wider attitudes at the time, including those held by Australia's musicians, and it is in terms of 'confidence' that Covell characterized Australian Music in the late 1960s:

> composers have not been content merely to imitate the latest musical fashions from overseas; they – or rather a few of them – have shown great confidence in attempting to find a synthesis of styles true to themselves and the society (local and international) for which they are writing.[2]

In the years after Covell wrote this in 1967 the opportunities for concerts for new music within Australia grew rapidly. Confidence comes with age, or with the 'coming of age', as James Murdoch has it, here writing in 1972:

Australia's music came of age in the 1960s: the life force and influence of our music world gathered momentum until it exploded onto the international stage.³

Peter Maxwell Davies's foreword to Murdoch's book also recounts his encounter with Australia in the 1960s in terms of confidence. In this case, Australia's lack of confidence is seen as a positive force compared with European complacency:

> The climate among young composers was quite unlike that in Europe, where there is an awareness (even if a rejection) of 'tradition', with a real tradition of performances, into which the composer fits (perhaps most uncomfortably), which generates (at the risk of a too general generalization!) a certain confidence, a taking of a situation for granted.⁴

'[T]radition' (whether rejected or not) and 'the modern' are formed relationally through 'confidence', and so confidence becomes a key to arguments about tradition and modernity. These arguments are also bound up with arguments about the relationships between Australia and Europe (or Australia and 'elsewhere', or 'local and international'). Meale, Butterley and Sculthorpe all talk about their experience of the 1960s and early 1970s in terms of their growing personal confidence, and there has been an easy slip between 'the personal' and 'the national', with earlier Australian music cast as having been written naïvely by composers who lacked the confidence of speaking with an original, individual voice – with the voice of modern Australia.

Part of what restricted that slippage in Britain was the diverse practical support for composers. In 1960s Australia, however, there was very little by way of infrastructure at either a city, or state or national scale that supported newly written music, beyond the activities run by lone composers.⁵ The main support came from a small handful of places: the Adelaide Festival, the Festival of Perth, Musica Viva and academic music departments in Sydney, Adelaide and Perth, though even with this list only a handful of people were highly influential, and many of the opportunities that they afforded had been newly established. The only significant national support came from the Australian Broadcasting Commission (ABC) and their orchestras. Until the 1972 election and the increased funding for the arts that it brought, there was very little by way of organizational support for professional music-making. When organizations were established they solidified the idea of the 'Australian Composer', and with that concept arose a newly 'personal' nationalism, centred on individual composers rather than a broad movement. Voicing the difficulty of matching national and personal identity, Lumsdaine, who had lived away from Australia since 1953, wrote to Banks:

> Perhaps you and I have made a great mistake in continuing to think of ourselves as Australians. We know the intrinsic value of Australian music in Australia and it should be no great disappointment to form no part of that scene. Except that it is! But the disappointment is not a musical one. It's probably a much more personal grief and as such, something to be overcome. Peter's [Porter] probably

had the right attitude all along. Everybody remains a stranger in that country, any country[,] and the only home we have a right to is within ourselves.[6]

For Murdoch and for Covell (and, indeed, most of those writing about composers based in Australia), the concept of 'Australian Music' is by the mid-1970s to be taken for granted. For individual musicians the concept is less clear-cut, and it varies significantly from composer to composer. For Banks the matter is never decisive, and although he was crucial for the organizations that were being formed, his priority was always that composers receive the funding that they needed to write music. In 1972, there was the potential for the consolidation of the movement of modernist composers in Australia, and for this to happen it needed central funding that was not concerned with promoting a distinctive form of music. Banks's attitude was open in this regard, and he did not favour a particular school of composition.

*

Having left Australia in 1950, in 1969 Banks wrote to Frank Callaway in Perth from his home in London about a possible return:

> Regardless of my active life here I have felt more and more the pressure of being an Australian composer away from my country. How long can I go on considering myself an Australian? I expect what has stopped me short in my tracks is the realization that next year it will be twenty years since I left home, and that if I don't make the attempt to return very soon, then perhaps I never will.[7]

Callaway invited Banks to lead a composers' workshop as part of the 1970 Perth Festival, an invitation that Banks accepted.[8] In 1972 he again visited Australia, for a longer stay as a Creative Arts Fellow in Canberra, only to find the position poorly paid and under-resourced,[9] and he was 'very glad [to have] return tickets'.[10]

In 1972 Banks wrote a statement in which composition was compared to sport, and it reveals Banks's desire for a well-funded national organization for composers:

> It comes down to a matter of the status and stature of the composer, and this is something which will not be reconciled until he is considered as important as a professional tennis player.
>
> I say this as an admirer of the talents of Ken Rosewall and Rod Laver, as here are people who have worked for years and years to perfect their craft. They know the percentages to play, the dedication which is required to attain the status of a 'professional' and justly reap their rewards.
>
> When will this happen to the composer? We have spent years as well to perfect our technique. We are concerned about the 'state of play' but are being denied the opportunity to protest to the referee and the linesmen when we are being misrepresented. And who are they? The organisations provide us with the platform for us to be heard, or the court to play on if you prefer.

> As tennis has grown into a situation of the 'professionals' versus the rest, then I'm afraid that for the Australian composers it's a matter of accept your 5 dollar fee (and a glass of red wine if you're lucky) and don't try to act like one of the big boys. But I must protest – as an ex-aptaite [sic][11] I play in the big leagues.[12]

Australian tennis players were doing well at the time, and Banks made the same comparison in a letter to David Ahern, in which he emphasized the systematic problem facing composers:

> This ['rough deal'] is international, but especially true of conditions in Australia where THE SYSTEM has so far relegated us to the very fringe of society. I've always believed that until we at least have the status of, say, a top tennis player, then we're only battling along and being overlooked.[13]

The opportunity to change the system came surprisingly quickly, and within a year Banks was in a position to make important changes to the organization of Australia's musical scene, establishing significant new structures to support professional composition; his return tickets to the UK were not needed. On Australia Day 1973, Banks wrote to Alan Woolgar, at his publisher Schott, with news of his new appointment:

> [T]here has been rather an extraordinary development for me out here. The new Government headed by Gough Whitlam is making some amazingly rapid changes (for the good) to life out here, and one of his projects has been to nurture the Arts. He has taken these under the wing of his own Prime Minister's Department [...] and to-day he has announced the formation of a new Australian Council for the Arts.[14] This will be a statutory body (like the ABC in a way) with responsibility to administer its funds in its own way. He has appointed a Council of some 24 members, but with its Executive arms being headed by Chairmen of 7 boards representing the various arts.
>   I rather anticipated John Hopkins would be chairman of the Music Board, but to my great surprise I was invited, and after seeking a 12 hours delay, accepted. So I am now Chairman of the Music Board effective as of to-day, and therefore the holder of the most influential post in Australian music.[15]

The changes made were *systemic*, providing not just more funding for music,[16] but better infrastructure for its development.

The appointment was made in the week before the announcement of the Australia Council,[17] which is indicative of the rapidity of the changes taking place. The formation of the Council came directly from the Prime Minister, who on 27 January 1973 expressed his new confidence in the arts:

> Vitality in the arts was frequently accompanied by innovation, by controversy and by challenge to established conventions of taste, belief and behaviour.

Artists need protection from unnecessary restraints and governments should be able to resist pressures from those who are disturbed by controversy and challenge.[18]

The board of which Banks was chairman comprised a wide range of practitioners, few of whom had held positions of administrative power in the previous era. In March, Banks wrote to Lumsdaine, giving brief biographical sketches of the board's members, who included:

> John Hopkins (ex Chairman CAAC [Commonwealth Assistance to Australian Composers]), Frank Callaway (ex CAAC and Music Committee), senior composer Bob Hughes (ex CAAC, ABC, APRA [Australasian Performing Rights Association]) Elizabeth Silsbury (Adelaide […] a fighter, teacher and real person), Rod Taylor (singer, businessman from Innisfail – 800 miles North of Brisbane – organized a Summer Conservatoire there and an Opera company using Italian cane-cutters and an orchestra [of] kids [from] all over Australia – real Bazza), John Painter (cellist-teacher at the Con, stirrer and fighter), Ken Tribe (solicitor – Secretary Musica Viva – solid with know-how and devoted to music), Winsome Evans (young teacher at Music Dept. Sydney, organises very good concerts […]), Kim Williams (extraordinary 20 year old composer – one of the first kids I met in Perth 1970 and may have influenced – he's my Dave Lumsdaine with the integrity, refusal to compromise, imagination, concern – all the things that mark you. […]) and Jeanie Lewis (jazz singer plus – kinda Cathy Berberian material […]).[19]

With so little infrastructure in place, the work required for the new board was extensive, and Banks's initial ideas give a sense of the task as he conceived it:

> I told the board I saw us as one concerned with policy, not policing applications as this we could relegate to others and thereby extend our 'ears' into the community. That we had to establish 'alternatives' to the present musical situation, seek out the many gaps in the fabric of musical life here and show initiative in plugging them, develop communications between groups, states and overseas, build an Australian Music Centre as an executive arm etc. etc. and etc.[20]

Banks referred to the document that came from the first meeting as 'our "manifesto"'; and his conception of the board's role was explicitly future-focussed and internationally minded, and less focussed on Australia than the Council was to become. The change that Banks's outlook brought was significant for Australia, ending a period during which the ABC was the primary source of employment for composers, and in which overseas study was mandatory for gaining the credentials of composition necessary for securing commissions.

The increased funding available through the Music Board coincided with an expansion in the universities, with many of the new positions filled by composers. Banks, at the same time as he was chair of the Music Board, was also establishing an electronic music studio at the Canberra School of Music. The funding for this was significant, and involved developing new technology. Banks had already established a studio at Goldsmiths, in London, and he had commissioned the VCS1 synthesizer from EMS Putney:

> I'm proud to own the Zinovieff EMS VCS 1 (serial 001) as I […] asked for it, and that my VCS3 is model number 003 (how did I miss out there?) and that the QASAR II is Serial number 001, and the Multimode 8 will be 001, and the Cardiff Sequencer is 001.[21]

With assistance from the Music Board in the form of two grants of $12,000 and $14,000 (1974, 1975), the Canberra School of Music was at the forefront of studio development, purchasing Furse's digital QASAR II in early 1975.[22]

In 1973 Lumsdaine returned to Australia for several months, brought back with Australia Council finance through Banks's support. Late in the year[23] Banks wrote to Lumsdaine about how he saw his role as chairman, and about the scale of the work to be done, and he did so in terms of their shared experience in London:

> You view from the outside still, but you know how much there is to be done? Where's our 1st rate chamber performing group? Why does the ABC still only have 5% Oz content? How best can we get composers out to primary schools? What about our Music Information Centre? These things need time and staff, and yet we have the money. BUT WHERE DO WE GET THE PEOPLE FROM? We need 7 Jamie's [sic], 2 Bill Collerans, 4 Michael Vyners, 3 Gary Howarths etc. to make things work and take the load off our backs.[24]

By 1976, most of what was to be done had been accomplished, and the scale of optimism and energy that characterizes this early period proved to be justified.

The most visible body founded by the Music Board was the Australian Music Centre (AMC). A music centre (information centre) was one of the first ideas that Banks raised, and it was needed to fulfil several functions. One was to connect to other information centres and better facilitate two-way knowledge about music being composed within Australia and abroad. It would also be a place for purchasing music published in Australia and elsewhere and it would house perusal scores and recordings. By participating in the transfer of music internationally those composers resident in Australia would be able to keep up to date with the latest developments in music, and through reciprocal arrangements those outside Australia would have better access to scores by composers based in Australia.[25] A further function was to act as both a local publisher and an intermediary for existing publishing houses, and by so doing to form a nexus for promotion. As such, the Centre's role was to open Australian composition to wider influences and to enable Australian composers to work more closely with their counterparts elsewhere.

As early as February 1973, less than a fortnight after the formation of the Australia Council and two years before Australia's Information Centre came into existence,

Banks sent James Murdoch a possible structure for an AMC. Murdoch would eventually become the AMC's first director, and his experience as an artist manager in London, in addition to his work for the World Record Club (which was the principal source for recordings of music by Australian composers in the 1960s) gave him the international perspective that suited Banks's plan for the AMC. Murdoch had also worked with Banks in London, where in the previous years Murdoch had managed a range of artists, including: Davies (whom he managed internationally); Hans Werner Henze (UK); Leo Brouwer (UK); London Contemporary Dance Company; Domaine Musicale and Gilbert Amy (UK); Stephen Pruslin; Cathy Berberian (UK); Roy Hart; and the Pierrot Players.[26]

It is worth considering the proposed structure, since even though the AMC's functions later differed from those listed, it nevertheless demonstrates how Banks was thinking about Australian Music. Banks lists six functions, starting with: '1 Library of Scores, Books, Tapes, Discs, Films, Research Material' and '2 Promotion of Australian Music and Musicians'. These would include: an 'Information Bureau' to maintain lists of compositions and of performers; the 'active encouragement of performances' (by way of subsidizing hire fees within Australia and rehearsal costs without); 'audio/visual facilities' for visitors to the Centre; a quarterly journal; and membership of international organizations such as the International Society for Contemporary Music (ISCM). The list went on: '3 "Educational" work with ASME [Australian Society for Music Education] and ISME, as well as "international exchanges"'; '4 Centre for Musicological Research' in 'Aboriginal', 'Early Australian', 'Pacific Area' and 'SE Asia' music; '5 Storehouse for performing equipment (Electronic and Exotic)'; '6 Social Centre' for 'Entertaining visiting VIPs', a 'Bureau for "Youth & Music" (Jeunesses Musicale)' and a 'paid membership body'.[27]

In the UK, the British Arts Council had just taken over the responsibilities of the local work of the ICSM, and the list of people involved in that formation covers a similar range of interests to those represented by Banks's ideas for the AMC. The people involved in the former were David Drew ('Chairman'), Martin Dalby, Alexander Goehr and Jonathan Harvey (both listed by Banks as 'Academic'), Keith Winter ('electronics'), Barry Guy, Roger Smalley, Alan Hacker, Stephen Plaistow, Kevin Stephens and Barrie Illiffe. Many of these people were close colleagues of Banks, with whom he was in close correspondence during this period.[28] This collection of people integrated the national broadcaster, independent musicians and academics, with Drew as an academic, producer and journalist bridging several fields, as Murdoch, too, was seeking to do.

The AMC was part of a larger plan, a physical manifestation of a concept that had been part of Banks's thinking from the very beginnings of the Music Board, in which the centrality of policy came with a focus on 'ideas':

> in fact what I did in London has been trebled (at least) because of the 'official' mantle which has fallen on my shoulders. I don't want this at all, the VIP, Commonwealth Car, attend official functions bit is against my nature, so I'll be a drop-out as much as possible – EXCEPT – that I'll fight to the death to get certain ideas and concepts through. The only possible advantage of being 'The Chair' is this[.][29]

One of the difficulties for Banks was that the Music Board was not yet a statutory body, and its recommendations needed to be approved by the Australia Council, which would then make recommendations to the prime minister. Negotiating this restriction in autonomy, the AMC was strategically to be located away from the Music Board's offices, to protect its offices from being co-opted by other parts of the Council in the competition for space.[30]

Banks had been unwell for several years, and on 2 December 1974 he wrote to Murdoch about his ill health, relaying his doctor's prescription to take 'a month's holiday ASAP! with no commitments at all', and asks: 'My prime concern is the AMC – was Ian Turner[31] forthcoming? Are we all resigning?'[32] (Banks's illness and the busyness at the Canberra School of Music prevented him from being at the board meetings at this time, but Ken Tribe, who had been deputy chair, was also working towards the formation of an AMC.[33]) In January 1975 Banks wrote to Colleran:

> The Music Centre came to the crunch this meeting. The Directors did not accept the compromise that the Board has suggested to them and want the amount they asked for in full – instead of the suggesting [sic] that they get an amount to establish the *structure* AND THEN apply to the Board for individual projects. I fully supported the view of the AMC director's [sic] and after much to and froing moved that they be given the amount requested and we just lay it on the line with the Council Finance C'tee and the Council itself that we are tired of fucking around and that this goes through *OR ELSE*! The Board was unanimous and we have stuck our necks out, so now anxiously await the reaction at the Council meeting on Feb 7. Jamie [Murdoch] has a hold on the Rocks area until then and I'm hopeful that the Council will realise that we are all tired of stalling and delaying tactics and I don't think they'll risk the turmoil the Board will create (resignations, conferences) if they refuse.[34]

In February, Banks was able to write to Woolgar at Schott with the news that:

> James Murdoch has been appointed National Director of the Australian Music Centre Ltd. This is something we have been fighting about for years, and after 2 years on the Music Board of pushing and pushing we've finally got it financed. I was determined right from the start it would not be a 'hole in the wall' operation so it starts with a bang! The premises are fabulous – 8000 sq. feet in a prime area of Sydney. Just off Circular Quay with views to the Opera House and Bridge in a location which a State Development Authority wants to make into a place where the arts will be encouraged, tourists enticed, wonderful restaurants, shopping arcades etc. […] Here will be the prime network for the promotion of Australian music and musicians. Computerised data on all works and repertoire of performers linked to every other city, listening booths, concert promotions, recording facilities, displays AND sales of materials of overseas as well as Oz composers. The Centre (from now on the AMC) will charge for services, but there will be nothing else to touch it in Australia.[35]

Murdoch's role changed from being a consultant advisor to the Music Board to head of the AMC, where he was to 'be a kind of co-ordinating figure to keep everyone informed of who is doing what/where'.[36] The desire, as ever with Banks, was for an open musical environment with well-informed composers.

The AMC was to be an 'executive arm' of the Music Board, undertaking a role that was part promoter, part manager and part publisher – the models being the Society for the Promotion of New Music (SPNM) and the British Music Information Centre in the UK, with Murdoch undertaking similar work to that which he had undertaken in London. In its early years of operation, the AMC did fulfil the role of a publisher, collecting hire fees and making sales. For example, Banks assigned his *Divertimento for Flute and String Trio* to the AMC, rather than to his existing publisher Schott, under 'the usual terms'[37] for hire and sales royalties, in exchange for the AMC producing performance materials.[38] The AMC provided the essential organization of music in Australia, and it also provided a centre for the promotion of Australian composers. With its foundation, the phase of Australian Music that was increasingly concerned with promotion, and later with celebration, began. Murdoch's 1972 book *Australia's Contemporary Composers* marks the start of what became the 'celebratory model' of Australian Music, which reached its dominance in the late 1980s.

Later developments, such as the 1976 Australian Composers and Performers Seminar, were initiated by Banks and Lumsdaine as a direct extension of the SPNM Composer Weekends that Banks, Lumsdaine and Anthony Gilbert had started in the UK, themselves modelled on the Wardour Castle Summer Schools, and on Dartington and Darmstadt.[39] The intention was to promote similar opportunities as had existed for Banks in Britain, with diverse support for new music. Banks had been involved with the SPNM since the mid-1950s, and served as a member of its executive committee from 1965. From 1967 to 1968 he was its chairman, and remained a member of the executive committee until he left for Australia in 1972. He was a founding member of the British Society for Electronic Music, and a member of their executive committee,[40] and with Margaret Sutherland he founded the Australian Musical Association in London at Australia House, which gave concerts of Australian music with British Council funding.[41]

Similarly, the Australian Contemporary Music Ensemble (ACME) was founded by Banks, Keith Humble, Larry Sitsky, Peter Platt and Murray Khouri, the latter keen to expand his solo career after working in London's professional orchestras.[42] Humble was appointed Professor of Music at La Trobe University, Melbourne, and the ensemble was formed in 1975. With its significant funding from the Music Board, the ensemble was a national one, and toured extensively.[43] In 1976 Lumsdaine's proposal for the Australian Composers and Performers Seminar refers to ACME as an 'ensemble ready made with similar aims to those of the seminar and which can be used even more effectively by working through the seminar with composers and other players on a national scale.'[44] He therefore tacitly connects ACME to the Melos Ensemble, which had performed this role at the Wardour Castle Summer Schools, as well as to the Nash Ensemble and the ad hoc groups that had come together for the SPNM Composers' Seminars.

In 1976 Banks wrote to Barry Tuckwell, telling him of the latest developments with the Music Board, including ACME:

> This has been a real break-through for us in that we have proved this year that we can produce an ensemble in Australia equal to that of the Sinfonietta![45]

The London Sinfonietta visited Australia in 1976 on a tour organized by Musica Viva (the head of which, Ken Tribe, was also on the Music Board). They performed works by a wide range of composers – Bach, Birtwistle, Debussy, Haydn, Gerhard, Ligeti, Mozart and Wagner – and also Banks's *Sonata da Camera*.[46] With the London Sinfonietta touring, one of the models for ACME was present in Australia in the year of ACME's launch. In his letter to Tuckwell, Banks explained that ACME aimed to 'present music by those composers who have made the most contribution to music in this century, to serve the Australian composer, and also to play significant music by American and European composers who are almost unknown out here'.[47] In the first year, two institutions hosted the ensemble, the University of Sydney and the Canberra School of Music, with players travelling to each for a week of rehearsals, performances and recordings. In the first concert ACME performed Stravinsky's *Octet*, Webern's Op. 22, Davidovsky's *Synchronism No. 2*, Shostakovich's Piano Sonata No. 1 and Gerhard's *Libra*. In the second concert they performed Schoenberg's Suite Op. 29, followed by '3 composers who have recently returned from overseas', Peggy Glanville-Hicks (*5 Portraits*), Lumsdaine (*Annotations of Auschwitz*) and Graham Hair (*Ensemble*), the latter commissioned for the performance.[48] Their plans for 1978 included a series of concerts at the Adelaide Festival of 'the complete chamber music of Roberto Gerhard and all the Webern songs with Jane Manning'. This programme itself recalls October and November 1973, when the London Sinfonietta had performed the complete Gerhard chamber works. The plan for ACME to perform Gerhard's chamber music did not eventuate, though they did perform Webern with Manning.[49]

Like that of the AMC, the significance of ACME was as a national entity that was international in outlook. This marks it out from the proliferation of ensembles that came into being in the later 1970s, which arose attached to specific cities (often to a particular university), or those that had come before, which were mostly local due to the commitments of players to the orchestra that provided them with work. This also made ACME highly dependent on Music Board funding. In later years it became more difficult to obtain funding from the Music Board for non-Australian music, and in the late 1970s ACME disbanded, at the same time that the visiting composers' residencies also ceased, as funding became focussed on activities within Australia, rather than activities that better connected Australia to other places.

One of the last 'composers in residence' was Salvatore Martirano, who in 1979 was brought by Banks from the University of Illinois to the Sydney Conservatorium, funded by the Music Board.[50] Martirano had, like Banks, studied with Dallapiccola, and he maintained a correspondence with Bank throughout the latter's life. In a letter to Martirano written in preparation for his residency in Sydney, Banks recalled an earlier SPNM seminar that Banks had organized for Martirano in London:

I remember you playing a tape of 'BALLAD' in London at the SPNM Seminar during one session and a lots of the guys didn't get it. Then you followed this up with an illuminating exposé of combinatoriality and its application and I was grabbed on the way by people like Elgar Howarth, Sherlaw Johnson etc. etc. saying how much it meant to them then as they could see what it was about and hear it as well, and who was Milton Babbitt? I also remember you saying 'why should I regurgitate this old stuff?' – but Sal – THEY DIDN'T KNOW IT! Boy, you proved a point that day. That cunning old deep-down craftsman who wasn't fucking about in the music he wrote and knew, and was in control of everything he was doing.[51]

The SPNM seminar to which Banks refers took place at Goldsmiths in London, where Banks had established an electronic music studio, and it was one of the series of seminars that he organized with Gilbert and Lumsdaine. In 1969 Babbitt had been their guest composer, and in 1970, Pousseur.[52] What Banks sought to establish in Australia were similar fora in which detailed technical conversations could take place amongst a group of composers.

In his correspondence Banks constantly voices the usefulness of his previous experience in the UK, and at the same time he was very clear about the problems he had encountered there. Similarly, a memo Lumsdaine wrote for his Adelaide residency in 1976, a copy of which is held in Banks's archive, outlined the need for better organizational support for new music at the same time that it questioned British practice, since the 'British musical scene is anything but Utopia'.[53] Indeed, Lumsdaine's proposal for an 'Australian Musicians' Seminar', written in mid-1976, makes explicit that the relationship between British experience and new Australian organizations is one of critique:

There are many criticisms to be made of the summer schools [such as Dartington]; not least, that there is too much opportunity for 'ego tripping', and consequently a certain amount of elitism; even so, young composers with initiative can make good contacts. In 1967, after the demise of the short-lived but highly successful Wardour Castle Summer Schools, Don Banks, Anthony Gilbert and myself devised and directed the first SPNM Composers Seminar which was at once a critique of the existing summer schools and a setting out in a new direction.[54]

Such is a reminder of the interconnectedness of the two places, and of the complexity of the relationships and extensive collaborations that go to form organizations. Banks's involvement with British musical life means that there was no straightforward transplantation of British models, since the British organizations were in part also formed/founded by him, making any clear designation of nationality of the models problematic.

The idea of transforming a model to suit a new environment as a form of critique underpins the whole expansion that goes with Banks's work with the Australia Council. That critique extends to issues of nationalism, especially given how frequently Banks and his correspondents wonder openly what Australian Music might mean, how readily conceptions of nationality shift depending on where composers live at the time and how flexible the concept can be depending on the work that they are undertaking. Given the emphasis that Banks gives to composition and the tension he feels between putting in place mechanisms that would help others and finding time to compose, the period between 1972 and 1975, when Banks was establishing so much, is an era in which his correspondents were able to question again where they lived and what they wanted to compose (in part because of that correspondence). Only rarely does Banks discuss audiences for music, and there is little sense of there being any existing scene from which more listeners might be attracted. Rather the scene is to emerge, and the excitement about that emergence is the desire to be part of what might arise. Allied to this is the desire to contribute to the new scene so that it does come to exist, and to realize the potential that the new funding and young population presents.

By January 1975, two years after his appointment as chairman, Banks was ready to leave the Australia Council, despite the possibility of staying longer:

> It's lovely to be wanted for your integrity, balance, perspective etc., but after 2 1/2 years of slave labour that's enough. Especially when I know the carve-up and empire building is already in operation so let it happen. At least I've given a valuable (?) breathing space for other influences to operate, but the career guys will win in the end as they use music as a 'product' and I want to produce. C*R*A*Z*Y*. Let's join the ranks of the exploited.[55]

Although Banks had succeeded in establishing the organizations that were lacking, the task of having to do this, in addition to his teaching and administrative work at the Canberra School of Music, left him very little time to compose. With the establishment of a well-funded national body for music, its work was newly surrounded by personal politics, and with that a new form of the idea of an Australian Composer arises, less internationally connected and less useful for those composers whose performers lived across the globe. The new 'Australian Composer' is indivisible from the new organizations, however much individualism and nationalism might seem at odds in their purposes. Just as the discussion about new quotas for Australian music goes with the industry to push for those quotas, so Australian music ceases to be open, flexible and internationally minded. Although organizations such as the AMC were founded to provide reciprocal arrangements with music centres internationally, those links proved to be insignificant compared to their work within Australia, and by the 1980s the AMC was responsible for formalizing the notion of a distinctively Australian Music, particularly through its journal *Sounds Australian*. This change in the conception of Australian Music combined with different (mostly neo-tonal) compositional aesthetics to end Australian Music in its modernist form.

*

In 1975 the only work that Banks composed was his first string quartet. In the previous year he wrote *Carillon*, a short piece commissioned by the ABC for the initial broadcast by ABC-FM in 1976, and *Prospects*, for the ongoing celebrations around the opening of the Sydney Opera House. In 1973 he composed *Take Eight*, a crossover work for jazz and string quartet. In correspondence with Martirano from December 1974, Banks described the work of the previous years, his poor health and his work for the Canberra School of Music:

> I've hardly written any music, I've been in all kinds of fights to establish the rights of the composer and performer out here, for a year and one-half – as an appointment by the Prime Minister – I was Chairman of the Music Board for the Australian Council of the Arts with a budget of some 3 million dollars (Aus.) – and although still a member of the Board I establish[ed] new organizations to fight (supplement?) what the Board has achieved under my Chairmanship. Like an Electronic Arts Society, Composer's [sic] Guild of Australia, and all the things we miss out here.[56]

Writing to Martirano in 1975 Banks charted the decline in his output over the previous years:

> Sorry if I'm in a down phase at the moment Sal, but with this month finishes my involvement with the Board after 2 1/2 years. The PM has asked me to stay on for another year, but I've [said] 'no way'. [...]
>
> You can look at a ratio of
>
> | | |
> |---|---|
> | UK 1971 | 6 major works |
> | OZ 1972 | 4 works |
> | OZ 1973 | 1 work |
> | OZ 1974 | 1 work |
>
> [...] I'm now for me.[57]

Banks had always been a prolific composer. Extending the list back into the 1960s would include not just major commissions from the London Sinfonietta, the London Symphony Orchestra and the BBC Symphony Orchestra, but also the music for nineteen feature films, advertisements and documentaries that he had composed since the 1950s.[58] The decline was not due to a wane in commissions, and his correspondence with Schott makes frequent reference to new opportunities. Rather, his time was almost exclusively occupied by forming the organizations that he saw as lacking in Australia at the time. The *String Quartet* marks a break with those efforts. He wrote to Bill Colleran at the end of August 1975 that

> I have had my head down at *composing* and a few hours ago finished my *String Quartet* (1975).[59]

He closed the letter by telling Colleran that he presumed the work would be the property of Universal Edition (Australia) by the time of the first performance, which was scheduled for 17 October.

Banks had been unhappy with Schott for some time. Michael Vyner had been Banks's promoter at Schott and he was now organizing the London Sinfonietta, and in a letter dated 3 March 1975,[60] Vyner recommended that Banks leave Schott. In his reply to Vyner's letter, Banks, on 11 May 1975, raised the additional complication of having heard that Schott had approached Denis James (of Ricordi[61]) to set up Schott (Australia).[62] On 7 May, Peter Makings (Schott's managing director) wrote to Banks, indicating that he had approached the AMC to act as a distributer in Australia as a precursor to setting up an 'Australian branch' through Allans (a local publisher). Schott and Universal Edition had jointly set up a branch in the United States, and the distinctiveness of each publisher was becoming more difficult to discern outside Europe, with the small size of the Australian market making it challenging for the major publishers each to establish a full operation with engraving, printing and effective promotion.

Nevertheless, there was a strong financial incentive for publishers to operate in Australia. In a letter to Makings,[63] Banks explained that since he was an Australian citizen in Australia, the Music Board would support one third 'of all costs in the production of scores plus assistance in the promotion of works'. Faber and Universal Edition had already taken advantage of that subsidy. A publisher registered in Australia received two thirds of those costs.[64] Recording companies were also able to apply to the Music Board for a guarantee against loss for releasing recordings of Australian music.[65] This subsidy is one of the reason why scores by Meale, Lumsdaine and Humble were published by the paradoxically named 'Universal Edition Australia'. With the publishers no longer having to invest significantly in the music they published, little promotion was undertaken, and little long-term revenue resulted. When Banks moved back to Australia in 1972 the agreement with Schott had been suspended, and by 1975 it had not been renewed. Between December 1974 and January 1975 Banks was negotiating with Colleran for a contract with Universal Edition. As he had composed so little in the previous years there was no significant impediment to changing publishers. His tenure at the Music Board ended on 30 June 1975, by which time he hoped to have delivered the *String Quartet*. In any case, by this time Universal Edition had already received $6,000 from the Australia Council, and more was allocated in the following year's budget for works including those by Lumsdaine.[66] Banks's piece was never published by either Universal Edition or Schott.

The complications of the period leading up to the quartet's completion affect the music, too, and Banks's correspondence from this period demonstrates the politics and the difficulties of securing funding for his plans, which together meant that he was having to refuse commissions.[67] In July 1975, Banks wrote to Murdoch about all the administrative work he was having to do for the Canberra School of Music, and of the difficulty of finding time for the *String Quartet*.[68] Where some of the works that he composed after 1972 were written quickly, the *String Quartet* was to be a major work of significant technical sophistication. In August, Banks wrote the following about the composition's serial workings and why they were chosen at the time of composition:

The series has been a tough one, and I think I chose it because after my 'lay-off' I needed a strict discipline to get the [...] compositional muscles working – hence the pitch/duration thing (which I have not tried before), in any case the series is so limited that I've had to pull out a number of stops I maybe wouldn't have tried before. I'm against doing my fast 'pro' bit (which I can do at the drop of a 2 cent piece – OK, we all have our price!).[69]

That 'pitch/duration thing' comes from Gerhard, and, as I will explain below, this is one of the features of the work that connects it to past practice, specifically to Gerhard's second String Quartet, and Schoenberg's fourth. Before detailing the composition, it is necessary to outline Banks's emphasis on technique, since his technical processes respond to the composers with whom he had worked.

In a lecture on form given at the Sydney Conservatorium of music (1977), Banks quoted Gerhard as saying that:

A composer needs grace (inspiration), guts, intellect, madness: and *systems* are a sine qua non, because the intellect can only work, only take grip, when confronted by a system.[70]

For Banks, technique was at the heart of training composers, and he felt that he brought to Australia the expertise to do this in a way that had not previously been possible, given a lack of 'serious disciplined craftsmanship':

Little wings burn up so easily when they have no membrane or fibre to support them. They need the guts of the matters that we were lucky enough to get, so their course will include a healthy diet of analysis, compositional techniques, analysis, historical perspectives, 2 part-writing, analysis, instrumentation, orchestration, analysis et al. [...]

A lot depends on the young composers for the 'models' they have. Too often here we have the PR guys who pass on their own ego trips and gimmicks and are not bloody well serious about music, so anything goes.[71]

Banks's letters are full of such remarks about the importance of technique and craft, which were not the priorities of the 'PR guys', who in Banks's opinion were more interested in promoting their careers than developing the technical capabilities of their students. Technique was important for Banks, and it was during his training with Dallapiccola that he began writing serial music, which he discusses here in a letter to Seiber:

At the moment I am struggling with my first 12-tone work as I felt a terrific urge to try my hand with the technique, so I commenced a setting of one of the Psalms for voice and piano because I thought this would provide me with a shortish form and a test to see if I could extract a good lyrical line from the row, besides the harmonic noises I like to make, and in any case one section just cried out for a crab-canon –

> so it seemed to be [an] interesting experiment. [...] I experimented over the weekend with the possibilities of a 'combinatorial' row a la Milton but this particular one gave me too limited a range of intervals to choose from and to arrive at the sounds I like [...] I don't know whether I really want to be a dodecaphonist but am finding it tremendously absorbing and am sure I'll eventually benefit from the work I'm putting in it now. 12-tone calls for so much imagination and invention![72]

The period that he spent with Dallapiccola (1952-3),[73] and briefly with Babbitt (1952), established the principal directions for his technique.

His *String Quartet*'s serial processes were important enough that in his letter to the Austral Quartet's leader Donald Hazelwood,[74] Banks wrote out the row, and briefly explained its combinatorial properties.[75] In the same paragraph he wrote that there was 'No need to worry about this as it will be obvious to your ears.' The contrast between written, strict, disciplined process and 'musical intuition'[76] is strong in this letter, as it is in all Banks's music from the time. But in the *String Quartet* especially, against the complexities of the previous years and the politics of publication, the opposition guides the music.

This opposition has a history for Banks, and connects his work with that of Gerhard. Their friendship was well enough known that Vyner asked Banks to write a statement about Gerhard, coinciding with the London Sinfonietta's performances of Gerhard's complete chamber music.[77] For Banks, part of Gerhard's 'enigma' was that:

> composers are not computers, and Roberto was a great believer in the balance between intuition and reason. The opposite sides of a coin as it were. He expressed himself this way in a talk we had shortly before his death when he said that often a musical impulse could only take you so far, then you would have to call 'Dr. Reason' in to examine what you had been doing. Often an impasse would occur which could only be solved by a logical examination of the preceding process, but as a person he was prepared to be guided by his natural reaction to sound and to push this to the limit.
>
> I believe that this was what made him so important to the younger composers of this country – his concern with the 'sound' of his music. This may be a trite thing to say but if one reflects on the music written in England in the 1950s, then Roberto was way ahead of his time. He was always prepared to let his ears guide him, and for one who had been an adherent, indeed a pupil of Schoenberg, this was no easy thing to do.[78]

For Banks's *String Quartet* 'the preceding process' takes the form of practices covering multiple decades, and the 'impasse' includes a lack of organizational structures for nurturing composition of the kind that had shaped Banks's experiences in Europe, and which he sought to establish in Australia.[79] It also includes a reassessment of his position in relation to his mentors (and their mentors) in addition to the specific demands of beginning a new work. These strands came together at this time, when his own health was uncertain, and writing a piece about the relationships with his mentors was one way of musically working through the arguments for better forms of compositional support in Australia. To overcome the malaise of the previous years, Banks called Dr Reason, and then set about composing the serial prescription for the *String Quartet*.[80] One can see these connections at work in the piece through Banks's use of techniques used by Gerhard, Babbitt and Dallapiccola.

The serial basis for the piece is this row:

C   B   G   A♭   D♯   E   G♭   F   A   B♭   D   C♯

Banks planned the all-combinatorial series to shuffle dyads within hexachords under consistent even (or odd) transposition. In other words, there are two fields, one that comprises the even transpositions, and one made up of the odd transpositions. As Banks explains, the:

> Series is based on combinatorial principles. Hexachords – and their interchange is all important – and are constructed from the re-shuffling of dyads within the hexachord – e.g.

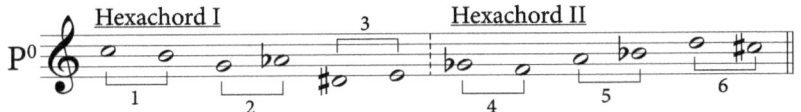

This means that this particular series may be transposed at steps of a tone and each Hexachord will consistently maintain its 6 notes with its group of 3 dyads (which will re-shuffle in order) whether appearing as Hex I or Hex II. Compositionally the result is that one may more freely select pairs of Hexachords from different transpositional levels to complete a 12 tone series which is consistent in intervallic content etc with P0's aggregate.[81]

The first sketch[82] for the piece shows Banks working out the permutations of dyads. The sketch begins with the row in prime form, broken into two hexachords with the first, second and third dyads of the first hexachord labelled. Transpositions of the row are shown (in the order listed here: T0, T2, T4, T8, T6 and T10), and the order of the dyads is indicated, similar to that found in his later explanation (see Example 2.1). In addition, the early sketch indicates the 'direction' of the dyads, marking the change in direction of each dyad's interval. (For example, dyads 1, 2, 3 in the first hexachord of P-0 are transformed into dyads 2R, 1R, 3R for the second hexachord of P-2.) Banks later explained[83] that the piece works with the polarity of 'even' transpositions (T2, T4, T6 …) and 'odd' transpositions (T1, T3, T5 …), rather than with the direction of dyads.[84] Within each polarity the rows are therefore related by whole-tone steps. The basic row is formed from two hexachords in which semitone pairs are related

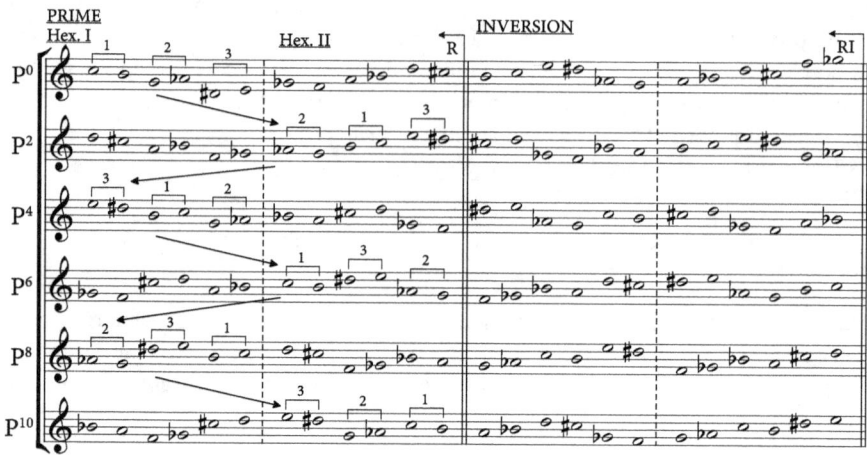

Example 2.1 Banks's row forms for *String Quartet*.

Table 2.1 The Order of Dyads within Banks's Matrix

	Hexachord I	Hexachord II
P-0	**1, 2, 3**	1, 2, 3
P-2	3, 2, 1	**2, 1, 3**
P-4	**3, 1, 2**	2, 3, 1
P-6	1, 3, 2	**1, 3, 2**
P-8	**2, 3, 1**	3, 1, 2
P-10	2, 1, 3	**3, 2, 1**

by T4 (that is, a major third). The result is that as the row is transposed up a tone, alternating hexachords have the same pitch content, and within those hexachords the dyads shuffle, as shown in Table 2.1.

Since there are only four transpositions of the [014589][85] hexachord, the first hexachord of P-4 is the same collection as the first hexachord as P-0. T2 is the complement of T0. Inverting a hexachord shuffles its dyads, and all the possible configurations of this shuffling are present. However, not all the possible configurations with intervallic direction are present, and between the early sketches and the composition of the piece, the importance of directionality was discarded.

The first hexachord, [014589] (Forte number 6–20), is also known as the 'augmented scale' (two augmented triads a minor third apart), and it is also a scale commonly used in jazz, of which Banks had extensive experience as a performer. A notebook page from Bank's student days shows him working with different scales, including one based on the [014589] hexachord, above which Banks connects notes that form an augmented chord, which he labels 'Aug triads'.[86] One of the properties of the row is that it does not contain an [012] trichord, and that suggests harmonies that are 'recognisably scalar'.[87] Each hexachord also contains either a major or minor triad. In using hexachords as ordered sequences of unordered dyads, the resulting music often outlines a fifth/fourth or major/minor third, since Banks often chooses to keep those intervals in the same register.

'In generalized form', Van den Toorn writes, '6–20 has a history, in other words, one that can be heard and understood to straddle different idioms and compositional methods.'[88] The [014589] hexachord features in Bartók, Scriabin, Webern's Concerto, Op. 24, Schoenberg's Suite, Op. 29 and *Ode to Napoleon*, and, according to Van den Toorn, in Babbitt's *Composition for Four Instruments* (1948).[89] The history of the row for Banks includes sketches that he made in a book of teaching materials. Only some pages have dates, and these are either 1970 or 1971 (the possibility remains that some pages were written later). One document begins with 'Statistical' permutations[90] and shows the derivation of an eighteen-note row by the permutation of trichords. He developed this into a twelve-tone row 'that would work by [segmentation into] 3, 4's [*sic*], and 6's [*sic*]'[91] He indicated its combinatorial properties, and then wrote:

actually divided into 2 AREAS:
Area I – P-0 transposed 2, 4, 6, 8, 10 gave same 4 note [i.e. 'tetrachord'] groups (on W[hole]/T[one])
Area II – P-0 transposed 1, 3, 5, 7, 9, 11 gave *new* 4 note groups[.][92]

Banks briefly outlined how the hexachords behave under transposition and then went through a similar procedure for the inversion. His conclusion was that with these procedures there is 'a great deal of latitude available'. He then connected all this with his 'tribute to Seiber', the *Duo for Violin and Piano*, which he completed in May 1951. The *Duo* won Banks the Edwin Evans Prize, which was presented to him by Edward J. Dent. It was performed at the 1952 ISCM festival in Salzburg (Dent had previously been president of the ISCM), where the piece represented Australia, and it was this performance that took Banks to Salzburg, where he stayed on to study with Babbitt.[93] The row construction used in the *String Quartet* therefore connects his music in 1975 with his earliest experiences studying in Europe and his first rigorous encounters with serialism.

Located in his archive amongst other manuscripts from his student days are what appear to be sketches that significantly predate the *String Quartet*, showing a very similar row (<0, 11, 7, 8, 3, 1, 2, 10, 6, 5, 4, 9>[94]) as part of Banks's analysis of Schoenberg's Fourth Quartet.[95] These pages show Banks methodically working through the properties of Schoenberg's row, including making alterations to see what effect they have on combinatorial properties. Banks notes the role of fifths in Schoenberg's row, and an example of the harmonic function of a fifth in the lowest voice is isolated.

The first sketch for the piece also shows Banks working out the inversion of the prime form.[96] The first I-row begins on E♭ and is formed in the standard manner. As for the prime form, several transpositions are shown (on E♭, C♯, F, A, G and B). The unusual order for these and the tables of dyads that follow suggest that Banks was more interested in thinking through how the shuffling dyads worked than he was in transposing the row form, which is hardly unexpected given Banks's long familiarity with serialism. By the end of this process an unorthodox inverse form has emerged, in which the first hexachord is as expected from the standard method, but in which the second hexachord begins two tones too high. Since transposition at T4 shuffles the dyads and keeps the pitch content of each hexachord the same, the inverse form still contains all twelve pitch classes. (No P/I matrix can be formed from the result.) This accounts for the inverse forms present in Banks's explanatory example, above.

In Banks's working copy of the serial material the direction of interval in each dyad is no longer accounted for, and it has the same placement of inverse and prime forms as shown above, beginning on what would typically be called I-11. This is not the case in the earliest of Banks's sketches for musical gestures (which precede specific pitches and rhythms), in which I-0 – which begins on B♮ – is the row next to P-0.

In the music, Dr Reason's prescription begins with a clear statement of serial workings. The first chord is formed from the first four pitches of the P-0, and then the cello solo moves through the row until its completion (see Example 2.2).

The work's characteristic semitone motif is established by this presentation of the series, and so too is a 'sequence of semitones' motif at the end of the second bar. The subsequent material is less readily able to be labelled, given the redundancies across the transpositions of Banks's series. The first four-note chord {A♭, E, G, E♭}, in bar 4, corresponds to the first four pitches of P-8, whilst the second four-note chord {B, C♯, D, C} corresponds to the next four of the same transposition. The third chord, of five pitches, could be drawn from the second hexachord of P-8 if the viola's G were an A, which the sketch[97] suggests may well be the case. But even if this is so, the bar is missing the F needed to complete the aggregate. Alternatively, the bar could be read as two hexachords distributed across the three chords, a kind of enjambement,[98] with the first hexachord of P-0 <A♭, G, E, E♭, B, C> including two pitches of the second chord, and the remaining pitches[99] in the bar coming from P-0's second hexachord. The

Example 2.2 Banks, *String Quartet*, bars 1–6.

next solo material (bar 5) is derived from the inversion of the row, hiding the 'upward semitone' between D♯ and E with a descending seventh. It is difficult to designate this according to row form. Following the nomenclature of Banks's explanation, the first six pitches fit I-4 as a move through the row in an ordered sequence of unordered dyads, with the first chord in bar 6 completing I-4's second hexachord. But bar 5 can also be described as a linear move from 1 to 7 through $_{orthodox}$I-3,[100] with the first chord of bar 6 completing the aggregate.[101]

Although most of the work can be traced to the prime row, the structure of this series and its implementation work against precise scheme-making. Indeed, my argument is that Dr Reason and intuition are balanced from the start of the pre-compositional[102] work; where one finds evidence of Dr Reason in action, one quickly finds the limits of the doctor's usefulness. The descending semitone in bar 1, which becomes one of the work's key motifs, is a choice of pitch class order within the predetermined order of dyads. Banks describes this bar as I-8 rather than P-0 (as I described it, above), due to the use of a descending E to E♭ in I-8 rather than an ascending semitone in P-0, though there is no greater consistency in implementation of the piece's serialism to be read from this decision, since the redundancies in the row's construction overwhelm specific melodic sequences. With such redundancies within the precompositional serial construction, the repetitive intervals tend to be emphasized in the composition.[103] The semitones are prominent, and so too are the major thirds. For example, the first violin's line at bar 4 is <E♭, D, F♯>, the descending semitone followed by a major third. Where there is a quick exposed series, such as in these bars, Banks tends to treat his rows as melodies, and so a semitone, rather than a ninth, say, is used motivically. (Nevertheless there are some moments where register is used structurally, as I will explain below.) At bar 15 (Example 2.3) a version of the opening occurs, with the same soft dynamic and cello solo. This section ends contrapuntally rather than with block chords, but again the semitone and major third are positioned prominently. (The annotation indicates I-4, as does Banks in his sketch, and an equally plausible reading is $_o$I-3.)

This melody begins with a rising semitone, diminished fourth (which here is equivalent to a major third), then falls a semitone to a G, which then forms a major

Example 2.3 Banks, *String Quartet*, bars 15–19, annotated with the serial structure.

third with the B at the end of the bar. The next bar, too, is built from semitones and major thirds. (The pitches at the start of bar 15 are a repetition of the cello at bar 12, where they are semiquavers rather than quaver notes, and better read as part of P-4.[104]) With such a flexible approach to transposition choice, Banks makes little attempt to build large-scale transposition-derived structures.

Combinatorial working suggests binary oppositions: between melody and accompaniment; of two hexachords; between tonality and serialism (and particularly Schoenberg's use of the [014589] hexachord in *Ode to Napoleon Bonaparte*); and between semitones and larger intervals. Only some of the historical implications of combinatorial working are followed through. Banks does not, for example, exploit the property that Schoenberg outlined whereby 'one can accompany melodic phrases made from the first six tones with harmonies made from the second six tones, without getting doublings'.[105] The combinatorial properties do raise basic questions about the segmentation of the row. The regular pulse often maintains groups of four semiquavers, which divide the row into three four-note groups. For example, the bowing of the opening cello line projects this segmentation. This is particularly applicable to the even sequences of semiquavers, and produces moments such as bar 166, where a kind of syncopation splits the four-note groups into 2+4+2 (see Example 2.4).[106] In the wider context of the piece the segmentation of the row easily comes in and out of phase with rhythmic groups, but in the metrical passages of semiquavers Banks does exploit segmentation with and against the rhythmic groups.

One might expect the homorhythmic chords that contrast with the melodic lines and contrapuntal sections to make the most of segmenting the row into tetrachords. Like the metrical moments that often go with tetrachord segmentation, there is a tendency away from the functions of hexachordal combinatoriality inherent in the initial row due to this work being for four players (with little double-stopping). This tension, however, is scarcely audible, especially since the properties of the row work against specific labelling by transposition (order of dyads), and the prime row's many semitones create a fairly uniform distribution of a small range of intervals. (This is reinforced when one seeks to address the problem of Banks's I and RI forms. Although

Example 2.4 Banks, *String Quartet*, bars 164–7.

one would assume the differences between orthodox and Banks's forms would be crucial, in practice there are so many chords, and so few places where Banks moves across a hexachordal boundary in I and RI forms, that the problem hardly arises.)

There are shifts between odd and even transpositions (the broadest level at which different hexachordal and tetrachordal contents emerge), and one of the clearest of these examples occurs with the rhythm, texture, timbre and voicing all working to generate one of the composition's most engaging moments. At bar 76 (Example 2.5) the music returns to the material of bar 15 for the first time. Bar 76 begins with an inversion of the intervals in bar 15 (P-1, I-4 respectively); the rhythm is also similar, with four quavers before a move to compound metre in both cases, but the bowing of the earlier instance generates more metric ambiguity.

This section comes out of an even transposition (R-2), and the change is definite, with the violin moving through P-1 from 1 to 6. At the completion of this hexachord Banks allows the melody to fold back on itself, repeating the fifth pitch (E), and then moving to the seventh and eighth pitches. At this point, crossing the hexachordal boundary, the melody repeats <G, F, E, F#, G> (7, 6, 5, 8, 7). This repetition goes against hexachordal segmentation, and the first violin repeats the central tetrachord of the row for ten bars, a full forty iterations of 5, 6, 8, 7. By this stage of the piece chords have alternated back and forth, but this level of repetition is new. The viola, also playing constant semiquavers, plays the last tetrachord of P-1, and the first tetrachord is played by the second violin. After their staggered entries the complete aggregate is constantly at play, and the combination of *sul tasto* and *a la punta* creates an airy cloud of pitches. This is a new texture for the piece, and accompanies a strongly pulsed, catchy melody on the cello playing a different metre.

The cello plays against the accompaniment, energized by its high tessitura, now well above the others. Its pitch material is from I-0,[107] an even transposition, making a contrast with P-1, the contrast being the one feature of the row's design that distinguishes two forms. The intervallic content of the row is so limited, however, that little real counterpoint emerges,[108] and instead of different transpositions generating distinct threads, all the material here consists of semitones and major thirds/minor sixths. The other intervals in the cello's row are positioned across the rests, between melodic phrases or registral changes. These changes of register align with hexachords: I-0 1–6 is a rising line, answered by I-0 7–10 (all we get before it is abandoned); and then there a change to odd transposition – R-1 1–6 is lower than the previous phrases and the phrase to come, which is R-1 7–12. After a surprise G (accented, higher than its surroundings and not part of serial working), we find I-6 1–6, low in the cello's range, and then I-6 9–12 (again, all we get before the repetition of a D/C# chord that brings the section to a close). The cello melody, then, plays with segmentations into hexachords and tetrachords, the ambivalence about that segmentation working with its different metre. The register of the phrases and bowing aligns (often with rests) to generate the segment boundaries, and the result is a texture of distinct layers. In terms of the functions of the series, little differentiates odd from even transposition here, much as little differentiates P from I.

If the passage is one of pseudo-counterpoint, there are passages that are rigorously contrapuntal. Dr Reason assumes a new role in these, which are carefully planned,

Example 2.5 Banks, *String Quartet*, bars 76–88, annotated with the serial structure.

strictly implemented divisions of the quartet into four clear lines. They also explicitly refer to Gerhard, as Banks explained in an unpublished explication of the work's serial premises:

> Rhythmic Procedures: Most of the piece is based on natural 'motive-type' rhythmic development with the exception of certain structures in the opening 'movement' of the piece. Here the interval is allied to duration in a serial sense (see Roberto Gerhard's 2nd String Quartet), but with my modification that any pitch given a specific duration need not be *sustained* for the period – i.e. I concentrate on an overall span or 'points of attack'. Basically the 'duration series' is calculated as follows from P-0 (given that the note middle C counts as 12 in its octave transposition) (and one counts upwards).[109]

Banks cites Gerhard's second quartet, but the first quartet also uses serialized rhythm.[110] In String Quartet No. 2 Gerhard assigns durations to pitches as Banks does. Gerhard included the row in his discussion of the topic in his article 'Developments in Twelve-Tone Technique' from 1956.[111] Gerhard writes that:

> the time-set is correlated to the pitch-set as an equivalent series of proportions expressed in numbers. The principle of common relationship therefore obtains in both dimensions. Rhythmicization in the Schoenbergian sense, as freely impressed from without, is thus replaced by rhythmical invention developed from within, i.e. analogically and hand-in-hand with the combinatorial operations concerned with pitch-structure. To put it in a nutshell: my proportions or time-set goes back to the Greek idea of number as the father of rhythm.
> In practice, however, rhythmical invention seems always to have proceeded largely (if not exclusively) from somatic rather than from intellectual inspiration. [...] number proposes but the body disposes.[112]

In 1961, in 'An Inaugural Lecture' that he gave at Tanglewood, Gerhard was less glib in opposing the mind and the body, and he was less keen on an opposition between 'reason' and 'practice':

> [L]et's consider what we propose to him [a student] about matters of method. Reason proposes, subliminal man disposes, but of course, *the whole man composes*, and nothing but the whole man will do for that.

Gerhard continued, talking about serial method:

> Musical organization is largely based nowadays on principles of serialization. Some of you may have come to feel that serialization is on the way out. This is possibly so. I for one am not prepared to defend any *status quo*.
> If serialization is on the way out today, it was nonetheless evident that classical serial technique, as in Schoenberg and Webern, has been the nursery where new

ideas grow. It is doubtful whether a young composer may safely ignore classical serial techniques. As with tradition, one does not escape its influence by ignoring it, only one suffers it in a more obscure and probably warped or maimed fashion.[113]

Gerhard's second String Quartet is also based on combinatorial procedures, though the work's row is not closely related to Banks's.[114] Even if Banks did not know the detailed workings of Gerhard's quartet from Gerhard, or from his own study, it seems likely that Banks received a copy of *The London Sinfonietta Programme Book: Schoenberg/Gerhard Series*, published in 1973 to coincide with the ensemble's performances of the complete Gerhard chamber works. This publication contained a short chapter by Keith Potter called 'Gerhard's Second String Quartet' that explains the work's form.

Only a few sections in Banks's piece use rhythm serially, and Banks does not use the rhythmic proportions for large-scale form, the technique that Gerhard used in his quartet. Banks's durationally serial sections are the only sections to consistently use multiple row forms simultaneously, and the only sections in which all four players are independent. They are, in other words, the only examples of faithful counterpoint. For the first section (see Example 2.6), the untransposed prime form is assigned descending durations from the first pitch. (For P-0, C=12 semiquavers, B=11, B♭=10, ..., C♯=1; violin I.) The retrograde form uses the same pitch–duration association (so for R-6, G♭=12, F=11, E=10, ..., G=1; cello). The inverse (violin II) and retrograde-inverse (viola) are similarly constructed, but since I-6 begins with F natural, that pitch is assigned the longest value.[115] Banks then gives a table of increasing durations, one based on quavers, one on triplet quavers and one on semiquavers; he indicates that these are implemented at bar 31, 105 and 146 (respectively), with a semiquaver + triplet quaver version at bar 137. Even here, Dr Reason is not entirely in charge, and in the first of these sections there is a slight deviation in the viola's part, only half of which follows the pattern. When the next canon takes place, Banks is less tied to the scheme, and by the third canon the structures are even more difficult to follow.[116]

Sketches that date from the early 1950s show Banks listing different serial constructions, mostly focussed on combinatorial and all-interval sets, with specific references to works by Schoenberg, Webern and Berg. On one page headed 'combinatorial sets of the first order', he shows the derivation of two whole-tone scales from cycles of fifths ('× by 7 [semitones]'). Under the subheadings 'Schoenberg' and '6+6', Banks then lists the whole-tone scale and writes 'complete symmetry – intervallic nature useless'.[117] The fifths in Banks's quartet recalls Schoenberg's idea that in 'the inversion a fifth below of the first six tones, the antecedent, should not produce a repetition of one of these six tones'.[118] On one hand, Banks's division of his material according to transposition by whole tones and his choice of transpositions for the canon do not follow Schoenberg's idea, since the operation that Schoenberg describes does not work for Banks's hexachords (which are too intervallically repetitious). On the other hand, Banks's fifths (and fourths) are tied to his basic material through the whole-tone scheme, which retains something of the basic procedures from Schoenberg, Webern and Berg that he had earlier explored.

Infrastructure, Serialism and Banks's String Quartet 57

Example 2.6 Banks, *String Quartet*, bars 31–41, showing the first durationally serial section (the serial annotations are Banks's).

Schuijer argues that: 'Schoenberg's idea was to simultaneously unfold two series-forms while not allowing octave-related tones to coincide',[119] and even if all of Schoenberg's choices are not all of Banks's, Banks is careful about where octaves occur, which is especially important given that he is using all four forms of the series simultaneously. The only octave relation in the quartet's rhythmically serial material is a unison A (bar 35, circled in Example 2.6) between violin 2 and viola. In a sense this precise position is arbitrary, since Banks delays the entries of each voice non-schematically (after 4, 12 and 16 quavers), but he makes the most of the unison by preceding the A in the viola part with a crescendo, and he accents the A by shortening the note before it, and with an accent mark on the A itself. The second violin also arrives on the A as a downbeat, making the most of what might otherwise seem a compositional flaw. The rhythmic phasing that enables this is contrived through Banks's adjustment to Gerhard's technique, which lets him repeat notes within a duration (fragmenting a long note into an uneven repetition of shorter ones, for example), and therefore the moment that begins the unison can be accented, and the previous anacrusis can be fashioned by inserting rests in the middle of the duration of the second violin's B♭. (The unison also marks a moment of retrograde symmetry between viola, which continues with B♭, G♭, F, and second violin, which has just played F, G♭, B♭.)

The canons are contained: they begin new sections and in each case end with repeated notes/trills. Their function is less structural at the level of the piece as a whole, compared to similar canons in works by Gerhard or Dallapiccola. Nevertheless, there is something from those mentors in Banks's composition, which is present in the canons in particular. Banks's training with Seiber and Dallapiccola also means that the canons are used effortlessly, since these techniques had been thoroughly practised well before Banks came to compose the quartet. The methodical way in which Banks develops his precompositional music also works against the canons sounding like ideas quoted from Dallapiccola and Gerhard, since the canons are embedded in the composition's energetic combinations of the four players manifest as changing textures. Indeed, in the construction of the piece the canons came first, since a sketch of the music labelled 'Discarded 1st thought'[120] groups P-0, R-6, I-6 and RI-8 with a tick. This is also the same piece of paper on which he sketches out the row and its forms.

Banks only attributes the strict time canons in his piece with Gerhard's second String Quartet, but the whole-tone basis for his series may also be a reference to Gerhard. Keith Potter identified the whole-tone scale as one of Gerhard's non-serial pitch formulations, and Potter provided an example of a passage that combines 'two forms of his whole-tone scale in simultaneously ascending form to produce a weird kind of whole-tone harmony'.[121] When Potter considered the chordal aspect of the work – the textures on which Banks's quartet is built – he found harmonies of 'overlapping major 3rds', [0145], which are used 'in various transpositions, sometimes with extra notes added' and with 'emphasis placed clearly on the harmonic aspect'.[122] These tetrachords are, of course, available to Banks. Indeed, they, and the whole tone, are the basis of his row's construction.

The single movement of Banks' piece was a new form for the composer:

There's a vitality in the 1st section which surprises me (I think) – and I've never tried to bring off a Fast/Slow piece before – not with a bang etc. […] I see it as dying out to nothing, so the form is > rather than <> or >< or >< permutations.[123]

Gerhard's late music is all in single-movement forms, including his second String Quartet, and Banks's choice here is likely a homage. So too is the combinatoriality that was important to Babbitt, and the canons from Gerhard and Dallapiccola.

By the second section (see Example 2.7), which begins at bar 255, Banks is audibly more at ease with the materials, and its opening semitone fluctuation, which is devised from the first bars of the composition, soon gives way to slow crotchets in the middle register – D, C♯, D, F and A, B♭, A, G♭ – in which the semitones sound like auxiliary notes that prolong an underlying pitch. The initial D/C♯ and A/B♭ semitones are familiar from the start of the piece, but the exposed D–F minor third comes as a surprise. Although this interval is part of the basic series, it is only in the second section that it is stated so clearly. The minor third is picked up by the first violin two bars later. Here it is rhythmically similar to bar 4, but the clear major third from that bar is now replaced with E–G, reinforced by the similar motion in violin 2 (C–E♭) and cello (G♯–B).

Example 2.7 Banks, *String Quartet*, bars 255–62, the beginning of the work's second section.

As in the first part of the piece, in the second part there is a passage (bar 273) where the cello is melodic against an accompaniment, but the juxtaposition is less strong, and it begins with a minor (G#–B), rather than major (E–A♭), third. The minor thirds continue to proliferate, and much of the music is neither serial nor dodecaphonic. Alternating chords and a small handful of repetitive intervals create local harmonic hierarchies. The principle is Gerhard's, with Banks privileging the initial row for its motivic potential, and the broadscale shift from major third to minor third referring to Gerhard's consideration of 'twelve-tone technique' as a 'new principle of tonality'.[124] The collection at the start of the second section might be described as the second hexachord of P-0, but the order goes against the motivic intervals from the first section, and radically disorders the row. Some of the second section is serial (from bar 297, or bar 321, or bar 330, for example), but much is not. For Banks, the move away from the row is not a critique of serialism, nor a questioning of its usefulness, as much as a confirmation of its role as a fertile starting place, and Banks's validation of method as a way of beginning more personal transformations of shared technique.

All this suggests that Banks returned to his early training at the time of composing the *String Quartet*, and that that early training was rigorous and methodical – concerned with establishing a role for Dr Reason in his craft. The quartet looks to the past both to differentiate itself from Banks's 'pro' output, and to reinvigorate his practice at a time when the music was not flowing easily, due to the work that he was undertaking to provide other composers with opportunities such as those he had had to develop his technique. The music shows Banks working with ideas that were familiar enough that careful and methodical working could give way to freer explorations of materials.

In the letter in which Banks wrote to Martirano about the decline of his output at the time when he was planning the *String Quartet*, he also wrote about his compositional models, and he named Dallapiccola and Gerhard, the former having recently died (on 19 February 1975):

> I've tried to tell Laura [Dallapiccola] what Luigi was to me as a model – as a concerned human being full of warmth as well as a composer – but nothing helps. Roberto Gerhard was another 'model' (you realise I use this term in its fullest, the guy, what he gave, the quality of the music, the dedication et al) [...]. I was one of the last people to see Roberto about 3 months before his death. I was able to do this as I knew his personal doctor. I can remember Poldi [Gerhard] saying as I left, if only someone would commission another String Quartet from him, as that's what he wants to write.[125]

Banks's decision to go back to Gerhard, and to Dallapiccola, for the path to his own string quartet is not without poignancy. Banks's musical relationships, like his organizational ones, are personally meaningful. They also align with a broader revisiting of Gerhard's music that was going on at the time, for example, the support it was receiving from the London Sinfonietta. The structures that Banks forged through the Australia Council drew on his experience in the UK, much as the musical structures that he establishes in the *String Quartet* connect his composition in Australia with his mentors in Europe.

3

Richard Meale I

Sydney

We get many composers who fade in, [and] fade out of history. I don't think that there are any ultimate judgments to be made on musical composers but there is only just what is happening now in relationship to them.

For me, this has quite an effect upon the way I work, because it means no one method is satisfactory. In any case, the constant application of one method for me would just lead to frightful boredom. I'm restless, it's my nature to look around, to do something else, not arbitrarily but simply because I am constructed that way, I am restless. So I subscribe to no set practice of music.[1]

The relationships between Banks's late music and that of other composers can be established through the personal connections that he maintained when he returned to Australia, for his absence from Britain resulted in extensive written correspondence in the 1970s with those who were not nearby. Meale's correspondence is scant and it rarely reveals much about what he was composing. Whilst Banks's musical responses tend to be to those with whom he had a personal connection – Babbitt, Dallapiccola, Gerhard, Martirano – Meale was self-taught, and his personal connections made little musical impression. Like many composers in this era, Meale had a formative experience abroad. However, the periods of time that he spent outside Australia were brief, and his musical responses are to those composers who had 'faded in' to history, whose scores and recordings were internationally disseminated, and about whose music articles and books were written, rather than to those with whom he had any personal connection. Meale's responses are less technical than Banks's, and prone to more rhapsodic ways of working. Meale's music also demonstrates some of the challenges of the time, particularly the difficulties of making sense of new ideas at a distance. But the gaps that emerge between his music and that of, for example, Boulez ought not constitute a criticism of either composer's work, so much as reveal the character of modernism in the 1960s and 1970s, a time when its ideas were better disseminated than ever before. This dissemination meant that formal study and personal contact was less necessary than ever, and Meale's relationship with those composers who developed the methods he uses is not one of student and teacher so much as one between fellow composers in an era of rapid change, for Meale's music was also widely disseminated. This ready availability of scores and recordings also worked against stylistic uniformity, and however much certainty serialism had provided earlier in the century, by the 1960s Meale no longer felt that path to be a secure one. Unlike Banks's music, which continued the serial attitude, at least as a basis for departure, Meale's music makes use of serial techniques in highly fragmented, non-formal ways; these techniques only occupy a small proportion of the work, though the fact that they have a presence at all is significant.

This chapter, together with Chapter 6, examines in detail several of Meale's compositions, focussing on *Homage to Garcia Lorca* (1964), *Clouds Now and Then* (1969), *Soon It Will Die* (1969), *Coruscations* (1971), *Incredible Floridas* (1971) and the first String Quartet (1974). The early works are all exploratory and assured, and they established Meale's reputation as one of Australia's leading composers. *Coruscations*, for solo piano, was performed often by Roger Woodward soon after its completion and shows Meale exploring specific technical challenges. *Incredible Floridas* was toured by the Fires of London, for which it was composed, and is far more diverse in its musical ideas. Comparisons of these works with Meale's music from the 1960s provides a sense of Meale's 'restlessness', and also his consistency. The String Quartet No. 1 is the last work of Meale's early period, and it ends Meale's modernist period. This chapter, and its companion chapter, Chapter 6, fall into three broad areas. One considers Meale's position as a progressive composer, indeed as the central composer in an 'Australian avant-garde', as it was termed. The role of the progressive composer dominates discourses about his music, including his own explanations. The second area considers Meale as Australian, the paradoxes of this designation and the ways in which it was formed through reconfigurations of the discourse of Australian Music itself. The third area is musically analytical and aims to provide the basis for future discussions of Meale's music by presenting new detail about how his music is put together. One of the features of existing work on Meale (as it is for Butterley) is that there are few close readings of his music, and many of the published explanations are based on some significant misunderstandings about how it works. Michael Hannan's 2014 monograph *The Music of Richard Meale*[2] is the only book to focus on Meale's music, and whilst Hannan's book provides an overview of the subject, few works are discussed in significant detail. Without Meale the movement of modernist Australian Music would hardly exist, and his work brings together a wide range of ideas from different places. By not studying in the UK he differed from others of his generation, and he established a new approach to negotiating modernist ideas in Australia.

Discourses about Meale's compositional output have focussed on a split between his early modernist work and his later return to tonality. Most writers have emphasized a major break in Meale's music before *Viridian,* and the following account is typical:

> In a program interview for his new orchestral work, *Three Miro Pieces*, Richard Meale, elder statesman among Australian composers, describes a film of Miro in his garden, waxing lyrical on the joys of weeding. For Meale, as for Boulez, whose avant-garde style once held Meale in awe before he walked away from it with *Viridian* in 1979, it seemed a good metaphor for the creative process.[3]

Covell was one of Meale's early and vocal supporters, and his influential book *Australia's Music* positioned Meale alongside Sculthorpe as a leading composer of the 1960s. He wrote that:

> Sculthorpe swims easily through society at all levels, makes friends readily and has a gift for finding the right opportunities at the right time. Until recently at least, Meale was much more the intractable rebel, the dark-natured outsider to whom favours did not come readily. This last quality – a wholly sincere continuation of the hero tradition in musical composition – has naturally helped make Meale a candidate for early deification by enthusiasts looking for a cause to champion.[4]

The contrast between Meale and Sculthorpe that Covell creates is dramatic, but has little basis in the composers' music, nor does it reflect the public profile of the two composers. Meale had, by this time, been performed by the Sydney Symphony Orchestra (SSO) for the Queen (of the UK/Australia), and his 'rebelliousness' was within the acceptable social limits of the time. Nevertheless, Covell's later characterization of Meale's career aligned with McCallum's in charting a move away from his 'avant-garde' music. In 1994 Covell wrote in a review of Meale's symphony that:

> It was true that he wrote a string quartet; but that was a very strange piece that seemed to mock the ideals of ensemble and cohesion contained in the history of the string quartet.[5] His second string quartet of 1980 was completely different in that it marked Meale's open avowal of a more traditional and empirical style and his frank return to melodic and harmonic principles of a pre-avant-garde consistency. The operas *Voss* and *Mer de Glace* confirmed this reversion to older methods.
>
> Even so, his decision to write a symphony indicated that his return to the forms associated with yesteryear had entered a new phase. [...] How well this material hangs together – it seemed to end with a disconcerting abruptness – is likely to be established by further hearings. Sufficient for a first impression is to note that this score is one of the most astonishing historical regressions in style in the annals of music.
>
> Put it beside Meale's *Incredible Floridas*, to be performed in Adelaide at the end of this week, and I very much doubt that many people would believe that these two works were by the same composer.[6]

In 1991, Covell similarly contrasted the second String Quartet with *Incredible Floridas*:

> Meale's Second String Quartet (1980) was the most extreme manifestation of his wish to resign from holding up the banner of modernism and allow himself the expression of a wider range of musical impulses, whether traditional or up-to-date. [...] Meale's instrumental ensemble piece *Incredible Floridas*, inspired by the poetry and vision of Rimbaud, demonstrated that the passage of 20 years since its first performance has not made it appear tame or house-trained.[7]

Covell's disappointment in Meale is clear, yet others went far further, and the further they went, the less they had to say about Meale's music.

What critics found difficult to square was the change that led the Meale who best fitted the image of the progressive modernist to become the Meale who wrote music that relied on large-scale tonal forms. Of course the problem was hardly unique to the Australian situation. Nor is Meale the obvious composer around whom this difficulty ought to have condensed, since his early music contains moments of triadic harmony that suggest that tonality was never fully obscured. These early works are evidence of the composer working with a variety of musical ideas, and their plurality does not sit easily with a neat opposition between not-tonal and tonal working. Meale's own response to the question of tonality in his music is less hard and fast than that of his critics, and it is worth quoting at length:

[Andrew Ford:] So when you look back at your pieces from the 1960s, and early '70s then, do you think of them in terms of having been written in a 'foreign language'?

[Richard Meale:] No, I don't think that. About the early works, yes, there was a selfconscious effort. I hope it doesn't show too much, but then it became me, and the Lorca for instance, had nothing forced about it, despite the complexities, hideous complexities of it. It was utterly now my way of thinking, as were various things including my move back into tonality. […]

[Ford:] You mentioned returning to tonality. There's several questions I wanted to ask you about that. First of all, was it difficult?

[Meale:] Terribly difficult. Harder to go that way than to atonal music. This time the selfconsciousness was totally different. I had to re-find a world which was actually natural to me, because I knew the language of (I hate the word) this tonal that we say but we'll just use it [sic]. It was part of my nature, I'd never lost it, it was part of my early expression.

It was really re-finding something within myself, but as soon as you start talking about these things, people say, Oh, looking backwards, nostalgia. No, it wasn't nostalgia at all, it's the fact that it was part of my life, part of my being, and it's a part that I respect and I respect tonal music more and more and more; but to turn my life around like that, it was difficult because I knew I was, in a sense, destroying what I had been making my name on.[8]

Meale's explanation of tonality's suppression is in modernism's terms: of the need for his practice to overcome the limitations of art's form, of a life led by art, and of the surfacing of a tonality that had always been 'part of my being'. Although it is beyond the reach of this book to deal with the complexities of the reception of Meale's music after the mid-1970s, the quotes above indicate something of the scale of investment in Meale as a modernist, and of the difficulty that an apparent change of style created for those who made that investment. As I will show, amongst pre-*Viridian* compositions one finds music that engages with the problems of writing both tonal and atonal music, and which is less uniform than the pre- and post-*Viridian* discourse implies.

In an interview in 2007 that looked back at the 'crisis' that had produced *Viridian*, Meale associated an 'avant-garde' with fashion, and he rejected the term as a description of his earlier identity.[9] Even if Meale shied away from the term, his music in the 1960s and 1970s does engage with the problems for which the designation 'avant-garde' is at least appropriate to investigate, since it puts into question the institutions of music in Australia, and Meale's relation to them. In his interviews from this period he frequently criticizes the social situation of music, and the systemic problems of being a composer in Australia. He does so far more often than he criticizes past musical practices. Indeed, the way in which he makes his criticisms of the role of the composer in Australia is by appealing to practices from 'elsewhere', be it Spain (in his criticisms in the early–mid-1960s), Japan (those from the mid–late 1960s), or France (especially in the early 1970s). It mattered less what the specific features of those cultures were, than that they formed a useful way of addressing the relationship between music and Australian society.

For Andreas Huyssen, considering the moment in the United States before the postmodernism of the 1970s, 'the 1960s can be regarded as the closing chapter in the tradition of avant-gardism', and broadly his argument applies to the Australian situation too, given Australia's involvement in the Vietnam War, and the similar 'promise of unlimited abundance', which later resulted in a comparable tension between modernism and postmodernity.[10] He argues that 'A major difference between the United States and Europe in the 1960s is that European writers, artists and intellectuals then were much more aware of the increasing cooption of all modernist and avant-garde art by the culture industry.'[11] Huyssen's argument further suggests that perhaps the 'avant-garde' that Meale was later to reject – a conception of the avant-garde conditioned by the discourses of postmodernism – is different to the 'avant-garde' being discussed in the 1960s. Nevertheless, the use of the term in Australia in the 1960s is problematic, since when Peart tries to explain Meale's 'avant-garde' through 'the post-Webern European school or with John Cage', the connections are vague, since the concepts are well outside Peart's primary field of expertise.[12] The important point to emphasize is that for Huyssen the avant-garde in the United States in the 1960s is in no simple way a belated version of a European avant-garde from forty years earlier.

In 1965 Meale was interviewed on the ABC for the 'desert island discs' programme *Away from It All*, in which he said that he intended to keep Australia as a base, and to keep in touch with Europe through travel: 'There's a touch of sanity when I get there [i.e. to Europe]. Everything seems normal about music. They're interested in cultural activities. The general people are much more aware of it.'[13] Meale had been working as a programmer for the Australian Broadcasting Commission, where he had responsibility for developing programmes of music for broadcast, and as a pianist introducing Sydney audiences to post-tonal music. Where Banks, for example, was involved in the concert life of London, and wrote music that responded to, and extended, past practices, the independence of Australia from Europe (for example) made it possible for Meale to refer to Spanish songs (as he does in *Las Alboradas*) without positioning himself in any specific lineage – for what experience of those songs did Sydney audiences have? His choice of a *sevillana* in the 1965 interview has nothing to do with Seville, and much more to do with the difference between Meale's aesthetic preferences compared with his local contemporaries, for it is 'a type of music not often heard in this country'.[14] Although his separation from 'the public' is apparent in this interview, so too is his desire to change the relationship between concert music and its audience:

> [Ellis Blain:] This comes back to your attitude that what you write is your own affair, and that you're not writing for public approbation or appreciation [...]
>
> [Meale:] No, I'm writing for 'public', but not in the sense of recognition or getting anything from them. I'm very interested in the contemporary society. In fact it is through this interest that I'm so insistent contemporary music should be written in a contemporary fashion. [...] This society is based so strongly on adoration of the past to an abnormal extent that this idea of emulating the past goes too far now.[15]

His particular 'contemporary fashion' is not one formed from local networks, but one defined in opposition to localism. This makes him an international modernist. Meale tended away from engaging with popular music in general, music he would have known well from working at Eric Anderson's record store. He worked there for five years, in part as record manager, and it is through this shop that he accessed many recordings of European music. When he chose Bob Dylan's *Desolation Row* as one of his 'desert island discs', his interviewer, understandably perplexed by the choice, asked Meale: 'Do you like this kind of popular music? Do you feel that it's worthwhile in any artistic sense?' To which Meale replied: 'I think popular music is important. It certainly has important communication with teenagers who do constitute a large proportion of the population today.' He then compared Dylan with the troubadours, before dismissing wholesale the music of the 'hit parade' and jazz.[16] The paradoxes of Australian connectedness to, say, France, alongside its significant geographical and cultural separation, mean that Meale's knowledge of Boulez or Messiaen could be used to seek a new orientation for musical society in Sydney (and later Adelaide).[17] Whatever the partiality of Meale's understanding that came from his rejection of the typical path of gaining insight through personal study with a mentor-composer (as Williamson, Banks, Butterley and many others did), he made the most of the LPs and scores that were available at the time of his 'self-teaching' in the 1960s. His use of this time to mine published resources rather than to study in the UK (as was the typical path for a composer at the time), amounts to a rejection and a critique of the institutional methods of learning. That critique is, however, soft-edged, and there is no *estocade* to tradition. In 1960 Meale was awarded a Ford Foundation grant, which he used to study at the University of California, Los Angeles (after which he returned to Australia via Britain and Spain). There he studied 'non-Western' music, and he returned to Australia as a composer with knowledge of 'Balinese, Javanese, Indian, and Persian' music.[18]

Although he later rejected the term 'avant-garde', as a performer and producer Meale's support for ideas from outside Australia aimed to undertake something similar to the project of the artists of the early-twentieth-century avant-garde: to 'de-familiarize a very specific set of institutional conventions: those modes of seeing [hearing] that have been canonized by the power of the dominant social discourse and the pervasive institution of art'.[19] The 1965 interview on *Away from It All* was Meale at his most negative and least comfortable with the conception of a composer that his interviewer describes, and he was keen to disagree with the conservatism of the questions that he was asked, especially in those moments where the questions sought to prise apart composition and life. Meale's desire is clearly to 'normalize' the music that he writes, something that he also sought to achieve through his radio programmes, in his work as a producer for the ABC and in his teaching. In *Away from It All* he sounds genuinely flummoxed by some of the questions, particularly those that assert composition as an occupation:

[Blain:] What are your ambitions for the future, professionally?
[Meale:] To keep on working in composition, and in music in general.[20]
[Blain:] Personally, do you have any ambitions?
[Meale:] No, just to keep on working.

And earlier in the interview:

[Blain:] How do you like to spend a holiday?
[Meale:] ... I don't know ... I've never thought of a holiday ... I've always worked ... or do something[.][21]

Blain had difficulty throughout the interview understanding Meale's point of view, asking a pointed question about Meale's attitude to marriage, for example. Blain was also taken aback by Meale's attitude to the British: 'You sounded a little bit anti-British to me, earlier. Does this carry through to your attitudes to the people as a whole?' Meale replied:

I'm afraid it does. I simply don't like the way they behave. To me they are simply pretending to a situation in the world which they don't rightly hold. They are trying to coast along on their past glories [...] London is one of the great entertainment cities of the world, otherwise I think it is a very empty city.[22]

Throughout this, and the other interviews he gave, Meale returns insistently to his music. In a lecture prepared for the 1976 Rostrum, Meale cautioned his listeners not to hear *Interiors/Exteriors* as being formed by his relocation to Adelaide in 1969, though he also gave a sense of the significance of the move:[23]

I must say, and it is important to say, that my move to Adelaide was a shock. At the time I felt I had moved from 'life' to 'limbo' (which is a place totally unsuited to me – I far prefer hell). My activities in performing and promoting seemed to be curtailed by the rigidly maintained conservativeness of the city – as it was then. Naturally I felt frustrated, and felt alienated.[24]

His lecture argues against materialism, of 'images of a world of ease, enjoyment, fulfillment and comfort', of 'Plastic sex [that] can be found in the Supermarket'.[25] The lecture lays out the paradoxes of the avant-gardist's position, confirming the separation of his experience as a composer and the task of the listener: 'You see, I believe it is not my job to provide solutions. In fact, I believe it is my job to respect you all as puzzled alienated humans, of sensibility – exactly the same as I am.'[26] He presents himself as a critique of that separation.

In his survey, McCredie argued that nineteenth-century Australia has no bourgeoisie, and that without this class the mechanisms of commodification that bind the artist and the institution (and which are necessary for an avant-garde proper) never materialized in Australia. Even in Meale's time Australia had no institutions of autonomous musical art against which to argue, though Meale did argue for his own music as autonomous: 'What I am trying to show is that an art work – if it is to be one – must transcend the temporal particular, by finding the tangible abstraction.'[27] Considering Meale in avant-garde terms poses a problem, since in the 1960s there were no significant bourgeois institutions of art; the institutions that did exist were overwhelmingly funded by the state, and so in making his argument against the Establishment, Meale positions himself against a version of Australian culture that was not present. Theorizing Meale as an avant-gardist requires European terms, which is nevertheless useful, since it emphasizes the differences between Australian and European markets, and it contributes to understanding Meale in the context of Australia. Recognition of those differences, and the difficulties they pose with regard to gaining audiences for orchestras and ensembles, is a reason for Peart's assertion that Meale belongs to an avant-garde. In other words, asserting an avant-garde promotes change that would be useful for composers whose music was progressive, supporting the kinds of institutions that may well have benefited Meale as a composer. Arguing for an avant-garde is also a way of pushing against the pragmatism that is characteristic of Australian culture, and which in the 1960s (as in the nineteenth century) privileged hand over mind.[28] Underlying all Meale's points is the sense of the world as 'wrong' (that is, in need of change) and 'alienating'.[29] Although the term 'Australian avant-garde' is often understood as a meaningless figuration, Meale's lecture on music is explicitly economic, concerned with 'the alienated labour' that underlies notions of 'technical progress'.[30] He concludes the lecture with Marcuse on the 'ivory tower' from the conclusion of *Counter Revolution and Revolt*, which was on Meale's mind as he considered his position as an academic at the University of Adelaide, a post that was created especially for him:

> The common denominator for the misplaced radicalism in the cultural revolution is the anti-intellectualism which it shares with the most reactionary

representatives of the Establishment: revolt against reason – not only against the Reason of capitalism, bourgeois society, and so on, but against Reason *per se*. And just as the indeed urgent fight against the training of cadres for the Establishment *in* the universities turns into a fight against *the* university, so the destruction of the aesthetic form turns into a destruction of art. To be sure, both branches of the intellectual culture, isolation and alienation from the given reality may lead to an 'ivory tower', but may also (and do) lead to something that the Establishment is increasingly capable of tolerating, namely, independent thinking and feeling.[31]

Table 3.1 List of First Australian Performances Given by Richard Meale[32]

Date of performance	Title	Composer
1959	Le Merle Noir	Olivier Messiaen
	Sonatine pour le piano	Daniel Ruyneman
	Pierrot Lunaire	Arnold Schoenberg
1960	Das Buch der hängenden Gärten	Arnold Schoenberg
	Drei Lieder	Anton Webern
1962	Sonata for Piano	Willem Pijper
	Variations for Piano	Anton Webern
	Vingt Regards sur l'Enfant Jésus	Olivier Messiaen
	Three Czech Dances	Bohuslav Martinů
1963	Sonata for Flute and Piano	Camillo Togni
	Cantéyodjayâ	Olivier Messiaen
	Monody for Corpus Christi	Harrison Birtwistle
1964	Neumes rythmiques	Olivier Messiaen
	Quatuor pour la fin du temps	Olivier Messiaen
	Laudes	Nigel Butterley
	Trope	Pierre Boulez
	Six Pieces	Arnold Schoenberg
1965	Piano Piece for David Tudor #4	Sylvano Bussotti
	Couple, for Flute and Piano	Sylvano Bussotti
	Gymel, for Flute and Piano	Niccolò Castiglioni
	Four Systems	Earle Brown
	Oisseaux Exotiques	Olivier Messiaen
1965	Serenade	Thea Musgrave
	Trois Poèmes d'Henri Michaux	Witold Lutosławski
1967	Songs of Earth and Heaven	Olivier Messiaen
1970	Catalogue d'oiseaux	Olivier Messiaen

Meale's vision for a better-informed, more open and progressive Australia was successful: he played a sufficient part in the reconfiguration of music to be rewarded with a lectureship, publishing contracts and opera commissions, all of which stem from his introduction to Australian audiences of so much post-tonal music, including through his own performances (see Table 3.1).

When Meale's style changed in the 1980s, so too did the programming of his earlier music. If the earlier music appealed to conceptions of autonomy and newness from outside Australia, its success brought a situation in which the abstraction of the earlier works served no further social function. Few of his early works are now performed. The two that endure are *Incredible Floridas*, the least obviously autonomous of the early works, and *Coruscations*, a tour de force of piano virtuosity and the most process-driven of all Meale's works. From *Interiors/Exteriors* onwards, 'Institutional frame and content coincide',[33] and Meale's growing standing as a mainstream composer and his use of 'high-status' practices from elsewhere – such as the use of Boulez's technique, or the prestige of having Paul Sacher commission him to write an oboe concerto – reconfigures music in Australia such that Meale is centralized by commissioning and discoursing institutions. By the 1980s this had taken place to a sufficient extent for Meale's earlier music to be a problem, which was overcome by diminishing the excesses of a young composer as having once been 'a bit of a rabble-rouser',[34] and a touch restless.

Homage to Garcia Lorca

[Blain:]   Do you think the fact that you live in Australia is a handicap [in making money as a professional composer]?

[Meale:]   Yes it's a terrible handicap. There're so few avenues for letting music out here that you have to depend on an overseas market, if you are going to even keep yourself in cigarettes.[35]

Meale's connection to an overseas market was through Boosey and Hawkes, which had signed him with *Homage to Garcia Lorca* (1964), a piece for double string orchestra. For those writing about *Homage* soon after its premiere, the musical problems it posed were about coherence. This is most clearly expressed by Stephen Walsh, responding to the London performance on 18 September 1965, in an article that engages with the work at a greater length than anyone else's. For Walsh the problems of organization are fruitful, and he ties these to the expression of emotion:

> The emotion of the Prelude is by design rather inchoate; the composer seems as bewildered as his listeners will be by the flood of half-formed impressions, and it is striking how well he controls the elements of his disorganization.[36]

The question of organization/disorganization is raised by Meale in his programme note:

The short *Prelude* is the embryo of the work. All basic rhythmic, harmonic and melodic structures are here. Particularly significant are the opening seven bars in which the basic intervallic series create the principal harmonic aggregations through their temporal appearance. [...] The *Postlude* consists of five sonorous plateaux related to the opening seven bars of the work. These accumulate and decay to end on their final intensity of sound produced by the methodical accumulation of the twelve tones.[37]

The key term here is 'embryo', and the sense in which it is useful is as a necessary precursor to 'death'. 'Death', such is its presence in the piece, precedes even the Prelude, captured in the lines of text above the score:

¡Ay, qué furia de amor, qué hiriente filo, qué nocturne rumor, qué muerte blanca!

Meale glosses this as: 'Ah, what fury of love, what stabbing edge, what nocturnal murmuring, what white death!' In his programme note, Meale is careful to distance his music from Lorca's poetry, emphasizing the tendencies of Lorca's style over the details of any particular poem:

As for the title of the composition, it refers to the Spanish poet and playwright whose work I have loved for many years; and whilst it is difficult to isolate particular features of such a rich and complex expression as his poetry is, a few outstanding characteristics do come to mind immediately – his intense passion, his overwhelming sense of humanity, his particular sense of death (which is only Spanish), his vibrant imagery which merges into surrealism, and the sonority of his lines. Certainly, these are some of the characteristics that have influenced me in the writing of the *homage*, though it never attempts to mimic Lorca in music.[38]

The nature of Meale's rejection of mimesis is intriguing, especially given the care with which Meale connects his response as an artist to Lorca's writing, but it nevertheless supports an argument for Meale's music as autonomous.

The first performance of the piece, by the Sydney Little Symphony Orchestra, took place in Sydney at the Cell Block Theatre, East Sydney Technical College, on 15 October 1964, which in the previous year had been the venue for a production of Lorca's *Blood Wedding*.[39] Joseph Post, 'at whose suggestion *Lorca* was written',[40] conducted Meale's work. It was performed alongside Schoenberg's *Verklärte Nacht*, Mozart's Violin Concerto in B♭ (K.207) and Haydn's Symphony No. 97 (one of the latter's 'London' symphonies, which suggests that the programming was thinking ahead to the orchestra's London performances).[41] The first performance of the work for enlarged forces was on 27 July 1965. The concert was reviewed by a breathless C. M. Prerauer,[42] and by an enthusiastic Covell:

Not many recent works could live next to Alban Berg's *Violin Concerto* [with Christian Ferras as soloist] without seeming diminished in the process.

> But Richard Meale's *Homage to Garcia Lorca* survived the proximity of its great companion in the first half of last night's Town Hall subscription concert with no loss of esteem.
>
> It seemed more than ever worthy of going to London later this year with Dean Dixon and the Sydney Symphony Orchestra, its performers of last night, as representative and witness of the vital new ferment in Australian musical creation.[43]

The Australian press coverage of Meale's piece was enthusiastic, consistently positioning him alongside contemporary European composers.

The SSO tour coincided with the Commonwealth Festival, highlighting art from member states. Writing about the literary aspect of the Commonwealth Festival, Leonie Kramer focussed on two publications that coincided with the festival, the *Times Literary Supplement*'s 'Sounding the '60s' and *The London Magazine*'s special issue, both devoted to 'The Commonwealth'. She reviewed Australian writing covered by the publications, criticizing them for failing to include the 'exploration by writers of varied talents and abilities of many aspects of Australian life' and 'the mood of self-criticism which has developed in the past decade' by writers such as Donald Horne, Manning Clark and Judith Wright. 'Australian music', she wrote:

> is represented by C. M. Prerauer on Richard Meale – to me the only sour note in the magazine, since Prerauer's praise of Meale has a decidedly parochial tone. Meale's merits do not need the artificial support of overstatement and of inaccuracies concerning the musical scene from which he has emerged. It is nevertheless pleasant to be able to cite this as an exception. In other respects the Commonwealth Festival is celebrated without self-consciousness, and, especially in *The London Magazine*, with considerable zest and liveliness.[44]

Reviewing the London concert (18 September 1965) for *The Daily Telegraph*, Peter Stadlen was not altogether positive, and took the opportunity instead to comment on the orchestra's 'Australian' identity:

> Leaving aside individual points of instrumental excellence the strength of our leading orchestras lies in the way the players are intimately attuned to one another.
>
> The most striking achievement of the Australians, on the other hand, is that perhaps owing to their splendid isolation they have completely assimilated the ideas of their conductor-in-chief.[45]

The Times was more positive, and more interested in the sound being made rather than national identity:

> The orchestra's chief strength lies in its strings, perhaps the violins most of all, who produced plenty of tone, always abundantly firm, and were consistently tidy in

ensemble. There are assertive, almost aggressive horns; and the woodwind section, if it gave us no particularly distinguished solo playing, showed an admirable corporate sense.[46]

The Guardian's Hugo Cole also made his criticisms in terms of players working together, connecting Meale's piece with Brahms's Symphony No. 1, which followed. For Cole:

> Homage to Garcia Lorca, by the young Australian composer Richard Meale [...] sounded dangerously opaque. The complexity of the music rivals that of those Schönberg chamber works which need 25 rehearsals before players can get round the notes, 50 before they can make sense of them. To play such intricately textured music with the full string orchestra rather than the 20 soloists allowed by the composer is to ask for trouble. I'm sure that almost all the right notes were played, equally sure that no one present had a clear idea of what the work should sound like, so that whatever order is present in score or composer's mind was lost in the general conflict and confusion.
>
> As if to point [to] the moral, the programme ended with a performance of Brahms' First Symphony in which every player clearly knew not only what he had to do himself, but also what his neighbour was up to.[47]

Bringing Brahms and Meale together underlines the problems of coherence and, to use Cole's term, 'order'. Meale's programme note declares that his first movement is a prelude and that the first seven bars set forth the subsequent music's material, which is a formal strategy that invites comparison with the Brahms. The opening of Brahms's symphony and its relationship to the subsequent music is a problem taken up by David Brodbeck, for whom the introduction to the work is considered a 'memorable afterthought'.[48] Raymond Knapp argues that the introduction was added to the symphony to balance the finale,[49] with adjustments made to already composed material to incorporate the addition. Walter Frisch comments that in the second movement of Brahms's First Symphony: 'unfolds one of Brahms's most sophisticated thematic groups, a splendid example of what Schoenberg was to call "musical prose", by which he meant thematic statements that avoid mere repetition or predictable patterns'.[50] 'Motivic-thematic coherence' is Frisch's concern in his analysis of the first movement as a technique essential to the symphonic genre.

Cole's other comparison, with Schoenberg, is more readily significant. Even if Cole's review raised Schoenberg as a token of 'difficult' music, the earlier programming of Meale's *Homage* alongside Schoenberg is important. The programming of Schoenberg's first 'fully mature achievement'[51] at *Homage*'s premiere presents Meale as a parallel composer, and therefore at the beginning of an Australian Music to come – a topic entirely fitting with the progressive idea of the SSO at the Cell Block Theatre.[52] *Verklärte Nacht* is also a likely musical predecessor to *Homage*, especially given the impact that it made on subsequent writing for strings.[53] *Homage* is closer to that work than to Stravinsky's *Apollo* or Tippett's *Concerto for Double String Orchestra*, though Bartók, in the *Music for Strings, Percussion and Celeste*, uses the orchestra antiphonally, as does

Meale. There are also some straightforward similarities between *Verklärte Nacht* and *Homage to Garcia Lorca*: both respond to poetry, and both are cast in five movements. Schoenberg's form follows his text; Meale's piece is less literally attached to his text, though he considered the work in terms of poetry:

> Five movements comprise this Homage – two outside ones framing three inner ones. The Prelude carries the inscription 'Ay qué furia de amor, qué hiriente filo, qué nocturne rumor, qué muerte blanca!' (Ah, what fury of love, what stabbing edge, what nocturnal murmuring, what white death!) The next three movements may be regarded as three poems, each of its own character. I refer to these movements as poems, not only for their general impression, but because the music is inclined to fall into sentences and stanzas. Before the last movement (Postlude) there is another quotation – '... y recuerdo una brisa triste por los olivos.' (... and I remember the sad breeze through the olive trees.) This movement is the most personal of all. It is irreconcilable as its plateaux of sound move closer and closer to the final noise.[54]

The music is evocative of the two brief texts, particularly in the third movement, which 'is distinctly nocturnal in atmosphere'.[55]

The previous year's piece, *Las Alboradas* (1963), took a less poetic approach to form. It was premiered on 31 May 1963, at the Cell Block Theatre, Sydney, and for Covell, it was 'a work by an Australian composer which [...] failed to sound as if it were a generation late in arriving'.[56] The performers were Peter Richardson (flute), Douglas Trengove (horn), Ronald Ryder (violin) and Nigel Butterley (piano), who responded to this piece in his own composition. For Meale the form of the *Las Alboradas* hinges on the relationship between 'total absorption in sound (in which all twelve semitones are present) and silence'.[57] The silences mostly coincide with section boundaries (such as defined by retrograde structures), and perhaps what Meale means is that the composition works against lyricism. Compared with *Homage*, it refuses momentum and is so fragmented that gestures involving all the instruments rarely last more than a few seconds. The point is that Meale was keen for the work to be understood in terms of sound, rather than in poetic terms. Its initial programme note emphasized construction: 'the work is formal – there is no picture painting'.

Las Alboradas was important locally at a time when new music performance in Sydney was flourishing (in no small part due to Meale's efforts). Programmed alongside *Las Alboradas* in its premiere performance were Birtwistle's *Monody for Corpus Christi*, Camillo Togni's Flute Sonata (which sounds very similar to Meale's own Flute Sonata from 1960, and very unlike *Las Alboradas*'s aleatoricism), Dallapiccola's *Quattro liriche di Antonio Machado*, arias by Menotti and Dallapiccola ('Annina's Vision', and 'Signore Fabien's Aria' respectively), *Two Poems by Sappho* by Petrassi and Messiaen's *Cantéyodjayâ*. Meale's composition was, by request of its audience, performed twice. Given that Meale worked extensively with soprano Marilyn Richardson at the time, it is notable that his composition, unlike the Birtwistle, eschews voice, even though there are specific 'Alboradas' on which his piece is based. Meale buries his source materials in abstraction, such that they are completely unidentifiable, where Birtwistle's piece works straightforwardly with its allusions and sources.[58] The Sydney concert was organized by the Sydney committee of the International Society for Contemporary Music (ISCM), headed by Peart, with Meale as a vice president alongside John Gordon and John Antill. The concert programme gives the dates on which Birtwistle's piece and Togni's piece were performed at ISCM festivals, which helps to position Meale's work as one of many in international circulation. With *Homage*, Meale had a piece that brought him international attention.

For Covell:

> An elaborate technical analysis of the work would be singularly unrewarding. No amount of row-hunting could add anything to the direct experience of the music. Meale, in any case, has absolved us from this task by acknowledging that no strict serial principles underlie the writing of the work.[59]

Anne Boyd's analysis of the opening Prelude in serial terms confirms that Covell is correct, though she argued that:

> The arrangement of the hexachords generates strong polarity between the notes that it contains.[60]

This is readily applicable only to the chords at the opening. It is difficult to see how this hexachordal arrangement 'effectively controls both horizontal and vertical aspects of the piece' as a whole. The pursuit of rows is especially unrewarding given that the work is not serial.[61]

Although the *Telegraph* review of *Homage to Garcia Lorca* refers to Meale as 'this Australian serialist', the work is not serially constructed. Rather, Meale's *Homage* is better understood as freely atonal, with a limited intervallic palate and careful registral control giving the work its motivic material. The opening is nevertheless carefully dodecaphonic, with the sustained pitches entering in the following order: <{A♭/B♭}, {C/D♭}, B, {E/F}, {F♯/G}, {D/E♭}, A> (see Example 3.1). The orchestration blurs the harmonies (using only strings keeps the timbre similar across the section), and some of the sustained pitches re-enter before all twelve pitch classes have been sounded. The subsequent sections repeat the intervallic materials – mostly semitones, often separated by fifths – without obvious serial transformation, and so broad are these materials that there is little motivic material to be transformed. When the third movement returns to the opening arco/pizzicato contrast, and also to the Prelude's preponderance of semitones, the material is more melodic but no less molecular. The chains are scarcely long enough to form motifs, especially in the more repetitive sections. The opening of the movement nevertheless offers a tantalizing glimpse of a chromatic descent: an initial leap from A to D is followed by C♯ and E♭ (already one senses uncertainty, and the potential for a cluster is undercut by the very high register and contrast between the pizzicato in the violin of orchestra II and the violin harmonic in orchestra I), then C, B (viola, orchestra II), B♭. However positive this assertion of line – Meale's registers

Example 3.1 Meale, *Homage to Garcia Lorca*, bars 1–4.

make this hard to follow – it evaporates into the pause in bar 6, and the following bars of repeating notes point more to the withholding of pitch material than its atonal unfolding or serial transformation. Even this movement's most melodic material, in the violas at bar 59, terminates with repeated notes that head nowhere.

Walsh reserved his most critical comments for the end of *Homage*:

> I venture to propose that it is a miscalculation, not because it does not make its effect in the manner intended, but because at the last moment when persuasion is almost complete and compulsion unnecessary, it takes us by the throat and compels us to experience its full horror. [...] The error of overexpression is a common one in contemporary music, particularly among young composers, who feel that they must at all costs oppose the drag of compromise. Meale has set himself a stiff task in attempting to make in music a worthy response to the work of one of the greatest and most humanitarian of modern poets, and it is not entirely surprising that the *Homage* is emotionally one-sided – one thing that Lorca's work never was.[62]

Meale's ending is underlined, italicized and emboldened, but its pitch material has little to say. The players are even directed away from pitch by 'dragging the bow flat across the string with pressure to produce a rasping noise'. Meale's expressionist decadence is a pithy response to serial idealism, coming as an ending to a work that repeatedly withholds the momentum of its material. To explain the ending, Walsh returns to the image of the plateaux of sound:

> These inner movements, says Meale, are like poems [...]; but in the Postlude the loose threads of emotion are taken up in five great planes of sound, which no literary parallel will meet. The first plane is [...] transfigured by a tragedy which, by the second plane, has become hysterical [...]. The level of intensity is held by the third plane, a rarefied plateau of sweeping string glissandi which eventually fade [...]; on this unstable podium the edifice of the final pages is built[.][63]

The alliteration of 'plateau', 'plane', 'podium', 'Prelude' and 'Postlude' is tidy, if not explanatory, and Walsh's descriptions all rely on transformation, when Meale's composition is notable for its lack of direction. Its first four movements do not head towards its final movement, and death is not configured as the necessary end of the music played. The work's intensity ('passion' as Meale has it) is in its refusal for that intensity to be deferred or anticipated, at the cost of coherence.

The Postlude's five sections have scarcely any melodic material and set out different harmonic fields. The first section is shown in Example 3.2. The second section is formed from block chords, more unstable than at the start of the piece, which become ossified in a fragmented chord of increasingly quick stuttering. A section of only glissandi follows, and though an immediate contrast to the stiffness of the repeated notes, the chords outlined are stable (see Example 3.3). The spacing of the repetition of glissandi is governed by interlocking rhythmic cycles, similar to those found in Birtwistle's *Tragoedia* (premiered in the month before the London performance of

Homage); Meale (born in 1932) and the slightly younger Birtwistle (born in 1934) responded independently to Stravinsky and Messiaen. The cycle lengths in this section of the Postlude are shown in Table 3.2 (within each group are two staggered entries). As the glissandi end, the double basses enter, playing E/B♭. This chord was first heard – and in the same register – in the second section of the Prelude, and here it returns as a stable bass. From bar 41 of the Postlude, the chord is tenaciously sounded, tremolo and *fff*. Departing from the B♭ is a chromatic row played canonically finishing in the

Table 3.2 The Lengths of Cycles in the 'Postlude'

Instrument	Cycle length, in crotchets
Violin I, Orchestra I	5
Viola, Cello, Orchestra I	4
Violin I, Orchestra II	7
Viola, Cello, Orchestra II	6

Example 3.2 The opening of the 'Postlude', bars 1–4.

Example 3.3 The second section of the 'Postlude', bars 26–9.

violins on A. If classical serialism promised much in the opening bars, the deployment of Meale's 'opening row' brings only degradation.

Meale's expression of the '*muerte blanca*' text at the end of his composition corresponds with Schoenberg's setting of Dehmel's text.[64] Although they might seem opposite in meaning, Dehmel's with its anticipation of new life and Lorca's ending with death, the opposition of the endings is undercut by the imagery that they share: Dehmel's *Ihr Atem küsst sich in den Lüften*, Lorca's *una brisa triste por los olivos*; Dehmel's *helle Nacht*, Lorca's *muerte blanca*.[65] The music of Meale's ending is both violent and introspective, and the flat bow that makes the sound of death is itself a kind of plateau that draws the music towards the sonorous rather than the poetic. The sonorous plateaux return in Meale's 1971 work *Plateau*, for wind quintet, in which Demel's '*Ihr Atem küsst sich in den Lüften*' returns in Meale's description of the work as 'rarified air'. *Plateau* was composed when Meale's music was at its most Boulezian.[66]

To focus on the music's poetry is to open up the problem of relationships between totalities and parts. The lack of a unified formulation, such as serialism, for Meale's piece means that the question 'what significance do the textural fragments of Lorca have for the interpretation of the work as a whole?' is less relevant than 'is there a concept of "whole" that Meale's quotation fragments?' For Hugo Cole, reviewing the work in *The Guardian*, such a question is an ethical one, at the centre of writing for orchestra: if the whole exists in the composer's mind or the conductor's score, then the decay that the individual instrumental parts present leads to 'general conflict and confusion'.[67] Furthermore, it is not enough for Cole that the right notes are played, since the relationships amongst notes remain unclear – it is the integration and coherence of the orchestra that Meale's piece undermines. Walsh grants a certain amount of that incoherence to Meale's compositional strategy when he writes that 'it is striking how well he controls the elements of his disorganization', yet the outcome of this disorganization remains the fragmented 'half-formed image', which the composer transcends emotionally despite his 'bewilderment'.[68] *Homage* is, following Walsh's argument, decadent, and the piece can be read within a tradition of decadence:

> [D]ecadence always involves the reification – petrification – of existing modes at the expense of future possibilities as well as past achievements, that is, of hypothetical utopia as well as tradition, of idealism as well as the truth that has been. Possibility and heritage – the not yet realized and the well-realized – are not simply neglected and ignored, but denied and expunged.[69]

Soon after the premiere, Covell used 'decadence' vividly to describe the composition:

> It may be enough to say that whole passages of the music are, in essence, strikingly varied ways of articulating a twelve-note chord. […] In other words, the basic aggregation of intervals may declare itself as a slow accumulation of registers, as a

series of whipcracks or as a toppling ruin; it may disintegrate like shattered glass in a hail of particles or it may settle into a close, thick, opaque neutrality.[70]

Emphasizing the connection with Schoenberg neglects two other scores that are also relatives of *Homage*. One is Humphrey Searle's *Poem for 22 Strings* (1950), which may well have come to Meale's attention by being premiered at Darmstadt (certainly Meale would have known Searle's translations of books about Schoenberg and Webern). Searle's serialism, like Meale's *Homage*, comes 'tinged with a sense of historical belatedness'.[71] Ben Earle gives the work's row as <E, B♭, A, G, D♭, A♭, F, D, B, F♯, E♭, C>, locating its prominent position at the start of the *Poem*, and perhaps the work has a more specific connection with Meale's *Homage*, which ends with a chord based on {E, B♭}. Earle points out that *Poem for 22 Strings* was written after Andrzej Panufnik's *Lullaby, for 29 Strings and Two Harps* (1947), citing Searle's memoirs *Quadrille with a Raven* (chapter 11), and that:

> the poem looks forward technically (in terms of tetrachordal revoicings of the aggregate) to the music composed by Panufnik's compatriot Lutosławski[72] in the late 1950s (see climax of *Musique funèbre* (1958)), and, so far as sonority is concerned, perhaps even to Ligeti's pieces a few years later: compare the opening of *Atmosphères* (1961).[73]

Musique funèbre ends, as Searle's row begins, with B♭ (spelt A♯), E. This is preceded by a series of wedge-shaped cascades that play out the essential semitonal material of the piece (its row consists only of semitones and tritones[74]): the final E is all that remains of the larger motif (played solo by the cello in bar 291) D, D♯, A, A♯, E. Lutosławski's piece is not explicitly connected to Searle's; nor does it stand alone – the score is prefaced with the phrase 'à la mémoire de Béla Bartók'. *Homage* and *Musique funèbre* are not obvious relations, though they do share some similar textures, such as a preponderance of repeated notes: *Homage* from bars 20–5 of the Postlude and *Musique funèbre* in the opening of the *Apogée*. Lutosławski's title is in the same poetic realm as Meale's music, especially if considered in its English translation as 'Music of mourning', 'a memorial tribute'.[75] One can hear the death in Meale's Postlude since it comes with the death rattle, rendered though the scraping of the bow 'to produce a rasping noise'.[76] A closer connection exists with Searle's *Poem* (even if, as a wedding present to his wife, Searle's subject matter is less dour) and in particular with its ending. Although the pitch materials are not the same, Searle closes the composition by introducing pitches one by one (<A♯, D♯, F♯, A, G♯, B, D, F ... >), with each sustained until the entire chord is sounded. The registral spread of pitches is similar to that of *Homage*.

Homage's musical ideas connect closely to those of Meale's contemporaries, whose music Meale had performed and broadcast (in programmes such as *Music of Today*, which he wrote for the ABC[77]). The Australian critics were keen for an Australian composer to fulfil the role that they had imagined for him, which came with technical rigour as taken for granted. In a 1965 interview with de Berg, Meale spoke about technique generally:

I think that a work should have this multiple nature about it, so it has often been perhaps an aim of mine that a work is always a little more than one can hear.[78]

And specifically about *Homage* and how it is put together:

I use durational patterns of rhythm, that is, movement of sound in time, not a dance rhythm but the sense of things happening, things happen quickly, they happen not so quickly, and these fall into various proportions of occurrence. I don't use a series of notes yet there is always a series of notes present in it. I move in and around these matters, so perhaps at one time when I'm writing I may be thinking of a certain inter-relationship whilst at another time I may not be almost thinking but I may be writing and the whole thing may just be simply the act of writing notes. In other words, my mind is turning from various areas of description about the piece of music to various others. In other words, perhaps I'm playing an impossible role; perhaps I try to be magician and a scientist in one given moment so that even I don't know quite what I'm doing, at any given one.[79]

Homage audibly works within musical boundaries, and the opening chords set the pattern for harmonies to come, but these boundaries are not established through external technical apparatus, and the 'durational patterns' and 'proportions of occurrence' come from within, not from without. Meale's achievement with *Homage* is in escaping his earlier, fractured writing and finding a more sustained music without extensive external structuring such as from serial technique.

Clouds Now and Then, Cicada

Clouds Now and Then is one of two works that were to form a triptych based on haiku by Matsuo Bashō, a seventeenth-century Japanese poet. The other piece composed was *Soon It Will Die* (henceforth *Cicada*[80]), and the third was to be *Ailing on My Travels*,[81] but the latter was not completed. *Clouds Now and Then* was written for the SSO, which performed the work at the Festival of Perth in 1969.

Like Boyd's early analysis of *Homage to Garcia Lorca*, Bright's study[82] of the pitch procedures in *Clouds Now and Then* extended from an assumed serial basis for the piece, but the value of Bright's work is its demonstration of a core harmonic working that is flexibly deployed. Although Bright sought to establish a serial basis for the piece, she reports Meale claiming that it was not serially conceived, and the result of her analysis confirms Meale's claim. Bright's analysis focusses on a few characteristic intervals, which she forms into three main groups: 'a: perfect fourth + semitone; or perfect fifth, or fourth, + tritone'; 'b: all semitones'; 'c: perfect fourth or fifth + major second'.[83] These groups could be used to describe most of Meale's music, though the flexibility of Meale's use of the constituent intervals makes the groupings difficult to sustain, and the harmony moves freely through the wide field enabled by this combination of intervals at various octave distributions.

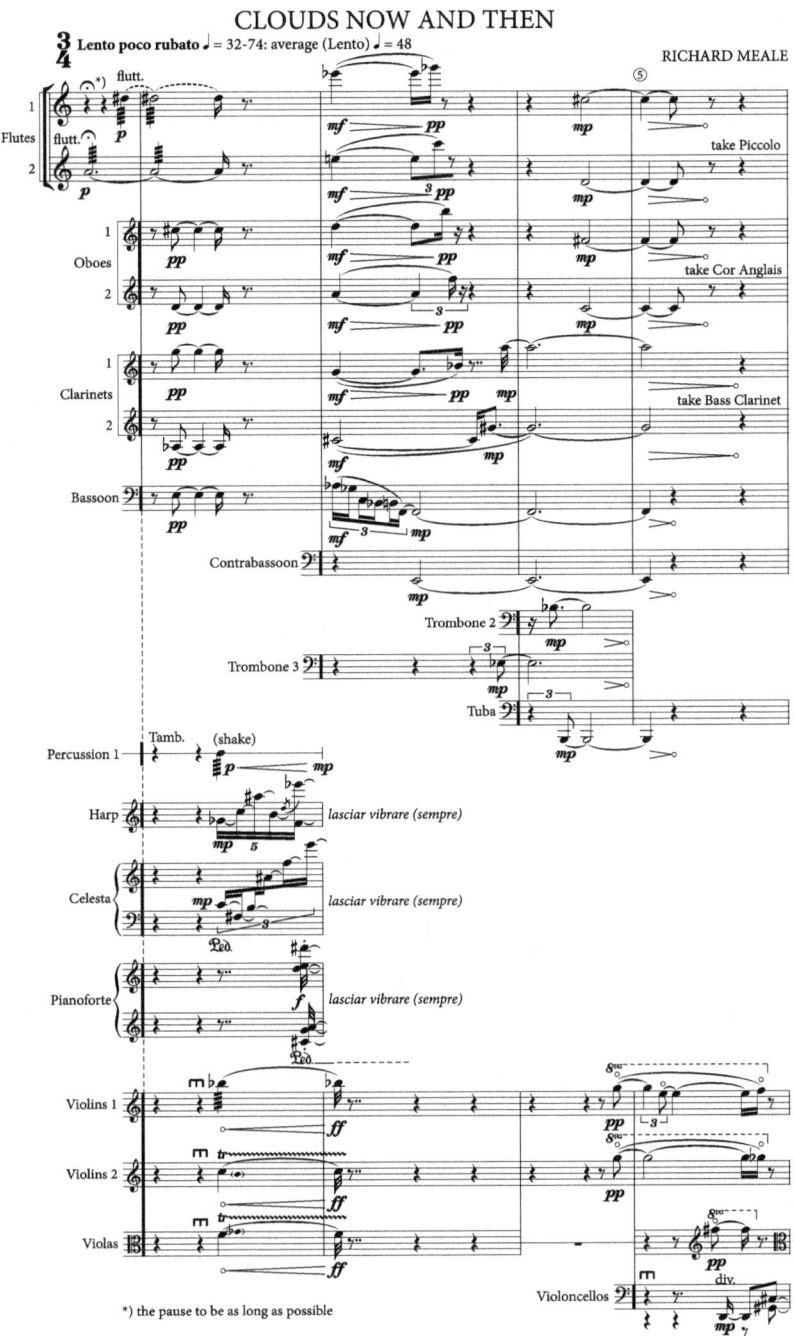

Example 3.4 Meale, *Clouds Now and Then*, bars 1–5.

The composition is colourful, with a limited palette, eschewing argument for slowly evolving, timbrally eventful blocks. These blocks, like the harmony, are formed flexibly. Bright cites Meale as dividing the work into three main sections, surrounded by an introduction and a coda:

Introduction:	7+3 [bars]
A:	8+5+5
B:	10+15
C:	5+5, 5+5, 5+5+5+5[84]
Coda:	–[No internal subdivision]

Bright writes that the last bar of B (bar 53) is also the first of C, but cites no further ambiguities of structure. Tracing these blocks audibly through the music is difficult since it fluidly changes texture, dynamics and instrumentation. Working further against any perception of the proportions is the tempo: 'Lento: poco rubato ♩=32–54: average (Lento) ♩=40.' The 'poco' is misleading, since the metronome marking is very wide indeed.[85] Given that the composition's rhythmic language is fairly steady, and that the piece makes as much of note endings as beginnings, the more constant tempo of recordings is not unexpected, and a steady tempo also supports the dynamic elements of the form already written into the rhythms. The 'Directions for Performance' in the score are brief, addressing only the tempo:

> The tempo should be very slow – in perfect calm – within various undulations as felt by the conductor but never must these be 'dramatic' – the work should always be poised and at the same time relaxed.[86]

Bright connected the bar structure to the syllable patterns of the haiku that appears at the opening of the score and gives the work its title: 'Clouds now and then giving men relief from moon viewing.' The English translation uses a 4–5–4 structure, but this is not clearly projected in the work's formal groupings.

In the sketches for the work several pages of different sectional structures exist. On one page a 'General Schemata'[87] is given, and on another the 'Principal Events' are listed, but they do not align. These schemes are summarized in Table 3.3, with the fourth and fifth columns drawn from subsequent sketches (note also that Meale's sketches indicate a section called 'Nexus', which is not part of Bright's scheme). So many of these schemes exist that most of the work's changes of instrumentation, texture and so forth can be attributed to one scheme or other, though none align consistently with, say, entries of woodwind or strings, or a particular harmonic move. The multiple sketching does highlight the significance of one-bar lengths as basic units, and it is not just at the junction of Sections B and C (bar 53) that sections overlap – every section overlaps. According to the scheme given in the last column of the table, each section begins with a one-bar introduction and ends with a one-bar coda, contributing to the work's long-term dynamism and creating a small-scale form that reflects the large-scale introduction–coda pattern. This kind of flexibility is characteristic of Meale's working

Table 3.3 Different Schemes for the Structure of Meale's *Clouds Now and Then*

	'General Schemata'	'Principal Events'	Sketch I*	Sketch II**
Introduction:	9⁺ [bars]	7	1+6+2	1+7
A:	9+10	9+5+5	[2]+9+9+1	1+19+1
B:	10+5+9	5+7+5+5+10	[1]+10+5+8+1	1+23+2
C:	9+10+9⁺	5+5+10+5(3+2)+4	[1]+9+10+9+1	1+23+1
Nexus:	2 (or 3)	3	1+1+[1]	1+1+1
Coda:	10+12	7+5+7+5⁺	10+12	1+21 [or] 1+4+2, 2+1+2, 12+

* Papers of Richard Meale, Box 34.
** Papers of Richard Meale, Box 34.

at the time, which had moved away from the amorphousness of *Homage* towards a more calculated form.

The least expected moment in *Clouds Now and Then* is its inclusion of a short tonal sequence within the pervading atonality, around the start of Section B (which evolves from Section A). Section A ends with a gradual proliferation of trills and tremolo in the strings and percussion, and the slow decay of held notes in the winds and brass (the harmony is dodecaphonic). At bar 28 only a low rumble from the tam-tam and bass drum is held over, and the cellos and basses play a C major chord. Although the F♯ in the bass at the end of the bar ought to destabilize the harmony, instead it blends with the strings and with the percussion, forming a yet more solid base for the entry of the flutes and clarinets, C major, *legato e dolce* (Example 3.5). The upper strings also enter with a C major chord, from which they immediately begin a slow downward glissando over four bars.[88] Those four bars are long enough to sustain a C major, G minor, C major move in the winds. In the fourth bar the clarinets play {C, E}, continuing the C major harmony, and they then contract the interval to {D♭, E♭}. At the same time the flutes play {B♭, F♯} and then {F♯, G}, which continues the G minor harmony. In the fourth bar a trumpet enters with {B, G♯} and by the end of that bar the tonal harmonies are lost. The flute and clarinet chords in the fifth bar, {D♭, B♭, G, F♯}, sound like most of the harmony of the work (the separation of the harmony into the {F♯, D♭} and {F♯, G} intervals overpowers a possible G diminished+major 7 triadic reading). (In the second bar of this short passage the horns play {C♯, B, G♯, D♯} and the trombones 'blow air through their instrument', an effect which combines more with the low rumbling and F♯ than with the high winds' clear triads.)

Each of the principal events in this passage – the beginning of C major, the entry of the winds, the shift away from triadic harmony – aligns with one of the sectional structures in the sketches. This passage hints at tonality, without fully enacting it, and it comes from a simplification of textures to reveal a C major triad and a few related chords. The beginning of bar 28 is a triadic moment made tonal only by association

Example 3.5 Meale, *Clouds Now and Then*, bars 29–34.

with works that enact functional tonal motion, but it nevertheless points to Meale's interest in tonality in the 1960s.

The clearest musical narrative involving tonality that Meale wrote during this period comes at the start of *Very High Kings* (1969). The piece begins with an E♭ major triad, *fff*, on the organ. Around this chord the flutes, percussion and strings play a shadow of other pitches, *ppp*. As these fall away the chord returns, followed by G♭ major over {A, E}, around which the same instruments create a harmonic haze. The progression repeats and expands: E♭, G♭ over {A, E}, C major. With the C major chord all the winds begin trilling, which saturates the pitch space. After this the organ is briefly bitonal, and then the diatonic working ebbs away (see Example 3.6). For Meale the harmonic conflict between tonality and atonality 'symbolizes two worlds, one the known, and the other unknown'.[89] He returns to this idea in *Incredible Floridas*, in which he 'tried to face the problem of "not knowing"',[90] in response to Rimbaud.

The second unexpected moment in *Clouds Now and Then* is at the start of Section C, the composition's midpoint. The passage is one of the most contested in terms of the sketched schemes. Bar 52 is a solitary central axis, defined through the overlap of possible forms (see Example 3.7), and it is marked with a piano flourish that ends on C natural, and begins a C–E♭ cluster. This is the region of the start of Section C. A gong at bar 53 adds to the sense of this as a new section; its dynamic increases from bar 55 to bar 58, where the gong is replaced by a metal bar and bells. The increasing dynamic and rhythmic spacing of these events creates a five-bar trajectory to bar 58, and outlines a subsection of Section C. The combination of gongs, bells and viola glissandi (which stand in for a kokyū) makes this the only section of the work that sounds in any way Japanese. The glissandi connect the piece back to *Homage to Garcia Lorca*, where they form the third 'sonorous' plateau of the Postlude. The glissandi also connect to the later piece *Plateau*, which Meale describes as follows:

> The sensations of the world of *Plateau* are completely those of a 'mental' music as opposed to an 'emotional' music. But by this I do not mean that 'Plateau' is cold or

Example 3.6 A condensed version of the organ's pitch material in Meale's *Very High Kings*, bars 1–16.

barren. It is 'an elevated tract of comparatively flat or level land' across which the mind can journey musically without reference to any 'emotional' anecdote. As an emotional work, it is one dimensional; as a mental work, it is three-dimensional. It operates under no technique. The writing was done intuitively. Even the title came after the work.[91]

Of course, titles matter, and *Clouds Now and Then* secures the work as one of Meale's 'Japanese' pieces,[92] no matter that its content has nothing clear to do with, say, the Japanese music Meale studied at UCLA.[93]

Example 3.7 Meale, *Clouds Now and Then*, bars 49–59, 'Section C', annotated with three possible structures.

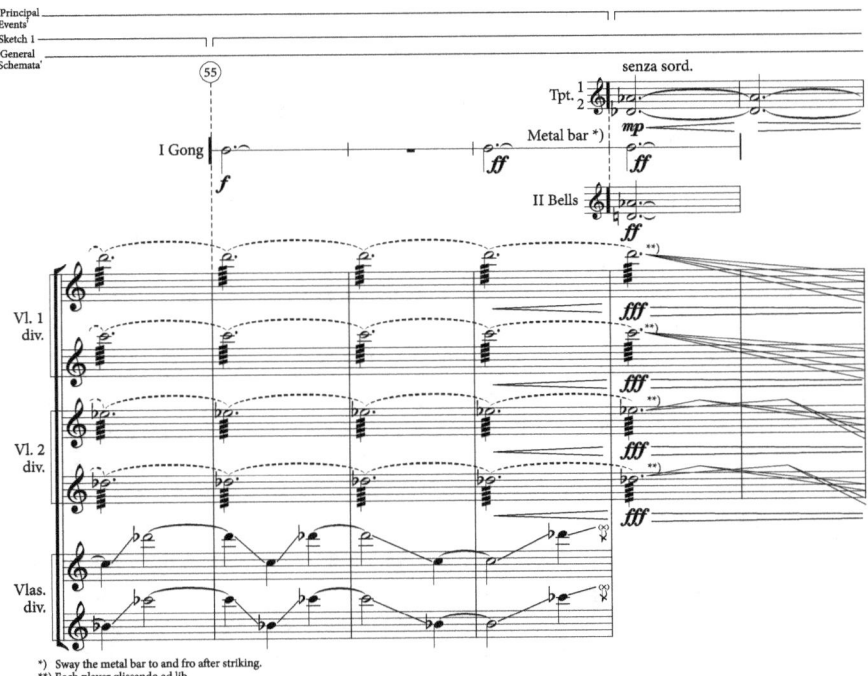

Example 3.7 *(continued)*

Meale's description of *Cicada* suggests that it was written in opposition to *Clouds Now and Then*:

> *Soon it will die* [i.e. *Cicada*] is a companion piece to *Clouds now and then*. Both were written during the first two months of 1969 and take their titles from two *haiku* poems by the seventeenth century Japanese poet Matsuo Basho. Furthermore, the two pieces are derived from the same basic materials but each is developed in an entirely different manner. [...] The music is a commentary on the sadness and anguish of the transience of life, but at the same time it is intermixed with the feeling of pure love of life as is symbolized by the cicada's screech. The piece is interwoven with the feeling of serenity as a result of the contemplation of these two basic sentiments.
>
> The placing of the players is important. Eight string trios of differing combinations are placed across the stage (four to each side of the conductor) to form little 'communities'. Between them and further back are trios of flutes, oboes, clarinets and bassoons. In front of them, but near the conductor, is the harp which provides a type of commentary. At the very back is a line of horns

and trombones, used solely to provide the last lingering chord. The woodwinds make frequently use of multiphonic sounds.[94]

Aitken argues that *Cicada* 'utilises strict dodecaphonic technique in the most absurd Schoenbergian fashion', except for the harp, 'which does not utilize serial methods'. For Bright, *Cicada*'s row applies to the harp too,[95] linked from the start to the other instruments' pitch material. The solo harp begins with C♯, D, E♭, E, which the strings then imitate; this cluster is then extended by the flute entry of E, F then F, F♯. The progression in the trios from bar 4 to 9[96] is: <{[013], [015]}, [014], [015], [014], [016], [016], [014], [016], [016], {[012], [015]}, [015], [014], [013], [016]>. None of this requires a twelve-note row, and the passage proceeds for the most part through common pitches and efficient voice-leading: <{[E, F, D], [C, D♭, A♭]}, [A, B♭, F♯], [C, D♭, A], [D, D♯, B], [C, D♭, G], [C, C♯, G], [G, G♯, E], [G, G♯, C], [A, B♭, E♭], {[D♯, E, F], [B♭, B, F♯]}, [G♯, A, D], [A, A♯, E], [C♯, D, B], [C, C♯, G]>. The local harmonies that these patterns create are shared across much of Meale's music from the time, which suggests that that serial working was less important than maintaining a consistent sound-world.

Whether or not the initial plans for the work made use of a row, the composition's harmonies are reliant on repetitions and modifications of a small range of chords. The most striking moments come with the wind multiphonics. These first occur at bar 25, a repetition of the opening harp chord, and with similar string material. Multiphonics are played by all the wind instruments, and are taken from Bruno Bartolozzi's *New Sounds of Woodwind*. This had been published in 1967, only a short time before the composition was written, and the work is an exploration of this newly disseminated resource for writing for woodwinds. The multiphonics musically render the cicada's screech that the composition's poem describes. The climax comes near bar 95, where the strings play closely voiced microtonal clusters, and the winds play multiphonics. Hollow harp harmonics cut off the screech with a perfect fifth. The harp then plays the only exposed twelve-note row in the piece, from bars 99 to 103. That sequence's four three-note segments are all [016], which suggests that the harp is less removed from the work's pitch procedures than might previously have been understood. The closing section is a mobile, in the manner of so many of Meale's works after *Las Alboradas*. The strings repeat hocketting, glissando-filled material which differs in dynamic with each repetition. The winds enter during the repeat of the string material and hold their multiphonics, which increase in dynamic until the conductor cues the final brass chord. This chord, the only time the brass play in the piece, is part of a cycle of fifths from D♭ to F.

Much more than the works composed only a few years later, *Clouds Now and Then* and *Cicada* present elemental material: simple harmonic formulations, textural interlocking, a fragment from a cycle of fifths and a simple triadic progression. These materials are partial, held together by the adroit orchestration of ever-changing timbres. That the work eschews classical serial procedures is part of what enables the 'cicada' multiphonics to sit easily alongside the non-microtonal music. There is no clear confrontation between worlds of technique, nor is the microtonal material restricted only to the multiphonics, since the strings also play microtonally. Like most of Meale's orchestral music, *Cicada* is better conceptualized as a chamber work, and the ease with which cicadas coordinate their song – beginning, pulsing and ending their sounds with seemingly perfect precision – suggests that the interlocking chamber groups ought to coordinate with equal ease.

The haiku that goes with each score might suggest a Japanese influence, but Meale's Francophilia is at least as important. As in Meale's *Nocturnes*, Debussy is not far away, his *Nuages* inhabiting *Clouds Now and Then*, the lunar ideas of all three works coming together, if not musically, then at least in Meale's charting of his musical lineage, though in his description of *Nocturnes* Meale cites Messiaen, rather than Debussy, as *Nocturnes*' muse:

> 'Nocturnes' (I had decided to concentrate on the movement of the moon) began at the beginning of 1965, while I was learning the solo piano part of Messiaen's 'Oiseaux Exotiques'. In a state of musical excitation, I would alternate between practice and composition. The result was the first version of 'Nocturnes', almost completed one year later.[97]

The process of continuing traditions, as well as finding new ways of bringing materials together, some of which are themselves new, is a project that Meale himself articulated, if only briefly, in the liner note to the LP on which his work *Plateau* was released:

> Very roughly speaking, there have been two divergent worlds in my musical thought – e.g. the abstraction of 'Las Alboradas' (1963) and the passionate 'Homage to Garcia Lorca' (1964). In the first two months of 1969 these divergencies began to meet when writing simultaneously my two 'haiku' works, 'Clouds now and then' and 'Soon it will die'. Afterwards, these differences became more intensified with the totally abstract 'Interiors/Exteriors' (1970) and the overtly emotional 'Quintet for Winds' (1970). The 'pure', or abstract line was followed further in 'Coruscations' (1971) and the denouement was reached in 'Incredible Floridas' (1971) where these two basic paths were to meet, in conflict, integration and resolution.[98]

This narrative, which differentiates his work strongly into 'abstract' and 'emotional' ideas, is more fixed than the examination of these pieces reveals. The serial explanations that Meale wrote, as well as his students and those who published on his music soon after its composition, stand for abstraction, and works written quickly, 'intuitively' and 'spontaneously', are emotional by virtue of their opposition to an orthodoxy of careful planning and precompositional strategy. Neither holds for Meale's actual musical practice, and the sketches now in his archive follow a similar pattern. They begin with ideas in fragmented form, rhythmic patterns, short segments of pitch materials, calculations of orchestral forces and other jottings of a handful of notes. The next stage is a short-score, often with initial ideas sketched in the margins. The third stage is a fair copy, ready for the final score. From the sketches that survive it is difficult to tell which works were being rigorously planned and which were composed 'intuitively'. The division that Meale describes arises out of an anxiety about system in a place and time where a progressive composer in the model of Boulez (say) was being sought. Given that there had been no prominent serialist working in Australia, and that serialism was seen as the dominant compositional method of the early twentieth century, escaping the parochialism of 'colonial' attitudes meant catching up with Europe, and that meant that a place for serialism had to be found. The place that was found was more often in the explanations of Meale's music than in than in the music itself. Werder overstates the argument, but nonetheless reflects its form:

> Quite apart from my own sort of personal experiences, the change in this country in the time I have lived here is just unbelievable. I think it is fair enough to say that between 1960 to 1970 now, in those ten years Australia has – well, not Australia, I'm sorry, Sydney has caught up a good hundred years. I would say that Sydney at the moment is right with what is happening in world affairs. I would say that Melbourne is lagging some forty or fifty years behind. The difference between the two cities is unbelievable, the difference between Sydney and Melbourne is about the difference between – what shall I say? the difference between Berlin and Birmingham. It's just unbelievable.[99]

If there was 'catching up' to be done, Meale accomplished it. The music that he wrote is not a case of cultural importation, but of a well-connected composer trying to work with the recordings and scores that were newly available, and with the quick flow of new ideas between distant places.

4

Nigel Butterley

Australian Music and Britain

Against the detail, swiftness and certainty of Meale's music, and contrary to the boldness of Sculthorpe's, Butterley's music is characterized by its slow dynamism, and his compositions, more so than Sculthorpe's and Meale's, fluctuate in their internal motion. Compared with Banks's *String Quartet*, which runs away with itself, increasingly certain in its purpose, Butterley's String Quartet No. 1 moves carefully through periods of remarkable stillness, and surprising outbursts. Compared to Meale, whose attitude to early-twentieth-century modernism is clear, Butterley's relationship with modernist ideas is cautious. Butterley's music often coalesces into what could easily be mistaken for solid sculpture, and yet within its solidity is always a sure sense of malleable curvature and flow. His music is in this sense the opposite of Meale's – the speed of which is immediate – and of Sculthorpe's – which resists transformation and development to favour highly stylized repetition. He is therefore an unlikely participant in a modernist movement, yet he challenged Sydney's audiences with the music that he composed, and he was aligned with Meale and Sculthorpe as a leader of progressive Australian Music.

In Butterley's music, the conjunction of nationalism and modernism relies on a dialectic of uncertainty and inevitability, of 'new emergence' and confidence, and no composer working in Australia at the time more wholly embodies these contradictions. This chapter therefore has two purposes. The first is to explain Butterley's modernist aesthetics. In explaining this my focus here is twofold: on the way that he works with serial ideas without ever fully embracing serial architecture; and on Butterley's religious ideas. The second purpose is to explain the relationship of his music to nationalism. This is a more complicated task, since his music often avoids nationalist statements, but this itself is Butterley's significance, since it reveals an aspect to Australian Music that is complex, contradictory and critical. The distance between celebratory nationalism and Butterley's music expands the notion of what Australian Music means, defining it much more broadly than recent discourses do.

Butterley's voice as a modernist was less radical than Meale's, deliberately more introspective and less polemical, and his music was less overtly nationalistic than Sculthorpe's. Whilst Meale's music is productively considered in terms of the sharp-edged problems that are typical of European postwar modernism, Sculthorpe's music is not usefully understood through those problems, and they map onto Butterley's music only with difficulty. As such, a different conception of modernism is needed. Butterley is the proudest Anglophile of the Australian modernists, and his aesthetics arose directly from his time in the Britain. Understanding that connection supports a more sympathetic reading of his composition in the 1960s and early 1970s, and it also explains how his music works against a definition of Australian Music based on isolation and national distinctiveness. Comparing Butterley with British composers also makes Butterley's Anglicanism less of a problem. In a place where 'There is no reason why an atheist could not write a good Mass',[1] there is no reason that a modernist could not either. Much of Butterley's music from the 1950s – before he went to the UK for study (1961–3) – is religious in nature and many works, such as *Prayer during Sickness*, and *Who Build on Hope*, begin a genre of small-scale pieces for voice that continued to be an important part of his output. Butterley's Anglicanism – however ecstatic it may sometimes be – quietly confronts Sculthorpe's spiritualism and Meale's atheism.

This chapter focusses on three pieces. With *Laudes* (1963), for chamber ensemble, Butterley was immediately established as central to Australian Music. It was Butterley's first work following his return to Australia after a period of study in Britain, and it announced the composer's new approach to composition. His first String Quartet (1965) was written for the Austral Quartet, which at the time was the foremost chamber ensemble in the country. The String Quartet's epigraph is by Henry Vaughan. *Fire in the heavens* (1973) was a commission for a performance in the newly opened Sydney Opera House. Its exuberance marked a turning point in Butterley's output, and it also ends his modernist period. I have favoured *Laudes* and the first String Quartet over the more technically consistent works of the late 1960s and early 1970s – *Voices* (1971), and *Pentad* (1968), for example[2] – for several reasons. The most important is that I am here interested in the work that was being done to form an Australian Musical modernism, and his two earlier compositions show less assured work that is also more ambitious, and therefore more important for the *formation* of the movement than the proficient compositions that come at the movement's height. The works that are my focus also reveal an aspect of the British–Australian relationship that is often overlooked in favour of a singular nationalism, and so they are here less as early examples of distinctly Australian writing and more for their engagement with the complexities of transnational ideas. From a musical perspective, connections between people and places are made in musical works, rather than existing independently of them, and in this sense Butterley's music stands neither for Australian Music, nor for British music abroad, but actually forms Australian Music in relation to British practices.

The Place of Praise: *Laudes*

Each of the four movements carries the name of a church. 'The music', says Butterley, 'is not meant to paint pictures or evoke impressions; but each movement has behind it the image of a place, and is intended to be a song of praise in the context and spirit of that place.' Perhaps it is remarkable that given the nature of Butterley's technique his music should in fact sound like songs of praise. Yet it does, and the Te Deum quotations can hardly be sufficient cause. The piece is enormously impressive.[3]

The planning for *Laudes* commenced soon after Butterley's return to Australia in 1963, and it was a response to four religious buildings that he had visited whilst in Europe. *Laudes* blends a personal conviction with what for Butterley was a new harmonic palette, responding to the buildings by creating new 'praises' for each place. Butterley does not evoke or describe specific locations; the spaces are instead conceptualized through their connections as part of an international community – which is what led Butterley to visit them – and this is expressed through the new musical language that Butterley developed during his time abroad. Butterley conceived *Laudes* during his studies with Priaulx Rainier,[4] who suggested that upon returning to Australia he should write an orchestral work. The opportunity to do so did not eventuate, but Donald Peart did ask Butterley to compose a piece for the Adelaide Festival, and Butterley negotiated a larger ensemble than was initially proposed. Although not for orchestra, *Laudes* is an orchestral work in miniature, and the instrumentation – flute, clarinet, horn, trumpet, violin, viola, cello and piano (an expanded 'Pierrot ensemble'[5]) – gave Butterley the opportunity to use the ensemble's winds, brass, strings and piano, in varying combinations. His orchestration uses the instruments in their family groupings, and as individual voices. Although not a narrative work, the instruments do sometimes act as *dramatis personae*; it is this movement between sonic combination and individual character – which dramatizes abstraction and introspection – that drives much of Butterley's music at this time, and it also accounts for the way that the music sounds intimate and distant, present and detached, engaging and difficult.

Laudes was written at a time of renewed interest in antique monuments and ancient narratives. In 1960 Butterley attended a performance of Sophocles' *Oedipus Rex*, one of the first performances undertaken in the Cell Block Theatre. John Tasker's production was very well attended,[6] the performers wore masks, and the set made the most of the daunting sandstone walls of the former prison, a space that was from the start of the 1960s crucial to Sydney's progressive arts scene.[7] In 1961 Butterley was involved in the first Australian production of *The Play of Daniel* (the mediaeval liturgical drama), which was inspired by New York Pro Musica's 1958 recording; the performances of this took place in the crypt of St Mary's Cathedral and were broadcast by the ABC's drama department. That year Butterley had transferred from working in the music department of the ABC to its religious department, which 'put me in touch for the first time, really, with oecumenical thinking and liturgical thinking in the Christian Church today'.[8] The year 1958 is also the date of the first performance of Britten's *Noye's Fludde*,[9] and Stravinsky's *Oedipus Rex* was performed in London a short time later, in 1960. Stravinsky's own take on the Chester/York Mystery Play, *The Flood*, was completed in 1962. Although it seems unlikely that Butterley knew *The Flood*, like *The Play of Daniel* it makes use of the 'Te Deum' melody, which features in *Laudes*. Whether that connection is a knowing one or not, Butterley had participated in the ongoing reverberations of earlier modernist transformations of Greek tragedy, filtered through the (mostly) British broadening of ancient theatre to include earlier music of other ritual dramas, of which Britten's theatrical works, and Tippett's *King Priam*, are exemplary.

The impetus for Butterley's year away from Australia was not just musical, and the churches that Butterley visited give a sense of his other purpose. He first visited Palestine, spending time in the old city of Jerusalem,[10] before travelling overland to London. After two weeks in London he visited the community at Taizé in Burgundy:

> I wasn't quite sure why I'd gone there. I went because I was interested in their music, their singing of Gelineau psalms, and the whole idea appealed to me, but it was a more personal sort of experience than I'd expected, than I would have wanted[.][11]

Aside from the musical connection (to which I will return), one of the reasons that Butterley gives for visiting the Taizé community was their idea of 'the revival of validity and, more particularly, the revival of validity in the context of Christian unity and the idea of the church in the world, the idea of the Christian being someone in the context of the everyday world and not someone in a separate little box'.[12] This type of ceremony therefore fulfilled Butterley's desire for a formal Christianity that was both distinct and quotidian. The opportunities for participating in such forms of ceremony in Sydney were very limited, though Butterley's experience of singing in St Andrew's Cathedral choir as a 19-year-old provided him with a working knowledge of the 'English choral tradition' in a liturgical setting.[13] This is all a long way from the importance of Greek theatre to Nietzsche, Strauss, Yeats and Pound, not quite so far from its importance to Stravinsky and Cocteau, and not at all distant from the theatrical innovations of Britten and Tippett.

Butterley's *Laudes* are four 'praises', each corresponding to one of the religious building that he visited. The first, 'The Basilica of Sant'Apollinare Nuovo', stands for the ancient world, Ravenna being the capital of the Roman empire in its last years. The basilica was built during the period in which Ravenna was held by the Ostrogoths, and was reconsecrated by the Byzantines. The second is the apse of Norwich Cathedral, which is considered one of the best examples of the round apse in England and exemplary of Norman architecture. In retaining the bishop's throne in its apse, the cathedral recalls the earlier layout of Byzantine and Roman buildings, which provides a link between Norwich Cathedral and the basilica at Ravenna. The third is King's College Chapel, Cambridge. The 'rich red and blue of stained glass', about which Butterley writes in his introduction to the score, links to the mosaics of the basilica, and the 'vaulted ceiling' represents the engineering progress that had been made in late Gothic architecture. Butterley's introduction describes the spaces in terms of changing architectural style – 'the mosaic procession', 'Norman Pillars', 'the vaulted ceiling', 'abstract stained glass' – except for his description of Taizé, the fourth 'praise', which he describes in terms of social function: 'praise expressed in involvement, compassion, unity'. *Laudes* recalls Butterley's experience of these spaces, and also his time singing choral music in Sydney:

> I was always in church choirs ... then when I was about 19, I had a friend who was in St Andrew's Cathedral choir [in Sydney] ... so I joined the choir there and this introduced me to all sorts of church music, mainly the more gentle sort of English school, Vaughan Williams, Herbert Howells, but also the older composers, William Byrd and Purcell [...]. My feelings for this type of English music developed, and my enjoyment of the sort of King's College chapel style of singing[.][14]

In *Laudes* the varied religious traditions that are associated with the different places are disregarded in favour of an ecumenical statement which is expressed in the published score through a quotation from Thomas Traherne: 'Are not praises the very end for which this world was created?'[15] At the same time, the listing of different places suggests a continuity of adaption of which Taizé is only the most recent manifestation. Of the musical precedents for *Laudes*, the quotation from Traherne suggests Finzi and his *Dies Natalis* (1938/9),[16] and also Butterley's own *Meditations of Thomas Traherne*, composed in 1968 for Britten-like forces of a children's recorder group and orchestra, which further supports a consideration of this piece in connection with British music. However, although the 'English school' informs most of Butterley's music from the 1960s, the music that he writes in *Laudes* is far from Howells, Vaughan Williams, Byrd and Purcell.

Butterley explains his approach to composing *Laudes* in the work's programme note:

> Part of my idea for the piece included contrasting different planes of sound, which is why I chose a group comprising woodwind, brass, strings and piano. Two note-rows are used, one with fairly relaxed intervals in the first movement, and a tenser one in the second; both of them are behind the material of the third and fourth. They evolved out of the music as it began to be written, and they're used quite freely, suggesting melodic phrases which recur throughout the work. Another thematic link is the Gregorian *Te Deum Laudamus*, a timeless symbol of Christian praise, which had become firmly ingrained in my mind when I was involved in the 1961 Sydney production of the medieval drama *The Play of Daniel*.[17]

Characteristic of Butterley's programme notes from the time, there is a brief explication of the technical means of pitch production, and in this case Butterley claims two rows for his piece. The question of using two rows is addressed explicitly in Josef Rufer's *Composition with Twelve Notes Related Only to One Another*,[18] in which Rufer argues, following Schoenberg, that 'one can also make good music with two series, or without any series at all, as in the early non-tonal music; or on a tonal basis, whether based on functional harmony or on the new synthesis with the experiments in serial composition'. For Rufer the principle implication of having two rows is formal, since 'it [i.e. using more than one series] not only contradicts the purpose and the function of creating form [sic] which belong to a twelve-note series, but actually abolishes this function',[19] and so the use of multiple series risks being ornamental rather than 'of organic importance'. This is the case unless the use of two series comes from '*musical necessity*'.[20] Nevertheless, Rufer argues against the likelihood of this necessity, given that Schoenberg had written *Moses and Aaron* using a single series. For Butterley, writing his first 'serial' work, these conditions are more technical and more restrictive than he needed them to be, since much of his music is not in practice serial. Nevertheless, the two rows are different in their character: the first row is made from (what in a tonal setting would be considered) consonant intervals, and the second row from dissonant intervals.[21]

The music's relationship with serialism is far from straightforward, which was a complication identified at the time. For Covell,

> further listening discloses a logic readily identifiable in the score [...] though it is typical of Butterley that the opening bars were conceived before a structural note-row was derived from them and not the other way around.[22]

In 1978, David Swale wrote:

> Most [...] of Butterley's mature works have used some form of serial technique. *Laudes* uses small note-cells, but in the works which follow twelve-note rows appear, often arranged in diatonic grouping[.][23]

Both Covell and Swale point to Butterley's 'ecumenical' way of composing, in which a variety of approaches are united over any single perspective. Nevertheless, there are materials that emerge strongly from the work that might usefully be analyzed alongside its serial elements. One is the use of the Te Deum melody, the intervals of which are significant to many parts of the composition. Another is the use of a non-serial, limited pitch space, which gives the work a coherent melodic and harmonic presence. Elliott Gyger's *The Music of Nigel Butterley* (2014) explains how Butterley uses two rows to guide the composition of the pitch materials, and Gyger's examples also give a strong sense of how flexibly Butterley approached serialism. Indeed, although Gyger traces the two rows successfully through some parts of the piece, the music deviates significantly from linear statements of its rows. Aside from a few moments where rows are explicitly stated, there is little here that explores the serial possibilities of his row. The result is a greater emphasis on a handful of harmonic entities than on large-scale serial structure. This is in part due to the challenges of embedding the Te Deum melody, and partly because for Butterley, like Rainier, composing obsessively with a few characteristic intervals was more important than forming large architectures. *Laudes* is not a musical equivalent to the basilica, cathedral and chapel to which it responds.

The first movement begins simply, with an arcing line in the trumpet, F, C♯, E, F, which is an early example of the rise and fall that one finds in so much of Butterley's later music (Example 4.1). At the end of the first bar, the movement's chief rising motif occurs in the flute, which joins a tritone and an augmented fifth, but the motif itself is

Example 4.1 Butterley, *Laudes*, 'I', bars 1–8.

best described as the ic vector 010101. The motif is played in bar 3 by the clarinet (G, E♭, A, not, strictly speaking, part of the serial unfolding here) followed by the piano (E, B♭, D), and then the strings (in bar 5). This motif is also found throughout the piece, such as in the second bar of the fourth movement's opening piano solo, where the rising motif contrasts block chords. The start of the first movement is motivically dense rather than serially driven, supporting the repeated rising motif. Much of the first movement is fluid, exploratory and also quiet and sparse, and it does not settle until the horn begins the Te Deum at bar 46. This melody here is harmonized in the strings with {E♭, B, D} ((014), the same as the opening trichord), then {C, E, G} (a rare trichord for Butterley in this period), then a return to {E♭, B, D}. At the same time, the piano plays {E♭, E, B}, then {F, E, A}, which are both made from ic1+ic5, a harmonic strategy that assumes clarity in the second movement (discussed below).[24] A greater sense of coherence comes with a coda (bar 52), in which the instruments play in their families, with back-and-forth sustained chords that elaborate an arcing gesture. The movement ends with: the strings playing the opening of the Te Deum <E, G, A>; a varied version of the chant played by the piccolo; and a chord played by the piano that is part of the chord that began the coda, and which is also the same trichord [025] as opens the Te Deum melody. In other words, over the course of the movement, dense motifs give way to more steady and focussed music, the pace slows, and the melodies grow longer and more lyrical as the pitch materials become more unified. This vector towards coherence is repeated in each of the movements, and as the piece progresses it increasingly stands for the way that a site of worship itself organizes religious praise.

The second movement raises the problem of the function of serialism in the piece. Gyger's analysis shows Butterley working with the following row: <A, E♭, D, G, D♭, C, F♯, F, E, B, B♭, A♭>. Gyger highlights the way that the movement emphasizes the row's 'characteristic intervals – semitones, fourths and tritones'.[25] Gyger divides the series into four trichords, though his analysis of the work mostly describes the piece in terms of pitch sequences. This description requires transposed and inverted forms of the row. It also requires some significant reordering and fragmentation. There are also some moments that sit completely outside the serial working, such as the chord at the end of bar 3 (and its recurrence at bars 8–9), which Gyger designates 'chord x'. For him these chords are solid blocks 'suggesting pillars on either side of an arch'.[26]

A different possible reading uses one of the rows from Nono's *Il canto sospeso*: A, <A♭, D, E♭, G, C, F♯, C♯, B♭, B, F, E>. This row suggests tetrachordal working, since each tetrachord has the prime form [0167], and the row is part of Nono's intensely symmetrical working based on tetrachordal segmentation. With this row in mind, the opening bar can be segmented into three tetrachords, 'a', 'b' and 'c' (labelled with solid, dotted and dashed lines, respectively, in Example 4.2). The first 'a' is a partial statement, missing an A♭. (Similarly partial statements characterize bars 7–9.) Crossing from bar 1 to 2 is a further iteration of the 'a' tetrachord, though there is here a question as to whether the first pitch – D – is separate from the first chord. One of the main ways that Butterley interrupts the serial writing is by elongating notes, which continually pose problems for analysis. The same elongation of pitches gives the music its continuity and flow, since the tetrachordal segmentation of this highly symmetrical row will tend to promote stasis.

Example 4.2 Butterley, *Laudes*, 'II', bars 1–12, annotated with serial structures.

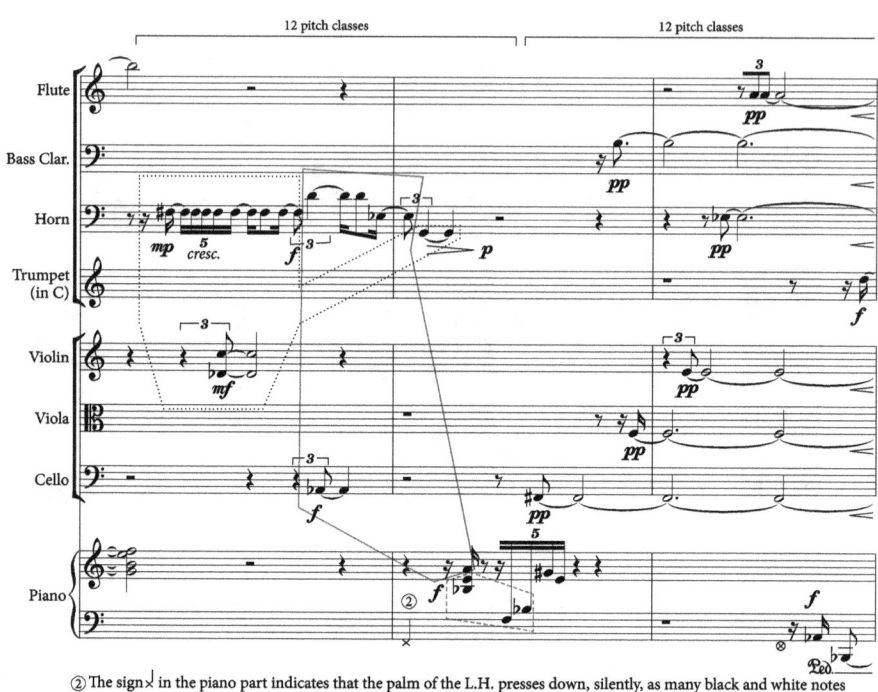

② The sign ✕ in the piano part indicates that the palm of the L.H. presses down, silently, as many black and white notes as possible, at the bottom of the keyboard. The pedal is not used unless indicated, and the hand is released at the sign ⊗

Example 4.2 (*continued*)

The rising figures in bars 4–6 are problematic for both Gyger's row and the row taken from Nono, though the final pitch of each figure (annotated in Example 4.2 with hexagons) outlines a motif that is important throughout the piece, since C, D, E is the 'second trichord' of the Te Deum.[27] Gyger also finds extensive whole-tone writing in *Laudes*'s fourth movement. The whole-tone segment points to a further property of Nono's row, which is that when it is transposed by a tone the pitch content of each tetrachord is maintained (if not the order of the tetrachords).[28] The other intervals in these rising figures emphasize ic1 and ic5, to continue Butterley's overall harmonic tendency. As is also typical of Butterley's working in *Laudes*, the opening of the movement is the clearest statement of the serial material, away from which he moves swiftly. Nevertheless, he more consistently thinks dodecaphonically, and the example is annotated with brackets to show three passes through the aggregate; bars 7–9 are similarly annotated.

If the row seems only tenuously in play, it returns more decisively in the polyphonic texture of bars 10–12. In this section many of the notes are repeated, often transferred to a different instrument, but the order of entry of pitches aligns with the tetrachords 'c', 'b', 'a', 'c'. As before, notes within the tetrachords are freely reordered.[29] Despite the sequence of tetrachords, this section tends not to emphasize audibly the sequence of pitches, and what sounds more clearly are the whole tones in the highest register, since Butterley favours {B♭, C, D, E} in the trumpet, violin and flute. This whole-tone material is a further extension of the second trichord of the Te Deum, which here is thoroughly integrated with the movement's serial process. Although these bars are not part of Gyger's analysis, using his row produces a similarly free arrangement of pitches within tetrachords, though it also requires beginning his row on its twelfth pitch.[30] Such reordering makes it difficult to be decisive in *Laudes* about the precise row that underlies the piece. Since both possible rows are highly redundant under the usual transformations (retrograde, inversion, transposition), and there are no larger serial architectures, it will not be possible to confirm a specific serial practice until sketches for *Laudes* come to light (none are held in the National Library of Australia, which is the central repository for Butterley's sketches). My alternative reading of the movement's opening raises the possibility of a different row, and tetrachordal segmentation, but quickly reaches the limits of considering the piece in terms of any particular row, which suggests that Butterley considers serial material as a resource from which to choose rather than a scheme to apply rigorously.[31]

Regardless of the extent to which this movement is serial, Butterley still made numerous decisions about the deployment of pitch material in terms of register, rhythm and motif. In the opening bars the same handful of intervals occur with their registers shuffled, and so it would be appropriate to characterize these as 'small note-cells' in Swale's terminology. The first three notes, for example, are a cell that recurs throughout the movement. The orchestration in the first six bars of this movement is discontinuous rather than structural, which changes at bar 7 with a rapidly repeating F♯ that suggests the changing syllables of a cantor who is holding a single note, and which initiates a long passage of greater lyricism than before. In bar 8 the piano 'presses down, silently, as many black and white notes as possible, at the bottom of the keyboard', evoking the rich reverberation of a cathedral. With this added resonance a polyphonic instrumental choir begins:[32] the cello plays a long F♯, *pp*, to which the bass clarinet adds B, the viola F, then the violin E, the horn E♭ and the flute A. The order of entries is a chain of paired pitches a semitone apart <{F, E}, {E, E♭}, {A, A♭}> separated by ic5 <{F♯, B}, {E, A}> (Example 4.3). If one considers only the long-held pitches, this pattern continues for several pages: <D, E♭, E, F, B♭, B, C, F♯, {B♭, D, D♭}, …>. Considering the movement as a whole, this pattern comes to the fore over locally serial moments.

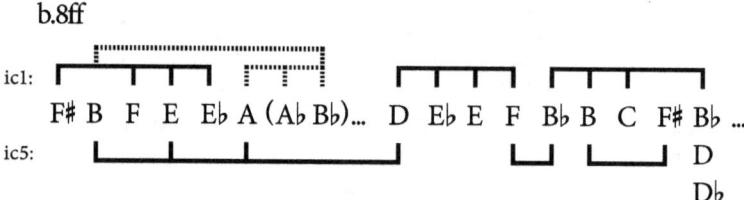

Example 4.3 This example shows the connections between long-held pitches in the bars after the section that begins in bar 8 of *Laudes*' second movement, with ic1 indicated above, and ic5 below. The dashed line shows that although some of the shorter durations also participate in this pattern, they do not contribute to its continuity. The elision indicates a short flute flourish in bar 10.

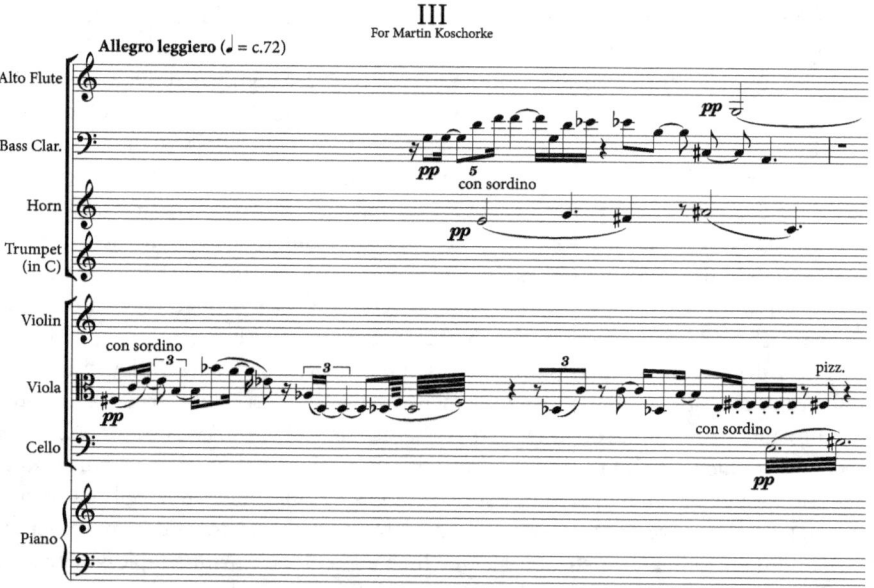

* In this movement the players are rhythmically independent of each other, except for the central barred section the conductor need only indicate entries. Strict rhythm and exact ensemble are not intended. In the first two piano entries the semiquaver is quite flexible and can be lengthened or shortened at discretion.

Example 4.4 Butterley, *Laudes*, beginning of 'III'.

Of *Laudes*'s four movements, only the third opens with a move through all twelve pitch classes (see Example 4.4). The viola solo presents the first eleven pitches, completed by the first pitch of the bass clarinet. The completion of the aggregate forms a structural cue for the second instrument's entry. But even here the relationship between the viola's first pitch – F♯ – the last in the viola's phrase – F♮ – and the first pitches of the bass clarinet {G, D} connects this movement to the proliferation of ic1 and ic5 that shapes the harmony of this piece. The rhythmic alignment of each instrument is loosely coordinated in this movement, which also works against the formation of strict pitch patterns. Long sequences such as at the opening of the movement do see the emergence of short motifs. For example, the horn's opening melody, which begins after the bass clarinet, is then replayed by the violin, which turns the intervals around in a free manner that emphasizes pitch cells:

hn	E	G♯	F♯	A♯	C	C♯	A	C	C♯	A	F	G	D	E♭	B	...
va	E	G♯	F♯	A♯	C	A	C♯	C	A	F	A	D	B	E♭		...

Some of the same pitch cells that emerge from this varied repetition are played early on by the bass clarinet. The horn's melody moves more slowly than the viola, forming a cantus firmus for the latter's more florid line, which includes a repeated F♯ that alludes to the earlier movement's syllabic chanting. The role of the cantus is taken up by the trumpet,[33] which enters with a single dotted minim D, before (some time later) repeating the D as the start of the Te Deum melody. The statement of the Te Deum is a dramatic moment, played *forte marcato* against hushed whispers, quite unlike the first movement, in which it was at the same dynamic as the surrounding instruments. It comes as the previously independent parts begin to be coordinated: it unifies their voices, which further reinforces the instruments as dramatic characters. The melody played is from the first two lines of the chant: 'Te Deum laudamus: te Dominum confitemur. Te aeternum Patrem omnis terra venerator', which returns to the opening quotation from Traherne: 'Are not praises the very end for which this world was created?' We can now reconceive the thirds and tones of the horn at the opening as presaging this melody. Although the melody is clearly and distinctly the Te Deum, its pitch material suffuses the movement, and Butterley's flexible transformations blur the melody's intervals and smooth over the disjunctions between dodecaphony and chant. In this movement in particular the compositional task of organizing pitches is secondary to the problem of coordination more generally, and he associates the instruments as characters in a drama with individuals in the Christian world, unified through a shared commitment to praise. Gyger summarizes the trajectory of the movement as follows: 'The final section returns to earlier linear material, but with only passing reference to the rows: the movement's own melodic material predominates. The epiphany of the chant thus effects a lasting transformation of the music.'[34] It is notable that this movement, and the previous movements, move quickly away from the potential of serial working, and gain coherence as they do. This suggests a repeated association of serialism with both order and disorder, and specifically with disorder in the world, since disorder and coherence, serialism and the chant, are not strongly opposed, even as one gives way to the other.

The idea of playing in rhythmic independence is shared with Meale's *Las Alboradas*, in which Butterley played piano at the premiere performance, and which was also composed in 1963. Its third movement begins with a similarly quasi-serial flute solo, and as in Butterley's opening section, Meale leaves the aggregate incomplete as a structural anacrusis to the entry of the other instruments. Meale's movement is decreasingly coordinated, ending with totally uncoordinated cells of materials played independently by each performer. *Laudes*'s fourth movement begins with a *fortissimo* solo, Meale at the piano,[35] a virtuosic moment in a composition that tends not to highlight solo performers, even though they are often independent characters. Both Meale and Butterley's compositions were performed at the 1964 Adelaide Festival, the year it hosted the International Society for Contemporary Music (ISCM). The chords that open the fourth movement of *Laudes* could be from Meale's piece, and, as with the start of the second movement, the intervals interlock to form chords that progress through ic1 and ic5 relationships. This is the first significant solo in the piece, much more lengthy than the brief viola solo, and it forms a cadenza that ends with a tremolando between two semitone clusters separated by a tritone, followed by a bell-like chord (of two ic1 dyads separated by ic5 (or two tritones a seventh apart)). The individualism of this opening solo is followed by a section of staggered entries in all the instruments in which, as before, Butterley is more focussed on intervals than a series, although the music is also carefully dodecaphonic. In the second movement this texture ended with the instruments coalescing into a homorhythmic chord, but here the texture condenses into a single, unison melody. This is a remarkable gesture of coming together in which the ensemble's individual players enact a moment of collective praise. The melody itself is an elaborated version of the first movement's rising motif, now both rising and falling. Rhythmically the tendency is for this shape to go with the augmentation and then diminution of durations, such that it produces a sense of expansion and contraction with the rise and fall of the line. When the melody stops at bar 30, it is replaced by a repetition of the first movement's coda. The repetition has no significant variation until its sixth bar, the point at which the Te Deum melody should return. Instead, the piano plays block chords, using mostly the thirds and tones of the Te Deum, and unrecognizable as chant. In the tenth bar of the first movement's coda, the strings play the [025] trichord that returned the coda to the opening of the movement. In the corresponding bar of the fourth movement's coda the strings introduce a new melody. This new material is, in the context of the piece, *radically* new. It is not the synthesis that ended the third movement, nor the slow, cohering counterpoint that ended the second, and it is not another version of the Te Deum that ends the first movement. It is, therefore, not a return to an ancient order, nor a rebirth, nor a restoration, nor new technical rigour, but new lyricism. *Laudes* ends with the challenge of lyricism itself, of voices singing in unison.

Even if *Laudes* was received as boldly new in 1960s Australia, it nevertheless remained tied to old ideas, presenting those ideas as its heritage. The music extends past practices, seeking to fulfil an ongoing tradition of praise. For all the grandeur of the buildings that give its movements their character, the work's intra-movement forms are not grand in their musical architectures, and so retain the scale, and openness to transformation, of a personal response. This is not music that transcends the boundaries of its component parts, be they 'serial', or from chant, and instead it presents a perspective from which materials and their differences are utilized for what they can offer at the moment that they occur. This is pragmatic work, presenting an optimistic case for something beyond the local or national. The composition's integration of the Te Deum and dodecaphonic working means that *Laudes* speaks of the end of an international modernist era (this is not a progressively 'post-serial' work), even as it exists as one of the early examples of a new period of Australian modernism. *Laudes* shows Australian music extending British ideas, participating in the transnational sharing of ideas that are transformed by Butterley's distance from the music to which he was responding into a personal statement about his place in the world. To extend the argument in reverse, it also shows British music not being limited by British borders. Certainly it demonstrates the ties that were being maintained between Sydney, London, Australian Music and a series of religious buildings.

Words without Voices: Unfolding Butterley's First String Quartet

Butterley's sketches for his first quartet are incomplete and fragmentary, mnemonics for a composer who also had a busy job working for the ABC. Perhaps due to the limited time that Butterley had for composing, the sketches were written to keep track of ideas, but they are also lucid, detailed and laid out with clarity. Their contents are carefully labelled, even though those labels do not always match the score, which says much about the importance to him of the early stages of drafting ideas and of the flexibility of this phase of composition. These drafts are full of text, and they mix prose with musical notation; both the sketches and the published score begin with a poem. The preface to the score explains the close connection between music and poetry:

> The work derives its structure, as well as its whole area of feeling, from Henry Vaughan's poem The Revival.[36]

Together with Vaughan's poem, this sentence is both explicatory and veiling at the same time, highlighting a connection between text and music that is both direct and ambiguous. Vaughan's poem is in the pastoral tradition, published with his *Thalia rediviva* in 1678:

> Unfold, unfold! take in his light,
> Who makes thy cares more short than night.
> The joys which with his day-star rise,
> He deals to all but drowsy eyes:
> And, what the men of this world miss,

> Some drops and dews of future bliss.
>   Hark! how his winds have chang'd their note,
> And with warm whispers call thee out.
> The frosts are past, the storms are gone:
> And backward life at last comes on.
> The lofty groves in express joys
> Reply unto the turtle's voice,
> And here in dust and dirt, O here
> The lilies of his love appear![37]

This springtime text is not only at odds with the string quartet as a secular genre;[38] its function in the preface is made uncertain by Butterley's description of music in the 1960s, which appeared in his 1999 Gordon Athol Anderson Memorial Lecture 'Words into Music: A Composer's Response to Poetry':

> The sixties, when my own style was beginning to emerge, was a time of great ferment. The old distinction between 'absolute music' and 'programme music' had little relevance in a world where serialism, music theatre, and electronic music were all new and exciting, and 'avant-garde' could mean anything that was different.[39]

Similar to the moments of instrumental drama in *Laudes*, the String Quartet exceeds 'purely musical' concerns, and it is closer to Butterley's vocal music than one might expect for a string quartet. The piece was written in 1965, and it was Butterley's most significant work after *Laudes*. More specifically than *Laudes*, the String Quartet demonstrates Butterley's response to British vocal music, which was important to him at this time, as he explained in 'Words into Music':

> The first 20th-century music I got to know was by English[40] composers, and the way some of them set words was an important early influence that probably still remains to some extent in my vocal writing.[41]

He goes on to mention the instrumental writing in Britten's *Serenade for Tenor, Horn and Strings*, and Walton's *Belshazzar's Feast*, in which it is 'the harmony that colours and conveys the words. The subtle manipulation of harmonic progression is a major source of the work's power'.[42]

Whilst studying in Britain, three events were formative. The first was the 75th birthday concert for Edith Sitwell, which Butterley cites as one of the most memorable concerts that he attended there.[43] This concert was organized by the Park Lane Group,[44] and it included Walton's *Façade* – which may well have prompted Butterley's later work *First Day Covers*, for Barry Humphries – as well as Peter Pears singing Britten's *Canticle III* 'Still falls the rain' (1954), the gloomy poetry for which fitted Butterley's typical sensibility better than Vaughan's springtime poem. The second and third formative events were the Coventry premières of Tippett's *King Priam* and Britten's *War Requiem*:

[I] went to the new Coventry cathedral, to the festival, and heard the first performance of the Britten *War Requiem* and wondered why [...] I wasn't moved by it. I was much more moved by Tippett's *King Priam* when I heard it the same week, and I realised later, and particularly after studying with Priaulx Rainier in London, I realised that the sort of struggle which Michael Tippett has to say what he wants to say is more meaningful to me than the wonderful schemes of Benjamin Britten which are realized with such definiteness and such expert skill[.][45]

He later explained his preference for Tippett over Britten with the following example:

The vocal melismas and wild piano figuration of *Boyhood's End* have a spontaneity and excitement that vividly bring W H Hudson's prose to life.[46]

Butterley's take on Tippett balances words and music, struggle and spontaneity, which describes his own music at least as well as it does Tippett's. On one hand words come to the fore: 'the rhythmic colouring of words like "dance" in [*Boyhood's End*], and "shine" in the madrigal *Dance, Clarion Air* made a lasting impression'.[47] On the other hand they are a place for Butterley to start, and also a place that can be abandoned in his sketching. This is a way of working that he traces to Tippett:

Tippett's aim was 'to destroy all the verbal music of the poetry or prose and to substitute the music of music'. He writes: 'The moment the composer begins to create the musical verses of his song, he destroys our appreciation of the poem as poetry, and substitutes an appreciation of his music as song.'[48]

David Clark's reading of *King Priam* raises the connection of music, text and the social world, since for him *King Priam* was 'intended to be a repudiation of Marxism – as well as Christianity – and in that sense we may see it as conditioned by Cold War politics'.[49] Christianity was a significant and challenging strand of Tippett's thought, as Tippett's earlier writing in *Moving into Aquarius* testifies. If nothing else, hearing *King Priam*'s performance in Coventry was significant for Butterley, in a manner similar to the effect on him of the other sites in *Laudes*. Butterley's String Quartet is not one of those of his works that bear an immediately resemblance to Tippett, and what Butterley found in Tippett was an alternative to Britten; as well as a composer whose music was audibly working with difficulty, and a composer whose music was not nationally placed.

Religious themes were consistently important for Butterley at this time, and although the music being performed in Sydney was not necessarily overtly religious, much of it did engage with religious themes. As a pianist, Meale was actively promoting the music of Messiaen, and we know that Butterley was present at many of the concerts Meale gave, because he, too, is listed in the programmes. The new British music being performed in Australia tended to have some connection with religion. Birtwistle's first piece to be performed in Australia, in the same year as *Laudes*, was *Monody for Corpus Christi*[50] (Butterley played the piano elsewhere in the concert), and religious seasons also come to the fore in Peter Maxwell Davies's *The Shepherds' Calendar* (1965), a work in which:

> the treble soloist cries out a prayer, 'Veniet Dominus et non tardabit' (The Lord will come and not be slow), which carries the double significance of a prayer for the advent of Christ and for the lengthening days of another spring – a meaning underlined by the final 'Ave, sol de stella' (Hail, Sun born of a Star) sung by the chorus. The cycle of the seasons is completed, and the way prepared for a renewal of the cycle.[51]

Butterley's String Quartet, also about renewal, premiered a few months later.

Butterley's String Quartet is a composition that explores the possibility of serialism. Most of the works he wrote after studying with Rainier are in some way serial (though often very loosely), though he had started thinking about serialism before he left for Britain. He writes that, on the ship to England, he had 'been trying to write a 12-note piece', and although Rainier 'didn't make me write 12-note music[,] I wanted to become familiar with this [way of composing]'.[52] As for so many Australians at this time, a journey to Europe came with specific technical challenges to be overcome, and on his return to Australia he tried out his new technical abilities. Serialism in the String Quartet is readily traceable, and Butterley's move to and from serialism within the work is structurally composed, since the 'unfolding' serial sections hold back the transformation of a second, non-serial 'unfolding' motif.

Serial Procedures

The poem begins 'Unfold, unfold!', and the quartet begins with a straightforward move through a twelve-note row: <C♯, D, A♭, G, B, A, C, E♭, G♭, B♭, F, E> (Example 4.5).[53] The long-held durations and repetition of pitches lessen the serial sound-world and create a slowly evolving harmonic mass. All instruments are in their low registers. The score's barring is pragmatic, even if the surfeit of double bar lines – not present in the fair copy – is eccentric. The rhythms are unpredictable. A new phrase begins in bar 5, by which time a second pass through the series is underway. Although this still sounds like an evolving mass of sound, the cello's moving part, and its sevenths in particular, do begin to form something at least potentially motivic. By bar 10 repetition itself has become a feature, the violin irregularly trilling {C♯, D}. These are the first two pitches of the row, and here indicate the beginning of its third pass, whilst the other strings play a chord that is held over from the row's previous iteration. In contrast to their earlier staggered entries, the second violin, viola and cello now play homorhythmically. In bar 12 the row ends, and the instruments end their chord. The brief viola solo, which begins C♯, D, quickly abandons the pitch series in favour of a strong statement of what Butterley calls an 'important figure' (of which more below). This opening is neatly serial, if fixed on P-0. The transformations that do occur are fragmentary: the row's second repetition (from bar 5) begins mid-sequence; the second pitch is absent (its presence has only just

111

Example 4.5 Butterley, String Quartet, bars 1–14.

Table 4.1 Peter Watters-Cowan's Summary of the Connection between Row Forms Used in Butterley's String Quartet. The Numbers Refer to the Intervals in Semitones

SQ1:01c	5	1	2	5	1	6	1	4	2	3	3			
SQ1:04r					1	6	1	4	2	3	3	3	4	5	1

ceased having been held since the third bar, where it was transferred to the violin from the viola after a little more than a crotchet's silence); there is no particular reason why the D should be repeated in bar 3, nor any greater structural reason why the phrase boundary at bar 3 fails to contain the pitch material. In other words, the implications of this particular row are secondary to a sense of growth, which is not predicated on serial writing. Rhythmically the music avoids the figurative formation that would come from a more focussed association of precise rhythmic repetition linked to changes in pitch class.

Other passages in which serial procedures are traceable have a tendency to obfuscate the opening of the row. Bar 38, for example, begins with the second pitch of the row, as does the second move through the row a bar later; bar 54 begins a phrase on the second pitch of the row. A different approach to the row occurs in the closing bars of the movement (from bar 75), which uses a variation of the initial series <F♯, C♯, C, D, A, B♭, E, E♭, G, F, A♭, B> in its RI form <F♯, A, C, B♭, D, C♯, G, A♭, E♭, F, E, B>. It comes with a clear break from the previous section through a three-crotchet rest, and it returns to the opening texture. This small-scale serial disturbance scarcely troubles the larger serial patterns (more significant disruptions do that), particularly in the sections that use serial procedures repetitively. The most obvious of these is Butterley's use of a varied row from bar 38 to the end of the movement. Peter Watters-Cowan neatly summarizes the connection between rows in Table 4.1.[54]

The row found in the sketch Watters-Cowan labels as SQ1:01c is used in P, R, I and RI forms, each beginning on F♯.[55] From bars 38 to 48 the prime form is used and accounts for almost all the pitches, moving six times through the row. From bar 49 the retrograde is used, passing through the row five times. From bars 62 to 74 the inversion is used, passing nine or ten times through the row (this is difficult to assess, since the row is used at varying speeds concurrently). From bar 75 to the end the retrograde inversion is used eight times. As usual for Butterley, no different transpositions of the row are used in the movement.

An Unfolding Motif

Against this sluggish use of serial transformations are a sequence of chords that are used palindromically, and therefore are not really in motion at all. These chords, which are conceived with a loosely serial approach,[56] form the work's second 'unfolding' motif. The sketches label them the 'unfolding motive[s]',[57] and they expand and then contract in pitch, rhythm and register. The content of the unfolding motifs in the first movement is shown in Table 4.2:

Table 4.2 Instances of the Unfolding Motif in the First Movement of Butterley's String Quartet

Bar	Chord I	II	III	IV	V	VI	VII
14–16	[0157]	[0158]	[0124]	[0136]	[0124]	[0158]	[0157]
19–20	[0136]	[0124]	[0158]	[0157]	[0158]	[0124]	[0136]
25–27	[0157]	[0158]	[0124]	[0136]	[0124]	[0158]	[0157]
35–38	[0157]	[0158]	[0124]	[0136]	[0124]	[0158]	[0157]

The first three instances of the motif are palindromic rhythmically, with increasingly long durations used to the midpoint. The fourth instance adds a quaver to each chord, moving from 1 to 7 quavers. Similar motifs are used in the second movement, as shown in Table 4.3.

Table 4.3 Instances of the Unfolding Motifs in the Second Movement of Butterley's String Quartet

Bars										
18–20	[0157]	[0158]	[0124]	[0247]	[0124]	[0158]	[0157]			
26–29	[0157]	[0158]	[0124]	[0157]	[0158]	[0124]	[0136]	[0124]	[0158]	[0157]
30–32	[0157]	[0158]	[0124]	[0136]	[0124]	[0158]	[0157]			
39	[0148]	[0148]	[0148]	[0148]	[0148]					
40–45	[0148]	[0148]	[0145]	[0148]	[0148]	[0148]	[0148]	[0145]	[0148]	[0148]	[0145]

The idea also unfolds in register. Example 4.6 shows the intervals (in semitones) between the voices in the section from bars 39–45 of the second movement (from one bar before Figure F, see Example 4.7), and it shows that irrespective of melodic shape, the vertical space between voices expands and contracts.[58] Whilst these 'unfolding' registers take place within a homophonic texture which retains distinct lines, that texture's internal structure does not follow Schoenberg's homophonic/contrapuntal opposition, in which homophonic textures emphasize the upper voices.[59] Butterley's homophonic passages privilege no particular part,[60] and Butterley's bass is, if not hard to pin down, then sometimes ambivalent. For example, in the second movement from bar 39, the characteristic shape of the 'unfolding' blocks arches in the treble from F♯ to E to B and back again, repeating the pattern in the following bars. The bass moves more or less in contrary motion, oblique relative to the inner parts. A more melodic move for the bass takes place from bars 41 to 42, with the cello moving into the treble clef, initiating the ending move into higher and higher tessituras. This section is the clearest unfolding of registral space in the piece, and the changing timbre of the cello emphasizes its new position in the middle register, destabilizing its role as a bass voice. When the violin was previously at its highest (Figure D), the cello counterbalanced it by playing at the very bottom of its range, which suggests that instruments are indeed tied to their roles even as their registral disposition works against role-register expectation.

114   Australian Music and Modernism, 1960–1975

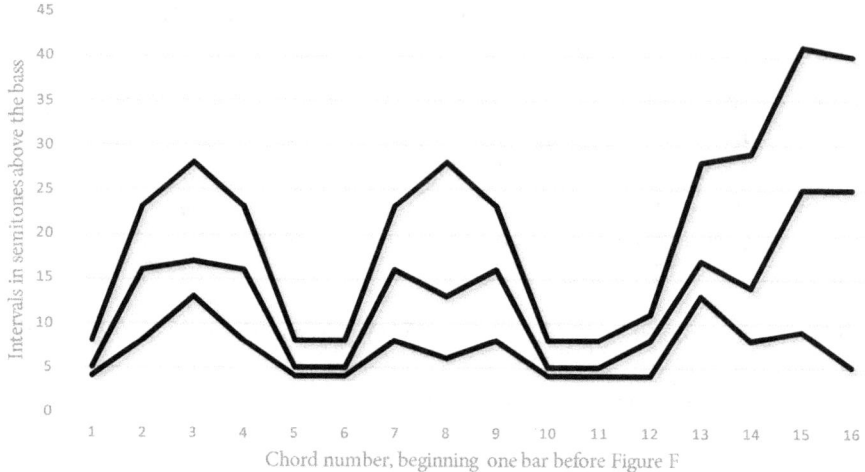

Example 4.6 The unfolding of register, measured in semitones, in the chords from one bar before Figure F.

Example 4.7 Butterley, String Quartet, 'II', final 8 bars.

The 'Important Figure'

Between each 'unfolding motive' in the first movement are 'important figure[s]',[61] each of which draws out a line from one voice in the palindromic chords. The first is for solo viola (from the end of the twelfth bar, see Example 4.5); the second develops the first figure, is longer, adds the cello, and is loosely contrapuntal; the third is for all four instruments and further increases in complexity; the fourth is the longest, is also for all four instruments and ends with a descending flourish through the retrograde of the row. The 'unfolding motive' in connection with the 'important figures' represents the flowering that the text implies. The sketches show these figures and the 'unfolding motive' directly above rows with which they have no serial relationship, though they, like the row, begin with <F#, C#>, further suggesting that the row is formative beyond its rigorously linear applications.[62]

The sketches show only basic forms of these 'important figures', essential shapes that emphasize characteristic intervals of minor ninths, sixths and tritones. The score sounds less like Tippett than Butterley's vocal music does, but the sketches provide glimpses of the kind of distilled, direct, powerfully modal writing found in Tippett's third quartet. Closer to Butterley's piece is Rainier's *Quanta*, which she was composing at the time Butterley was studying with her. Timothy Baxter describes the change in Rainier's music that occurred just before *Quanta*: 'After 1960, a more chromatic vein became evident with the wide use of harmonic clusters in which the semitone became more prominent, melodic lines more angular and the style more fragmented.'[63] *Quanta* and the String Quartet are motivically formed around the 'semitone', which in Butterley's piece is expressed through the leaping major sevenths and minor ninths, and which are also characteristic of Rainier's disjunct lyricism.

The relationship between the 'unfolding motive' and the 'important figure' raises the question of how the instruments relate to each other and to the ensemble. The 'unfolding motive' brings the instruments together, and the 'important figure' unravels the ensemble by isolating lines from homorhythmic chords. A third textural possibility is the opening counterpoint. The second movement begins differently, with the instruments only loosely coordinated (Example 4.8). In *Laudes* such a texture can be related to the individual/congregation idea through the work's religious narrative. The String Quartet's second movement begins the 'springtime' flourishing of the second part of the poem. Musically the second movement is a highly elaborated version of the first, in that it also begins with a twelve-note row, traceable through the cello, viola and second violin. The registral expansion that is part of the unfolding gesture of the first movement is in the second movement greatly exaggerated, and precise coordination is not required ('the three upper parts are independent of each other, but each player should relate his part fairly closely to the cello part'). All the instruments head in the same direction, as plants springing from the frost-free ground. The poetic gesture is of hope, but the music reveals that close to the surface lies the immense, disrupting energy of individual lines, given that the uncoordinated polyphony in the second movement corresponds to the opening of the piece (Example 4.5).

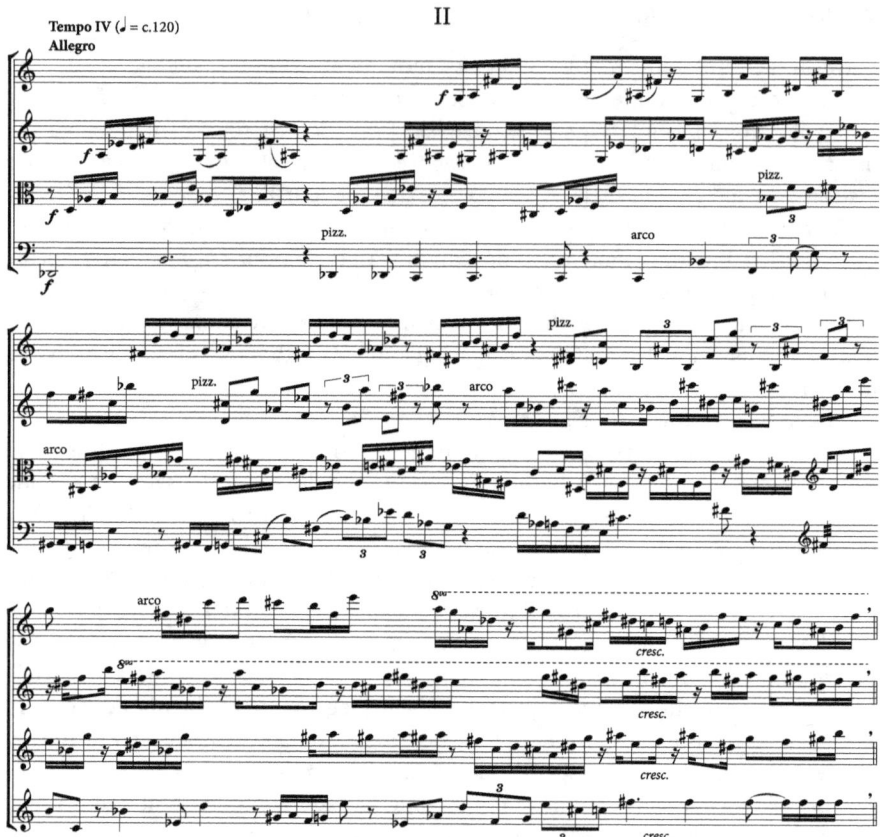

Example 4.8 Butterley, String Quartet, 'II', opening section.

In the sections that follow, in which instruments are coordinated rhythmically, Butterley's homorhythmic music is strikingly similar to the effect achieved by Tippett between Figure 1 and the start of the fugue of the third String Quartet. Butterley's irregular accents, if not directly imitative of this passage in Tippett's quartet, are characteristic of Tippett's competing metres and rhythmic jostling. The tempo of the corresponding passages in both quartets is the same.[64] The similarities also mark their differences, and at the start of Butterley's second movement the uncoordinated instruments do not properly form contrapuntal lines, since the relationships between those lines are not specified beyond their approximate relation to the cello. Other resemblances are less specific, but they keep the contrapuntal and the (not-)fugal ideas at play: Tippett's preoccupation with fugal movements and flowing lines is similar to Butterley's preoccupation with homophonic 'flowing', the 'unfolding motive' and the solo and contrapuntal passages; the way Tippett's lines fold back on themselves (see, for example, Tippett's second movement, with its convoluted melodic lines) sounds similar to Butterley's motifs. When Tippett's fourth movement repeats its opening semiquavers they are marked *declamato*, a direction that implies some connection with text, rhetoric or speech. In his quartet this passagework quickly begins to calm (*calmandosi*) and within a few bars the music is marked *molto tranquillo*. Much of Butterley's quartet is also declamatory, and it follows a similar trajectory, even if its ending is less straightforwardly tranquil.

The moves in and out of counterpoint in Butterley's music have the potential to join together its serial and non-serial unfoldings through a longer history. Ian Bent, in his book *Musical Analysis in the Nineteenth Century: Fugue, Form, and Style*, quotes Koch's 1802 definition of the term '*Durchführung*' for the way that '[o]ld and new, fugal and non-fugal definitions are juxtaposed',[65] a turning point at which:

> the mutation from formalized 'subject' to less-structured 'idea' is striking, as too is the change of implication that *durchführen* undergoes from restatement to transformation. From about this time, the verb took on some of the meaning of *entwickeln*, 'to unfold', and came into the orbit of the French *développer* and its English cognate 'to develop'.[66]

Unlike Tippett's fugues, Butterley's contrapuntal sections never become fully formed,[67] and so the question arises: is the 'unfold motive' a motive that unfolds? Or is it a motive of a gradual unfolding? In connection with the 'important figure' the question becomes: is the formation and transformation of the unfolding motive itself part of the drama of the musico-poetic narrative? In other words, how does the homophony relate to the counterpoint dramatically? In the first instance of the 'unfolding motive', the viola solo (bar 13) immediately comes up against solid homophony, the palindromes of which constitute it as a solid object. The second attempt at fugue is slightly more successful, but only a little progress is made beyond repeating the characteristic intervals before the next palindromic block. Subsequent contrapuntal sections still resist transformation into formal counterpoint, and neither the first nor second movement contains anything that can properly be considered fugal. Compared to more classicist modernist work, Butterley's music is full of unrealized potential, most poignant being the moment where the non-counterpoint of the first movement's coda (from bar 75) is not transformed into coherently interrelated voices in the second section – indeed, the opposite happens, and the voices are uncoordinated. Is this, then, a staged rejection of classicism, or a modernist statement of the impossibility of coherent development? The third possibility is that this is a work that is dramatic in its here and now, framed as a narrative that privileges individuals over centralized direction. If that is the case then the piece is a matter of conviction rather than of critique.

Ambivalence may here be the point, formed as a refusal to take an external point of view from the compositional matters at hand, such as might be implied by technical feats of complex polyphony (serial or otherwise). Indeed, 'ambivalence'[68] itself provides another avenue to Tippett. Whittall has argued for what can be conceived as ambivalence in Tippett's relationship with formal models:

> in spite of the tonal centre of the first movement, it is difficult to feel that a single process, a 'String Quartet in C' has been concluded: it is more that a harmonious balance between various possibilities has been achieved. The quartet is as

ambivalent about traditional forms as it is about traditional harmony, and in this ambivalence Tippett was to find a rich stimulus for future developments, and a future relationship with more radical tendencies.[69]

In the music Butterley was writing in the mid-1960s the relationship with traditional forms is unresolved. For example, in Butterley's interview with de Berg he raises 'developmental form' as a problem that Rainier identified in his music:

> she pointed out something which I hadn't realized, that [...] I was putting things into a readymade mould, a mould developed during the 19th century where something here is contrasted with something there and developed and the music progresses and develops[.][70]

There is no trace of sonata form, in any guise, in *Laudes* or the String Quartet. There is no central role for Beethoven either, which suggests a different relationship with developmental models to Tippett or Matthews, for whom Beethoven is significant.[71]

Gyger also associates Butterley with Tippett, arguing that in Tippett he found a 'problem-free'[72] approach to integrating ideas, as Gyger explains:

> The affinity I feel between Butterley's oeuvre and my own has several aspects, but the most fundamental one is perhaps the shared absence of a problem: the problem of the challenge of modernism. Many – perhaps even most – composers writing in Australia between about 1960 and 1990 seem to have felt acutely that they were faced with a stark choice: between progressive, modernist intricacy on the one hand, and direct, personal expressiveness (often tied to some version of tradition or tonal thinking) on the other. [...]
>
> Butterley's own models for this inclusiveness were Michael Tippett and Olivier Messiaen, but their much more extrovert, indeed extravagant musical personalities allowed them to relish the incongruous juxtaposition of seemingly incompatible elements within one piece in a way quite alien to him. As I suggested in my programming for the Sydney New Music Network's 2005 Butterley celebration, a closer parallel may be found in the music of British composer Jonathan Harvey, a close contemporary of Butterley's with remarkably similar philosophical interests, musical influences and aesthetic preferences. For Harvey and Butterley, allegiance to tradition and fascination with modernist experiment both remain subject to the higher imperative of stylistic integration.[73]

Butterley's programme note for the String Quartet also presents a problem-free picture, reflecting on the music in a way that reveals nothing of the complexities that characterize its construction. The programme note also downplays its modernist credentials in favour of a description in which music supports the poetry:

> The Quartet derives its structure, as well as its whole area of feeling, from the poem 'Revival' by Henry Vaughan. A note-row evolves out of the opening few bars, and the

music gradually unfolds quite freely from the four forms of this row, each one in a transposition beginning on F♯. In fact, the form of the work could be described as a series of variations on the idea of 'unfolding'. As the music unfolds it 'takes in' more light and warmth, joy and quietness. So while the first of the two movements is rather restrained, in the second the music has unfolded enough to contain both the energy of the outburst with which the movement opens, and the serenity of the closing bars.[74]

Although both Gyger and Butterley cast the music as 'problem-free', Whittall's argument about the tension between fragmentation and classicism, together with the musical features explained above, suggest that the idea of 'problem-free' composition in this period ought to be historicized. For Matthew Riley, modernity in Britain: 'was referred to […] obliquely – Corbett's categories of concealment, allusion and deferral are appropriate – while, in typically British fashion, the music's public face preserved the outward appearance of harmony'.[75] Butterley's quartet extends from the British music described by Riley. That music is not problem-free, and so neither is Butterley's.

To return to the poem, for Butterley the immense activity of much of his string writing – decorated and lively – aims to achieve a serene and flowing state. For Vaughan, the rebirth of spring and its new activity combines his religious imagery with personal growth, the two forces connected in the collection's title 'Pious Thoughts and Ejaculations'. For neither author are these forces fully reconciled. For the String Quartet, Vaughan's poetry provides a structure and an imagery that is at once direct and also ambiguous, its ecstatic moments pulling together long-established tropes far grander than the poem's small-scale form. That concision is hardly a precursor to fragmentation, and is not fragmentation itself, since the poem is part of a larger collection that is theologically consistent. The same cannot be said of the String Quartet, in which the range of allusions that Butterley's music makes – both opaque and very faint – exceeds the form that Butterley's uses, given that this form is dictated largely by a single poem. In this sense its ideas are too large for its structures, but that, too, is not inconsistent with the compositional strategy of the English choral tradition, such as Warlock and Finzi, whose music frequently refers to grand ideas in small musical forms.

Given that so much of Butterley's output is choral and that the work has a poetic text, it is hard not to read the quartet as a vocal ensemble. Such a reading also makes sense of the way that long-held notes are interrupted for short rests before beginning again: rests in vocal writing are similarly untroubling to the musical arguments, purely practical breaths rather than problems of repetition within serial structures. Few phrases are too long to be sung. The non-serial unfolding chords are a choral texture, and the quasi-counterpoint is a feature of the choral music Butterley knew as a singer. Butterley's direction to the players – 'flowing' – returns to the seasonal change of Vaughan's poem: 'Hark! how his winds have chang'd their note / And with warm whispers call thee out.' Later in the poem Vaughan refers to the tur-tur call of the turtle dove, which for a composer well versed in English song immediately brings forth the other Vaughan – Ralph Vaughan Williams – and in particular his setting of 'The Turtle Dove'. The second feature is the text of Vaughan Williams's song, which plays out the trope of the migrating bird, seasonal change and loss.[76] The humming choir at the beginning and end of 'The Turtle Dove' is distant if not exactly drowsy, and it is certainly wintery. The voices are required to sound even and homogenous, disguising their breathing, and they sing without text as an embodied version of a mechanical organ's continuous sound. This is the sound that Butterley miniaturizes in the unfolding chords. David Clarke argues that the slow movements from Tippett's Concerto for Double String Orchestra, the Triple Concerto and *The Rose Lake* translate 'the humanising power of song into the language of instrumental music',[77] and a similar translation occurs in most of Butterley's instrumental music in the 1960s and 1970s, certainly in *Laudes* and the String Quartet. Precedents in the music that Butterley knew from Britain offered him a way of writing in which radically different ideas might be brought together with a minimum of fuss, an unfolding tradition.

Of the various unfoldings that are connected to this work, the idea takes two specific forms. Firstly, according to Jones, 'the idea of the structure of a work "unfolding" came from Butterley's lessons with Rainier. Rainier's idea of "unfolding" meant taking an idea or ideas but then to resist fitting such musical ideas into pre-existing form or structure.'[78] He then explains this by quoting Butterley:

> So that's why the Henry Vaughan seemed to encapsulate that [idea of unfolding] but it also had the spiritual dimension which gave the work an added focus, but the unfolding was also a technical thing – that is, what the ideas were supposed to do – gradually unfold.[79]

The second aspect of unfolding comes well after the composition of the quartet, at the end of Butterley's lecture 'Words into Music', and provides a way of understanding his take on 'unfolding' that retains a poetic meaning aside from technical concerns, and that lightens Vaughan's reference to the Augustinian[80] *incurvatus in se*.[81] Butterley ends his lecture by quoting a letter that he received from the poet Kathleen Raine:[82]

> As Kathleen Raine put it in a letter to me, quoting Yeats at the end: 'I'm glad you find my poems good to set to your music. I suppose that is because I use as few words as possible, and that leaves space for the music to unfold, "to prolong the moment of contemplation"'.[83]

Butterley does not comment on the Yeats, nor does he expand on its context, but it is worth quoting Yeats more fully, to reveal the text's musical content:

> The purpose of rhythm, it has always seemed to me, is to prolong the moment of contemplation, the moment when we are both asleep and awake, which is the one moment of creation, by hushing us with an alluring monotony, while it holds us waking by variety, to keep us in that state of perhaps real trance, in which the mind liberated from the pressure of the will is unfolded in symbols.[84]

The rhythm of Vaughan's poem is indeed hypnotic, cast strictly in iambic tetrameter. Butterley's rhythms, by contrast, are not metric, and only in the palindromic 'flowing' motif and arithmetical rhythms of the end are they 'hushed'. Butterley's music may not be obviously repetitive in the same manner as the poem's metre, but it does repeat its ideas (musical, poetic) again and again. In this way, Butterley does not set Vaughan's poem for a listener's unfolding so much as present music as an unfolding of Vaughan's poem; the work is contemplative, not evangelical.

Laudes and the String Quartet show Australian Music tied to England, and Butterley's extension of their musical practices proved no problem for his position as 'the third of the triumvirate (the others being Sculthorpe and Meale) which has transformed the creative outlook and image of Sydney since 1960'.[85] The religious ideas in Butterley's music were no impediment to considering Butterley a modernist. Indeed, for McCredie:

> His religious background has been of signal significance in determining his intellectual approach to music, in which a deep rooted but universalised Christian mysticism is balanced with technical sophistication. It is precisely this type of intellectual idealism which from the outset differentiates the musical personality of Butterley from Meale on one hand and Sculthorpe on the other.[86]

The argument for 'intellectual idealism' considers Butterley as removed from the immediate politics of the world, but in the music that he writes religious practice is not 'universalised', since each movement of *Laudes*, for example, connects to a specific place, each with its own traditions of praise. Whatever his personal beliefs, the music that he wrote does not present 'Christian mysticism' as a transcendent, universalized ideology, and in the String Quartet the music itself emerges as more significant than the score's epigraph. Butterley's 'technical sophistication' is also not 'universalised', and 'technique' does not balance 'religion', since they are not opposed. If Jones is right and the 'unfolding' of the quartet should be considered in terms of Rainier's conception of 'unfolding' – 'taking an idea or ideas but then to resist fitting such musical ideas into pre-existing form or structure'[87] – then the quartet resists its poetry in resisting the wider implications of Vaughan's poetic structure in such musical moments as the uncoordinated start of the second movement, and in the ethereal ending that departs from Vaughan's earthiness.

Even if Yeats looms rather too large for us comfortably to declare (in terminology after Badiou[88]) that Butterley is an ardently 'faithful' modernist subject, Yeats's own position within modernism might clarify the problem. In Daniel Albright's consideration of Yeats in relation to the later modernism of Pound, Auden and Eliot, he argues that: 'Yeats could stimulate his successors precisely because his rhetorical vehemence seemed disconnected from any discipline except the discipline of poetic form.'[89] Butterley's composition is not a straightforward representation of Vaughan's poetry, nor a return to Vaughan Williams's music. The presence of serial thinking in Butterley's work counters the 'reactive subjects' in the 1960s for whom modernism was a period that was long extinguished. The connections that Butterley's early music forges with English music also move outside the existing opposition of Australia and England that is constructed as a temporal and spatial move away from the colonizing/colonized opposition of the colonial period. Covell considered the 1960s in terms of an ongoing distancing of Australia from Britain, but the 1960s was not a long-delayed move away from Britain, nor a spatial move away from Britain in a reconfiguration of Australia's 'place in the world' (as we shall see for Sculthorpe in Chapter 7). The change that Butterley's music presents is more radical, since the String Quartet and *Laudes* are more thoroughly outside the antagonisms conditioned by nationalism, which Meale's rejection of British culture, and Sculthorpe's 'distinctively Australian Music' continue. Butterley's music is more positive. The English music that had been shipped to Sydney, and which Butterley sang in the choir of St Andrew's Cathedral, is given a properly modernist setting in Butterley's music. His music is therefore critical, since it draws the English music that is often considered reactionary within a newly modernist Australian Music.

Explorations

There are few works by Butterley that do not have some kind of text. *Letter from Hardy's Bay*'s title highlights its lack of one. So too does that of Butterley's other instrumental work from 1971, *Voices*, for wind quintet. *Voices* is an assured, technical and abstract work, and the last of the pieces of Butterley's 'early period', which also includes *Pentad* (1968) for wind and brass ensemble, and *Explorations* (1970), for piano and orchestra. These compositions are some of Butterley's most impressive music from the era, and the high point of his modernist idiom. As such they represent a consolidation of Australian Musical modernism that coincides with Meale and Sculthorpe's compositional maturity, and which came just before Banks returned to Australia from Britain. At no earlier time in Australian history was there a compositional movement of such significance.

This zenith also coincided with the 1970 bicentenary of Cook's landing in Australia. *Explorations* was written for the highest-profile concert of the bicentennial celebrations, a concert on 2 May 1970 in which the Sydney Symphony Orchestra performed at the Sydney Town Hall with Queen Elizabeth II in the audience. Butterley's *Explorations* refuses the invitation for nationalist celebration. Even though it was commissioned by the Captain Cook Bicentenary Celebrations Citizens Committee,[90] it is difficult to conceive of a work that is less about Australia, nationalism, celebration, colonialism or provincialism. Indeed, perhaps the refusal to participate in the 'celebrations' is a more powerful, if less decisive, critique than a polemical work that defined itself as nationalism's or celebration's opposite would have been.[91] Such antagonism would inevitably tie a work to that which it opposed. Alongside the main items in the programme was a fanfare by Robert Hughes, and also Hughes's arrangement of the National Anthem 'God Save the Queen' (it was not exceptional at the time for the Sydney Symphony Orchestra's concerts to begin with the National Anthem). It is worth considering how much had changed between 1970 and the celebrations of the Jubilee of Australian Federation in 1951. In 1951 Hughes won second place in a composition competition to celebrate both the Jubilee and the formation of the ABC orchestras (one in each state capital city). The competition was open to 'composers who originated in Australia, Great Britain and Canada',[92] and it was judged by John Barbirolli, Arnold Bax and Eugene Goosens, of whom only Goosens had a relationship with Australia; he was at the time conductor of the Sydney Symphony Orchestra and head of the NSW Conservatorium of Music. Hughes came second to David Moule-Evans, who described his winning composition as 'an answer to all the ugly wrong-note music written these days',[93] and although Hughes was less conservative than Moule-Evans, his own symphony is a long way from Butterley's composition. If Jones is right and Butterley suggested that the ABC add Vaughan Williams's *Towards the Unknown Region* to the 1970 programme alongside his own work and Beethoven's Fifth Symphony,[94] then the decision provided the programme with the outward energy that might be expected from such an event, which would also have freed Butterley to write as he wished. *Explorations* is nothing like *Towards the Unknown Region* and although it shares with *A Sea Symphony* a quiet ending (the last movement of the *Sea Symphony* being 'The Explorers'), Butterley's music does not sound like that of Vaughan Williams.

Explorations derives its row from Ian Farr's Cello Sonata, though here again Butterley was not tied to serial writing; one of Butterley's advanced sketches for the piano solo includes the note: 'This [Figure L] need not all be derived from a row. Parts (e.g. first bar) may be quite unsuitable for a row.'[95] Similarly, he reminds himself: 'No need to do a rhythmic plan first. Write middle [chords in the piano] then add others [i.e. other notes] – not very extensive, but adding a jerky aspect to the dominating slow static basic rhythm. Middle part both hands.'[96] Even in those sections where the use of a row is apparent, such as from Figure A, the row comes second to other compositional considerations: 'In A sections where more notes are needed, these can be taken from the row and inserted where needed. Where there is too much material for the section it can stop before the end.'[97] Generally speaking, each new section evolves from the ideas of earlier sections, and Butterley returns to those sections for his pitch materials, rather than to an external scheme.

Farr was the pianist for the first performance,[98] and in the sketching Butterley devoted most attention to making sure that the solo part was pianistic, and that the textures were carefully differentiated. The work's most striking feature occurs after its short orchestral introduction, when the piano plays what at first seems like the building of a monument, a sequence of 114 crotchet chords at ♩=42, all but the last few of which have the same highest pitch. For Gyger this is 'one of the most audacious passages in all Australian music', and he describes it in terms of landscape:

> Those chords evolve, especially at first, by incremental change; each differs by only one or two notes from the chord preceding it. The prevailing impression is the gradual and methodical mapping of a landscape. The romanticised image of the explorer as visionary is deeply embedded in Australian culture, but Butterley here evoked the more prosaic (although no less impressive) drudgery involved in charting an unknown continent.[99]

The piece has nothing to do with landscape, and instead it asserts Butterley's newly confident use of the ideas of musical modernism, since the model for Butterley's chords is surely Stockhausen's *Klavierstück IX*, which begins with 229 repetitions of a single chord. The dynamic profile at the beginning of Stockhausen's piece – a long diminuendo with a sudden increase in dynamic – is also the profile of Butterley's repeated chords. Stockhausen visited Sydney at the beginning of April 1970, where he gave three lecture-recitals about his music. The press reported these lectures extensively, including an article in advance of his arrival declaring him (in large, bold type) an 'explorer'.[100] Although Stockhausen's visit would have been too late to have been the basis for Butterley's composition, it is evidence of the particular importance of Stockhausen in Sydney at this time. It is also likely that Farr had been working on *Klavierstück IX* when Butterley was composing *Explorations* for him, since Farr performed *Klavierstück IX* in recital in September 1970.[101] In the same concert Butterley and Farr performed Ives's Three-Page Sonata, and the programme also included Ahern's AZ Ensemble. Ahern had previously been a student of Butterley, and he had also by this date been Stockhausen's assistant. Much of Stockhausen's music that had been performed in Sydney during the 1960s featured in concerts alongside Butterley's music. There is therefore both an extensive background to Stockhausen's influence in Sydney in the 1960s, and a specific musical connection between the two composers. As such, Butterley's insistently repeating chords are not the exploration of landscape but a clear statement of the musical world in which he saw himself, and to make this statement in the year's most significant orchestral concert shows the confidence that he had.

Don Banks wrote the programme note for *Explorations*, having been invited to do so in a letter that Butterley wrote on 3 January 1970, and which included an explanation of the composition's connection to Cook:

> I'm writing a work for piano and orchestra commissioned for the Captain Cook Bicentenary concert next May. The piece has no connection with Cook except the title (Explorations for Piano and Orchestra) and the money! It's quite a big work, and I've been wondering what to do about a programme-note. I don't want to do it myself, as there's no extra-musical background to talk about, and I feel all I could do would be to give the bare bones of it's [sic] shape. John Hopkins feels there should be a reasonably substantial programme-note, and suggested that you might be persuaded to do it.[102]

Banks was in London, preparing to travel to Sydney, and Butterley suggested that they discuss the piece when he arrived. Banks's programme note gives the 'bare bones' of the piece, and then equates the *Exploration* of the title with the composer as explorer:

> The composer *is* an explorer working in the world of sound, and it is in this context that we must think of Nigel Butterley's piece. There is no programmatic element here, for the composer is concerned with the exploration and exploitation of his musical material.
>
> This is something which can really be said of all composers of all ages; we can think of Haydn in his later years, still experimenting with musical ideas and forms, or of Stravinsky not only charting a new world in his *Rite of Spring*, but also

annexing other people's territory, as he did with Pergolesi and Tchaikovsky, and absorbing their music into his own[.][103]

Even though Banks knew that the piece had nothing to do with geographical exploration, he nevertheless worked hard to bring Cook's exploration and musical 'exploration' together, but the combination is forced. Though Gyger also considers Butterley's musical relationships in terms of feet-on-the-ground exploration, there is nothing in the piece to support such a reading, which belongs to more recent discourses about Australian Music, and the celebration of the Australian landscape. The programme note says more about Banks's thinking about the bicentenary than it does anything about *Explorations for Piano and Orchestra*.[104]

In a letter to John Hopkins, dated 21 June 1969, Butterley sought reassurance that he could write the piece that he wanted to write, rather than fulfil the expectations of the Committee:

> This is an important and exciting commission, so I want to be as sure as I can be that what I write will be a really good piece. From the terms of the commission it's clear that the committee hopes for not just a routine occasional piece, but a vital and important contribution to Australian music.[105]

This is one of the few instances of Butterley articulating the tension between nationalism (Australian Music) and his 'present style'. Butterley wanted to write a piece for Farr, and had been thinking about a piano concerto for some time, and so he was keen not to write the nationalist statement that he felt the Committee[106] was expecting.

Butterley's confidence in writing a non-celebratory piece comes from being part of a wider movement of like-minded composers who were similarly pushing the boundaries of new music in Australia, asserting a newly open outlook and resisting the celebration of nationalism. This piece is unlike those that were to come with the commissions for the 1988 bicentenary of Australia's colonization, which are all immediately celebratory and politically charged. The differences between earlier and later forms of nationalism show the high-profile support for musical modernism even in an event designed to strengthen nationalist ideals, with Butterley's composition only superficially related to the celebration of Cook's bicentenary.

Fire in the heavens

In 1973 Butterley left the ABC to take up a lectureship at the Newcastle Conservatorium,[107] which was an appointment that recognized his prominence as a composer. The conservatorium opened officially in 1952 as a 'Newcastle branch' of the NSW Conservatorium of Music based in Sydney.[108] It formed another component in the expansion of postwar infrastructure for music, and it supported Butterley's move away from the ABC. This represented a larger cultural change: until the 1960s the principal places of employment for composers in the state of New South Wales were the NSW Conservatorium of Music or the ABC, either as a conductor, teacher or producer.[109] The foundation and growth of tertiary institutions in this era meant that for the first time in Australia, composers were employed as composers. With this came a growth in the number of composers, as well as a proliferation of centres for music away from Sydney and Melbourne.

Fire in the heavens (1973) is, with the second String Quartet, the last work before Butterley's mid-1970s shift towards more dramatic music in the first of the Whitman compositions – *Sometimes with the One I Love* (1976) and *Watershore* (1978) – which are also more overtly modal. *Fire in the heavens* (with its small 'h', as Butterley frequently reminds) was written to celebrate the opening of the Sydney Opera House. By the time of the Opera House's opening, its role as a tourist attraction – and therefore an icon of nationalism – was clear, and the two poems that Butterley chose do support the mythologizing of 'landscape'. *Fire in the heavens*'s premiere took place a fortnight before the building was officially opened by the Queen, in a concert by the Cleveland Orchestra, programmed alongside Schumann and Brahms, and conducted by Lorin Mazel. The commission had come on 3 August 1972 from John Hopkins at the ABC.[110] Hopkins's next letter clarified (at Butterley's request) that the commission need not specifically relate to the building, but also that 'if the composer wishes to bear in mind the opening of this great building and the effect of such a building at large, he is quite free to do so'.[111] Hopkins had similarly reassured Butterley about the composition of *Explorations*, three years earlier. Unlike *Explorations*, Butterley wrote *Fire in the heavens* with the straightforward energy of a celebratory work.

The score of *Fire in the heavens* begins with poetry, in this case two lines from Christopher Brennan's 'Fire in the heavens':

Fire in the heavens, and fire along the hills,
and fire made solid in the flinty stone ...

and four lines from Judith Wright's 'Silence':

Silence is the rock where I shall stand.
Oh, when I strike it with my hand
may the artesian waters spring
from that dark source I long to find.[112]

They are not the most obviously musical texts to use, though they are both located in Australia. Both poems also weave sound and silence, and they contrast the physicality of earth – with its 'solid', 'flinty' consonants – with other places, either above or below: 'heaven', or 'artesian'. Their version of Australia is a place of exile and isolation. Brennan's text is part of a lengthy collection *Poems (1913)*. Even without Wright to make the silence explicit, it is an essential part of Brennan's collection, since its second part – which includes 'Fire in the heavens' – is entitled 'The Quest of Silence'.[113] Brennan's Australia is not literally silent, since his sleep is interrupted by 'the cicada's torture-point of song', but for Brennan, as for many other Australian poets, the lack of the noise of industrial modernity was sufficient to consider a place as silent. No matter the precise setting for Brennan's poem; for an Australian reader of Brennan's time the 'brimstone lake' would have resonated with the previous century's search for Australia's inland sea (which lasted even as late as Bourke and Wills in the 1860s), about which Brennan often wrote. The lack of an actual inland sea, or fertile lands, strengthens instead the cultural importance of the flinty stone from which Wright hopes to strike water. When water is found, it was not for the maid's pale, as Brennan would have it, but for the grazier's beef. In the collection Brennan labours his contrasts hard, to make apparent the Europe where he was not: 'the rosy mist!'; the 'pale absence of the ruin'd rose', which once 'saw the rose of heaven bloom'. It is an awkward collection, atypical of the nationalism popular at the time, which, being forged by hard-headed mercantilism, was rarely fond of unreconstructed pastoralism.

In quoting briefly from Brennan's poem, Butterley cuts through the inundation of myths past (and the messiness of Brennan's text, its problems and its complaints about distance), containing the sprawl of past literature to cleanly focus on some of the few striking moments in all of Brennan's writing. The programme to the first performance of *Fire in the heavens* gives a little more of the poem than the published score, and it connects Wright's silence to 'the silence of the new concert hall'. The programme note then becomes more artful, with more lines from Brennan, and then – in quotation marks – lines from Butterley: 'the quietness out of which some new experience comes', 'power hidden, untapped, likely to be released'. With these lines go a new persona, the quotation marks making sure we do not miss that these are about the compositional process. The same persona asks a question (no quotation marks this time, and so not Butterley): 'what new energy will spring through the hall's silence?' Then more lines from Brennan:

> the heart's silence between beat and beat
> in which myself and silence meet

Clarifying, as far as this programme note seeks clarity, the persona of quotation marks returns:

> in any piece I write there's some involvement with another person. my music is essentially related to people in two ways: when starting, it's in the light of a relationship with a person or people which affects the way I write and makes me want to write it[.][114]

The wordiness of this silence is reminiscent of the prolixity of Cage, whose (then) recently published collection *Silence* informs the second page of the programme note (not by Butterley), in which a scattering of words across the page is prefaced by more Wright:

> the silence between word and word,
> in which a truth waits to be heard;

The programme note's literalization of Wright's 'silence' via Cage now reads awkwardly (and perhaps it also read awkwardly at the time). Below the scattered text is the declaration of the note's author: 'annotation by Ian Farr'. Farr is a pianist with whom Butterley had worked closely; they had played piano duets together, and they were colleagues at the ABC. Piano music is the transition in the programme note between Brennan and Wright, and the scattered text, in which a few brief sentences read most like a traditional programme note:

> *Fire in the heavens* is dedicated to Rodney Wetherell. It's 'the other side of the coin' from its introspective companion piece *Letter from Hardy's Bay* for piano, of 1971, the new piece was written in Sydney and Newcastle between January and May 1973, discovering new confidence, expansiveness, exuberance
>   'after I've written a piece I want it to be a means of my relating to other people … the hearers'.[115]

'Exuberant' is an apt description for *Fire in the heavens*, and Butterley positions his piece as a breakthrough work, marked by its 'concise' form that was 'not rambling'.[116] According to Butterley, Hopkins wanted a 'brilliant' work, not something 'slow, gloomy, concentrated, [and] reflective'[117] for this commission, leading Butterley to initially suggest that it might better suit another composer. Hopkins insisted that Butterley accept the commission, and that he compose a work unlike those he had written before that date. The piece succeeds in fulfilling the commission, even if the middle section, when the solo flute emerges from the orchestra (bar 83), is surprisingly involuted.

The composition is audibly sectional, though its form is far from straightforward, having been worked and reworked a number of times. Butterley's early drafts include a fourteen-section structure, reformed as a nine-section structure; this was then subdivided, a thirteen-section structure was imposed, and then this was grouped into four larger sections, 'the material of all of them being related'. In the sketches, he finally comments: 'to the listener it will be one flow of sound – not five sections or any other standard formal structure'.[118] He uses at least four types of pen to refine the sketches of the structure, and although each structure is traceable to the score, there are so many complications to each that, as Butterley suggests, no one form exists. The stable materials are: 'upward surges', such as at the opening, and which are interspersed with silences; lyrical wind writing with horns and strings, such as at bar 83 and bar 111; a cellular idea at bar 50 and bar 132; and a final 'virtuoso' section from bar 150.

The opening is a fanfare of springing arpeggios played by the reeds. The sketch for this suggests that Butterley originally had brass in mind, but for dramatic purposes the brass are delayed until later in the piece. This melody is labelled 'Exuberant theme, capable of extension, variation becoming "vulgar"'.[119] The opening D is established strongly, and not destabilized by the piano's dissonant E♭ and C a dotted crotchet later. The main melodic move to F suggests a tonal seed, one sustained through the subsequent E if only because the melody then continues <A, F♯, F♮, A♭, D, F♯>: the opening bar is D major, minor and diminished all at once. The next bar is a dominant-seventh chord of sorts – {A, C♯, C♮, G♯} – moving back and forth between pitches, not quite managing to state the E before a B enables an outline of either a major seventh ({C, B}) or the midpoint of a G♯ diminished chord. When the trumpets enter (with first trombone) at bar 4 they each hold a single pitch, iterated irregularly, ringing out an [0347] tetrachord that is characteristic of Butterley's later harmonic language: voicing aside, as a D♯ major/minor chord it connects to the opening harmonic ambivalence.

Repetition is important, but the specific musical materials that are subsequently repeated quickly follow different paths. For example, the opening returns at bar 7, a long-held F replacing the opening D, evaporating the background tonality of the opening. The fragmented triplets also return, initially transposed a minor seventh higher, but then pursing their own direction. The trumpets play a three-note chord ({A♭, D♭, E♭}) that, like so much of Butterley's music, derives from fifths, and which is appropriate for this fanfare. A homorhythmic quaver prepares for silence in bar 6. A later interjection of the piano begins in a *senza misura* section where the conductor cues grace notes from percussion, trombone, horn, bass clarinet, cor anglais and piccolo. The *senza misura* texture connects the piece to *Laudes* and to the first String Quartet, and also to Lumsdaine's *Flights*, which Butterley performed with Ransford Elsley in the Opera House in the same month as the first performance of *Fire in the heavens*. All the silences that interrupt the fanfare are moments of reduction from full orchestra that emphasize the space of the concert hall. A different audition of the hall's resonance occurs after the third opening (bar 19) where the solo flute holds a long D, and the orchestra interrupts with a staccato chord, *ff*. (The chord is a larger segment of a stack of fifths, <A, E, B, F♯, C♯>, with an added F♮.) The flute, which is already playing *pp*, then decrescendos into silence (into the hall's resonance), beginning again, *pp*, several crotchets later. Here the flute is testing the limits of audibility in the space: how soft can the flute be for its detail still to be heard? How does that balance with the decay of the orchestra's chord?[120]

From the flute's D a sequence of slowly changing chords emerge (bar 22). The first [0247] is played melodically by the first violin, and harmonically by the wind, and then brass.[121] The other strings play different pitches (Vn II: [0126]; Va: [012357]; Vc: [0134]), which are not held chordally. The violin then completes a melodic arch, returning within the [0247] collection. The *pp* chord at the end of bar 26 is an octatonic collection [013679]; this chord is repeated in the winds, and then *ff* with vigorous repetition in the strings,[122] against which the horns play a simple melodic/harmonic move using [013469], which is also octatonic. The passage is leading nowhere, but showing off the orchestra's control of the voicing of the chord, whilst shifting in timbre, which is a further moment for assessing the acoustics of the space. Pitch-class saturation is achieved in bar 35, though it hardly matters. The harmony is made up of the nearly octatonic [0134568] set played by the trumpets and trombones and an [01357] chord played by the winds (held from bar 34). Such octatonic passages are reminiscent of Stravinsky's tour-de-force orchestral writing. So too are bars 50–72 and 132–49, which is a cellular idea, reminiscent of Stravinsky's *Symphonies of Wind Instruments*, in which cells are 'repeated, deleted, or reshuffled'.[123] The cells are mostly short, between one and three crotchets in length, and repeat with variation. In both sections the strings do not play, strengthening a possible connection to Stravinsky's

Symphonies of Wind Instruments. This section presents on a smaller scale the overall form of the piece, as it kaleidoscopically reorders a set of short cells, most of which are between a quaver and a minim in length.

From bar 104 (Example 4.9), a melody that has been only partially heard is revealed, initially shared amongst the strings (the melody is always the highest pitch). The section realizes the earlier, quiet sections, showing that the music that the fanfares otherwise crowd out is lyrical, and also melancholic. The intimacy of the passage is a brief chamber moment in an orchestral score, adventurously tonal, and smooth. The harmony here is consistent and clear. In the closing bars (from bar 162), the trombones, piano, percussion and double bass play chords, either staccato or held. These chords revoice the same pitches – {A♯, B, D♯, F♯} – to ring the changes of a pseudo-tonal

Example 4.9 Butterley, *Fire in the heavens*, bars 104–7, the lyrical music.

progression. The metrical chords also mark a change in the fanfare from monody to homophony, with the thickening texture emphasizing the broadening of the harmony.

Gyger writes that

> The overall harmonic vocabulary suggests a particular strain of French influence in Australian music between about 1968 and 1986, also to be found in Barry Conyngham, certain works of Richard Meale including *Very High Kings* and *Viridian*, and even Peter Sculthorpe's *Mangrove*. The passage [from b. 104] stands out as unusually rich for Butterley, but its wayward tonal slips will emerge as part of his mature vocabulary a few years later.[124]

Gyger is undoubtedly correct about his later music, but the tonal moments here are not slips, but an original part of the plan for the composition. Six bars before bar 104 is a string cluster from A to E, which in the initial conception of the piece was intended as a dissolution of a section based on an A minor chord.[125] The string melody from bar 104 would therefore have existed in a more overtly tonal setting. Similarly the 'ending section' was also to be more obviously tonal: 'Throughout it all (?) brass chord (eg E♭ major, but possibly changing, both subtly and suddenly) pierces and glows.'[126] This chord was qualified in the sketching of the actual music, and what remains are a predominance of fifths between E♭ and B♭, and the dominance of E♭ more generally, especially from about bar 120 until the end – in the final bars the only long note is a high horn D♯. This return to tonal harmony is also present in some of the melodic details, and in the sketches Butterley reminds himself that tonal allusion is permitted: 'All the figuration can be full of tonal shapes.' Following this comment his sketch includes the note: 'e.g. I can write <B, D, B♭, E♭, D♭, E♭> whereas I would previous have written at least <B, D, B♭, E♭, D♭, E>'.[127] The resulting shapes contribute to the 'glowing' harmony that he was seeking, but this change in his music also shows just how self-conscious his earlier avoidance of tonality was. One also wonders whether Meale's *Very High Kings*, and its opening E♭ major triad, was on Butterley's mind. Perhaps Butterley felt that such a gesture was too overtly tonal, and so he clouded *Fire in the heavens*'s tonal beginnings. Although in retrospect it lacks the tonal nuance of his music from later decades, it nevertheless succeeds in producing the kind of luminosity that he was seeking for such a celebration, and which had not been part of his previous music. Later music would achieve such luminosity more straightforwardly, but in 1973 the obfuscation of tonality was a defining part of his aesthetic, just as his music before 1973 avoids celebration.

With the composition as a whole in view, the work's double structure becomes apparent. One strand is a fanfare and the other is a lyrical melody, a hymn sung by the strings. The former begins the work; the latter starts in silence, from which the lyrical line emerges. Attached to these two strands are the work's two texts. In an early prose plan for the piece, Butterley commented:

> The 2 sections are both necessary to each other. The Judith Wright poem must flower into something, and the exuberance of Brennan (or the music emerging from it) needs something to prepare its way. The release of exuberance that comes

out of silence. [The following is different ink:] Both poems are full of pent-up energy – the kind of energy that can only be released by listening to silence.[128]

He later noted that 'The influence of both poems is very free. For instance, there need not be any silence very soon after the opening but the activity out of which silence comes can be established first.'[129] This is a more direct response to text than in his music since the first String Quartet, quite uncharacteristic of his music in the early 1970s, and a rare example of Butterley writing music that invokes conceptions of Australian 'landscape' (which is a practice more often associated with Scultthorpe). For Gyger: 'The imagery of the two texts is diametrically opposed – fire and the harsh brilliance of the noonday sun for Brennan, water and subterranean darkness for Wright – but they are connected by their "quest for silence": a search for spiritual grounding, on the bedrock of the Australian landscape.'[130] This is to say that the introspective and the ecstatic, the core poles of all Butterley's music, are here combined in a moment of excitement for the new national icon.

Fire in the heavens utilizes the successes of its modernist canon – Stravinsky, Messiaen, Bartók – and it builds on Butterley's earlier orchestral music to form a response to the occasion that is both celebratory and consistent with his earlier music: he finds a way to mobilize silence more purposely than in his earlier contemplative compositions. *Fire in the heavens* also marks the end of his thoroughgoing modernist composing, and his next orchestral work was not until *Symphony* (1980), a piece in three movements that nevertheless contributes to the rehabilitation of the genre, and the move towards tonal forms that that genre represents. In the intervening years he was less prolific, but he also composed the formative work *Sometimes with One I Love* (1976), which began the flourishing of a more confident lyricism, a more overt if ambiguous tonality and a more seamless integration of sung text and instrumental line. The year 1975 therefore emerges in Butterley's music, as it does in Meale's and Banks's, as a key date in Australian Music, a boundary that marks the end of the modernist movement to which Australia's most prominent composers had contributed.

5

Peter Sculthorpe

Australian Music and Nationalism

Peter Sculthorpe consistently promoted a nationalist vision of Australian Music, and as a nationalist he was also a traditionalist, promoting earlier nationalisms. In this way he is exemplary of modernist Australian Music as a movement that sought a unique Australian idiom akin to such as had occurred in literature and painting, an idiom 'irreducible to the mere importation of European or American modernism',[1] and which was also anxious to define a national sound. This makes him a different kind of modernist to Banks, Butterley and Meale. Nevertheless, Sculthorpe's music incorporates aspects of modernisms from other places, including those of Britain and Europe, in a way that transcends nationalism. And at the same time he situates Australia as independent, reconfiguring existing conceptions of geography to propose new relationships between places. Sculthorpe's modernism is defined by his nationalism, and the principal pillar of his nationalism reconceives landscape in musical terms. As I will explain, this brings a new sense of 'spatiality' to Australian Music, particularly in connection with Sculthorpe's conceptualization of the central Australian landscape as flat and unchanging, and with this he radically reconceived Australian Music as a spatial rather than a historical problem. This new musical conceptualization of landscape combined with Sculthorpe's interest in Aboriginal culture, and in music from various parts of Asia, to reform Australia's national boundaries – defining what is within and without – so as to challenge existing discourses of music about Australia at the same time that it defined Australian Music through established ideas.

One of the problems of Australian Music as a defining discourse is the extent to which a handful of urban composers come to represent Australia's diversity. To make a claim for 'Australian' anything is to raise this problem, and so the very notion of Australian Music is inherently problematic. Australian Music was desired rather than a descriptive term, and the composers in this book are the people around whom it was considered that a national music might form, rather than composers who had already defined a distinctively Australian sound. In a radio interview in 1982, Meale, looking ahead to the performance of *Voss*, was asked about his attitude to 'Australianism, that is, a nation character for Australian Music'. (The opera is, in part, about changing ideas of nation in the nineteenth century, and the connections between urban centres and remote places.) Had his attitude changed with his new compositional approach?

Not in the sense that a lot [of composers] are attempting to get a nationalism into Australian Music by deliberate ploys. I disagree with that form of what I call jingoism.[2]

Nevertheless, he declared his interest in Australian 'subjects', and considered his works as 'Australian', adding 'I'm an urban Australian.' And so were Banks and Butterley. The situation is more complicated for Lumsdaine, whose part in Sydney's intellectual cosmopolitanism contrasts with the extensive time he spent away from urban Sydney. In the late 1940s Lumsdaine was one of a loose collection of people who were later known by the formulation the 'Sydney Push'. In Lumsdaine's time, well before it was written about (for there was scarcely any 'it' about which to write), and before the era of Germaine Greer, Clive James and Robert Hughes, who made it famous, that 'push' was equally the 'putsch'. The former term referred (not seriously) to the 'Rocks Push', via the (anonymous and nearly cotemporaneous) reworking of Henry Lawson's poem 'The Captain of the Push' as 'The Bastard from the Bush', a retelling of the meeting between urban and rural Australia. The latter referred to the European libertarianism influenced by the former communist, former Trotskyist and libertarian professor of philosophy John Anderson.[3] Lumsdaine moved easily in these Sydney circles, as he did in Australia's non-urban areas, to which the extensive catalogue of birdsong recordings that he later made attests.

Well before the 1940s, Australian nationalism relied on an urban/bush opposition that was more mythical rather than lived. Nevertheless there remained a preoccupation with that contrast. Sculthorpe's music, and, indeed, Sculthorpe himself, embodies the extension of those currents. Sculthorpe was born in Launceston, Tasmania in 1929. He moved to Melbourne in 1946 and studied there until 1950, before returning again to Launceston and the family's 'Huntin, Shootin and Fishin' shop'.[4] For Michael Hannan, Sculthorpe's association with these pastimes confirms the essential ingredients of Sculthorpe as a *solitary* man.[5] In 1958 Sculthorpe moved to Oxford, and although he studied briefly with Edmund Rubbra and Egon Wellesz, his time there might better be described as a period during which he became acquainted with England, for the studies were less significant than the connections that he made outside Oxford, perhaps especially with Wilfrid Mellers, whose public and private support was significant.

The end of Sculthorpe's early period is, for the composer, marked by his departure from Oxford in 1960:

Unfortunately around this time, my father got prostate cancer, and I didn't finish my degree because I returned home to Tasmania at the end of 1960. After my father died, everyone wanted me to go back to Oxford. In those days England was a long way away and I couldn't afford it. In any case, I only wanted the doctorate for him. Instead I wrote a work in my father's memory called *Irkanda IV*. It was my first mature work, and the first work that received wide critical and popular acclaim.[6]

Irkanda IV, for solo violin (Example 5.1), strings and percussion (1961), reworks material from several earlier pieces: the opening is a repetition of the opening of

Irkanda II, and further material is drawn from the Sonata for Viola and Percussion, and also from his previous setting of D. H. Lawrence's 'Sun in Me', in Sculthorpe's 1960 composition *Sun*.[7] *Irkanda IV* is straightforwardly formed, and it repeats its opening semitones and minor thirds again and again. *Irkanda IV* is also the basis for other music. The marking '*con disiderio pieno di malinconia*', for example, returns in the fifth movement of *Port Essington* (1977), a piece that 'tells the story in musical terms of the attempted settlement of Port Essington, in the Northern Territory,'[8] and whose 'Arietta: Farewell' intends to convey the 'feeling of the settlers, rowing out to their rescue ship'.[9] In this section there is a musical unison between the string trio (representing the settlers) and the string orchestra (the bush) which play a variation on the Aboriginal 'Djilile' melody. *Irkanda IV* also establishes '*malinconia*' as an essential part of Sculthorpe's music, which brings him into the sphere of a long history of melancholic Australian Art. For Ian McLean, melancholy is a feature of the colonial period, which he traces from the art of convict Thomas Watling through 'the psychology of exile, and its two principle motifs, landscape and Aborigines' which 'set the pattern for the dominant themes of Australian art to this day'.[10] Mellers argued that *Irkanda IV* established the essential relationship between Sculthorpe and Europe:

> It is about death in that it is a requiem for his father and for the past his family had stood for, but also in that it is a relinquishment of Europe. Several European ghosts, Bloch and Bartók among them, are laid, while Mahler's threnody for the old world is obliquely recalled. Gradually the outback engulfs the self as the solo violin's chant wavers microtonally[11] between diminished fourths and major and minor seconds, while the string band evokes an eternal solitude by way of telescoped concords, sul tasto and tremolando.[12]

With *Irkanda IV* 'silence' and 'stillness'[13] come to be significant compositional materials, and with them Sculthorpe's melancholy is written in the language of Australian landscape.[14]

The decade after *Irkanda IV* was a prolific time for Sculthorpe. Alongside a series of string quartets, his most significant works in the period to 1975 are the large theatrical work *Rites of Passage* (1972–3), and String Quartet No. 6 (1965), which was commissioned for the Austral Quartet by Musica Viva (they performed the work at the Commonwealth Festival of Arts in England in 1965). String Quartet No. 7 (1966) was commissioned for the Yale Quartet (Sculthorpe was a visiting fellow at Yale), String Quartet No. 8 (1969) was premiered by the Allegri Quartet at the Wigmore Hall and in 1975 String Quartet No. 9, also for the Austral Quartet, was commissioned for their eight-week international tour, alongside Banks's String Quartet (1975). *Sun Music I* was written for performance by the Sydney Symphony Orchestra for the Commonwealth Festival of Arts in England in 1965. *Sun Music III* (1967) was commissioned by the ABC for the West Australian Symphony Orchestra. *Sun Music II* (1969) was for the Sydney Symphony Orchestra's ABC Promenade Concerts, and *Sun Music IV* was commissioned for the Melbourne Symphony Orchestra to perform at the Montreal Expo '67.[15] These works are, therefore, markers of Sculthorpe's international

Example 5.1 Sculthorpe, *Irkanda IV*, bars 1–5.

success,[16] and indicate how connected Australian Music was to other places. They were all composed soon after Sculthorpe began to lecture at the University of Sydney in 1964, and during the first period in which he lived in Sydney. He arrived there at the same time that Butterley returned from the UK, at a time when Meale was increasingly prominent as a composer and performer, and when the International Society for Contemporary Music (ISCM) concerts were supporting new music of all kinds. It was the right time to be in Sydney with an influential post in composition. Before I explain how the ideas in these pieces relate to ideas in literature and painting, it is worth revisiting how these works came to be understood within Sculthorpe's output. This chapter pulls apart the central ideas for considering Sculthorpe's music in the 1960s and early 1970s: music and landscape; isolation, alienation and rejection; 'indigeneity'; and representation. I will do this through the work of Hannan, whose book on Sculthorpe, published in 1982, was essential for the mainstream understanding of Sculthorpe's music that has dominated conceptions of his earlier work since the book's publication, and also through the writings of Roger Covell, whose 1967 book was also crucial for establishing ideas about Sculthorpe and his music.

Reading Sculthorpe through Hannan

Hannan was Sculthorpe's assistant at a time (1969–71) when no other Australian composers had assistants. Hannan's book *Peter Sculthorpe: His Music and Ideas* (1982) was a published version of his PhD thesis, and it therefore marked a change of generation, a change that came very soon after Meale's 'silent' period (which is also the time of Edwards's silent period), after Banks's death, and at a time when composers internationally were reconsidering tonality. In brief, the moment is Sculthorpe's, and he was able to build on his earlier reputation to confirm his position as Australia's best-known composer. Sculthorpe's centrality to discourses about Australian Music emerged gradually in the 1960s and 1970s, and definitively with Hannan's study. Nevertheless, Andrew McCredie, for example, singles out Sculthorpe from Butterley, Dreyfus, Meale, Sitsky and Werder, as 'at present the most frequently performed of Australia's younger generation in overseas centres, [and he] has made perhaps the most widely varying experimentation over a long period of stylistic development. [...] The foundation of this development rests on natural lyrical gifts combined with a sophisticated professionalism.' Like others, McCredie is convinced of Sculthorpe's 'musical intellect', and Sculthorpe is set aside by an 'overt Australianism' not shared by his contemporaries. The other key attribute that McCredie identifies, and for which Hannan provides musical detail, is Sculthorpe's 'ethnomusicological interests in the indigenous music of South East Asia'.[17]

According to Hannan, 'Sculthorpe considers that the diversity in the European landscape and culture is mirrored by the complexity of European art, or more appropriately by the inordinate activity, for it is possible to achieve a great complexity without much diversity or activity.'[18] Complexity without activity is also Hannan's reason for Sculthorpe's interest in 'Asian music', since 'he sees below its surface a complexity which belies the superficial simplicity or seeming monotony'.[19] As an Australian, Sculthorpe has, the argument goes, the ears to hear the subtleties of Javanese music. For Prerauer, Sculthorpe's music exceeded such as had been achieved by Antill's *Corroboree* – which Prerauer argued also 'translated' the landscape into music – because Sculthorpe's was 'absolute music' rather than programmatic ballet.[20] So to begin, it was the abstraction of Sculthorpe's music, rather than any depiction of landscape, which made the music significant.

The particular path to abstract Australianism begins, according to Sculthorpe, or perhaps Hannan, with a crisis of serialism. Sculthorpe had been working with serialism 'without any knowledge of Boulez or even Webern', but having read Krenek's *Studies in Counterpoint* in 1948, which led to 'silence. Besides I had a feeling that this had little to do with myself and that I was handling something quite alien. [...] I began to clutch at the idea of being an Australian most aggressively.'[21] And so there is an 'identity crisis as well as a compositional one', and this relationship between Sculthorpe and his music is a foundational myth of Sculthorpe and Australian Music, which works against the sense of autonomy that might be expected from abstract music.

The work that most clearly demonstrates the serial exercise is *The Loneliness of Bunjil* (1954), a thoroughly quarter-tone work, and Graeme Skinner, following McCredie, accepts the invitation to read the piece as autobiographical – the character of Bunjil 'became lonely', having 'made the world and all things in it except man'[22] – and Sculthorpe is then identified with the 'Great Australian Loneliness'.[23] The Sonatina (1954) is 'a naïve, unsophisticated piece',[24] which makes it Australian, in contrast to European complexity, and made all the more Australian for having been composed in the 'isolation of Tasmania'.[25] Having been written on an island that is isolated from an island that is isolated from Europe, the place of composition itself makes the work a double rejection of European music, if not a rejection of the opportunity that the first performance afforded Sculthorpe, since the piece had its performance at the ISCM festival in Baden-Baden.

The next major change came with the *Sun Music* series, which for Hannan was:

> an attempt to remove his music still further from such European notions as 'motive', 'development of the motive', and, to a large extent, from harmonic progression. [...] The choice of [...] material was designed to purge the music of melody and tonal relationships as much as possible, to eliminate the fulsomeness of its harmonic textures and to create a more impersonal language, but at the same time a language which was capable of evoking emotional associations that were different from those recognizable as being especially European.[26]

Sun Music for Voices and Percussion (1966; originally *Sun Music II*) is pure rhythm, including the voices, which declaim deconstructed texts as unconnected consonants. *Sun Music I* 'has a spaciousness and calmness perhaps brought about by the composer's efforts to evoke the loneliness and the desolation of the Australian landscape'.[27] But it is in *Sun Music II* (1969) that the rhythms take on a new meaning. The piece includes the rhythms of the Balinese *ketjak* (its original title),[28] which was later used in String Quartet No. 8 (String Quartet Music). Its second movement is based on 'Balinese rice-pounding'[29] music (Example 5.2). If the music here does not sound overtly 'Balinese', *Sun Music III* (1967) certainly does. Having read Colin McPhee's *Music in Bali*, Sculthorpe composed *Sun Music III* using both Balinese melodies and gamelan textures (as he also does in *Tabuh Tabuhan* (1968)), and the piece has come to represent Sculthorpe's clearest statement for hearing Australia as a part of Asia.[30]

Music for Japan (1970) goes the other way, being a piece about Australia written for performance in Japan, and although it includes some minor references to Japanese music, the majority of the piece is made up of clusters. This is Sculthorpe at home in the sound-world of European modernism. Hannan considered the work 'an additional *Sun Music* as it exploits the possibilities of orchestral sonorities rather than pitch relationships'[.][31] In Hannan's explication, some of the pitches are organized through 'Nono's all interval row', which makes it different from the other *Sun Music* pieces in practice and in principle; Sculthorpe later wrote that the composition 'evokes Australia's bush and city, desert and ocean. The very last chord is the opening chord of *Irkanda IV* (1961), which for me always recalls images of loneliness and landscape.'[32] (I will return to *Music for Japan* in Chapter 7.)

The challenge of writing about Sculthorpe is to accommodate a diversity of often contradictory positions. He is a Romantic when he invokes Mahler. He is a cosmopolitan modernist when he goes to study with Wellesz and through his involvement with the ISCM. He is a nationalist when he writes *The Fifth Continent*. The resulting collage of ideas enables narratives that shift from piece to piece, or through the same piece as it is reconceived through successive anecdotes, including his own, and by those who have been close to him. However, many of the arguments made for Sculthorpe were first

Example 5.2 '*Ketjak*' in Sculthorpe's String Quartet No. 8, 'II', bars 1–12.

articulated in other fields well before he began composing, and existing descriptions of his work have assembled those ideas in new ways – through Sculthorpe – to describe Australian Music synecdochally.

The discourses about Sculthorpe have tended to conflate the music and the person. In Malcolm Williamson's 1971 article 'How Australian Can Australian Music Become?', he wrote that:

> Sculthorpe has thought out new sound devices from a musical inner prompting. […] Head and heart collaborate in his compositional processes in proper proportion to each other. He stands to upset the cerebral listener on account of his innate romanticism, or the romantic listener on account of his cerebral brilliance, but it is a whole music, adult and integrated.[33]

Sculthorpe and his music are central to current ideas of Australian Music. In the following example, Skinner describes the 1954 Sonatina for Piano, setting out Australian Music's essential ideas of Australian landscape:

> Though coming after his serial crises, it was still self-consciously an exercise in modernism, and – the 'European Australian landscape' of his Nocturnes, Seascapes, Sketches and Reveries notwithstanding – an attempt at evoking

Australian landscape. The narrative structure he chose [...] was also strikingly new, following a journey described in a real, if repackaged, Aboriginal legend, 'The Adventurous Journey of Yoonecara, the Head Man', from W. E. Thomson's *Some Myths and Legends of the Australian Aborigines* (1923).[34]

The serial crisis is a personal crisis for Sculthorpe as a (belated) Romantic, the 'exercise in modernism' operates at a distance (and is, therefore, a modernist study of modernism) and the 'Aboriginal legend' is commodified and 'repackaged' for trade. Such glosses as Skinner's reflect a flexibility of discourse through which Sculthorpe's music moves. Sculthorpe encouraged such readings, and his work and the discourses around it tend to smooth over the edges of problems that for other composers (Meale, Lumsdaine) are their music's vitality.

Sculthorpe, centred by a range of such narratives, has come to be the culmination of the modernist phase of Australian Music. Meale's move away from modernism was difficult and produced a significant stylistic and technical break, dividing his earlier music from the more obviously tonal works of the 1980s, but his earlier music retained its reputation as uncompromising. Sculthorpe's music slowly evolved, and it/he symbolized the compressed but direct journey through 1950s and 1960s modernism to an unequivocally nationalist music, the swiftness of the journey made possible because it was 'late', and the directness of the journey created through his success. The broad question that arises is: how can Sculthorpe's contribution to Australian Music in its modernist phase be better considered historically and geographically? In other words, what happens if one approaches the period in a way that does not presuppose his centrality to Australian Music? More specifically, finding equivocality in his music can form an important counterweight to the ideas of progress on which coherent conceptions of nationalism rely. Did Sculthorpe give institutional legitimization to the earlier arguments, aestheticizing them in new ways for a middlebrow audience that was increasingly unconcerned with the politics of progress?[35]

Reading Sculthorpe through Covell

Of the academics who wrote about Sculthorpe, it was Covell who most clearly forwarded a nationalist vision, defined by 'the lack' left by the expansion and contraction of Europe:

> As a result of the expansion of European settlement to all continents of the world, the situation has developed in which a considerable part of the world's population of European stock is existing, and creating art, within a transplanted and more or less subsidiary culture.[36]

Not only is Australian culture defined by the absence of a long history, but even the history of its settlement is defined by a lack of history:

> Had Australia been settled two centuries earlier than it was, a familiar pattern of musical evolution might have repeated itself. The traditional songs the settlers

brought with them would have come from a stronger, richer folk tradition instead of from a partially or wholly deracinated industrial society.[37]

As such, for Covell it is the lack of the 'isolation' necessary to develop a distinctive nationalism that is Australia's founding problem, and its peculiar nationalism is defined in negative terms. And so for Covell the musical problem with Australia's colonial period is that the settlers 'came from countries whose trained musicians had adopted a second-hand variant of central European musical culture', and that that culture was ill-suited 'to understand what the Aborigines were about in their music'.[38] The British are dismissed, therefore, as amateurs, lacking proper historical awareness, and Australian music is given a middlebrow history, as well as a post-industrial one. In other words, the belatedness that defines Australian Music is itself a belated version of Britain's belated music.

Covell departed from many of his contemporaries in noting that Australia's landscape is, in fact, far from silent, and he reversed the 'empty and quiet' discourse, since the country's birds are 'as capable of brilliant and beautiful melodic flights as their European counterparts'.[39] Australia's nature also lends itself to 'an effect not unlike an early study in the sonorities of *musique concrète*',[40] which might, Covell suggests, mean that 'Australia will become one of the first nations to discover its own characteristics in sound through the musical possibilities of the tape-recorder or, in other words, through that organization of naturally occurring sounds characteristic of *musique concrète*'.[41] Australia by nature already sounds modernist, which is why, in this period, the music that represents landscapes is already modernist, too. Australian Music therefore had the potential to be modernist before Europe, in a configuration of space and history that inverts the directionality of belatedness, so long as the music sounds like the landscape. For example, when Sculthorpe collaborated with David Matthews for the film *Manganinnie*, Matthews wrote 'Schubertian' lyricism to represent the 'so-called civilised world' and Sculthorpe wrote 'Manganinnie's music [...] for solo cello and, in order to mirror the landscape, I also wrote music for string quartet'. Their collaboration came together with 'some *musique concrète*, suggesting Aboriginal spirit voices'.[42]

This general argument regarding modernity is described by David Carter:

> Let me attempt to describe the recurrent form of this argument as concisely as possible. It is to claim that Australia has always already been what European or American culture has only recently discovered as its own modernity. What emerges in the metropolis as a new philosophical or art movement [...] is defined in Australia as the *Australian* condition. The aesthetic or the epochal is rewritten as the very essence of Australia. [...] Australia is not modern by the sophistication of its high culture, by its intellectual or aesthetic avant-gardes. If anything, the absence of these cultural structures is the first principle of the argument. Emphasis falls instead on what we might call the *pre*-cultural, even the pre-historical: nature, environment, landscape.[43]

For Carter the argument involves a paradox, since it 'proclaims Australia's modernity and lack of modernity in one breath', and this enables its recurrence, since it is a '*type* of argument'.⁴⁴ This argument runs parallel to the argument of belatedness put forward by Werder, quoted at the end of Chapter 3, and the 'coming-of-age' narrative put forward by Murdoch, quoted in Chapter 2. The argument of belatedness is itself late – repeating colonial discourses that in other fields such as literature had been criticized some decades earlier, and late, too, is the repetition of Romantic notions of cultural evolution. All that lateness makes belatedness an inescapable way of describing Australian culture, even – perhaps especially – when it is about an era too late for it properly to apply, since lateness makes it *Australian*, rather than passé.

When Covell came to Sculthorpe in particular, rather than Australian Music in general, he faced a problem, since he was keen to read Sculthorpe as exceptional, outside the wider discourses of Australian Music that describe Sculthorpe's contemporaries. Covell did so through the inscription in the preface to *The Loneliness of Bunjil*, which he quoted as follows: 'In the beginning, Bunjil, the Great Spirit, created the world and all things in it, except man … he became lonely.'⁴⁵ This is similar to the given meaning of *Irkanda* (the title to a sequence of pieces) as 'an Australian Aboriginal word meaning "a remote and lonely place"'. At the same time, Sculthorpe's use of 'Aboriginal titles and Australian-oriented subject matter provide no guarantee of recognisability in music'.⁴⁶ Covell nevertheless argued that:

> Sculthorpe does seem – and the impression, of course, must be subjective – to convey in satisfactory and often moving musical terms the loneliness and sadness induced in many sensitive observers by some of the typical elements of Australian landscape. Whether the loneliness and haunted melancholy are specifically Australian in music is impossible of proof; all that matters is that the music should make its own way in a purely musical context.⁴⁷

To be isolated is to be Australian, with Sculthorpe as the sole composer of the topic. Culturally this places Sculthorpe with other modernist writers of alienation and isolation, through for Covell it is more significant that Sculthorpe is isolated than that he is grouped with other isolated artists. In Covell's argument, the music that is representative of the Australian landscape is abstract ('purely musical') and distant from the work of other composers. Sculthorpe's special status, or his music's special status – the two are the same because '[o]f all younger contemporary composers in Australia Sculthorpe speaks [musically, that is] with the most personal voice'⁴⁸ – transcends the problem of representation of landscape by transcending subjectivity. (Conversely, the requirement for transcendence here guarantees Sculthorpe a special place.) And with this accomplished, the 'shared emotional experience' of Australia itself is Sculthorpe's to write, free from the contextual and subjective problems that arise in the voice (musical or otherwise) of other composers. Covell mobilizes Romanticism to solve the problem of bringing together the individual and the national: through Sculthorpe's *will* pure music and elemental Australia are transcended. For the first time Sculthorpe, and Sculthorpe alone, *is* Australian Music. The result is that Sculthorpe is positioned as exceptional through several (competing) narratives, each of which constructs him as simultaneously central and outside (outside the discourse for the others, who are less exceptional).[49] In an interview with Hannan published in 1974, Sculthorpe described the extent of the alienation idea: 'My theme, in almost all my music, is man's alone-ness, the solitary figure in the landscape. I'm Australian; it's as simple as that.'[50] Such ideas were the currency of many of the artists of the time, of which Francis Webb's *Eyre All Alone* (1961) is exemplary.[51] As I will explain more fully below, the 'lonely' discourse is also significant due to its impossibility, and in the musical exchanges that draw together Sculthorpe and listeners, performers and other composers, their very collectivity in the face of 'alone-ness' expresses the desire for sociability (of which nationalism is one manifestation).[52]

Music and Landscape Painting

The British composer David Matthews's essay *Landscape into Sound* might well have been titled 'Landscape Painting into Sound', and his short book is richly illustrated with images of paintings by Turner, Lorraine, Kandinsky, Collins, Bocklin, Mondrian, Friedrich, Titian and Schoenberg. Many are paintings of landscapes, and their meaning is symbolic:

> The most appropriate symbols of infinity in nature are mountains, forests and the sea, and for the British the sea is the most potent of these.[53]

Matthews and Sculthorpe first met in 1971 when Sculthorpe was living in Glynde, Sussex, and when Matthews was working for Faber Music. In 1974 Matthews worked as Sculthorpe's assistant in Sydney.[54] Roger Scruton, writing about Matthews's music, casts his work as 'right out of the pastoral tradition', a composer of landscapes after Vaughan Williams. Scruton considers Matthews a wanderer who 'has been profoundly affected by the landscape of Australia',[55] specifically heard through the music of Sculthorpe. In Sculthorpe's own contribution to *David Matthews: Essays, Tributes and Criticisms*, almost all the anecdotes that Sculthorpe tells are of Matthews's encounter with Australia in colonial terms, of the writing of Kipling and Lawrence and the architecture of the Georgians and Victorians, as well as the modernist (and otherwise) writings of T. S. Eliot, Rupert Brooke and T. E. Hulme. Sculthorpe explains the understanding of places and cultures that he shared with Matthews. Although he hints that the 'savage ... rhythmic resource' of Matthews's second String Quartet must surely have come from his writing of it in Australia, Matthews composed it on Sculthorpe's 'back veranda' in Woollahra, which is Sydney at its most genteel. And, as Sculthorpe confesses, when he drove Matthews to the bush, 'I'd probably stay in the car', letting Matthews roam on foot. Sculthorpe writes that '[b]oth Ross [Edwards] and I had long satisfied our curiosity about the bush'.[56]

In his essay, Matthews writes about the Australian painters Russell Drysdale, Fred Williams, Sidney Nolan and Arthur Boyd as 'those painters whom Peter [Fuller] singled out as having achieved a redemptive vision of contemporary landscape',[57] and there *is* something redemptive, if utterly prosaic, about the image of Sculthorpe in his car while Matthews walks in the bush. The significance of the idea of redemption here is that it works against earlier readings of Australian landscapes as 'savage'. For Sculthorpe the bush was something to which one could drive – 'the bush' is somewhere visited rather than somewhere without people. (These landscapes are a world away from the Danish landscapes around Carl Nielsen. Daniel Grimley describes Lundbye's landscapes as possessing 'a sense of edginess: the preferences for long, flat horizons, gentle hills, fields, hedges, and seascapes' as 'an attempt to render the Danish landscape scenically within a broader romantic tradition of prospect and melancholic contemplation'.[58] Many of the ways in which Grimley characterizes Danish nineteenth-century painting are similar to the way that Australian modernist painting is often described – 'their tendency towards abstraction', 'a geometrical play of lines, colour planes, and textures'.[59] Grimley argues that, for Nielson, 'Ploughing effectively becomes a form of writing or inscription, of tracing a line through the earth. But this mark is one that can readily be erased or reploughed.'[60] Such cannot be said of the capacity of Australian landscapes. It is against such metaphors of fecundity that Australia's landscapes are considered barren and unchanging, a conception forged by those who sought to use European farming technologies and failed in the process.) At the same time that Sculthorpe's individualism is declared through the redemptive moment in the bush, so too is Sculthorpe's Antipodean status; Matthews no doubt identified, through Britten, the redemptive attitude Sculthorpe derived from Mahler.

In this relation to the bush, the difference between Sculthorpe and Lumsdaine is most apparent. For Lumsdaine nature is lived and present, provoking endless curiosity, where for Sculthorpe nature is visited, elsewhere, at another time, and his curiosity is readily sated.[61] Unlike Matthews, for whom changing understandings of the violence of English landscapes alter their significance,[62] Sculthorpe's bush is relatively static: ready to be depicted, rather than a resource for ongoing exploration. In this sense it is part of the new vision of Australia, since a savage landscape is an active one, savaging the land's inhabitants (trees, birds, people).

Sculthorpe's most iconic response to landscape is conveyed in the anecdote that describes the genesis of *Irkanda I* (1955), 'for violin alone':[63]

> [W]hen I wrote *Irkanda I* for solo violin, I was living in Canberra, working at the Playhouse there. And I certainly thought that I would trace the 360 degree graph of the landscape around me, and then write music that followed the contour of the landscape. And so that is exactly what happened.[64]

Hannan compares *Irkanda I* with the *Sonata for Violin Alone* (1954–5) and with a melody from Mahler's *Das Lied von der Erde*,[65] showing Sculthorpe's response to Mahler's 'extensive use of appoggiatura', but the comparison relies on the not insignificant difference between Mahler – 'who uses the gamut of chromatic triadic harmony as the framework for melodic appoggiatura' – and Sculthorpe – whose framework is 'limited to one chord'; and so not only is there no synthesis between Sculthorpe and Mahler, there is no dialogue with nature that the birdsong in Mahler's music sometimes symbolizes.[66] Mahler the modernist does not play a role in Sculthorpe's music, and Mahler stands in Sculthorpe's music for melancholic high Romanticism.[67] At the same time, if the 'vehicle for the expression of the Subject in Mahler is the traditional but exhausted one of Romantic melody',[68] then Sculthorpe's tracing of Canberra's mountains, or the borrowing of an Aboriginal melody, might be understood as a search for a new and viable subject. Sculthorpe later (1964) described the melodic material in the Sonata for Viola and Percussion as 'a yearning Mahler-like melody', in contrast to the work's 'architectonic blocks', but the 'two ideas simply alternate with each other: there's no attempt to bring them into synthesis',[69] which is a description that is apt for much of Sculthorpe's music's formal construction in this early period. In *Irkanda I*, the *Sonata for Violin Alone*, and the later String Quartet No. 7 (1966), for example, there is no internal transformation of material. There is scarcely any external transformation of material either, and the multiple works share strikingly similar ideas. Skinner's account of the reuse of ideas tends to consider them as pragmatic solutions to close deadlines. As ossifying processes they support the picture of Sculthorpe in a desiccated landscape. In his music of the 1960s the essential Australian landscape is a flat desert, the line of melody approaches a drone, and the composer becomes the only possible subject. Rather than being a statement about landscape, for Sculthorpe landscape offers only one figure, that of the artist, as environment gives way to his perspective. But one needs no redemption from geometry.

It has been easy to consider *Irkanda I* as an attempt at a musical depiction of landscape in a realist manner, but Sculthorpe's anecdote about its melody is remarkably similar to the following anecdote by Stockhausen (speaking in 1971), also about the composition of a work in 1955:

> I had a little room in Switzerland for three months, and there was a small window in front of my desk through which I could see the incredible shapes of the mountains on the other side of the valley. There are quite a few groups in *Gruppen* which follow exactly the shape of these mountains: I became quite expert in drawing outlines during that time.[70]

Stockhausen's *Gruppen* is one of the monuments of postwar modernism;[71] and, following its example, Sculthorpe's treatment of Canberra is not straightforwardly realist,[72] nor especially Australian. The radical simplification of a place (austere, remote and almost silent, save the sound of a few birds[73]) considers the landscape as a line, one-dimensional, melodic. Insofar as modernist painters transformed landscape into line, Stockhausen's tracing of landscape belongs to the tradition of the sonic translation of visual ideas. This has nothing to do with the appoggiatura-filled melodies that Sculthorpe identifies in Mahler. Nevertheless, with his anecdote about *Irkanda*'s composition, Sculthorpe rethinks earlier oppositions of 'urban' and 'remote'. Canberra is Australia's only planned city, and is 'the Bush Capital',[74] and therefore 'the bush' at its most populated: the almost outback made thoroughly urban, with looping roads for swift travel, insulating the explorer from discovery. The remote, made populated.

Sculthorpe's definition of *Irkanda*'s title emerges in fragments over several decades. On BBC Radio in 1960 he gave the title's definition as 'the name of the huge silent scrub-country of Central Australia',[75] which he later revised to the even less particular 'remote and lonely place'. In these early accounts of the work's creation Sculthorpe constructs *Irkanda I* as 'detached' from any particular place, and his use of the indigenous word of its title is taken from a specific language from one area of Australia and applied to an abstract, unvisited, uninhabited 'remote Central Australia'. So, although the anecdote about tracing the hills around Canberra claims a new way of conceiving Australian landscape (in general), it also makes claims to this being the realistic way of hearing a place (the place where Sculthorpe was living and working). It does so more through a series of abstract transformations of ideas of realist art than it does of a particular landscape, or a specific experience of Australia, or of hearing a precise place.[76]

Writing about *Art in Australia*'s 1926 issue 'A New Vision of Australian Landscape', Carter contrasts the 'Australian landscape translated "into the curt speech of the present day"', new, modern, and contemporary, with a 'logic' that is 'ultimately realist, for the Australian landscape "lends itself to a simpler, harder treatment. It is severe in form and outline"'.[77] In Australian landscape painting one finds planes of colour for plains of land, and with these planes/plains the Australian landscape is flattened. This comes from a reductionist approach to a flatness of contour and new approaches to colour and light. From the perspective of landscape painting, Sculthorpe writes 'landscape music' in a modern movement of experimenting with colour, with planes of colour, and of the rejection of draughtsmanship and academicism. (In this sense he also writes against Prime Minister Robert Menzies's desire for morally uplifting academic pastoral landscape art.[78]) This music has less to do with particular places, and more to do with landscape *painting*. In arguments about Sculthorpe the phrase 'Australian Music and Landscape' is perhaps better considered as containing a significant elision of its full form: 'Australian Music and Landscape Painting'. His landscape pieces are not detailed and contoured depictions, but modern responses to the new forms of art that were trying to come to terms with what it meant (and indeed, whether it meant anything) to depict Australia.

There is a long history to Sculthorpe's conception of landscape. The early twentieth-century, postcolonial Australia is described by Carter as follows:

> The landscape is no longer prehistoric but once again its unconventionality, its difference, can only be apprehended through the otherness of modernity. Once again it is nature not culture, not history but a lack of history, which is figured in terms of the modern. The colonial figure of belatedness is reversed – but at what cost? In a sense [...] at the cost of history, which might be why we are condemned to repeat the argument.[79]

In Carter's argument modernity was 'not English but weird or unconventional American or Continental. Precisely because of the colonial relation no English modernity can be visible: modernity was anti-English.'[80] Although for the composers of the 1960s and 1970s this is no longer such a clear-cut case, their use of Asian music functions similarly by being not only not English, but also not North American and not European. At the same time, the Asian music to which Sculthorpe refers is far from simple exoticism, and he is sometimes – if not always – careful to distinguish particular melodies, for example. In other words, the conception of landscape has a long history, but the argument had moved on by the time of Sculthorpe's work, and the reversal that Carter finds in the early postcolonial situation no longer adequately describes the later composers, for whom a more fragmented situation exists, and in which culture and nature are no longer opposed, since one drives to/through the bush.[81] Certainly, when considering Sculthorpe's music, the sense of Asian music as 'other' ought not be considered his attempt to escape from the moral complexities of the time and place in which he lived and worked.

For Sculthorpe, the Australian landscape is bright and flat. Such a landscape comes from landscape painting. In Australia, modernist thinking about landscape was dominated by painting more than by photography, and the flatness of the horizon's contour was rendered through blocks of colour, at a time when photography was still limited to black and white. Sidney Nolan's paintings contrast red earth and blue sky, and in Drysdale's paintings the sky, too, is red, as if the landscape itself, even with its flat horizon, dominated by light, also fills the sky. Nolan commented 'I gradually forgot all about Picasso, Klee and Paris ... and became attached to light.'[82] The literary scholars Bill Ashcroft and John Salter argue that the idea of landscape is itself built on 'concerns that had persisted since the nineteenth century', and the Ned Kelly series – Nolan's most significant 'landscape' works – make 'representation itself' the 'subject of this painting'. Nolan 'appropriates "modern" forms of representation and disrupts them'.[83] Gaile McGregor argues that Drysdale's 'stickmen' figures depict 'humanity damaged by its transactions', and his art has 'to do with the relations *between* individuals. This is a world, as well, in which, ultimately, everyone is alone.'[84] I will return to these ideas about landscape painting, and Sculthorpe's music, in Chapter 7.

Isolation, Alienation and Rejection

Sculthorpe's music is far more rooted in the arguments about Australian nationalism and modernism than other composers of his generation, and also more closely connected to the history of Australian colonization and postcolonial art. The scholar Ian McLean has used the idea of 'White Aborigines' to help explain Australia's twentieth-century art. For him, the work of the artist Margaret Preston and the anthropologist A. P. Elkin, as modernists who looked to 'Aboriginal art [as] the source for a distinctive Australian identity', combines with the contrasting approach of Patrick White, Russell Drysdale and P. R. Stephenson, for whom the 'very alienation of Aborigines made them exemplary Australians'.[85] For McLean, 'Aborigines are emblems of alienation',[86] a conception conditioned by British colonialization. In Australian Music, discourses of landscape became the place in which the colonial ideas continued to play out, and the 'indigenous' new music that Covell and others imagined is just that, imagined rather than realized: 'There is no redemptive moment. The possibilities of convergence are only imagined.'[87] For McLean 'Russell Drysdale's paintings [...] picture the "white blackfellow" that characterised mid twentieth-century Australian national identity, hence making his images the most emblematic of the so-called "Australian-type".[88] Sculthorpe placed himself as something like this figure in his description of waiting for Matthews, sitting in the car, alone, 'satisfied' in his 'curiosity about the bush'. No exploration was necessary, since Sculthorpe was already of this place. Nevertheless, Sculthorpe did not wholly reject British perspectives of Australia, since he was sympathetic to D. H. Lawrence's writing about the country, using Lawrence's texts in his 1960 song-cycle *Sun*,[89] and the *Sun Music* cycle.[90] According to Skinner, in the planning for *The Fifth Continent* Sculthorpe wrote to the Prerauers: 'I wish that I could have found a book by an Australian ... but Lawrence moves me to music.'[91] The end of *Irkanda IV* includes material from the song he wrote to Lawrence's 'Desires Goes Down into the Sea'.[92] Skinner rightly associates Sculthorpe's time in Oxford (where he had read *Kangaroo*, at Mellers's suggestion) in Lawrence's terms, but in reverse, with Sculthorpe longing for the Australian sun.[93] The gesture is of modernist alienation from a centre of the academic world, and a return to the place of pure alienation, the composer alone, under the sun, with the personal alienation of the artist aligning with the alienation of the continent. At the same time, the gesture rejects Oxfordian academicism, and casts it as peripheral to Australia (and, for that matter, to the English countryside around Glynde, where Sculthorpe later lived briefly).

The cycle that used Lawrence's poem 'The Sun in Me' was written for Wilfrid and Peggy Mellers. The 'eternal solitude' that Mellers, writing about *Irkanda IV*, identified with Australia is a colonial one that views the centre of Australia as empty of 'selves', 'engulfed' by the land itself, a preserved space of absolute otherness;[94] for McLean such discourses are of a type in which 'the creation of oceans was not stopped, as if once having successfully crossed the Ocean, the European invaders had to preserve a space of absolute otherness within the continent'.[95] The poem of Lawrence's that Sculthorpe uses is a good example of the trope: 'A sun will rise in me, / I shall slowly resurrect, / already the whiteness of false dawn is on my inner / ocean.'[96] The ongoing creation of oceans is a process that means that 'Australian culture constructs within its very centre an absolute alterity that stubbornly refuses [...] idealised border exchanges as redemptive spaces. In their refusal, in their stubborn antipodiality, Australians preserve their origins as Europeans. To be an Antipodean in Australia is to be a European.'[97] On one hand *Irkanda IV* performs the redemption of a border crossing that refuses the Antipodean position. And on the other hand, as Sculthorpe later wrote: it 'is expressionistic and full of yearning, a yearning, perhaps, for the civilisations of the Western world'.[98]

The early criticism of *The Fifth Continent* (1963) also connected the work with Drysdale.[99] In 1963 Sculthorpe wrote that: 'Tas [i.e. Drysdale] was a role model ... I admired his approach to craft, the way he used layers of paint to come up with the right colour and texture. I also admired the way he worked and reworked his material.'[100] Sculthorpe was clearly impressed with Drysdale himself, including his approach to embodying the nationalist ideal. At least as significant as Sculthorpe's responses to musical modernism are his relationships to artists such as Drysdale, which connect him to ongoing debate about Australian nationalism very differently to Lumsdaine or Banks. The 1965 String Quartet No. 6, for example, was composed in Drysdale's presence,[101] and the two artists spent much time together, especially in the early 1960s, the period in which Sculthorpe's nationalism matured.

For Mellers, Sculthorpe's music could be likened to 'the obsession with emptiness in the works of Drysdale, Nolan and White [which] implies an Asiatic immobility, rather than a concern with consciousness and the will. The new generation of Australian composers seems to be bypassing the Bartókian phase of personal and national consciousness.'[102] Sculthorpe's non-developmental treatment of immobile landscapes attempted to escape the pastoral landscapes of Britain. As Bernard Smith argues, the 'parched, harsh inland [is] the antithesis of pastoral prosperity'. And yet such landscapes 'remained [in the visual arts], until the 1940s, a land without people or visible signs of the twentieth century, thus retaining the feeling of purity of the landscape. In terms of pictorial organization it resembles the pastoral image with its shallow space, its unified and specific structure.'[103] Sculthorpe's musical simplification of forms repeats the visual depiction of the landscape as pastoral. We ought not to move too quickly from flat musical geometries, to Australian landscapes, to Lawrence, since for Lawrence 'the landscape is so unimpressive, like a face with little or no features, a dark face'.[104] Sculthorpe's musical structures are more sophisticated than the rhetoric claims, and Lawrence's equation of the featureless landscape with the 'dark face' in *Kangaroo* demonstrates the limits imposed by the colonial perspective, which are limits of seeing.[105] Although Sculthorpe's individual sections within individual pieces might be described in simple terms, these sections never last more than a minute or two, and the totality of Sculthorpe's 'landscape music' is far from featureless. If Drysdale's nationalism is figurative, Sculthorpe's music is not a neat translation of this into music, since even if the figure one encounters is Sculthorpe himself, the constant reworking of pieces into new compositions presents a highly fluid figure, one who often moves away from earlier themes into new areas. Nor is it a mimetic transformation of landscape into sound, and certainly not representation in Lawrence's terms.

Indigeneity

Jonathan Paget's article 'Has Sculthorpe Misappropriated Indigenous Melodies?' argues that 'it is unavoidable to conclude that, to some extent, Sculthorpe's identification with Aboriginality perpetuates his position at the spiritual heart of Australian musical composition'.[106] Paget focusses on Sculthorpe's later work, though he also refers to the earlier 'Jindyworobak' movement in literature in connection with Sculthorpe's music.[107] The Jindyworobak movement was the most prominent artistic group of the 1930s and 1940s, which sought to include what it saw as Aboriginal ideas about Australia in art. As Paget understands it, through Covell's interpretation:

> 'Jindyworobak' is an Aboriginal word meaning annexing or joining, and its application to western literature implied a cultural renewal through the absorption of Aboriginal culture. As Covell described in his book *Australia's Music*, the

Jindyworobak movement aimed 'to seek a closer identification with the Australian landscape through Aboriginal traditions and even through borrowings from the languages of the Aborigines'. As Covell points out, the borrowing was 'basically a longed-for "short-cut" to cultural maturity and national identity'.[108]

Paget's focus is on Sculthorpe's music after the period with which I am concerned, and although some of the composer's titles, such as *Irkanda* or *Bunjil*, fit the movement's use of Aboriginal terms, his music makes greater use of Aboriginal melodies after 1974, especially in works from the late 1980s such as *Djilile* (1986), *Earth Cry* (1986) and *Kakadu* (1988).[109]

Mostly conceived as naïve nationalists, the Jindyworobaks have been reconsidered for their role in Australian modernism by Ellen Smith. For her, they were 'a nationalist poetry movement, invested in local literary communities and the poetics of place',[110] and she identifies two competing positions for their work. One position, held by the poet Max Harris, opposes 'metropolitan modernism, cosmopolitanism, international culture, the elite, the avant-garde, and the contemporary' against 'national literature, jingoism, provincialism, backwardness, and a dependent and derivative mentality'.[111] Another position, held by poet Victor Kennedy, 'suggests that a kind of modernity might inhere in the circulation of provincial, local, and national cultures'.[112] Smith argues that 'the period from the late 1930s through the mid-century sees modernist energies redirected away from the transnational and cosmopolitan towards landscape and the consolidated local'. This 'begins to break down the structure of oppositions that Max Harris works within and moves towards a pluralised modernism that is as deeply invested in the American small town (Faulkner) or the English pageant play (Woolf) as it is in the hybrid and cosmopolitan forms associated with high modernist texts like Pound's *The Cantos* or the Eliot's *The Waste Land*'.[113] As such, 'the Jindyworobak movement provides a new formulation of the relationship between the local and the modern'.[114] There is no Covellian 'short-cut' here, and in connection with the Jindyworobak movement Sculthorpe's music is better read as part of the musical response to nationalism at a time when localism, nationalism and cosmopolitanism were rapidly shifting in meaning, along with the changing organizations and the politics of the 1960s. Most significantly for Sculthorpe studies, then, is that the Jindyworobaks tried to find a 'language [that] might fully inhabit its subject', and the use of Aboriginal words was, in Ingamells's manifesto for the movement, 'to express something of the Australian place spirit which baffles expression in English words'.[115] This returns us to the landscape topic. Smith rightly criticizes the collapsing of language and landscape in the quest for a distinctively Australian idiom: 'the bearer of national destiny remembers German and English romantic nationalism'.[116] Such romanticism played a significant part in Sculthorpe's time studying in Melbourne in the 1950s, as Skinner argues:

> He later said that during his five years on the mainland [that is, away from Tasmania] he had become 'acquainted with a different landscape', not only physical but musical, explored first via Mahler and Delius, and later through Bartók and Ernst Bloch: 'I equated Bloch's biblical wilderness with the Australian wilderness and loneliness'.[117]

David Symons, in 'The Jindyworobak Connection in Australian Music, c.1940–1960',[118] quotes Sculthorpe as follows:

> While Jim Penberthy and I were well-aware [sic] of the Jindy movement, and shared many of the ideals, we did not feel part of it. In those times, there was something of a chasm between music and the other arts.[119]

Symons explores the difficulties of connecting the literary movement to composers, including Sculthorpe. Nevertheless the movement is one of the most prominent in the era of Sculthorpe's musical development; the arguments of Smith and others provide ample evidence of discourses of Australian modernism aside from those viewing it as derivative, and she follows Ingamells's argument to explain the paradox of the Jindyworobak's 'somewhat counterintuitive' idea that 'internationalism is attained by focusing on the local and parochial rather than by reaching out to the world'.[120] The role of Jindyworobakism in Sculthorpe's music is therefore audible in its resistance of 'wishy-washy pastoralism'.[121]

Whatever his relationship with 'the Jindy movement', Sculthorpe did have an ongoing interest in Aboriginal music, and in the period before the mid-1970s at least, this interest was connected to landscape and landscape painting. In a 1974 discussion with Sculthorpe about *Rites of Passage*, Hannan suggested:

> you reject the heroics and the despair of humanistic endeavor,

with which Sculthorpe agreed:

> Yes ... as it is certainly because the importance of ritual to man is most strongly manifested in primitive cultures that I have used poems from the Australian Aranda tribe. It is not only that the feeling one gets from the Australian landscape is permeated with the primeval religious presence of the aboriginals, and also the fact that the imagery of their ritual poems is, of course, related to the natural history of Australia, but also that their rituals are archetypal.[122]

The topics of 'landscape' and of 'aboriginality' are totally conflated, in that Aboriginal art is synonymous with 'Australian landscape' as that landscape is synonymous with 'the natural history of Australia', whilst that history is totally separate, at least implicitly, from the 'non-primitive' cultures that work with 'archetypes', the art of primitivist modernism. The choice of the Aranda language is 'because it sounds very like English as spoken by Australians; certainly, it is as much part of our country as the rocks of the desert'.[123] Hannan attributed the Australian accent, as so many others did, to the 'almost closed mouth' needed to keep out the sun and wind.[124] In *Peter Sculthorpe: His Music and Ideas (1929–1979)*, Hannan explained Sculthorpe's 'rejection of European music' through Sculthorpe's interest in what Hannan referred to as 'the monotonous repetition' of Aboriginal music, and the 'feeling of a constant tonal centre. For Sculthorpe these aspects of the music represented the flatness and the sameness of the Australian landscape' and therefore the 'flatness of Aboriginal music and speech and the flat quality of the English language as spoken by Australians' are a direct result of 'the flatness of the country'.[125] The Aranda language[126] came with a rich modernist heritage of abstraction, having been used by Tristan Tzara in his *Poèmes Nègres* (1917), which he based on transcriptions published by Carl Strehlow.[127] These poems abstract the sound of the language in multiple translations. For Ann Stephen, 'Tzara saw how a literalness that bordered on abstraction arose when the meanings of the Aboriginal words were rubbed between two foreign tongues.'[128] And she reminds us of the 1920 Dada manifesto, in which Tzara wrote that 'thought is made in the mouth'.[129]

Sculthorpe's first use of an Aboriginal melody and text is in *The Song of Tailitnama*, a piece written for the film *Sun Music for Film*, a documentary about Sculthorpe's music, and dedicated to Matthews. *The Song of Tailitnama* combines the 'Groote Eylandt Melody' as transcribed by Trevor Jones (recorded by Elkin on the Dutch-named island off the coast of Arnhem Land),[130] the 'Northern Aranda' poem that gives the composition its title, as transcribed by T. G. H. Strehlow (from central Australia), the Japanese 'Etenraku' melody[131] and the Japanese *hirajoshi* scale.[132] The instrumentation (high voice, six cellos, percussion) is from Heitor Villa-Lobos's *Bachianas Brasilieras*, the fifth of which gives Sculthorpe's work its opening vocalise.[133] The 'Groote Eylandt Melody' was also published in Covell's book,[134] in which the author argued that:

> the value of Aboriginal music as a source for Australian composers will not lie in direct imitation but in the assimilation of those elements of it – notably of rhythm, scale structure and microtonal intervals – which seem to explore territories of music relatively untouched by the standard varieties of European music. The first requisite of creative accessibility of this kind is that the music of the Aborigines must be scientifically and accurately recorded.[135]

As before, for Covell this might be compared with the English experience: 'The exploration of sixteenth century polyphony, coupled with research into the then neglected territory of English folk song, helped Vaughan Williams to discover a convincing personal synthesis of musical style at a time when it was very difficult for an English composer to escape from wholesale imitation of the dominant German traditions of the previous century.'[136] Similarly, the influence of 'Asian traditions in music on Western composers will continue to grow and that this will have exceptional importance for a country of Australia's Asia-fringed geographical situation'.[137] Such may not have been Sculthorpe's thinking, and Paget makes the point that 'the composer's note to *The Song of Tailitnama* does not explicitly mention that an Aboriginal melody has been adapted. It would appear that Sculthorpe himself was more reticent to present this melody as being Indigenous in origin than was Hannan, his eager disciple.'[138] Nevertheless, Sculthorpe came to adopt a similar attitude to Hannan, in print, at least: 'Usually, I employ Japanese aesthetic and musical ideas when they're related to my own, or when they can be easily incorporated into my musical language. [...] The actual sound of the work, however, doesn't suggest anything Japanese.'[139] In his discussion of the work, Sculthorpe differentiated between his earlier and later music, and the change of period that occured in approximately 1974: 'Unlike some of my more recent pieces, however, I didn't quote the chant directly: it's considerably reworked. In my reworking, I noticed that, with a few intervals added, the pitches of the melody formed the Japanese *hirajoshi* scale. Almost hidden in the last part of the work, the scale appears exactly as it does in gagaku. I like this coming together of two ancient musics.'[140] The music might not sound 'Japanese', but its interlocking rhythms are reminiscent of both Jones's transcription of the didjeridu in the 'Groote Eylandt Melody' and *String Quartet Music*'s (1968) rhythmic mobiles (the 'rice-pounding' music), just as *The Song of Tailitnama*'s opening expanses of secure modal material is a simplification of *String Quartet Music*'s opening *con dolore*. *String Quartet Music* (later String Quartet No. 8) is 'a resolution of all the influences of the Balinese music' that Sculthorpe had been exploring,[141] but *String Quartet Music* is also, as Skinner argues, a development of Sculthorpe's pre-Balinese music, such as String Quartet No. 6, which was 'a summing up of my Irkanda period'.[142] This does suggest a sense of continuity not just across several works, but across cultural references that might otherwise seem incompatible.

The opening of *The Song of Tailitnama* is also similar to Sculthorpe's *Music for Japan* (1970): they are both unmistakably on E, with the E drones in the double bass supporting evolving clusters. The distance between those works is indicative of the change in Sculthorpe's relationship with modernist ideas, for *Music for Japan* is much more overtly part of the modernist aesthetics of slowly evolving pitch-clusters. *Music from Japan* was composed for 'Expo '70', which was held in Osaka. For Joel Crotty, Sculthorpe's visit there 'gave Sculthorpe the opportunity to advocate the incorporation of Asian musical knowledge into an expanded, non-Eurocentric compositional palette'.[143] The problem for such a repositioning of Australia was that 'His ideas apparently fell on deaf Japanese ears, as Sculthorpe notes: "[t]he Western European avant garde seemed to them [to be] the salvation of Japanese music"'.[144] It is therefore problematic to conclude, as Crotty does, that 'his aesthetic was currently attuned so closely to Japanese musical ideas',[145] given that 'Japanese musical ideas' were actually focussed on the European avant-garde. Such are the problems with the existing discourse that seeks to position Sculthorpe's rejection of Europe as an embrace of Japan.

The difficulties of disentangling Sculthorpe's different compositions and their relationships with different cultures has contributed to the discourses that have shaped his career, and where other composers such as Butterley or Meale were distant from those who wrote about their work, one finds a close alignment between the reviews of Sculthorpe's music and his own statements about what that music means. Skinner's biography demonstrates the connections that Sculthorpe had with critics such as Covell and the Prerauers, as it is often unclear whether the critics gave public voice to Sculthorpe's ideas or whether Sculthorpe adopted the critics' ideas about his music. Significantly, the music itself provides little material with which to untangle this situation, which further supports Sculthorpe's claim that his work is intimate and personal rather than mediated by established techniques.[146]

The ethics of Sculthorpe's music have only begun to be addressed by scholars such as Paget. He concludes: '[i]n some ways, Sculthorpe's methods may be vestiges of a bygone era, methods that future generations of composers should perhaps avoid. However, posterity may find it is the celebration of Indigenous culture which is the true legacy of Sculthorpe's musical "appropriations".[147] Like so many other recent interpretations of the 1960s and 1970s, Paget's does not raise the ethical problems associated with 'celebration'. What Paget also neglects is that the 'bygone era' discussed here was not one contemporaneous with Sculthorpe, but one that was already 'bygone' by the 1960s. There were no significant composers amongst the 'Sydney Moderns',[148] for example, and the energy for nationalism in the other arts had waned by Sculthorpe's time.

An Argument between Sculthorpe and Meale

The ethical questions that went with new geographical formulations were not absent from discussions at the time. In 1971, leading up to the first performance and broadcast of *Incredible Floridas*, Meale wrote a short article for *The Listener*, in which he explained his attitude towards Australian Music, raising the topic of representation and race:

> There is no such thing as an Australian school of music. [...] The Australian composer of today can either attach himself to specific current European movements – an operation which can be as decisive as sterilisation – or, now that we have discovered that our neighbours are in South-East Asia, he can produce music that can only be described as a 'musical world of Suzie Wong'.[149]

'Suzie Wong' refers to the 1957 novel *The World of Suzie Wong* by Richard Mason, which was made into a successful play that ran in New York and London and was then released as a film of the same name in 1960. The two main characters are Suzie Wong, a 'Hong Kong bar girl', and Robert Lomax, a British (in the novel)/American (in the play and film) painter.[150] Meale referred to the novel/play/film as an exemplar of ethically problematic ideas of orientalism. He contrasted this with his own awareness 'of the richness of indigenous cultures of our South-East Asian neighbours', and he wrote that 'I have benefited from the textural aesthetics of non-Western music, as I have from the structural examinations and discoveries of Boulez and Stockhausen, and the conceptual factors of indeterminacy'.[151] For Meale, abstraction assuages appropriation. To avoid 'sterilization' and orientalism, Meale proposed a third way:

> to be a 'stateless' musician in a 'global village'. To work this way is a unique pleasure because one can give more attention to the creative act *per se* than to the inflections of foreign nationalistic pressures, orientalia and intellectual covens.[152]

Furthermore, he argued against the 'formation of an Australian school of music [...]. It would be an artifice, a denial and would have to be illiberal'. The 'geographic isolation' was no problem for Meale, since 'knowledge is disseminated easily and rapidly through broadcasts, recordings, scores and article – not to mention live performances'.[153] Given that he was writing this for a BBC publication ahead of a London performance, that dissemination overcomes isolation both ways. Meale's reference to the 'musical world of Suzie Wong' is specific in its criticism, and his target was Sculthorpe. In an interview with Belinda Webster,[154] Sculthorpe recalled Meale's criticism of *Anniversary Music* (*Sun Music III*) as 'Suzie Wong music',[155] and he laughed off Meale's criticism.

Even though Meale was critical of Sculthorpe's response to the music of South East Asia, his own response was extensive in the 1960s, and in earlier interviews he described himself as 'intensely interested in music of other cultures today'. For him it was also a matter of geography: 'Australia has only just recently wakened up to the fact that Indonesia is our neighbour. This is why I'm interested in South-East Asian music.'[156] Between the 1960s and the 1970s Sculthorpe's attitude changed, with his public stance reflecting the increased and more widely held interest in 'South-East Asian music' over this time period, which was not often characterized by the abstraction that Meale favoured. Sculthorpe mentioned Meale, in an article written in 1969, as a composer who shared his own interest in Asia, but who wrote different music in response:

> In 1968 I wrote music for the film *The Age of Consent*, based upon a novel by Norman Lindsay. In this score I decided, again, to use Asian music. The thought had occurred to me that, instead of desperately looking to Europe for ideas, one should look to the Pacific and to Asia. Our political and economic future is bound up with Asia, and for this reason there must be tremendous cultural inter-action. If, for instance, our light music composers, instead of reaching out to England and the States, looked to Asia, they would find there unique rhythms and sounds which could be used to create a unique light music of our own. We belong geographically to this area. Richard Meale has written *Images (Naguata)* based on Japanese Kabuki music, and in this work he has put Asian music through his own personal sieve, and written music which is quite different to my own Asian-inspired pieces. For me, the East is re-vitalising my music and I hope that one day it will become part of the Australian manner, the Australian style.[157]

The future of Australian Music as a distinctive, national style is one that is inspired by music from Asia.

In her 1989 interview, Webster pressed Sculthorpe about the influence of Asian cultures on Sydney in the 1960s:

> [Webster:] Why were you so adamant to insist that we are part of Asia and to bring that Asian connection into your music? When really, and especially at that time, Australia was still (and probably to a large extent still is) a European place? The impact that Asia was having on Australian society, culture, music, aesthetics, philosophy, politics, anything you could name, was minimal really.
>
> [Sculthorpe:] Oh, do you think so? All the bamboo furniture, thongs ... I think even then it was profound.

[Webster:] Really?!

[Sculthorpe:] Without us realizing. And our economy, even then Japan was incredibly important to us ... But it really has to be said right now that I was forced into saying things like that. I was just getting on doing things that were right for me, and then somebody comes along and interviews you ... Suddenly one is forced into inventing a whole world that isn't really what one is about.[158]

Sculthorpe then explained his personal and long-standing interest in Asia.[159] This exchange is crucial for understanding Sculthorpe's music and the discourses that surround it. Webster's first question moves quickly from Sculthorpe's insistence that Australia was a part of Asia to Sculthorpe's music, which is a line of thought that assumes that a straightforward link between geographical conceptions and musical expression is possible. Nevertheless, the question is an implicit critique of two ideas that are usually taken for granted. The first of those ideas is that Australia was becoming less European and as increasingly understood as part of Asia. The second is that Sculthorpe's music represents this move. This critique gets to the nub of an often-repeated misunderstanding about Sculthorpe. His music has been read in terms of the extensive commentary, reviews, criticisms and interviews associated with it, and the multiple fictions of different kinds of representation have been elided. Indeed, this elision is seen as itself distinctively Australian, an unfussy, straightforward and middlebrow approach to complex topics. Webster's question pulls apart what has often been easily mixed together. Sculthorpe's work has been characterized by unarticulated shifts between places in particular, 'landscape' in general, wider cultural shifts, new geographical conceptions and musical aesthetics.[160] Sculthorpe's reaction to Webster is to parody the 1960s suburban understandings of Japanese culture. Sculthorpe was rarely so confrontational, and although one ought to be very cautious about reading the whole of Sculthorpe's work through this one exchange, it does underline two significant points. Firstly, that is it important not to move too quickly between 'Australia' and 'Asia' in seeking to explain Sculthorpe's music. Secondly, that there are discussions of his music that have (perhaps) very little to do with what is taking place musically.

A similar problem to that of understanding Sculthorpe's attitude to the music of Asia is that of trying to understand the relationship between Sculthorpe and Meale, and that difficulty has tended to stabilize a handful of ideas about Australian Music. The first problem is that of representation. Meale and Sculthorpe have often been cast as opposites, with Meale interested in abstraction,[161] and Sculthorpe rejecting abstraction as European, as in the following statement from the latter: 'All my pieces are somewhat programmatic. There is a certain visual element to all of them. They are never abstract. The idea of European music is that it is abstract.'[162] In an unedited transcript of an interview held in Murdoch's papers at the National Library of Australia, Murdoch typed (in uncharacteristically red ink):

you [Meale] write music which is itself whereas Sculthorpe writes music about the walk in the paradise garden.

Meale responded:

Peter writes music ...

which was corrected to:

Many contemporary composers still write music which uses a lot of symbols of tonal language. We associate this sort of sound with that of western culture while I am not at all concerned with that aspect of it.[163]

If Sculthorpe's version of Australia is idealized,[164] a no-place-in-particular, Meale's concern is with sound. Elsewhere in the interview Meale argued against 'the concept of a museum of orchestral work', saying that 'there is no such abstract thing or concrete thing [as a Beethoven symphony]'.[165] His argument against representation, and the privileging of performance, is at the heart of this period of Meale's rhetoric, and although this underlies his criticism of Sculthorpe, his arguments against Sculthorpe's musical representations are also applicable to some of his work. In the same interview Meale gave the example of the 'percussion cadence' at the end of *Images* as an Asian gesture to replace the European 'harmonic cadence'.[166]

Representation

For Sculthorpe, matters of representation are fluid, and his music often changes form rapidly in response to changing situations. For example, in 1966 Sculthorpe was at Yale as a Harkness Fellow, and the opportunity arose for him to write a work for the Yale Quartet to perform at the Norfolk Chamber Music Festival.[167] The material began as *Three Pieces for String Quartet*, but on 'the day before the performance, I made them into one piece, & called it Teotihuacán, for String Quartet. (More Sort of Sun Music)'.[168] Whether or not there was a musical transformation behind the change from music written as a homage to New England, to music that carried a title from Mexico, is not clear. The piece was later published as *Red Landscape*, becoming Sculthorpe's String Quartet No. 7. Despite all this complexity, Sculthorpe's music provides *the* narrative for understanding what Australia sounds like. Where other composers worked on specific places in Australia or people living in Australia, Sculthorpe's music was accepted as being about Australia itself. At a time when other composers engaged with national character only to parody it,[169] Sculthorpe's music took titles that spoke of Australia and had musical ideas that were general enough to be adapted by his wide audience. The music falls into two categories: desert music and inhabited music, *Earth Cry* and *Small Town*. None of his music *sounds like* any particular place, since it is about Australian nationalism, which is not a particular place. Sculthorpe is less of a realist than Meale thought.

In response to an exhibition of Kazemir Malevich's art at Tate Modern in 2014, Tony Wood ends his review with a discussion of the artist's late work, and apparent return to representation. 'These final canvases', he writes, 'suggest some private allegory or code at work, a kind of representation that suggests a mysterious absence.'[170] To make sense of this contradictory move away from abstraction he asks two questions:

> The Russian term for abstraction was 'objectlessness'; what if the objects in figurative art bear no more relation to the physical world than geometric forms do, inhabiting some separate realm of their own? And what if the task of painting were not to depict, but to wall off one piece of that realm after another?[171]

Stephen Adams, writing for the ABC soon after Sculthorpe's death, made a similar argument about the connection between music and landscape as setting forth what is actually also *dis*connection. In his argument, the distance between the reality of Sculthorpe's situation and the vision that he offered is actually the reason for the composer's significance:

> As a student I couldn't help feeling that it seemed strange to devote so much creative energy to portraying distant desert or tropical landscapes rather than engaging with the urban landscapes that most of us actually inhabit. But then, that was something for me to kick against. And as the years pass I can see how that vast landscape in some sense embodied a cultural lacuna – representative of the colonial realities of the violence and oppression in our history of colonisation that we can all too easily forget and turn away from; something hidden behind the comfortable life I and my fellow descendants of our first boat people have enjoyed as we focus on our cities, beaches and what lies on the other side of our surrounding oceans.[172]

In the 1960s and 1970s, prominent writers, critics and concert programmers all aligned their understanding of Australian music in terms of its connection with landscape; the optimism of the time came with a desire for something new, and that something new was Australian Music, with Sculthorpe as the defining composer. The simplicity with which Australian landscape and Sculthorpe's music are brought together speaks of Australia's urban centres, and of the decreasing amount of time that people spent outside (sub)urban areas. Sculthorpe's early music also reinforced a conception of Australian landscape as a state of mind or an attitude. In this his perspective was close to that of the author Patrick White, through whose work the realist tradition gave way to the anti-realist emphasis on myths over traditions, the mind over the land. Sculthorpe's music never provides the level of detail of White's literature, and his landscapes are never as detailed as Lumsdaine's (Lumsdaine being the composer of this generation who was most influenced by White, with *Aria for Edward John Eyre* the culmination of this influence, directly engaging with White's metaphysics[173]); nor were the myths of which Sculthorpe spoke thoroughly dramatized in his music. Sculthorpe's opera *Rites of Passage* – for which White was to be the librettist – 'uses a kind of Pacific mythology that I'm inventing,'[174] and so it is new, and not about representing the rites of particular people; this is ritual music, rather than music for a depicted ritual. '*Rites of Passage* is not concerned with psychological relationships, but with spatial relationships.'[175]

Such aesthetics are also shared with the aesthetics of Australia's visual arts. The artist John Coburn (1925–2006), for example, is Sculthorpe's contemporary in portraying the sun. If from London the Australian sun appeared endlessly parching, Coburn's artworks reveal abundant plant life, even though his plants are frequently in flames, as in his tapestry *Curtain of the Sun* (1973), which was designed for the proscenium of the Sydney Opera House's Opera Theatre. Coburn's flora are energetic under the bright sun, and through his work's use of block colours and Matisse cut-out shapes, the burning plants resemble dancing figures.[176] The *Sun Music* series contains the early forms of ideas that later made up individual pieces. More recently, Sculthorpe became known as a composer who had honed his characteristic motifs, such as his seagulls endlessly flocking,[177] and most of his mature work is constructed from a few basic ideas. Sculthorpe's centrality to the Australian Music narrative of landscape was secured through the *Sun Music* series and its 'scorched earth kind of music, from which nothing as green or fertile as a tune or rhythm could grow',[178] or so it seemed to the *Telegraph* critic writing in London. The *Sun Music* pieces are not as uniform as this review suggests, and the diversity of the series is one of its striking features, alongside its evocation of tropical places. Those works that take the name of a particular place, such as *Port Essington*, are not about that place, and in *Port Essington*'s case the work is about the challenges of colonizing Australia and of the land's resistance to colonization. But even this is done as a 'repainting' of some earlier ideas that were no longer necessary to experience first hand; indeed, this is a repainting of ideas that could not ever have been experienced first hand because the ideas are always already depictions. In this he is the opposite of Meale, for whom first-hand experience was of primary importance. For example, Skinner writes (citing Hannan) that 'the Bali visit [Sculthorpe's first, in 1974] virtually signalled the end of Sculthorpe's use of actual Balinese musical materials',[179] whereas Meale's music mostly comes after his experiences of a place. Although Meale claimed to favour abstraction in opposition to Sculthorpe, no clear-cut opposition between the two composers can be sustained.

The reception of *Rites of Passage* (first performed at the Sydney Opera House in 1974) predictably focussed on its 'Australianness', which makes it a good case study for examining the idea (after Wood writing about Malevich) of Sculthorpe seeking a separate, 'walled-off' realm. The following is exemplary of the critical reception:

> There have been many attempts to write an Australian opera. None have succeeded as Sculthorpe has since none have dared to disregard all conventions and build from the native ground up … a new world that has drawn from several worlds. Sculthorpe has been a long time discovering this place. Now in *Rites of Passage* he has populated it with people moulded and formed by it.[180]

Ever since Sculthorpe had signed with Faber in 1965 there had been calls for Sculthorpe to be an Australian Benjamin Britten.[181] Despite the critic Brian Hood's insistence on the work's unconventionality, the form of *Rites of Passage* is that of an oratorio, close to Britten's *War Requiem* and to Tippett's *A Child of Our Time*, particularly in the way that chorales/choruses are employed dramatically. The fourth chorale in Sculthorpe's

Rites of Passage uses a Javanese melody, for example, as a gesture towards a universal spirituality, which functions in a way that is not dissimilar to the spirituals in Tippett's *A Child of Our Time*.[182] Sculthorpe composed *Rites of Passage* when he was a visiting professor at the University of Sussex (1971–2), and it was written with the assistance of Matthews, who had previously worked for Britten.[183] Matthews's contribution highlights the distributed effort in composing the work, whilst Skinner's account of its long and very complicated development provides a basis for appreciating the complexity of connections that make it up, since although Sculthorpe's music has been understood as personal and solitary, it is also collaborative. Skinner connects Sculthorpe's ideas for staging *Rites of Passage* to having seen Davies's *Taverner* in 1972:

> Davies's work was traditional in dramatic structure, though the production called for both stage and pit musicians, and had a single set – a flexible, arena-style performing area, similar to that Peter [Sculthorpe] was now envisaging for *Rites*.[184]

According to Skinner, in 1973, the director Jaap Flier

> envisaged the work [*Rites of Passage*] as a 'scenic oratorio', an 'abstraction of a life cycle' [… One of] his innovations in production was to move the performers of the Chorales from the pit, where Peter originally intended them to be, and put them behind and around an arena-like stage area, partly to accentuate the 'oratorio' feel.[185]

In so doing Flier connected the work with ancient Greek theatre, and therefore with other works such as *Oedipus Rex* (and Butterley's *Laudes*). Sculthorpe's comment that it 'is a religious work, a statement of my belief in the divine, the sacred in nature',[186] aligns with the modernist view of Greek theatre as 'regarded as a religious ceremonial, as an act of homage to the god'.[187] Matthews would surely have felt at home in what Sculthorpe was trying to achieve given his own knowledge of the way that Britten responded to Noh and Balinese music.[188] Britten had met McPhee in New York in the 1940s, and Sculthorpe was later to describe McPhee's *The Music of Bali* as 'one of the greatest books ever written on any kind of music'.[189] Philip Brett argues for *Curlew River* that it 'engages with the music of Asia on terms that are not at all patronizing, because they put so much of Western musical history at risk in an attempt at a genuine relationship that acknowledges and celebrates difference'. For Brett,

> Britten opened up conditions in which he was able to pay homage to Eastern tradition by adapting and imitating some of its musical and dramatic procedures without patronizing it, and without using it as a vehicle for the projection of Western fantasies. It is a project that tries hard to avoid the colonizing impulse, though of course it reflects the romantic utopianism also associated with the phenomenon of Orientalism in the West.[190]

For Anthony Sheppard, 'Brett's attempt to redeem Britten from charges of Orientalist thinking is misdirected, for the Japanese remained Britten's ultimate exotic. Far from putting "Western musical history at risk" in these works, Britten played it safe by recasting Noh in a Christian musical idiom."[191] *Rites of Passage* is post-Britten, and Sculthorpe's music is as much a criticism of 'the colonizing impulse', and, indeed, of 'Western musical history', as it is a continuation of the conceptual framework.

Composers throughout Europe were engaging with Japanese culture in the middle of the twentieth century, and so the extent to which Japanese music can function to reposition Australia as part of Asia is questionable, since similar music did not function similarly to position Germany, say, as part of Asia. For example, in the same year Meale composed *Images (Naguata)* (1966), one of Roger Smalley's notebooks contains an outline of the history of Japanese music, scale forms, 'Noh drama-form', instruments and situations in which the music functions. Both composers were keen to distance themselves from mainstream anglophone composition, and both were influenced by Messiaen's *Sept Haïkaï* (1962).[192] John Exton's music from the early 1970s shows the influence of Cage and Zen (in *Ryoanji*, for example). In the early 1970s Stockhausen's *Inori* makes plain his interest in Japanese music, and in 1968 Boulez's 'Music of the Orient' was published in *Music and Musicians*, in which he declared that 'Noh remains the peak of oriental music.'[193] Similarly, composers outside Australia have long been interested in the ideas and ideals of landscape (and its functionally similar counterpart, seascape, or, indeed, the intertidal zone, such as in Sculthorpe's *Mangrove* (1979)). The pillars of Sculthorpe's nationalism, in other words, are paradoxically part of a movement of a transnational musical modernism, and need not be read as uniquely Australian for them to make sense.[194]

Sculthorpe's *Sun Music* series sounds his connection of music with place, with light and flatness translated into music as melodic and harmonic stasis.[195] This is an understanding of the need to connect time and place, and for that connection to be multiple. Friedman's call to 'Always spatialize!' as the counter to Fredric Jameson's 'Always historicize!' suggests that, awkward and nascent as his efforts may have been, Sculthorpe was working against the dominant understanding of music as a temporal art as opposed to painting's spatiality; if Sculthorpe's music sounds like it 'doesn't want to go anywhere' then this is because the music is problematizing 'where' and 'go', presenting place and time as problematically enjoined in the politics of nationalism. The incomplete philosophical position that the music presents (its occasional awkwardness, say), can productively be read as resisting a nationalist uniformity derived from imperial Britain.[196] As such, Sculthorpe's music forms a postcolonial response to shifting relations between time and space, and Sculthorpe's understandings of music from anthropology present the modernist paradox of time as both unchanging and constantly in flux, and of space as both fixed ('ancient', for example) and constantly renegotiated through experience. The Australian landscape is not 'empty' as a metonym for the failure of imperial reach, of a perceived restriction of empire's ability to totalize uniformly the Australian nation and the landscape due to the latter's vastness or inhospitableness. Similarly, when Banks writes about the task being to 'seek out the many gaps in the fabric of musical life here and show initiative in plugging them' he writes about the active creation of lacunae that emerge in the 'musical situation' that brings Australia and Britain into a new relation; new, that is, at the time of the 'seeking out' and 'plugging',[197] since these are not gaps left by the end of British imperial control, or by post-imperial influence. (Similarly, Hannan's consideration of Meale's *Las Alboradas* as 'a work whose idiom suddenly closed the stylistic gap between Australian composition and that of the European avant-garde'[198] does not describe a gap that existed before Hannan's textual formulation brought Australia and Europe into temporal and spatial relation: temporal in that it happens 'suddenly' and in the immediate past, and spatial in that it posits both a gap and then the movement of its closure. Implicit in Hannan's phrase is a contrast between a nationalist mindset and a transnational one, since Australia is a single nation state and Australia-Europe (with the 'gap closed') transcends national borders.)

McCredie is partly right when he writes that 'For Sculthorpe, it is the fascination of the sounds, textures and structures of this music which appeals, not its ethnological significance primarily',[199] since McCredie's concern here is with Sculthorpe the modernist. Considering Sculthorpe's music in 1960s Sydney supports a reading of him as actively addressing the overlooked politics of place at a time when the politics of temporality were highly charged, and when there was an emerging scholarship of place as political in its guise as inhabited landscape, associated with the growing land-rights movements. The politics were even more pressing in those parts of Australia where the problems of colonialism were most obvious (sites of cultures that had apparently divergent notions of space and time) and which had withstood colonial uniformity. An example of the latter also includes, for Sculthorpe, the music of Bali, which in his opinion was 'flourishing as never before. Contact with Western music had, in fact, not meant its demise: it had helped bring about a renaissance.'[200]

Even though the axis of 'contact', within and without Australia, continues to define ideas about Sculthorpe in the 1960s and 1970s, his music can contribute to rethinking relations between places and periods. Combating the centre–periphery model with Australian uniqueness increases, rather than decreases, distance, since 'distance' itself is emphasized, resulting in a surfeit of the isolation discourse. By way of such a dialectical inversion anxieties of distance are turned into distance's celebration, and Sculthorpe's desire for Australia to be a centre rather than a periphery confirms the Antipodean model. Such a conception of distance distances Sculthorpe, in turn, from his contemporary composers, which is useful in terms of celebrating Sculthorpe's success, and of understanding the important place of modernism within Australian Music more widely.

6

Richard Meale II

Adelaide

In 1969 Meale resigned from the ABC and was appointed Lecturer in Music at the University of Adelaide. Through the Adelaide Festival of Arts the city had come to be favourably regarded as an artistic and cultural centre, and the festival itself was a substantial undertaking. In 1968 there were 326 performances, in 1970 there were 284 and in 1972 there were 344.[1] In 1970 the English Opera Group performed Britten's *Curlew River* (1964), *The Burning Fiery Furnace* (1966) and *The Prodigal Son* (1968); that year Britten also conducted the South Australian Symphony Orchestra, and he and Pears gave a recital. In the same year the Warsaw Philharmonic Orchestra and Bartók String Quartet performed alongside local ensembles such as the Adelaide Singers, as well as university groups. Meale performed in the recital series, including in the premiere of his composition *Interiors/Exteriors* (1970, for two pianos and percussion). Outside festival time Adelaide was less musically attractive, and for Meale the move to Adelaide 'was a shock. At the time I felt I had moved from "life" to "limbo"'. He wrote:

> My activities in performing and promoting seemed to be curtailed by the rigidly maintained conservativeness of the city – as it was then. Naturally, I was frustrated, and felt alienated.[2]

He accounted for the composition of *Interiors/Exteriors* as follows:

> I woke up in my sterile bedroom and thought 'I am in here, and you are out there.' *Interiors/Exteriors*. It suddenly because clear to me that the composition (triggered by my 'I hate Adelaide' syndrome) would be in the form of a declaration – a declaration to re-establish my alienated identity.[3]

Despite giving this account, he cautioned that 'this personal anecdote does in no way provide a key to this piece of music. And this personal account of its psychic genesis [...] should not be considered whilst listening to the music. Otherwise, you, as an audience, would be guilty of anecdotal listening.'[4] As with *Las Alboradas*, and the other works that hide their histories, Meale wanted his music to 'transcend the temporal particular, by finding tangible abstraction'.[5] Nevertheless, the move to Adelaide was a significant one, providing Meale with a salary to support his composition, and it began a prolific time for him.

In 1972 Meale proposed the 'Formation of Special Studies in Composition' at the university. The aim was to establish a specialist course for training composers, led by a composer (himself) rather than, as other institutions offered, a training model that was based on musicology. In the document he cited the University of York as a model,[6] and he also suggested that, if funded, the programme could form a 'far-reaching cultural wave as did that of the famous "Bauhaus"'.[7] Meale argued that the 'common practice' period gave way to one in which – and here he quoted Boulez – 'The world of music today is a *relative* world, that is to say, one where structural relationships are not defined once and for all according to absolute criteria, but are organised instead according to varying schemata'.[8] The quotation is from *On Music Today*, a text to which I will return in my analysis of *Coruscations*. Meale quoted Boulez on music as a way of thinking through the problem of 'moulds' for teaching composition. At the same time he warned against 'laissez-faire' attitudes that understand compositional ability in terms of the 'myth' of a creative 'gift'. Meale considered the proposal as a necessary 'new structure' to address 'Australia's *isolation* from the mainstream of contemporary music',[9] since 'despite broadcasts, recordings, musical scores and local concerts, information flows into Australia at too slow a rate'. The proposal requested funding for Meale and students to travel abroad, and for the university to invite 'A-grade' composers from elsewhere. The outcome saw a new position for Meale as Senior Composition Fellow, arranged directly between the Minister of Education, the State's Premier and the Vice Chancellor and paid for by the state,[10] and providing support for Meale to 'work freely and with proper facilities and within an environment conducive to the art of composition'.[11] Some travel funding was included, through significantly less than he had requested.

Incredible Floridas, Coruscations and the String Quartet, which are the focus of this chapter, were composed against the backdrop of this new support for composition. *Coruscations* demonstrates the influence of Boulez on Meale's composition, for it is a highly schematic work, and *Incredible Floridas* shows Meale finding a way out of Boulezian rigours. *Coruscations* is the high point of Meale's modernist music, and *Incredible Floridas* returns to earlier twentieth-century ideas of serialism and pantonality, raising a crisis of modernism that the String Quartet explicitly writes. These works bring the period of Meale's musical modernism to an end.

Coruscations

Light is a topic that returns again and again throughout the twentieth century,[12] and it is light in its strikingly plastic form that caught Meale's attention: light in the form of an aurora, evolving shapes of massed light, both quick and brilliant, and pliant and chaotic. The early twentieth-century avant-garde's obsession with speed is there too: Meale's *Coruscations* flow.

Roger Woodward's premiere of *Coruscations* took place on 25 April 1971,[13] at London's Queen Elizabeth Hall. With the piece completed in early March, there was little time to learn the work, and Woodward recalls that it only arrived a few days before the performance. The composition was written quickly too. If an aurora is light slowed down, then Meale's *Coruscations* is composition at pace. Ross Edwards, whose *Monos II* was in the programme,[14] and who was at the time based in the UK, wrote programme notes for the concert, including this for *Coruscations*:

> *Coruscations* for piano was written especially for Roger Woodward. Richard Meale defines the title as 'a series of rapid flashes of light such as that coming from the Aurora Borealis'. The work is constructed from a total of 10 inter-related sonorities which are subjected to a rigid system of transpositions and permutation. Despite its closely organized structure, *Coruscations* has an inherent flexibility, leaving many secondary interpretive decisions to the performer.[15]

Coruscations is one of Meale's most performed works, and although the published recordings have different approaches, they all follow the score published by Universal Edition. This score leaves many of the rhythmic decisions to the performer, and all the recordings grasp the essential character of the music: the fast, fleeting, forceful flow of notes.

The composition of those notes was determined according to a precise pitch scheme, with everything else chosen by the composer as the piece was written. The sketches provide information about the mechanism of the work's scheme, as well as Meale's choices in using that material, and they also raise some questions about the accuracy of the published score.[16] The work is unusually systematic for Meale, and it explores some of Boulez's 'chord multiplication' ideas in a relatively direct manner; as such it is useful for considering Meale's attitude to technique.

Meale's sketching began on The University of Adelaide's letterhead, a single page of typed letters and numbers that set out the scheme. His typed scheme consists of two cycles, one of ten chords designated by letters (A–J), and the other of their twelve transpositions (1–12). The pattern begins with the two cycles in synchronization:

A1	B2	C3	D4	E5	F6	G7	H8	I9	J10

The transposition cycle continues, matching a transposition number to every second chord:

A11	C12	E1	G2	I3	B4	D5	F6	H7	J8

To form the subsequent rows the transpositions continue to increase incrementally, attached to every second chord of the previous row:

A9	E10	I11	D12	H1	C2	G3	B4	F5	J6
A7	I8	H9	G10	F11	E1	D1	C2	B3	J4
A5	H6	F7	D8	B9	I10	G11	E12	C1	J2
A3	F4	B5	G6	C7	H8	D9	I10	E11	J12

Each of these six rows is then used to determine a block. In all, six blocks of 'sonorities'[17] are produced, within which the chords are shuffled against the transposition numbers. The first block is:

A1	B2	C3	D4	E5	F6	G7	H8	I9	J10
B1	A2	D3	C4	F5	E6	H7	G8	J9	I10
C1	E2	B3	D4	A5	H6	J7	G8	I9	F10
E1	B2	D3	A4	C5	J6	G7	I8	F9	H10
G1	I2	C3	E4	A5	F6	J7	B8	H9	D10

The aim here is to shuffle the 'sonorities' (i.e. chord + transposition), not to generate patterns that enable structuring symmetries in the music. The result is a block of material where some sonorities repeat much more frequently than others, and where some transpositions are not used. (In the first block the chords are not transposed by 11 or 12.)

Meale's conception of the two series (chords, transpositions) as being brought together to form the sonorities in the scheme-making phase is clear from a typewriter alignment problem. He abandoned typing the second block of material when the transposition numbers were out of horizontal alignment, exposing the chord lettering that was awaiting its transposition numbers. The process of forming these blocks is significant, since it suggests at least two levels of recognizability of chords: when they return transposed (i.e. when they are 'sonorities'), and when they return untransposed. The frequency of each 'sonority' is noted by Meale in the table with a handwritten subscript numeral that indicates how many times the sonority has occurred.

The chords permuted in the above scheme were formed by using Boulez's chord multiplication technique. Meale began with five chords of between one and four notes (all twelve pitch classes are used), and he multiplied these to form six of the chords used (see Example 6.1): 1×3=E; 1×4=F; 1×5=G; 3×4=H; 4×5=I; 3×5=J.[18]

The other four were generated by first inverting the base chords about D,[19] and then multiplying as follows: 1×3=A; 1×5=B; 3×4=C; 4×5=D. Unlike all the other chord multiplications, 1×5 generates B12, a semitone lower than the B1 used in the scheme. This suggests: firstly, that the transposition/chord cycles are indeed more about shuffling sonorities than about rigorous pattern-making; secondly, that the music was

Example 6.1 The derivation of the pitch material for Meale's *Coruscations*.

being composed at speed; thirdly, that the piece is being composed with procedures that were new to Meale, rather than ones that were thoroughly practised.

The latter point is reinforced by the date of composition, which reads: 'Adelaide, Australia 7-3-1971'. The multiplication procedure that Meale uses first appeared in the book *Boulez on Music Today*.[20] This was first published in 1963 in French and German, but not translated into English until 1971. In his 1965 interview on the ABC's radio programme *Away from It All*, Meale said that he was particularly interested in modern French literature, reading Jean Genet and Nathalie Sarraute in translation. It seems likely, then, that he was also reading Boulez in translation, and that *Coruscations* is an immediate exploration of the chord multiplication technique.

The condensation of a row into five building blocks for transformation is pure Boulez:

> Take another example: the case of a homogenous complex of pitches. Suppose the groupings of absolute values are made (still in the domain of the semitone, with the octave as model) and that the result is a succession of complexes of variable density – still fulfilling the essential condition of non-repetition –: 3/2/4/2/1, that is, all the twelve semitones of the octave.
>
> If the ensemble of all the complexes is multiplied by a given complex, this will result in a series of complexes of mobile density, of which in addition, certain constituents will be irregularly reducible; although *multiple* and *variable*, these complexes are deduced from one another in the most functional way possible, in that they obey a logical, coherent structure.[21]

In Meale's case the density is 3/1/2/4/2, which keeps close to Boulez's example. Meale does not follow Boulez precisely, and the ten chords he produces from the multiplication are not subjected to transposition according to the basic material, but are used in all twelve transpositions, with the block scheme creating variable relationships (as generated by the frequency of the occurrence of a sonority). Again, Boulez's writing in 'Music Technique' seems more than apt:

the advantage of transformations – or transpositions – lies in creating regions which are privileged in relation to others; the interplay of these functions of privilege can frequently sustain a dialectic of interconnections, entailing structural consequence which can be the basis of form. In addition, when the elements are *placed* simultaneously in their relative tessituras, they follow or oppose the acoustic proportions 'of least resistance' (I am referring to simple relationships which we call the 'natural' harmonic series); from this very fact, they acquire reciprocal functions, the one corroborating or destroying, reinforcing or negating the other, and these give the material its internal profile, its energy potential, its malleability and its cohesive properties. These are all extremely important characteristics, whose structural consequences will be no less essential in the establishment of a form than serial linking. Thus, it is a mere illusion to conceive of sound points that are completely independent of a directional field[.][22]

Meale's sketches contain a diagram on the same paper as some experiments in chord multiplication.[23] The diagram begins with a chord, the notes from which (with some additions) are then distributed across the stave, and the pitches connected with lines (Example 6.2). The lines demonstrate possible connections between pitches, and unlike other sketches for this piece, the register of the notes is important for revealing the vectors of the network. The lines indicate the flow of material across the page. It seems more than coincidental that the bar line in this diagram aligns with the intersection of three connecting vectors, suggesting a latent structure that comes from the intersection of vectors generated by the registral and temporal distribution of notes.

Edwards's programme note describes 'a rigid system', which raises the following question: just how rigid is the composition? The sonorities that Meale develops for the piece are mostly used linearly, spread into fast flourishes. Occasionally chords punctuate this texture. The flow of the piece is established at the start, the pitches from A1 distributed over two and a half octaves. There are no particular registral boundaries generated in this short moment, and both the pianist's hands are used; the 2, 2, 1, 1 alternation of hands presses forward (see the beginning of Example 6.3). A brief pause and 'upbow' mark the end of its flow and generate a spikey, rising object. The upbow symbol is explained by Meale in the score's preface:

> it [the group preceding the mark] is to be thought of as an enclosed group followed by an appropriate pause before proceeding.[24]

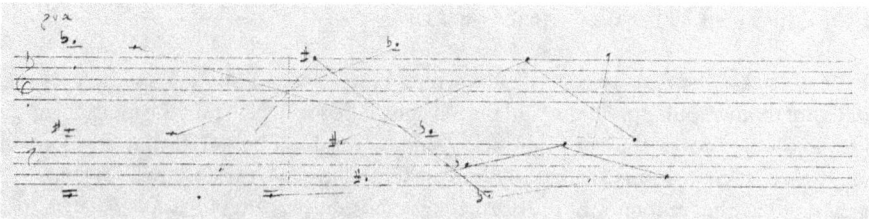

Example 6.2 An early sketch for Meale's *Coruscations*.[25]

Example 6.3 Meale, *Coruscations*, p. 1; the first system is annotated with the sonorities used.

The next group is less bounded, a dashed beam connecting it to the following group, itself connected with a dashed beam to the next, which ends with a comma. The comma 'indicates an enclosed group with an appropriate hesitation before proceeding'; the dashed beam indicates 'an enclosed group which should be followed almost immediately by the next. The hesitation is minimal.' These three semi-connected groups use pitches from four sonorities, with the D4 and E5 overlapping – the G and E♭ belong to them both (see Example 6.3). The overlapping of sonority fields becomes more interesting after the comma, since G7 also has the E♭ with which F6 finishes, though there is no strict overlap here since G7's own E♭ quickly follows. The hesitation that occurs here is significant, since it avoids the risk of inadvertent octaves. The D♭, D that surrounds the second E is a cluster that similarly distracts from the octave.

One of the specific warnings given by Boulez finds a positive use in Meale's music. Boulez writes that 'actual octaves must be avoided at the risk of structural non-sense'.[26] For the most part Meale follows this advice, choosing an order for pitches that avoids octaves. Troubling, then, is the unison between consecutive notes in G7 and H8. The first A♯ completes G7, and the second A♯ (B♭) begins H8, but the rhythm and dynamics[27] work to group A♯ and B♭ together, since the whole of the '*uguale*' group is separate from the flow of the music. This deliberate use of a unison suggests Meale had noted Boulez's warning about octaves weakening the structure, and that Meale had then used the 'weakening' specifically to punctuate the otherwise smoothly flowing coherence; this transforms a potential structural weakness into the articulation of structure itself. A similar *uguale* moment occurs to mark the end of the next flowing section, and again the octave is hidden with the quickest notes of section. Meale also makes the most of the opportunity to recall the close intervals of the first *uguale*. Here again a unison is used. The third flowing phrase brings the third *uguale*, and the return of G8 enables the same pitches, now an octave higher (a structurally exposed octave?).

Even if Meale is working with unisons and not octaves (and therefore diverges slightly from Boulez's warning about octaves and triads), the specific shape of the group, and the intervals Meale uses alongside the unison, is surprisingly similar to Boulez's example of the octave:[28]

Example 6.4 Webern's Op. 27/ii, bar 21, used by Boulez as example 6 in *Boulez on Music Today*.

One can well imagine Meale playing through Boulez's examples, and finding this pianistic example particularly relevant. It also makes use of the alternation of hands that is so important to *Coruscations*. One of the reasons why the octaves are so effective as phrase markers is that they introduce registral separation through the exposed octave displacement of a pitch. The surrounding music is all in one register, since there is no way consistently to group pitch with timbre, octave, or hand placement in a way that also suggests meaningful registral differentiation.

A fourth phrase is created by a more emphatic marker: two accented chords (B2 and D3, p. 1, stave 4). By now it is clear that the pitch scheme is not generating the work's structure, since B2 does not occur at the start or end of a cycle. The next time a chord occurs (p. 2, stave 1), it mixes both G1 and I2. What this suggests is that not only are chords transformed into pitch fields, but that the fields can also be compressed, bringing together multiple fields in one chord. The overlapping of potential field boundaries in this section of the piece is considerable, and most of the neighbouring groups share pitches with neighbouring sonorities, so that even when a group boundary coincides with a sonority boundary, that boundary is somewhat porous. Combining G1 and I2 into a single chord also reduces the repetition of pitch classes. G1 {F, A♭, E, G, A} and I2 {F, A♭, E, G, A, B♭} are very similar sets, and the immediate repetition of such similar material would in any case disrupt the average rate at which pitch classes vary. The eliding further suggests: firstly, that tessitura and rhythmic grouping are not enough to overcome the repetition of pitch, even if the order in which pitches appear need not be the same for G1 and I2 (this is another way of saying the octaves do not generate useful structural relationships); that Meale is aware of the overlapping of pitch classes from one sonority to the next; and that there is a desire to limit the degree of overlapping.

One can see in Meale's sketches that there is an understanding of where in the scheme he is, and the sketches are annotated with the sonority to be used.[29] The sketches show that the composition process involved Meale working on one group/sonority after the next, rather than working architecturally. There are occasional groups that were erased and recomposed, but most of the work looks quickly written, the alternation of hands very much part of that process, suggesting a transcription of his work at the piano one group at a time.

Only a few of the sections of the piece are sketched separately, and these involve some of the more contrapuntal music. One such passage occurs on page 6 (Example 6.5). Meale's sketch of this passage is shown in Example 6.6. Only a photocopy is present in his archive, but the manuscript paper is of the same type that was used for the diagram of connecting lines (Example 6.2). The sketch begins at B9 (the first bar of Example 6.5), and all the pitches are in close position unrelated to the registers found in the sketch of the score. The order of pitches is written on the stave in (more or less) prime form. The sketch clearly shows the connection between pitches in neighbouring sonorities. The B in common with B9, J10, F10, A12, E1, C2 and I3, is held throughout the passage. To go with the recurring B, Meale repeats pitch cells beyond such as are enabled by the sequence of sonorities – see, for example, the F, E, F that occurs in the first and second bar. The blurring of pitch fields from different sonorities increases in the fourth bar, with the held B♭, then held G, surrounded by repetitions of D, F♯ and the repeated E♭.[30]

Although the scheme produces only pitch material, Meale does include articulations in the score, and the sketches show him working through different possibilities. For example, in the sketches Meale is undecided about the articulation of the first system of page 6 (the section which leads into the long-held B). He opts to give the performer

Example 6.5 Meale, *Coruscations*, p. 6.

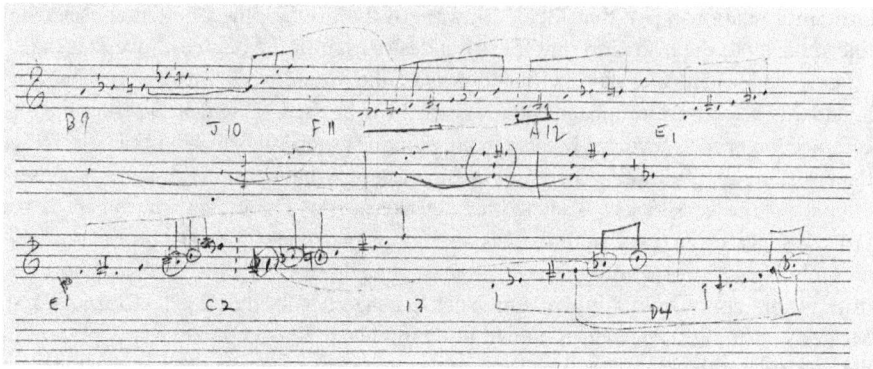

Example 6.6 Meale's sketch for *Coruscations*, showing his early stages of working with the sonorities.[31]

no more information than at the start of the piece. Relative to the opening this section is much quieter, and the hesitations between groups is more substantial. In the sketch, 'secco' is written underneath the first group, and 'stacc.?' beneath the second, and each group is slurred. The idea is closer to the slurred notes in the following bars (see Example 6.5), with their final accented notes. This is also closer to how Roger Woodward, who commissioned the piece, recorded it;[32] he emphasizes the final note of each group, bringing out the paired repetitions: C♯, C♯, E, E, F, E♭, E♭.[33] The melody that emerges prepares for a later legato bassline (p. 6, system 3), which is a further example of the way vectors are created across pitch fields.

The performances that bring out the melodic lines in this and similar sections help to reveal the polyphonic aspects of the piece. Although it is unclear exactly which part of the piece the sketch (Example 6.2) of intersecting lines refers to, the pitches that surround the B drone of page 6's second system are those that begin the diagram (where they are gathered into a chord). The accents that are performed, whether those indicated in the score or others added by the performer, create the composition's dynamic form. Meale's sketches shows him thinking through the implications of these accents, and then deciding that they need not all be specified.

Having derived his material in the manner of Boulez's method, Meale went about distributing that material linearly. The transformation from vertical to horizontal is one that Boulez mentions, when he gives a general example:

> This method gives us, so to speak, sound 'surfaces' using either the true continuum or a rough approximation of this continuum by the aggregation of all the unitary intervals included within the given limits; these are called clusters in the vertical sense or glissandi in the diagonal sense.[34]

Boulez made this remark after a discussion of fields, which is too flexible a concept to be traceable directly to Meale's music. Nevertheless, Boulez's comment that 'musical thought can move in a world which evolves from existing objects to ensembles of probable objects'[35] fairly well describes the process of schematic forming of material into patterns for 'creating regions which are privileged in relation to others'.[36] The B in this section is a very specific privileged 'region', about which material is distributed (both in terms of tessitura and in the procession of pitches and groups). Within this section there is a hierarchy of pitch that includes the redundant repetition of pitch sequences, and only one frequency band (that is, one register): 'the frequency band represents a field completely filled with amorphous material'.[37] The sonorities may be premade, but they form new and less defined fields once Meale has chosen their order, tessitura, dynamic, articulation and phrasing. The fields' instability is inherent (the scheme only guarantees that they cannot last), and held notes begin to accumulate in the fifth cycle of the piece, but they then vanish almost instantly.

For Meale, this amorphousness is at the heart of the piece. It is central to the image conjured by its title, of an elusive, unpredictable light show, which is chaotic and brilliant. And it is central to the composition process. An early programme note for the piece is held amongst the sketch material, which explains the process more fully than the note written by Edwards:

> From a row of grouped notes, I transposed each group upon the other to obtain a set of inter-related sonorities. There were ten of these (I to X). These were each transposed twelve times (I_1 to I_{12}). The ten sonorities were permutated to vary their sequence as were their transpositions. Results were that one sonority might occur frequently in the one transposition, whilst it may never be heard in another transposition. Furthermore, frequently note repetitions would occur in sets of adjacent permutated sonorities. The articulation of each sonority and its octave disposition, became a question of my decision. That is the most important point.[38]

The grouping of pitches from a row into the essential material that forms the sonorities is a condensation into uneven groups. These are permuted in such a way as to also form uneven blocks (from the point of view of the frequency of repetition of chords). These processes are schematic. A freer process takes place in arranging pitches to form the music. Allied to the choice of register is the grouping of pitches according to the hands that play them, forming a finer grain of rhythm than that defined by 'hesitation' or 'pause'.[39]

Through this amorphousness some clearly defined moments emerge. At the point when all the sonorities have been heard, a reprise of the opening block occurs (p. 10, see Example 6.7), which also introduces a new texture. Until now almost all the music has been a single stream of pitches. The reprise brings two layers at once, formed from two simultaneous sonorities, one in each hand. This is therefore not only a change of texture, but also a change in the rate at which sonorities pass and a change in the harmonic fields (since sonorities are now heard simultaneously). Tuplets adjust the rhythms so that sonorities in each hand align. There is a larger structure of alternation of hands here too, for in the first group the right hand is given *internal* rhythmic groupings ('3×2'), and the left hand is to be played smoothly. The situation reverses for the next group, with the right hand playing smoothly and the left hand striated.

Until this point the alternation of hands had been a latent property of piano playing, or something chosen to detail a long flowing passage, but it now seems more like one part of a large-scale formal strategy, a feature that is core to the very business of piano playing itself. Perhaps here, too, Meale had Boulez in mind: 'we shall have [...] *non-homogenous time*, where striated and smooth time will alternately be superposed'.[40] If Meale is making this connection, then the alternation of hands, at high speed, is one of the work's core temporalities.

If the opening is slick and quick, the reprise is less straightforward. At the end of page 10 (see the last system of Example 6.7) each hand is given separate material, alternating one note at a time, and then they come together in the longest mobile of the piece. The internal rhythmic groups – 4, 4, 4, 6, 4, 6, 8, then 8, 6, 4, 5 – compensate for the to and fro of hands that provides no rhythmic groups of its own.

The 'reprise' is a dramatic moment, which is emphasized structurally by a crescendo, from *pppp* to *ffff*, the latter dynamic coming with a layering of sonorities that considerably increases the density compared to the opening. It is not surprising that the text 'reprise' is not present in the score (it appears in the sketches) since there is little repetition beyond the repetitions of the sonorities that obsessively comprise the piece. The next few pages of the score notate material that is more differentiated in dynamics, articulations and register than those of the earlier stages of the piece. The idea of a central note returns on page 11 as a simple melody surrounded by

Example 6.7 Meale, *Coruscations*, p. 10, the reprise of the opening.

more percussive, short durations. At this point there is even greater contrast between continuity (slurred melodic lines) and discontinuity (unpredictable, staccato, chordal placements). A series of short sections (p. 13ff), indicated by changes of tempo or by double bars, progressively simplifies matters, and increases the contrasts between quiet notes and *agitato* music. This leads to the work's defiant downward gesture, ending the piece *fff*, '*prestiss., brutale*'.

Meale's first idea for the ending was *pppp*, 'rapide leggiero' (Example 6.8). This shows how radically different possibilities might have been pursued from the same material. In the closing bars, silence is used more than at any other point in the work, pointing to the problem of 'ending' itself. Meale ends *Coruscations* with a final flourish that is strikingly similar to the following 'endings' in Messiaen's music: *Vingt regards*, 'XX: Regard de l'Eglise d'amour' (and the structurally similar *Vingt regards* 'X: Regard de l'Esprit de joie'); 'Potançiagourou' in *Cantéyodjayâ*; the eighth *Prelude* 'un reflet dans le vent'; the last of the *Quatre études de rythme*, 'Ile de feu II'. The ending of *Coruscations* comes from outside the flow of the rest of the piece. The relationship that is formed here with Messiaen's music reinforces the significance of Meale's performances of Messiaen's piano music throughout the 1960s, and it underlines the fact that Meale's composition of *Coruscations* took place at the keyboard.

The ending includes some of the more problematic changes from sketch to score. There is an F in the first bar of the example where the sketch has a G – the G is called for by the I11 sonority – and the four-ledger-line E in the final flourish, a pitch not predicted by the D12 sonority ({A♭, G, A, C, F♯, B}) from the scheme, and which Meale indicates in a sketch is the sonority used. The sketch gives a G here, which

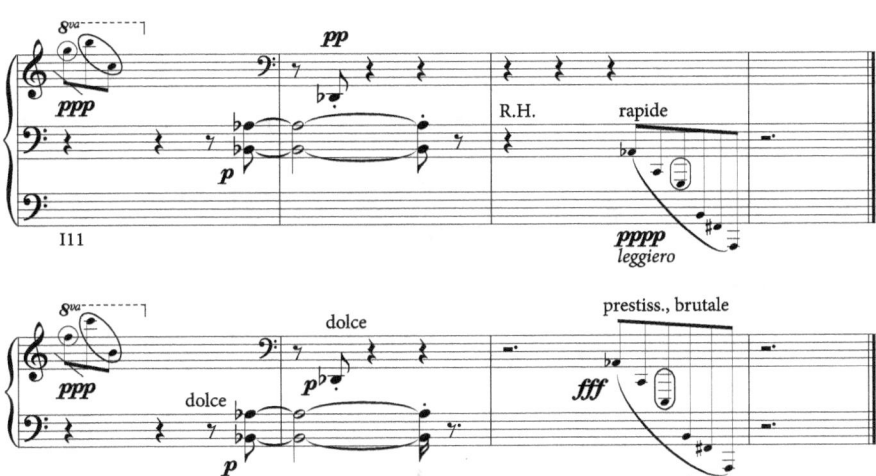

Example 6.8 A typeset version of the sketch for the ending of Meale's *Coruscations* (above), and the final score (below), with the different pitches annotated.

is needed. Given that every recording plays an E, the 'creative engraving' is now the performance practice. One of the biggest changes from sketch to score is a passage on page 9 (Example 6.9). In the sketch all the material is in the bass clef, and in the score all the material appears on a staff with a treble clef. The E♯ in the treble clef indicates the mistake, since Meale uses F rather than E♯ when he wants that pitch class. With Universal Edition routinely printing 500 copies of its new scores, it would be difficult for Meale to change this after printing, and very soon after the first performance the work had been recorded and was becoming well known. In a work that is very much about performance, the engraving too emerges as creative. Given that Meale's programme note emphasizes his 'decisions' about deploying the scheme as 'the most important point', these changes (errors) present no structural problem. Nevertheless they reveal much about his compositional process. One of the significant differences between sketch and score is in the first bar. The sketches show Meale's use of an eraser to correct mistakes, but only in the first flourish is an earlier version still clearly visible, at 50 per cent of the opacity of the surrounding pitches (see Example 6.10). Here, Meale's composing and Boulez's procedure are only partially distinguishable from each

Example 6.9 A sketch for Meale's *Coruscations* (above), and the final score (below), with the different clefs annotated.

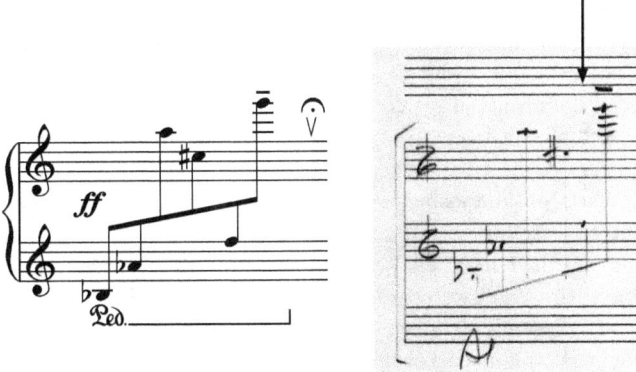

Example 6.10 A sketch for the beginning of Meale's *Coruscations* (right), and the final score (left).

other, and Meale, Boulez's book, the pencil and the eraser co-create the music. If the final note of the first group were an E, the sonority would be completed as predicted by the scheme. But a G occurs in the score. And the sketch clearly shows an E with three ledger lines erased, and a G written next to it. The erasure results in the last two pitches of that group being more assertively pencilled than the first four. This change from sketch to score is therefore not an error, and it is unlikely that Meale could have overlooked the number of ledger lines when the two pitches are next to each other; and it is more likely that the change deliberately added a ledger line. The G is more dramatic, giving a more strongly rising shape to end the flourish, and also means that the opening registral span is not exceeded until the end of the stave.[41] This shows how crucial the sketching stage was, the flexibility of Meale's decisions and how little he felt tied to the scheme.

This use of the eraser does not correct an error, in the sense of reinforcing a plan (Meale is not a draughtsman). The adjustment comes after the scheme, but before a musical object. In other words there is an immediate avoidance of a musical object formed from the scheme, and therefore to speak of repetition and variation of sonority A1, even if several cells in the piece carry that label, is to engage in a process likely to set up unhelpful structures at odds with the plasticity of the piece and its dynamic form. The chord labels in the sketches are also less certain than they might appear, given that the chords are transferred to pitch sequences in which the order is not determined by the precompositional processes, and which work to undercut the planning of the scheme by forming flexible fields of pitch material.

For Edwards,[42] the piece is split between the composers' decisions and those of the pianist. Given that many of the rhythms of the work are projected through the hands of the pianist, and that Meale is himself one, a strict separation of composer and performer is difficult to maintain. The work is pulled in two directions: one direction is spontaneous, with Meale writing a piece for his own instrument, concerned with speed and immediacy; the other direction is carefully systematic, with Meale consistently accounting for the results of his compositional decisions. For Boulez, the task of the composer is to establish a system within which spontaneity is organized:

> if *at the start* [of composing] one settles on a plan of immediate action, of instantaneous reaction, of stimulated impulse (a kind of 'automatic writing' of actions and their function, set in motion to order by exact but unforeseen information) this empirically adopted idea is immediately falsified; one should find a system which will inevitably engender these 'provocations' and stimuli rather than writing them according to a fixed disposition whose surface logic can never assume a generative function so as to *organise* the action.[43]

Whether Meale's piece inevitably connects system and action or not depends on how embedded the performer is in the piece. It would seem from the sketches that the piece is very much a performer's response to a technique, and to the material that the technique produces, the book in which the technique is discussed and the music of that book's author. In other words, Meale's 'system' is markedly widened to encompass a greater sense of the performer within the compositional process than Boulez discusses.

Meale's work is not centred in the anglophone world, and the 'cultural recycling' that characterizes Davies, for example, hardly operates in *Coruscations*, which is rather more concerned with music that is internally energetic than it is with parody or homage (in this it is different from Banks's music, too).[44] What, then, is to be gained by recognizing Boulez's ideas in Meale's composition? For sure, few of Meale's audience would have understood the connection. In any case, the *Boulez on Music Today/Coruscations* relation is an abstract one of pure technique, free from specific musical experiences, much as *Boulez on Music Today* is musically detailed but without explicit ties to particular pieces. In making this argument I am attempting a generous explication of the Boulez/Meale nexus, which addresses Meale's music as significant, rather than derivative, in which *Coruscations* is more than a platform for demonstrating *Boulez on Music Today*'s influence. In the writing of *Coruscations* Meale thinks through (pencil in hand, fingers on keys (of the typewriter and the piano)) the connections of action and thought, and impulse and organization.

Schiffer and Oakes are half right when they write that:

> The piece has an intricate impersonal glory like an heraldic frieze. Dynamic variety is great but the music refuses to bear specific emotional messages because rhythmically it is free from linguistic associations; its sounds act not as words but as electricity going straight to the nervous system.[45]

The half about which Schiffer and Oakes are right is when they come closest to Deleuze and Guattari:

> The work of art is a being of sensation and nothing else: it exists in itself. Harmonies are affects. Consonance and dissonance, harmonies of tone or colour, are affects of music or painting. [...] The artist creates blocks of percepts and affects, but the only law of creation is that the compound must stand up on its own. The artist's greatest difficulty is to make it *stand up on its own*. Sometimes this requires what is, from the viewpoint on an implicit model, from the viewpoint of lived perception and affections, great geometrical improbability, physical imperfection, and organic abnormality. [...] Standing up alone does not mean having a top and a bottom or being upright (for even houses are drunk and askew); it is only the act by which the compound of created sensations is preserved in itself – a monument, but one that may be contained in a few marks or a few lines[.][46]

The piece's 'impersonal glory' is its technique, in the way that Meale can be associated with Boulez through Boulez's explication of his technique, even when Meale does not follow his scheme. The accessibility of Boulez's book makes it (potentially) a matter of common experience, and this opposes the labels of 'difficult' and 'avant-garde' attached to Meale by early commentators. More importantly, Meale positions himself through Boulez as a member of a community of those who understood the significance of Boulez's music. That community need not be in the same place in order to function, since tapes, LPs, books, articles and performers were all moving from place to place. Such a notion works against ideas of nationalism such as 'Australian Music'.

Meale departs from serial processes, and from tonality (both of which return in *Incredible Floridas*), and turns to Boulez's chord multiplication, in which the internal attributes of chords are used to pass those chords into new sonorities. *Coruscations* looks to the future, perhaps like all works composed quickly and in response to new ideas, and it takes this view from Boulez, even as it departs from what Boulez writes; for Boulez's musical examples are abstract, about *The Music of Today*, not of yesterday, and therefore they do not explicitly cite an existing repertory. Although it can be seen that Boulez's examples do relate to music he had composed, this is not the book's point.

If modernism is to be considered a transnational movement, then the dissemination of ideas internationally is essential. The work of Bradshaw and Bennett in translating Boulez's text is therefore crucial; so too the distribution networks that moved books between the printing presses in Oxford and Meale in Adelaide. Meale's use of Boulez's technique contributes to an international movement that sought mutual comprehensibility, to which he was able to contribute through the materials of his publisher, Universal Edition.

The idea of comprehensibility through musical composition is itself raised by Woodward in an interview he gave in 1982, in which he spoke of auditioning for Boulez, playing Boulez's *Second Sonata*, and Meale's *Coruscations*:

> It stunned Boulez. In Baden Baden he sat on his couch and said 'who wrote that?', and I said 'Richard Meale'. And he smiled and he said: 'Please play it again.' And he was full of the most warm and generous praise for this piece. He was fascinated

by it, as was Olivier Messiaen when I played it to him at my Los Angeles debut in 1973. [...] Xenakis [...] loved it. Berio liked this piece. Berio was very fond of *Interiors/Exteriors* too, I remember.[47]

Clearly proud of his commission, Woodward continued with anecdotes about playing the work for Stockhausen, Cage, Feldman, Davies and Birtwistle. My point is less about the prestige that might be transferred to the work through the favour of a series of high-profile composers, and more about Woodward's own telling of the story, since Woodward groups *Coruscations* with other modernist music, asserting all the composers as members of a single communicative community. Implicit in the account is that Woodward, too, is part of that community, as the pianist whose performances make the international links material. Various programme notes and Woodward's early recordings were published internationally, going alongside performances of which little trace survives. The score, published by Universal Edition Australia, itself demonstrates the international ambition of that publishing house and of the Music Board of the Australia Council, which funded the score's printing.

If Meale's *Coruscations* is to be physical, in the manner of the plastic arts, then the hands of the pianist matter greatly. Although Meale was active as a pianist throughout this period, there is no recording of him performing *Coruscations* (there are no concert programmes listing him as a performer, either), and therefore the clearest autobiographical elements are in the sketches, which do trace a kind of performance. The opening erasure of an E in favour of a G is just such an event. Such an autobiographical opening has a history, too, as in the opening of Michel Leiris's *Aurora*: 'I was not yet thirty when I wrote *Aurora*.'[48] Although it is tempting to pursue Meale's love of French literature in seeking ancestors for the work, its immediate debt to Boulez is too great, and the speed of its composition too swift for careful genealogies (at the same time Boulez is a referent easily overemphasized, and there is a danger of distracting from Meale's achievement here). The piece contrasts with one by Vincent Plush, who wrote to Meale in 1972 about his new work based on Valéry's *Aurora*; however, in Meale's case, Valéry does not seem to inhabit the composition, even via Boulez.

In the same year as Meale composed *Coruscations*, he also composed *Incredible Floridas*, which sets Rimbaud, and makes different connections to French culture.

Incredible Floridas

In his authoritative history of modernism T. J. Clark argues that:

> [modernism] takes its own technicality and specialization as guarantees of truth. But at the same time it knows these qualities are potentially smug and philistine, always threatening to turn into a Bauhaus- or École de Paris-orthodoxy. Modernism's disdain for the world and wish for a truly gratuitous gesture in the face of it are more than just attitudes: they are the true (that is, agonized) form of its so-called purism. Wilde and Nietzsche are this agony's spokesmen, Rimbaud's its exemplary life.[49]

Modernism is a long project, with an extensive history for a composer working in the 1970s, by which time the core texts that established the ideas of the mid-twentieth-century musical modernists were all readily available and it was possible to take a long view of the music of the early twentieth century. *Coruscations* is Meale at his most technically distilled, and his next work, *Incredible Floridas* is Meale's composition at its most flexible, and also most troubled. *Coruscations* shows that Meale was technically up to date, which makes *Incredible Floridas*' gestures towards tonality and serial sections emblematic of the crisis of modernist Australian Music. This crisis is typically attributed to the 'silent period' in the mid-late 1970s shared by Meale, Sculthorpe, and Edwards, after which they composed more 'accessible music'; but for Meale the crisis is embodied in *Incredible Floridas*.

It took some time for Meale's *Incredible Floridas* to come to fruition, even if the pencil-on-paper stage took place swiftly in 1971 (the eightieth anniversary of Rimbaud's death). The idea of a work in homage to Rimbaud came at about the same time as the writing of *Homage to Garcia Lorca* (1965). In a letter dated 1 March 1965, Curt Prerauer asked Meale: 'How far is Rimbaud? Is it in a state where one may have a look? Or even ready, for an "analysis?"'[50] In a later letter (12 March 1965) to Wolfgang Fortner, Prerauer referred to 'Homage to Rimbaud' as an orchestral work.[51] On 25 June 1965, Meale described its form in a letter to James Murdoch as:

> bigger than Nocturnes in all respects. Not that I am aiming for a gradual increase in length and orchestral size, it has all just happened this way. In this work, as in Lorca, seating arrangement will be important. There will be two string orchestras, behind them a block of woodwinds, on either side of the W. W. a brass choir. Five horns spread across at the back of the woodwind block to link with the brass choirs so that a 'wall' of brass is also possible. Separating the two string orchestras is a piano (lid off and facing the conductor), whilst deploying at various points throughout the orchestra are the other percussive – melodic instruments – vibes, harp, marimba, glockenspiel, xylophone, celeste and tubular bells. At the back of the orchestra will be four percussion players plus timpani. Each movement will be separated by a setting of a Rimbaud poem for soprano (and orchestra). The work can be performed three ways. As a song cycle with only the vocal movements, as an orchestral work without the vocal movements, or in its entirety. Estimated length – approximately one hour.[52]

In 1971 Murdoch was managing the Fires of London, and the opportunity came for a new commission for Meale. The earlier plans were revised, and a smaller-scale score was composed, to go alongside other Australian works and a composition from Peter Maxwell Davies in a concert for an International Society for Contemporary Music (ISCM) festival:

> [Donald] Peart has sent four scores: Nigel's [Butterley] Variations; Keith Humble's *Archetype IV*; Helen Gifford *Of Old Angkor* and your *Interior/Exterior*. Max has rejected them all except yours, and so has the ISCM London, as being just not good

enough. Because of the difficulty of 2 pianos and three percussions and the fact that it would most certainly only get one performance – we, and Plaistow of the ISCM/BBC would dearly love you to write a new work, based on the instrumentation of the Fires of London (Pierrot Players) for the Festival and so that we can travel it around, especially when we come to Australia and New Zealand for a tour in 1973. Plaistow is writing to Peart and Carter strongly suggesting this. So please, do you think you can manage a work (music theatre work?) so that we can have it by late April? Why no work by Sculthorpe, or David Ahern or B. Conningham? [sic][53]

Given that *Coruscations* was not finished until the beginning of March, it is remarkable that Meale was able to complete the score of *Incredible Floridas* early enough to be performed at the ISCM festival in July.[54] Both works demonstrate that there were no problems of 'time-lag' between Australia and Britain, the music being performed in London immediately after its composition in Adelaide. Murdoch wrote again shortly after Woodward's performance of *Coruscations* (25 April):

Please don't let yourself falter about Floridas at this stage. The fight has been too long and we have won. At this stage of your career – changing publishers especially[55] – it is so important for your work to be performed at this Festival and that you are here for it. [...]

There has been unbelievable politics behind this concert which I won't bore you with now and I've nearly lost it altogether several times. It has finally been settled as follows:

Butterley – Variations
Sculthorpe – Tabu Tabuhan [sic]
Interval
Meale – Incredible Floridas
Davies – Revelation and Fall

The first half of the programme will be performed by London Sinfonietta because Max refused to do them, and the second half by The Fires of London. Max refused to have Tabu on the same programme and threatened to cancel Revelation and Fall if it went on but because it had become very complicated, finally agreed so long as the programme was split in two and the other group performed Tabu. [...]

Ross [Edwards] is working around the clock copying the parts [of *Incredible Floridas*] and I await anxiously the second part.[56]

Meale's decision not to use the soprano must have been an artistic one rather than for practical reasons, since it is the only deviation from the ensemble's usual forces.

Meale's interest in other cultures emerged over the decade prior to *Incredible Floridas*. His first trip abroad was enabled by a Ford Foundation Grant in 1960, which took him to UCLA to study *gagaku*, as well as Javanese and Balinese gamelan. The foundation's funding had been awarded on the basis of his Sonata for Flute and Piano, which in 1963 was performed at an ISCM festival. Following his studies in the USA, Meale travelled to England and Spain. It was on his return that he composed *Homage to*

Garcia Lorca and *Las Alboradas*. By Meale's second trip to Spain he was less enamoured with the country, writing to Murdoch on 20 August 1966 that:

> Spain was disappointing. I'm older, and so is it. Although I'd still like to live there, I'm not enchanted any more. So, no more works with Spanish titles!

On the other hand, he found new energy for France, having travelled there for the Paris Rostrum:

> Paris was marvellous. How terrible to come back here after being in that milieu that was truly intellectually alive.[57]

The Spanish works of the mid-1960s were interrupted by several compositions based on Japanese themes. By the early 1970s Meale's Francophilia again had the upper hand, but the title *Incredible Floridas* picks up the journeying theme from *Very High Kings*,[58] the subtitle of which – 'The Mystical Voyage of Christopher Columbus' – underlines the Europe/USA link that Columbus enabled, as found in Rimbaud's poem:

> I have struck, do you realize, incredible Floridas, where mingle with flowers the eyes of panthers in human skins! Rainbows stretched like bridles under the seas' horizon, to glaucous herds![59]

A programme note explains one account of the work's genesis:

> Ten years ago [later versions of this note give 1961] the idea of writing a work as a tribute to [Arthur] Rimbaud occurred to me whilst I was re-reading his poems to pass away the long flight from London to Sydney. The 'hermetically sealed' atmosphere of the plane, intensified his burning, passionate violence (sensually and intellectually) and I was stunned once again, as I had been when I first encountered his work in my teens. My reaction to his work is entirely personal, and I feel justified in taking such a reaction to his writings since they, themselves were entirely personal. In fact, despite many, valuable efforts, much of his work cannot be 'broken down'. They [sic] remain locked in the mystery in which he created them – his own alchemical world.[60]

First movement

Incredible Floridas begins with members of the ensemble declaiming the following text, from Rimbaud's poem *Voyelles*:

> A noir, E blanc, I rouge, U vert, O bleu: voyelles

The colours and five vowels align with the gradual entries of each instrument at the start of the piece: the cello begins, playing its lowest string, C, tuned down an octave (this pitch returns throughout the composition at structural moments); the bass clarinet is next, an octave and a tritone above; then the alto flute with G; and then the viola with a {D, A} chord. These instruments are all able to sustain their sound, and so the introduction of notes is also the formation of harmony itself. The specific configuration enables both a cycle of fifths in order of entry, C, G, D, A, E (ignoring the F♯), and two interlocking major chords: C and D (the latter of which includes the F♯). The percussion then adds {E♭, B♭} to make possible an E♭ major triad (see Example 6.11). With these chords, and a cycle of fifths, Meale gives us a glimpse of a tonal or modal working that is not characteristic of his music at this time, though it is also not without precedent, given the tonal moments in *Clouds Now and Then*, and *Very High Kings*. The pitch entries that enable the three triads coincide rhythmically with the declamation of red, green and blue. 'Black' aligns with the {C, F♯} tritone, and 'white' with the {C, G} fifth. Meale's opening therefore presents the essential stuff of sound, vision and speech, and immediately following the declamation of 'voyelles', the piano plays a twelve-tone flourish.[61] These bars establish the harmonic materials of the work, which bring together a set of repeated intervals (semitones, fifths), diatonic triads, dodecaphony, all unfolding over a stable pitch (the cello's C).[62]

The opening presents the composition's clearest relationship between text and music. The initial declamation ends with: 'Je dirai quelque jour vos naissance latentes.'[63]

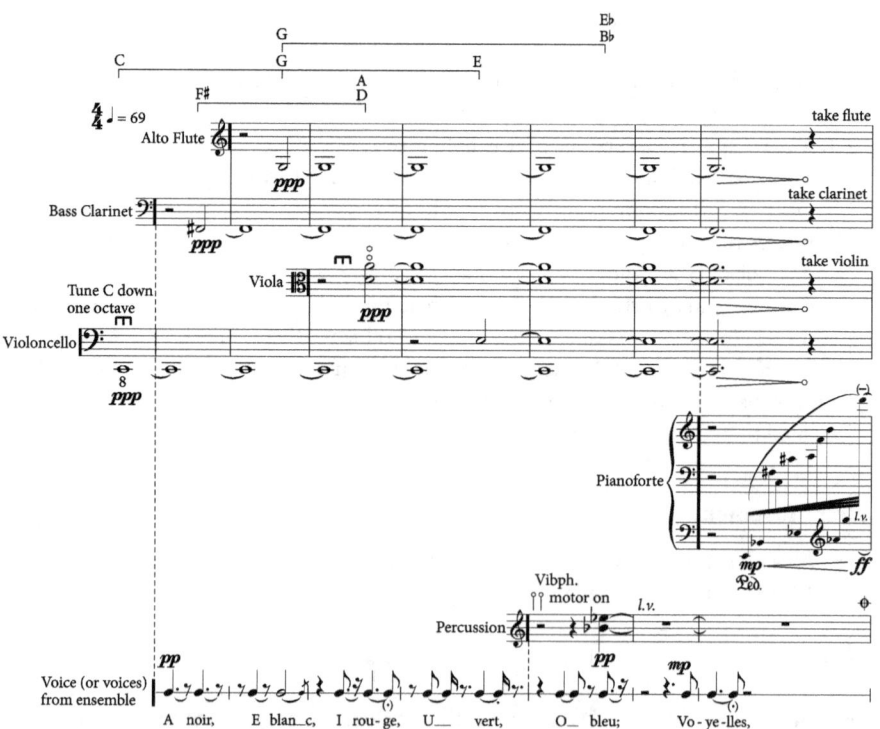

Example 6.11 Meale, *Incredible Floridas*, 'I', bars 1–8 (all instruments sound as written).

The following music is appropriate to that text, in that it is about essential pitch materials, being formed by an E♭–A cluster (bar 12) and semitone chords. At bar 21, various performers again declaim 'A noir, E blanc, I rouge, U vert, O bleu', the vowels and colours now overlapping, to accompany a simple flute melody. The melody is built from semitones, tritones and a perfect fourth (the two tones are better conceptualized as semitones away from a preceding pitch), so the two strata are linearizations of semitone clusters (see Example 6.12). The pitch fields here are closer to Meale's music from the 1960s than the sonorities of *Coruscations*.[64] With no more declamation from the instrumentalists, it is impossible to attach securely Rimbaud's text to the music. This is not a setting of Rimbaud, but Meale's homage, written almost a century after the poems it admires.

The writing in *Incredible Floridas* is orchestral, and its details aim to maximize the timbral possibilities of the instruments, even (perhaps especially) in timbrally similar combinations. The result is music with internal vibrancy, in which lines cohere into harmonies that maintain the energy of discrete components. The constantly rearranged semitones keep the music fluid, enabling transformations that maintain the consistency of harmony and highlight the variable tessitura, timbres and textures. The music is most impressive close up, in the details of each moment. For example (see Example 6.13), following the opening declamation, the music's tempo slows, the rhythmic values elongate and a narrow registral band is used. The passage's constituent lines are also differentiated, since the violin and cello are given different performance directions: the violin 'ord., *mp*'; the cello '*intenso e appassionato*, M.V., *ff*'. The cello's higher tessitura adds significantly to the impression of a line that is distinct, even though it is registrally close to the violin, whilst the violin's open G string restricts the possibility of vibrato (which is therefore not specifically denied in the score), and its mute creates a part that shadows the cello. Throughout the piece the instrumental

Example 6.12 Meale, *Incredible Floridas*, 'I', bars 21–5, melody.

Example 6.13 Meale, *Incredible Floridas*, 'I', bars 26–31, violin and cello.

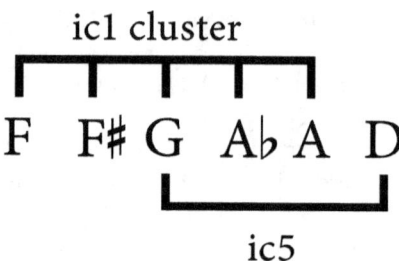

Example 6.14 Showing D in relation to the midpoint of the cluster.

writing is careful, detailed and vibrant even in its restrained textures. In this way Meale explores a wide range of timbres, much as Rimbaud's poetry derives its meaning from his use of five vowels.

In *Coruscations*, musical objects are tenuous. *Incredible Floridas* is full of neatly bounded sections, marked by silences and abrupt juxtapositions of texture, which keep the focus on the present sound. The harmony is repetitive, and static. For example, at bar 67 the clarinet, violin, cello and vibraphone suddenly play a single chord repeated in rapid homophonic triplets. Against this the flute plays a simple melody: <F, F♯, G, A♭, D, A>; in other words an F–A cluster with an added D (see Example 6.14). The accompaniment is quasi-octatonic {B♭, C, C♯, E♭, E, G}, which is to say that it comprises semitones spaced at the interval of a third, with an ambivalence about the quality of that third. Reading this as octatonic also connects the section with the composers Meale most consistently admired, Debussy and Messiaen. Meale next elongates the held A (which makes up the aggregate with the pitches in the piano's flourish), with the violin taking it over before the flautist runs out of breath, and he repeats the piano flourish three times to create a moment of stasis that emphasizes the {A, C} between flute/violin and piano. With only a small number of instruments in the ensemble, the movement's harmonies tend to contain only a handful of notes (which is also to say that the piano is often treated melodically), and the melodies are also limited in their scope. This sense of limitation is one of the ways in which the movement achieves its intensity, just as the wide variety of timbral shifts often disguise similarity in the music with what has gone before.

Second movement

The second movement, 'fêtes de la faim' (Example 6.15), begins with discontinuous material in the manner of Stravinsky's *Symphonies of Wind Instruments*, Debussy's *Jeux* or Ravel's Le Gibet.[65] The opening is rocky, tilting to and fro from percussion and piano, to flute, clarinet and violin. The cello's repeating {G, A} chord, *ff*, provides

Example 6.15 Meale, *Incredible Floridas*, 'II', bars 1–10.

Example 6.16 Meale, *Incredible Floridas*, 'II', bars 28–33.

an unsteady base for the upper voices. The piano's chords[66] are slowly reconfigured by transposition and additional notes. The flute/clarinet/violin is clearer harmonically, with semitones, fifths, fourths and tritones (at various octaves).

Six bars before the end of the movement the percussion begins, *pp*, and the drum, hi-hat and cowbell introduce the piano, flute, clarinet, and violin, which play the music from the start homorhythmically, with the hocketing now ironed out into dance-like rhythms (see Example 6.16). The ending therefore reveals a relatively straightforward song for three instrumental voices accompanied by piano, defragmenting the opening exposition. At the same time the reprise reveals the movement's source in popular music, which is unusual for a composition by Meale (at least in this period of his work) – since in interviews from this period, Meale consistently asserts his music as 'abstract' – though it repeats a process used previously used in *Las Alboradas*. In correspondence with Murdoch, Meale explains that *Las Alboradas* is both abstract, and very much based on specific existing music:

> I had long been impressed by the enormous amount of non-flamenco music in Spain, and as an amateur ethnomusicologist decided to study some of it. I obtained a collection of music from Extremadura. Included in it were three Alboradas which I began to study. I conceived of the idea of using their structure as the background to a composition, which I did. Hence the title – *Las* Alboradas (*The* Alboradas). Because these melodies have been treated in an abstract fashion, there is no surface trace of them in the composition. In other words, Las Alboradas doesn't sound at all like Spanish music! However, far at the back of them, these three melodies live in secret – so to speak. Already I have forgotten where and how they lie. Furthermore, I would not be interested to know again. Still, although I specifically state the non-Spanish sound of the music, I cannot in all respects say the final product has no direct relationship with the implications from the title. For instance, an Alborada is a love song sung by a young man to his girl at dawn on a feast-day beneath her balcony. I still regard my Alboradas as being love-songs, though this may not be immediate to the listener. However, they are characterised by their intensity and their lyricism (an almost abstracted lyricism which I would describe as a hyper-lyricism, the essence of all that is lyrical). As well there is the 'caressing' character of the melodic structures – for instance, the opening solo flute passage which is a crystallisation of the melodic shapes. The intensity of feeling which I mentioned, is probably most noticeable in the way chords accumulate their tones in crescendo throughout the work and the way in which the episodes (particularly for the first movement) renew themselves and become more eloquent in each instance.[67]

The melodies that form the basis of *Las Alboradas* are beside the point, since Meale, like his contemporaries, was not interested in playing 'spot the tune'.[68] As in *Las Alboradas*, in the second movement of *Incredible Floridas* Meale rewrites music ('jazz') that is essentially tonal or modal. This transformation retains – in its fragmentation – something more continuous and consistent.

Third movement

The third movement is titled 'Sonata 1: Le Bateau Ivre', and it is formally more complicated than the two earlier movements. Although it is not entirely clear what Meale means by 'sonata', on one hand the term emphasizes the composition's nature as an instrumental work, free from the texts of vocal music that the opening of the composition raises, underlining an absent soprano. On the other hand this sonata might be better considered alongside the following two movements, which are designated an 'Interlude' and a 'Sonata II', to suggest Cage's *Sonatas and Interludes*, even if the music has nothing to do with Cage's work.[69] Perhaps the term aims to capture the alternation

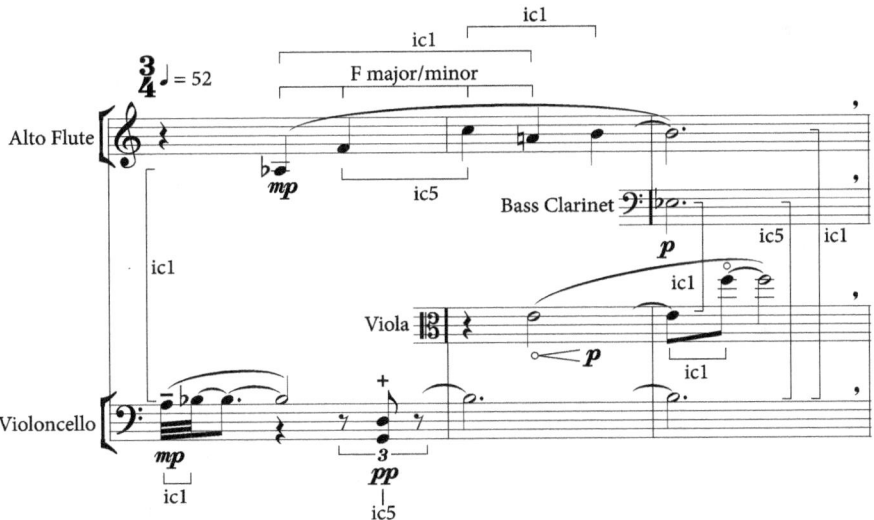

Example 6.17 Meale, *Incredible Floridas*, 'III', bars 1–3, with the pitch relationships annotated.

of solo lines and group chords.⁷⁰ The movement begins with precisely these textures (Example 6.17), with an alto flute melody that, like the opening of the first movement, gradually unfolds. Its intervallic construction is also familiar – semitones, a fifth and a tritone – with the opening two-bar incipit containing the material for both F minor and F major triads. The other instruments do not support a tonal reading, since the cello's B♭ is held throughout the opening six-bar section, and even as the B♭ combines with G and D,⁷¹ and later D and F, there is too much happening at once for this to sound like anything other than the expansion of a pitch space based on B♭.

Fourth movement

All the surviving sketches for *Incredible Floridas* relate to the fourth movement. Meale's archive also contains a partial analysis of some parts of the movement.⁷² If the opening of the composition gives the vowels intervals, sets out a pitch centre on C and suggests triadic chords, taking five steps along a cycle of fifths for the five vowels declaimed musically by five performers, then the opening of the 'Interlude' transforms elements into arching triads. The C pitch centre is preserved, held under a series of major triads: C major, then E♭, F♯, D, C, E, B♭, C, E♭, F♯ and D (see Example 6.18). The roots of these chords were introduced in the first seven bars of the first movement.

Like the second movement, which begins with fragmented music that is later given in greater coherence, the start of the fourth movement reorders the beginning of the piece, gathering together the latent triads into an explicit sequence of parallel chords.

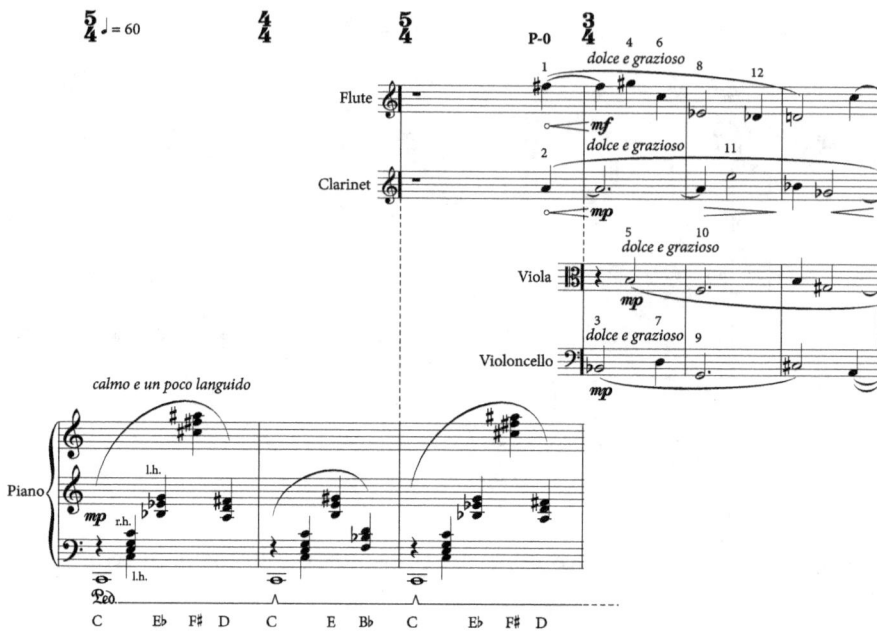

Example 6.18 Meale, *Incredible Floridas*, 'IV', bars 1-6, with the pitch structures annotated.

This is a moment in the work where the poem that Meale uses as a subtitle is useful to consider:

> Quand le monde sera réduit en un seul bois noir pour nos quatre yeux étonnés, – en une plage pour deux enfants fidèles, – en une maison musicale pour notre claire sympathie, – je vous trouverai.[73]

That 'manifest sympathy' is the pantonal language that goes, again, straight to the composers most significant to Meale: Messiaen and Debussy.[74] For Meale writing in 1971, the simplicity of the fourth movement's opening is wilfully naïve, playing on the familiarity of a major triad, and returning to C major three times before the flute and clarinet enter. When they do, it is with A and F♯, slickly aligning the D major chord with the first two pitches of the row, for the bulk of the movement is serial. With *Coruscations*' rigours so distant from this work, much of it gives the impression of intuitive, instinctive writing, yet here the tonal/serial interface is elegant and seamless.

The pitches of the flute, clarinet, viola and cello enter as predicted, if counting along the first row of the matrix held in Meale's archives (Example 6.19):[75]

Example 6.19 Meale's sketch of the matrix for *Incredible Floridas*.

The 'P numbers' in this example are determined by order number, not transposition. So too are the 'I numbers', though Meale inconsistently numbers these above and below the staves to which they refer. How the R and RI number are determined is not clear, though the few that are labelled in the sketch do match Example 6.20. For ease of use, the analysis here will use the P/I matrix shown in Figure 6.1.

The serial writing begins straightforwardly, and with a slight rearranging of pitch order, Meale facilitates a transition from P-0 to I-1, and then back to P-0, which then overlaps with R-0. By bar 18, P-7 and RI-6 are happening at the same time, and a few bars later RI-12 is mixed with R-0, P-5 and I-1. At bar 23, I-4, P-3, R-1 and RI-5 all occur simultaneously. A page of sketches shows Meale planning this increase in the density of simultaneous row forms (Example 6.20).[76]

With maximum density reached, the four instruments fade, and the piano returns, repeating its first two bars (Example 6.21). If the transition from D major to serialism was seamless, the return to C major is not quite so elegant. The piano repeats its chords

	I-0	I-3	I-4	I-2	I-5	I-6	I-8	I-9	I-1	I-11	I-10	I-7	
P-0	F♯	A	B♭	A♭	B	C	D	E♭	G	F	E	C♯	R-0
P-9	E♭	F♯	G	F	A♭	A	B	C	E	D	C♯	B♭	R-9
P-8	D	F	F♯	E	G	A♭	B♭	B	E♭	C♯	C	A	R-8
P-10	E	G	A♭	F♯	A	B♭	C	C♯	F	E♭	D	B	R-10
P-7	C♯	E	F	E♭	F♯	G	A	B♭	D	C	B	A♭	R-7
P-6	C	E♭	E	D	F	F♯	A♭	A	C♯	B	B♭	G	R-6
P-4	B♭	C♯	D	C	E♭	E	F♯	G	B	A	A♭	F	R-4
P-3	A	C	C♯	B	D	E♭	F	F♯	B♭	A♭	G	E	R-3
P-11	F	A♭	A	G	B♭	B	C♯	D	F♯	E	E♭	C	R-11
P-1	G	B♭	B	A	C	C♯	E♭	E	A♭	F♯	F	D	R-1
P-2	A♭	B	C	B♭	C♯	D	E	F	A	G	F♯	E♭	R-2
P-5	B	D	E♭	C♯	E	F	G	A♭	C	B♭	A	F♯	R-5
	RI-0	RI-3	RI-4	RI-2	RI-5	RI-6	RI-8	RI-9	RI-1	RI-11	RI-10	RI-7	

Figure 6.1 A P/I matrix for Meale's *Incredible Floridas*.

exactly as at the start of the movement, the serial music having made no impact in the intervening bars. The last serial chord – {G, B, E, E♭} – connects to the major/minor thirds of the piano's chords. The G in the bass is by choice rather than dictated by a scheme, and Meale's sketch indicates that he was aware of the continuity of the G in the last three chords, something that a situation demanding greater tonal/serial integration might have emphasized.

None of the viola/cello counterpoint from bar 28 to 40 appears to be serial, and the harmony is as for other movements, based almost exclusively in a flexible ic1/ic5 field. The next transition from serial to tonal writing begins when P-0 returns at the end of bar 48, and ends above a low C from the piano. The harmony at bar 50 ({C, F, C♯, E}) is two semitones ({E, F}, {C, C♯}) separated by a fifth ({C, F}), which is typical of Meale's ic1/ic5 harmony in this period of his music; it can also be understood as a pair of semitones ({E, F}, {C, C♯}) a third apart ({C, E}, {C♯, F}), which means that it bridges

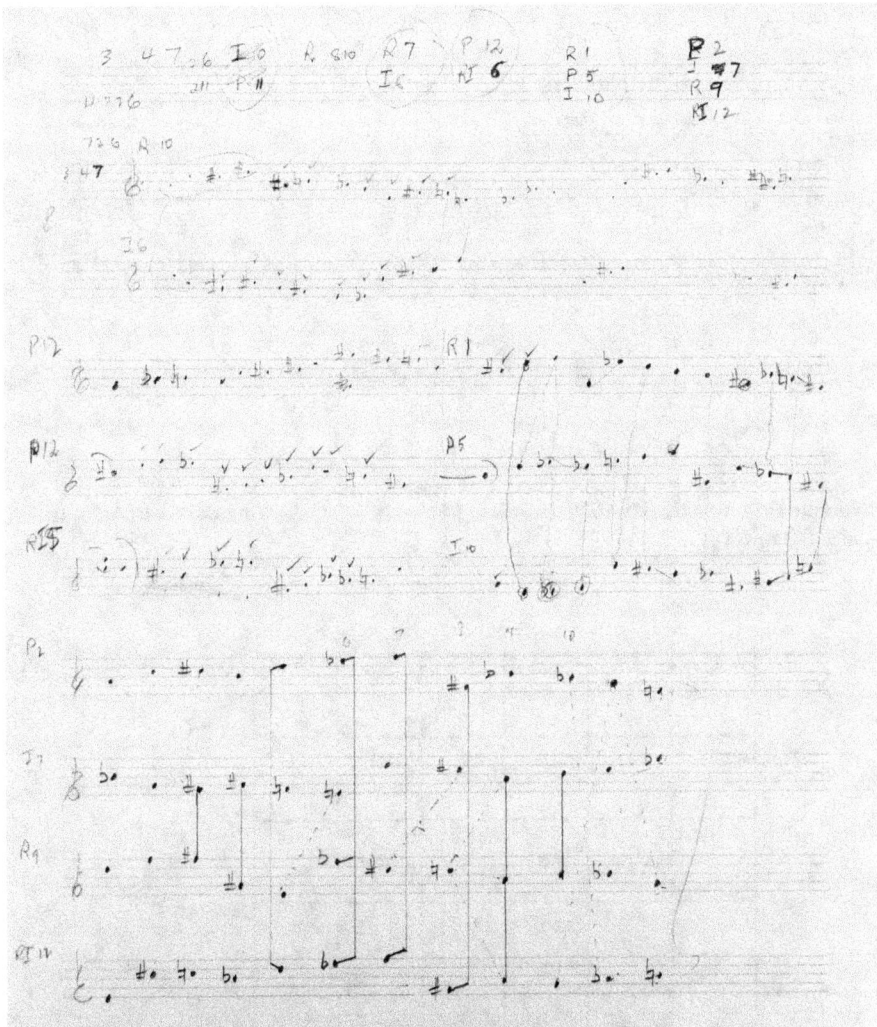

Example 6.20 Meale's sketch showing his serial workings for *Incredible Floridas*.

the series, the tendency towards ic1/ic5, and major/minor triads (indicated in Figure 6.2 as 'ic4'). Example 6.22 shows an annotated excerpt of the score. Figure 6.2 shows the conjunction of Meale's multiple harmonic systems on a *Tonnetz*, to demonstrate how neatly the systems come together.

Although his interface is carefully controlled, parallel triads and serialism are essentially incompatible, which poses a problem for Meale: beyond the simple interface of a row that begins with a third, is further integration possible? This question returns to the more general question of coherence. The opening of the composition dealt with

194 Australian Music and Modernism, 1960–1975

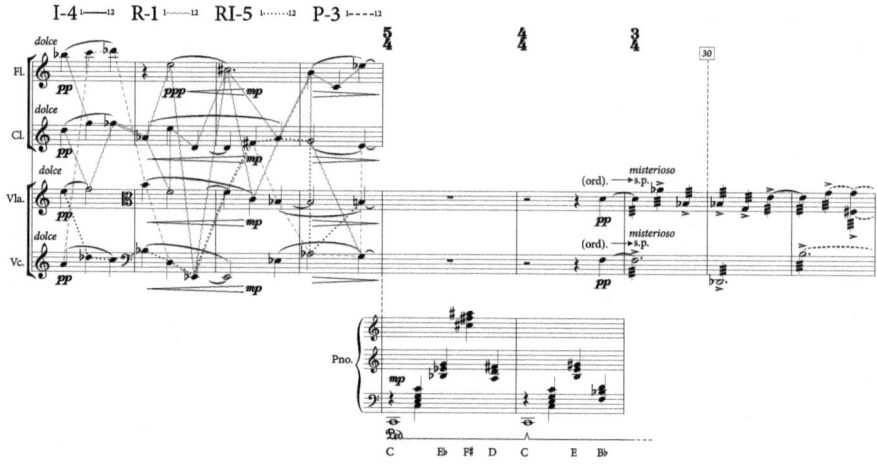

Example 6.21 Meale, *Incredible Floridas*, 'IV', bars 23–31, showing the interface of triadic and serial music.

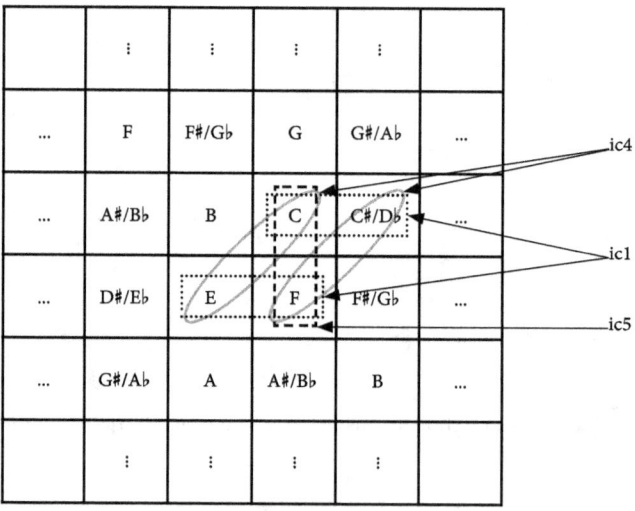

Figure 6.2 The conjunction of ic1/5 and 'major thirds' (ic4) at bar 50 of *Incredible Floridas*.

Example 6.22 Meale, *Incredible Floridas*, 'IV', bars 48–52, with the pitch structures annotated.

the problem of coexisting systems by avoiding it, since the triads interlock in a way that hides their presence, and the block structures cut off the section after a dodecaphonic flourish, but in the fourth movement both triadic and serial elements are fully exposed. Meale has set up the problem through alternating sections, but from bar 65 he brings the two systems into direct conflict. As a first step, Meale introduces new serial patterns from bar 53. Where earlier sections move through the rows linearly, with only slight deviations, now the row is broken into three-pitch segments (which is also a new kind of fragmentation) (Example 6.23).

Example 6.23 Meale, *Incredible Floridas*, 'IV', bars 53–8, with the serial structures annotated.

The principal line here is the violin's, shadowed with a more active and softer flute, and marked by the vibraphone's sparse rhythms. Although the speed of each line is different (with the vibraphone slower than the violin, which is slower than the flute), the rate at which the series progresses is similar in all parts. This gives the impression of dynamism within a constant rate of structural unfolding. At bar 65 the violin simply stops, and the vibraphone continues the material that combines its earlier fragmented material, with the flute's rolling triplets in a melody marked 'cantabile'. This is not serial, though it sounds as though it could be, and takes place alongside a slow-moving chorale (see Example 6.24).

The chorale is the centrepiece of the movement, and one of the most extraordinary moments in Meale's music from the early 1970s. Each chord in this chorale is a major/minor tetrachord. It begins with a chord on C ({C, E♭, E, G}), and continues with chords based similarly on E♭, E, D, F, F♯, G♯, A, C♯, B, B♭, G. The order of these chords follows P-6:

<C, E♭, E, D, F, F♯, G♯, A, C♯, B, B♭, G>.

The minor/major interval itself comes from the series, which can be divided into three-pitch segments as follows:

<C, E♭, E>, <D, F, F♯>, <G♯, A, C♯>, <B, B♭, G>.

Three of these segments comprise a minor and a major third, and Meale adds the fifth to complete the major+minor chords. The transposition used (P-6) is at the tritone and Meale's sketch of the matrix has a line through the sixth pitch, which is also a tritone higher than the first. The chorale is 'triadic', the movement between each major+minor chord functioning 'serially'. In other words, this section distorts the associations with both tonal and serial practice, transforming one through the other.

Where the triadic reading of the composition's opening is less convincing than a scalar or cycle-of-fifths explanation, the latent possibility of major chords from those pitches is explicit in the opening of the 'Interlude' and necessary in the chorale, which unites the work's serial, modal and triadic patterns. Meale does not set up a scheme to do this automatically, and he contrives the unification of ideas by adding notes to complete the 'triads'. When he does so, the chords formed are consistent with the

Example 6.24 Meale, *Incredible Floridas*, 'IV', bars 65–70, with the pitch structures annotated.

harmonies (conforming to an ic1/ic5 field) of so much of his non-schematic music. The movement ends definitively with a C-major chord in root position.

One of the three poems that Meale associates with the 'Interlude', 'Veillées', has the following lines (its second part):

> L'éclairage revient à l'arbre de bâtisse. Des deux extrémités de la salle, décors quelconques, des élévations harmoniques se joignent.[77]

Reading the second sentence with a musical translation for 'harmoniques se joignent' describes *Incredible Floridas*' harmonic transformation, and this description configures *Incredible Floridas* as the culmination of Meale's harmonic practices from the 1960s.[78]

As such, *Incredible Floridas* is a significant retreat from the technical explorations of *Coruscations*, and although he does later use chord multiplication in the oboe concerto *Evocations*, that work has none of *Coruscations*' brilliance. *Incredible Floridas* is the most impressive of Meale's works from the 1970s, though stylistically it belongs with his music written in the 1960s.

*

In the years leading up to *Incredible Floridas* Meale worked hard to introduce Australian audiences to modernist French music. In the 1960s his work responded to music from Japan, Indonesia, France and Spain. These responses are idiosyncratic, specific and deliberate, rather than globalizing.[79] By 1971 Meale was more certain about his musical interests; his music more keenly responded to French culture, and simultaneously his response to Rimbaud became more modest. The long genesis of *Incredible Floridas* is, in part, its own material, the work loosening its ties to Rimbaud throughout the late 1960s, to the extent that only a handful of relationships can be drawn. The technical developments that continued to drive his music form a less important part of this work, though Meale's return to tonality and serialism create the music's most striking moments.

Incredible Floridas and *Coruscations* are the high point of Meale's modernism; these are compositions that realize the technical ambitions of earlier works, fulfilling their possibilities. They also exhaust Meale's possibilities. If *Coruscations*, written entirely from chord multiplication, is an attempt to impose a way of working from without, *Incredible Floridas* responds to Rimbaud as modernism's 'exemplary life', and in so doing questions the composer's capacity to sustain a modernist attitude in Adelaide.

Those eager to believe Meale when he declared that his music was abstract, and those who were keen to embrace his later tonal music for its new-found 'expression', did so at the expense of the music that actually works with the differences between diverse approaches, and the music that generates its materials from contrasts, restrictions, syntheses and excesses. The early supporters who championed Meale's modernism, who saw modernism as a transnational project in which they too were newly engaged, configured Meale as a figurehead of Australian Music's 'avant-garde'. Meale's music neither solidly supports this designation, nor, critically, undermines it. The point is that Meale, as a late-twentieth-century composer, has serialism, chord multiplication, tonality (including such as developed by Satie, Debussy and Stravinsky), modality, atonality, dodecaphony and any number of other strategies on which to draw. His tonal methods after *Viridian* may have been more consistent, but they are not without precedent in his most 'modernist' compositions from the 1960s and 1970s.[80]

Later arguments about Meale's 'plurality' take on the following general form: diverse musical interests inform the person, who then writes music about music, with coherence guaranteed through single authorship. However, his music rarely bears the hallmarks of experiences manifesting as stylistic imitation, borrowing or appropriation, and in the interviews from the time, Meale again and again stresses that his compositions are absolute music:

> There is in the long run a piece of music to which one listens. In other words, I don't believe that music is full of meaning [...] we should be totally concerned with its relevance today [rather than what an historical work might have meant, or how it might have been performed]. [...] For the creative artist today I think this realization is most important. From it he can gain what is generally called artistic freedom. He gains it by knowing all the factors surrounding the work, as many factors as he can. In other words, he does study techniques but to my mind only to forget them. These things become part of oneself and one goes, so to speak, beyond any specific technique in itself. [...] We speak of understanding music, but I cannot see that there is anything to understand. All we essentially do is listen to it. When people say 'I do not understand this piece', I really don't know what they mean and I doubt if they know what they mean [...]. So essentially I think that there is no understanding music, there is no understanding art: one merely looks at it or listens to it, and depending on the complexity of one's relationships to music or to any art form one derives more experience, that is, the experience of listening or looking is more complex, dependent upon whether you have gathered the complexes of these arts around you.[81]

The personal/absolute dialectic is Meale-the-modernist's usual way of explaining his work, with technique mediating experience and music. That strategy is more useful for *Coruscations* than it is for *Incredible Floridas*, in part because of the quick composition of the former and the long genesis of the latter. At the same time *Incredible Floridas* comes with its travels, as its title implies.

Meale's explanation of his own Spanish travels in relation to *Las Alboradas* relates to the composer's voyage of self-discovery – Meale as an expressionist – rather than discovering anything specifically Spanish:

> [Travels in Spain] produced two works which have direct Spanish reference. *Las Alboradas* I wrote when I came back from Spain. I was so disturbed at losing this country that I had to do something myself to try to recapture it in my own mind. The music itself has got no Spanish reference at all, but is more my own feelings towards the country[.][82]

This is, as we know from the unpublished interview with Murdoch quoted above, not entirely correct, as *Las Alboradas* is specifically related to three songs, but this incorrectness only further underlines that the songs were ones that Meale happened to hear, rather than songs for an audience to go and seek out in order to understand the piece. Meale's attitude might also inform our understanding of *Incredible Floridas*, and also explain some of the reasons for the dramatic differences between that work and *Coruscations*.

The first String Quartet (1974)

Given that Meale's String Quartet No. 2 (1980) is one of his most performed works, it is surprising that the first quartet is almost never played. (Meale's previous work, the oboe concerto *Evocations*, has also rarely been performed, despite having been written for Heinz Holliger and Paul Sacher's Collegium Musicum Zurich.) The first String Quartet was premiered at the opening of Sydney's Seymour Centre, played by the Carl Pini Quartet, on 20 September 1975. Until 2014 there was neither a commercial nor a private recording available, though the original quartet recorded it for the BBC.[83] The parts, too, have been unavailable for performance, which is a problem for a work that has no performing score. The set of parts held by Universal Edition are heavily marked by the original quartet. There is a letter to Murdoch from David Worrall which may explain this:

> please find enclosed:
> 1. Score and parts to Richard's String Quartet. I have not erased all the scribblings on the parts [...] To let you see what sort of respect Australian performers have for Australian music.[84]

The first string quartet comes just before Meale's 'silent period'. For Michael Hannan this is 'a period of five years contemplative silence',[85] but Meale was actually working on several pieces (notably a piano concerto for Roger Woodward) that were not completed. His next acknowledged work is *Viridian*, shortly followed by String Quartet No. 2.

The sound-world of the first String Quartet is a long way from *Incredible Floridas* or *Evocations*. It is Meale's bleakest piece, and it represents the end of Meale's modernist period. The string quartet opens with a four-note cluster, followed by a series of near-clusters, the last of which merges into a cloud of harmonics. The next section divides the quartet in half, with violins playing together and the viola and cello together. In the third section of the score the instruments are connected by wavy stems, indicating that no precise coordination is required. Subsequent sections explore changes of texture against a consistent approach to the harmony. These are labelled as 'Variations', but quickly the formal structures of the opening sections break down into constantly varying textures (Example 6.25). The rhythms are only lightly constrained by the ictuses in the score that mark out time, and although the score indicates that they represent 'one to two seconds', Meale's directions to the performers say that 'it is even possible that these duration divisions can be less than one second or more than two, depending on the discretion of the ensemble'.[86] As the textures become increasingly complex, the music is formed by the close interaction of performers, who react to each other in placing their notes, rather than the work's nominal structure.

Example 6.25 Meale, String Quartet No. 1, pp. 1–2.

Example 6.25 *(continued)*

The flexibility that Meale affords the players is surprising, especially given that he had moved away from such freedoms after *Las Alboradas*. In the document 'Directions to Performers', which is not published with the score, Meale writes:

> Additional ornamentation may be used on sustained notes (e.g. momentary quartertone deviation, change of bow pressure, simultaneous arco-pizz, momentary tremolando, variation in vibrato, quick encircling arabesque returning to primary tone, rapid harmonics […]). These should be used discreetly.[87]

The striking word is 'additional', for what is ornamental about this music? Cast in solid blocks, the textures change but remain texturally in focus, and the work's sharp edges are starkly non-ornamental. (His invitation to the players freely to ornament their parts is an invitation best refused, as the Kreutzer Quartet did on their recent recording.[88])

The second section is subtitled '*far away*'. For this:

> it is preferable when acoustically and visually suitable, for the players to leave their chairs and take new positions towards the rear of the stage. This new seating position should be as dispersed as possible, so that there appears to be no visual contact between the players. It is also necessary for the players to perform with their back to the audience. [...] The aim is to create a visually remote and contemplative atmosphere.[89]

The section begins with a 'harmonic cloud'. Through the harmonic cloud three 'Tropes' – as Meale labels them – are audible. These are slow-moving sequences of pitches, to be played 'espressivo'. The term 'trope' refers obliquely to Boulez's Piano Sonata no. 3, the movement of Boulez's music that enables the performer to reorder their music. Although Meale sets the order of the tropes, there is nothing to distinguish one from the next. The only structural feature that suggests some kind of order is that in the first trope there is an approximate division of the sequences of pitches in halves, and those halves are about 6 pitches long, recalling the other meaning of the term 'trope' as a 'synonym for set', which implies 'the content of a collection but not its order.'[90]

The variations do not vary; the faraway clouds are unordered pitch sequences of background harmonics that are unpatterned, and foreground lines that are undirected. The challenge to the performers (whose instruments have also just been differently tuned) is to address the constantly slipping tunings with attentive adjustments, and to fiddle with the placements of pitches at the micro level, even as the macro level gains no higher structure. The quartet is therefore a decadent one, which fits Stephen Downes's definition of decadence: it is 'excessive, [...] artificial, [...] esoteric', based on 'fragmentation, dissolution, deformation and ornamentation'.[91] The dissolution of Meale's nominal structures for music that projects individual, localized performance decisions also fits Paul Bourget's literary definition:

> A decadent style is a style where the unity of the book decomposes in order to give way to the independence of the page, where the page decomposes to give way to the independence of the phrase, and the phrase to give way to the independence of the word.[92]

Meale argues, like Banks, that a composer 'does study techniques but to my mind only to forget them'.[93] In Meale's music of the mid-1970s technique quickly gives way to sonority; far too easily, from, for example, the Boulezian standpoint. *Coruscations* totally collapses ornament and structure, and the String Quartet is neither ornamental nor highly formal: even the players abandon their chairs halfway through, to gesture at the listening – pure sonority – that they (and, therefore, we) are to do. But listen to what? To the players? They sit with their backs to the audience, and they refuse to perform to us anything like the music that we associate with either modernist

Example 6.26 Meale, String Quartet No. 1, 'II', showing the cloud of harmonics through which a single line is played.

verbosity or argumentative string quartets. We are all equally alienated here. Meale's performance, too, is in question, with the parts mixing requests for 'sounding pitches' and directed left-hand actions, forcing (frustrating) the player to ask what 'sounding pitch' means in a part that hovers between transposed and not.

Meale's String Quartet makes the distance from Europe audible. Its harmonic clouds reflect the 'perfect calm' of *Clouds Now and Then*.[94] The sequences of pitches in the second half, 'far away', are indeed far away from the tropes of Boulez or set theory, and far away from the (European) traditions of the string quartet as a genre that organizes a verbal argument. The quartet comes after Meale's *Incredible Floridas*, where for Meale 'these two basic paths [abstract and passionate] were to meet, in conflict, integration and resolution'.[95] Although the most significant transformation in Meale's music is typically traced to his 'silent period', an earlier transformation takes place in *Incredible Floridas* and its most pithy manifestation is the String Quartet, in which music is sonority. In this sense it is a total break not just from the passionate music of folk song or tonality, but also from the functional abstraction of *Coruscations*, which connects him with modernism internationally.

The excitement of the 1960s and early 1970s introduced and ended modernist Australian Music, an end present in *Incredible Floridas*, and audibly fulfilled by the String Quartet. The organizational support that came in the early 1970s gave 'Australian Music' capital letters, and this brought a newly defined assertion of locality (whether focussed on California, Spain, Japan or Asia – the scales vary) alongside international modernism in the 1960s. By 1975 modernist music in Australia had Australian publishers, promoters and funders. With all those new organizations keen to celebrate Australian Music's leading composers, the modernist form of Australian Music ended.

7

Landscapes in Painting and Literature

Lumsdaine and Sculthorpe

This chapter is in two parts. In the first I discuss David Lumsdaine's *Aria for Edward John Eyre* (1972) in connection with literature. In the second I use the context of landscape painting to rethink Peter Sculthorpe's 'musical landscapes'. Together they form a different way of addressing the relationship between music and landscape, one that is not reliant on connections to particular places, and which instead works through connections to other artistic practices. This chapter contests the primacy of 'Australian Music' by exploring some of the ways that connections between artists transcend national identity, particularly when they are of a personal nature.

Aria for Edward John Eyre is notable for the way that it articulates ideas repetitiously at the same time as it follows direct lines through matrices, and indirect paths through lines of text. The section that is my focus stands apart from the composition's typical music, forming a singularity in musical style to express a precarious moment in its narrative. I show that the section's basis is about literary connections, rather than about the explorer named in its title. This part of the chapter extends from my existing writing on the composition.[1] However, where my earlier writing about the piece is mostly technical, my focus here is textual.

Sculthorpe's music is well understood from a technical perspective; nevertheless the technical aspect of his music's connections to painting have been subsumed within a broad discussion of 'landscape'. In this way, Sculthorpe's music can be seen as a particular instance of the wider problem posed by modernist music written in and about Australia, in which the explanatory discourses of a general type run ahead of detailed understandings. In this chapter the significance of landscape painting to Sculthorpe's music is demonstrated through the composer's relationship with the paintings of Russell Drysdale.

Part I: Singing Seahorses: Eyre and the Air

In 1968, the poet Peter Porter wrote a letter to Don Banks about the latter's Violin Concerto, in comparison to the music of Karlheinz Stockhausen:

Music is always less voluptuous than sound, it has something to do and somewhere to go.²

Porter was well aware of the vagueness of 'somewhere', as in the closing lines of his poem 'Caliban v. Prospero':

Calm seas and prosperous trips begin
[...]
With Mother waving from the wharf
And genius, dry-eyed, heading North.³

The poem was written for David Lumsdaine's sixtieth birthday, in 1991, and it draws on Porter and Lumsdaine's similar experience of leaving Australia for London, where they shared a flat in 1953.⁴ There they collaborated on several works, including *Annotations of Auschwitz* (1965) for soprano and ensemble (which is now Lumsdaine's earliest acknowledged composition), *The Groaning Mountain* ('a gothic pastoral after Æsop' for chamber choir, written 1953–4, recomposed 2013) and *Temptations in the Wilderness* (withdrawn), and they planned many more. Lumsdaine's interest in literature finds its easy musical home in works with a text, such as *A Tree Telling of Orpheus* (1990), *My Sister's Song* (1974) and *The Ballad of Persse O'Reilly* (1953, recomposed 1981), and also in music without voice, such as *Caliban Impromptu* (1972), *Sunflower* (1974) and *Looking Glass Music* (1970). Lumsdaine's 'Australian' works tend to be more abstract, for instruments rather than voice: *Kangaroo Hunt* (1971) is for piano and percussion; *A Dance and a Hymn for Alexander Maconochie, Norfolk Island, May 25 1840* (1988) is for chamber ensemble; *Shoalhaven* (1982) is for orchestra; *Kelly Ground* (1966) and *Cambewarra* (1980) are for solo piano. *Aria for Edward John Eyre* (1972) is the exception, both for its solo soprano, who sings from Eyre's journal, and for its use of loudspeakers that surround the audience. These two forces in particular enliven literal and abstract explorations of space and text. *Aria for Edward John Eyre* is the lengthiest of all these compositions, an hour-long, single-movement form. The piece is, by design, challenging for a listener, since it is far from straightforward in its direction, and this combines with its long duration and surround sound to form an epic composition, in which distance and travel are explored.⁵ This chapter focusses on one moment from *Aria for Edward John Eyre* to demonstrate something of the relationship between literature and music about Australia, offering a new perspective on the artistic discourses of Australian landscapes.

Aria for Edward John Eyre begins before the first notes sound, since we can read in its title the composition's elemental pun. When translated fully into English the title reads 'Air for Edward John Eyre'. The air and an aria, as element and melody (particularly meaning a melody for voice, as in *The firste booke of songes or ayres* by John Dowland), is etymologically thoroughly entangled, and spellings travel between French, Italian and English.⁶ This hidden homophone that awaits discovery emphasizes the role that sound can take in textual understanding, joining melody and element to begin the wordplay that guides the music, as much as its 'musicplay' then guides possible understandings of the sung text. If we identify the person with the melody (the character with the musical line), then we begin to understand the centrality in this composition of air, indeed, of 'the elemental' more broadly; the line – the melody – is how music makes its journey.

The play of the title also comes with a sense of transformation in the European/non-European/Australian/English dislocations that were ongoing in the early 1970s, and which were particularly important for Lumsdaine, who had been living away from Australia since 1953.[7] In Porter's poem 'Caliban v. Prospero', quoted above, the 'airs' of the isle that is full of noises are of 'midges stinging in the dark' rather than a 'thousand twangling instruments', a swipe at the composer Pierre Boulez:

> Through all the airs of colleges I hear the voice of Prospero
> (a neutered Senior Prefect just like Boulez)
> boring Miranda, patronising Ferdinand, teasing Ariel
> and belabouring the monster he won't recognize
> in his own body.

Porter was no admirer of the music that Boulez was composing, and Porter writes of the 'loss of intensity' in his collaboration with Lumsdaine that came from Lumsdaine's changing technique: 'I had always been fixed on an approach to music which owed much to the Britten/Auden axis. After beginning study with Mátyás Seiber, David changed his approach to composition. I have always hated serial composition and Schoenberg's music in particular. When Webern swam into my ken I found I disliked his music even more.'[8] Even so, Porter's correspondence with composers makes clear that his distaste for serial music was well informed, and that he did not avoid hearing it in concert.

Porter's comment about Banks's Violin Concerto having 'something to do and somewhere to go' is equally relevant for Lumsdaine's *Aria for Edward John Eyre*, which engages head-on with the idea of music as exploration, and with the notion of music as a temporal art form.[9] *Aria for Edward John Eyre* is at the heart of Lumsdaine's musical engagement with the mid-century literature on exploration. The 'exploration' topic aligns with the new modernist discourses of discovery in postwar European composition, and, in Lumsdaine's work, Eyre's quest for 'King George's Sound' – with an emphasis on *sound* – maps onto Lumsdaine's own search for musical materials.

The topic of travel had new relevance in the late 1960s and early 1970s, as it was a time when the composers who had left Australia in the 1950s were returning, and as they did they reformed Australia's relationship with Britain, and wrote new musical conceptions of 'place' and 'distance'. For Lumsdaine, the exploration of Australia in *Aria for Edward John Eyre* is done through memory, since he had been away from Australia for half his life at the time of its composition. Even after this composition, his movement between the UK and Australia has emphasized the importance of memory in writing about a journey.[10] Banks, who was Lumsdaine's close friend, was one of those who returned to Australia. The distance between Canberra and London became a motivating factor for an increase in correspondence between Banks and Porter, and although by this time neither Banks nor Lumsdaine were collaborating with Porter on new works, the archives of the National Library of Australia hold their ongoing correspondence. Between Porter and Banks this amounts to a few dozen letters, approximately the same volume as between Lumsdaine and Porter. This collection of letters is very much incomplete, with many letters not retained by correspondents, and, of course, it captures none of the discussions that they had in person. What we can read is characterized by open, candid conversation, and the correspondence speaks of a close social network that was established quickly in the mid-1950s, and which endured for several decades.[11] The letters frequently include concert reports, keeping all the correspondents up to date with the latest performances.

Porter collaborated with Banks on *Limbo* (1970) and *Tirade* (1971), the latter a satirical triptych of Australiana. *Tirade* itself is a piece of myth-making, a sequence of clichés hemmed in by clichés, of 'ghost towns ghosts won't visit'.[12] The triptych is divided into past, present and future, though the 'future', in which 'superfluity is god', is as much about the present as it is the past, and the past is made present in a series of still-potent 'public icons', from 'Kelly', to 'Phar Lap' to 'Burke and Wills'. The piece is very much about Banks and Porter in London, and about the relationship of Australia with the UK. In the composition Banks directs the following text to be delivered as a 'quasi lecture': 'A northern race living in the south, myths in reverse, all journeys inland.'[13] These are lines to be spoken, rather than sung, ensuring their comprehensibility, though at no point in the composition does the music overwhelm or even disagree with the text. One senses that Porter's frustration with Australian culture may have been greater than Banks's, with the latter's correspondence full of the kind of slang that is never found in Porter's. *Tirade* (first performed in Paris in 1968), is both a tirade denouncing Australian culture, and a 'Tirade' – with the emphasis at the start of the word, as in French – 'a set speech from a classical play, a sort of phillipic'.[14] And it is also, Porter writes to Banks, a 'triade', by which he means the musical 'triad', as it is spelt in English, which was in the 1960s so out of favour as a harmonic device. Porter knew that Banks was not a 'triadic composer', and so he gave a further understanding of the term, noting the recent performance of *Triade* ('pour orchestre divisé en trois groupes') composed 1966 by Gilbert Amy.[15]

Alongside Porter, Patrick White was a significant writer for Australian music. His influence on Meale, for example, is well known through Meale's opera *Voss* (1985), and his association with music more widely is increasingly acknowledged.[16] He is remembered within the music community as a writer who attended concerts. There are some concrete, if fleeting, references to White and music in the archives of various composers, such as a letter from Murdoch (who at the time, in 1976, was head of the Australian Music Centre) about the early-stage planning of an opera by Lumsdaine based on *The Aunt's Story*, and which indicated White had given his approval for this to go ahead.[17] The opera did not eventuate – indeed, it may be a surprise to those who know Lumsdaine's music that such an opera was ever conceived, given that Lumsdaine's output contains no staged works – though it would have formed a companion (literary, if not musical) for *Aria for Edward John Eyre*. The composition is Lumsdaine's transformation into music of ideas from White's *Voss*.[18] This is a tangent that, like so many of Lumsdaine's works from the period, is born of a collaboration between the composer and literature that is difficult to assess, but which is no less significant for that difficulty. Bringing *Voss* back to Eyre's diaries by way of solo soprano takes us back to the elemental, and to Laura Trevelyan's words at the end of the novel: 'the air will tell us'. It also recalls White in London during the Blitz, reading Eyre's diaries and Alec Hugh Chisholm's *Strange New World*: 'I wanted to give my book the textures of music, the sensuous of paint, to convey through the theme and characters of *Voss* what Delacroix or Blake might have seen, what Mahler and Liszt might have heard.'[19]

Aria for Edward John Eyre is scored for two narrators, solo soprano, solo double bass, ensemble and two mixers (who control two tape players and the amplification of the instruments, which is projected through the speakers surrounding the audience). The two narrators read from Eyre's journal, one speaking full sentences and reading out the dates as they arise, the other fragmenting the journal's text. The soprano's text further transforms the diaries. The particular section that is this chapter's focus comes from the latter part of this composition (bars 175–202), where the music shifts and one hears material that sounds more driven by a unified style than what has come before. This section stands out in the composition for its strong sense of pulse. Most of the piece eschews metre for complex rhythms in multiple layers, but here the lines come together with relative rhythmic uniformity, and significant energetic activity. The section is also notable for its different use of pitch; where the earlier music either leaps virtuosically, or settles into slowly evolving counterpoint, this section maintains a steady register, with each part moving within a narrow pitch-region of an octave or so. The rhythms here are mostly additive, grouped into threes and twos, with a strong tendency towards sixes (see Example 7.1). This is not itself wholly unusual in Lumsdaine's music from the period, and in his later compositions these rhythms are attached to ideas of dance, especially in works such as *A Tree Telling of Orpheus*, a piece that sets Denise Levertov's poem of the same name, written in 1968:

> The wind, the birds,
>   do not sound poorer but clearer,
> recalling our agony, and the way we danced.
> The music![20]

Nevertheless, dance is not the most obvious choice for a work that deals with Eyre's journey across Australia's south coast to Albany, and given how different this section is from the surrounding music, we might be pushed by its incongruousness to look to the words that are present in the section in order to make some sense of it. The soprano sings a text that Lumsdaine constructed from Eyre's journal:

> Deep wells of night, rambling in and out and in and out among the belts of scrub. Dark seahorses, flecks of scud and nimbus threading through the moon grass honour bound for the northeast tracing round every point bay curve afflicted by swarms of sea horses, neighing stamping biting, tossing writhing into the sea itself inevitably destroyed.

These words come from various parts of Eyre's journal, and form a jumble of text that brings together such fragments as: 'swarms of large horse-flies, which bit us dreadfully'; 'They literally assailed us by hundreds at a time, biting through our clothes, and causing us constant employment in endeavouring to keep them off'; and 'At other times we were forced to go between these banks of sea-weed and the sea, into the sea itself, on which occasions it required our utmost vigilance to prevent the wretched horses from drinking the salt water, which would inevitably have destroyed them.'[21]

By the time that the section occurs in the composition a significant amount of text has been read by the narrators, and we have a sense of a version of that text that gives us a narrative, and a version that is fragmented. The soprano, rather than reproducing the narrator's words with melody, *sings* the text, which emphasizes the sound of the words, stretching vowels and consonants. There is nothing secondary about this material (in terms of making semantic sense) since the composition begins with the soprano humming, and it is through the soprano that we first encounter

Example 7.1 Lumsdaine, *Aria for Edward John Eyre*, bars 191–203.

Landscapes in Painting and Literature

Example 7.1 *(continued)*

Example 7.1 *(continued)*

Eyre's writing. Her first words are 'I will', the initial vowel extending for so long (some 10 seconds) that the end of the word merges with the long notes from clarinets and brass, embedding the soprano in the ensemble, and combining text with music. The soprano then speaks the words 'I wilderness', with a similar slow pacing; this enables 'I will' to be distinguished from the fuller 'I, wilderness.' These fragments allude to Isaiah: 'I will even make a way in the wilderness, and rivers in the desert.'[22] They also allude to White's novel *Riders in the Chariot*, which opens with William Blake – 'The Prophets Isaiah and Ezekiel dined with me' – and also to the 'wilderness of garden' that White's character Himmelfarb explores.[23]

The process of elongating and contracting text distances it from a coherent sentence, and such moments are therefore less about practical communication than an expression of interiority (which begins with the opening of the composition, when the soprano hums rather than sings with full voice), and of temporal transformation. Against the soprano's expressive vocality, the narrators are matter of fact, reading out the dates from Eyre's journal to provide a counterpoint to the composition's other temporalities.[24] Where some composers might seek a synthesis between music and text – setting the text – Lumsdaine keeps the differences between them in play, making the most of the different technologies at his disposal. The tape player distorts the temporality of live performance; the journal captures each day of the expedition (the plot, to use an appropriate term for the expedition's mapping). The soprano's technique, forged by long traditions of vocal practice, is also significant, audible in the work's virtuosities. And the myriad of small details speak to transformations that emphasize the sounds of the words – 'wrrrrriiiiiithing' (with a trilled r and elongated i) – over their combination.

Aria for Edward John Eyre uses a matrix to generate the order of its pitches. Through this device the small details of pitch order are consistently related to larger structures. Figure 7.1 shows the matrix used in this section of the piece. The matrix is composed as a territory through which paths can be traced, and the shapes of these paths form the sequences of pitch use in the composition. The pitches for the harp are derived from paths (indicated with arrows) from an E (circled in the example). Because this matrix is constructed from many mirrored patterns, following the paths in any 'cardinal' direction from that E (for Eyre? starting at either end of his name) produces the same set of six pitches. In the music, the harp plays a mobile of this six-note set, continually reordered, a musical representation of geographical confusion, a moment of pitch disorder. (In other words, confusion does not require stepping outside technique.) The direction to the mixer in the score is 'bring up harp to solo level, let its harmony dominate the general texture', and so the harp's unordered set dominates the sound, forming a harmonic backdrop for the voice. The mobile of the pitches employed go with the mobile of the text, no longer given in coherent order, and speaks to Eyre's precarious position following the murder of the overseer.

Lumsdaine's use of a pitch matrix also has an idiosyncratically literary aspect. In reference to the 1967 piece *Flights*, Michael Hall writes that:

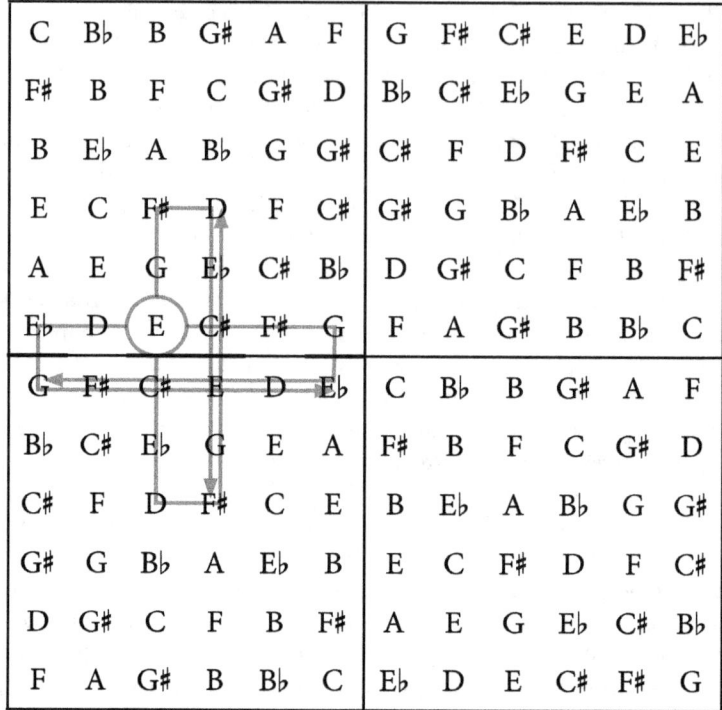

Figure 7.1 The matrix for Lumsdaine's *Aria for Edward John Eyre*, annotated to show possible paths used to generate the pitch material for the harp.

The magic square which generated the material for *Flights* started out as a 12×12 'magic square' in which the prime of a twelve-note set is placed in the first horizontal line and the first vertical column, and then permuted down and across the matrix into its retrograde. This matrix, however, was abandoned after reading Patrick White's *The Solid Mandala* which had been published in the previous year.[25]

It was replaced by a matrix that connected two six-pitch sequences in a tighter and more complicated fashion, which Lumsdaine referred to as a 'Gemini matrix';[26] he also reconceived the piece for two pianos rather than solo piano.

Aria for Edward John Eyre only partly responds to Eyre's diaries. The narrators speak Eyre's text, but the principal musical voice is the soprano. In White's novel, Voss and Trevelyan are joined, and in the music so too are the soprano and Eyre. In his programme note for the composition, Lumsdaine asks: 'To what extent does Voss exist outside Laura's mind? Where would Ulysses be if Penelope forgot him? A Labyrinth is conceivable without an Ariadne, but could it structure a myth?'[27] The questions are pursued through conceptions of memory. The recording devices that Lumsdaine brings together are all technologies for remembering, and their materials are all literally present: the diaries are read from cards held by the speakers; the taped recordings of the soprano are fed through their machines in the performance; the notated score and parts are on the performers' stands.

Memory is also explored musically. The section we are considering ends abruptly: Eyre is by now in the sea with the horses, and the end of the section of music comes with a sudden silence that is indicated in the score with rests, and also with Lumsdaine's performance direction 'evaporate' (another turn of phrase that joins 'air'/'Eyre' and water). The sudden ending is a typical one for Lumsdaine, and a few years later it is found in *Mandala 3* (1978) at the end of a transcription of Bach's music for chamber ensemble, which ends just as suddenly: at the point of greatest harmonic expectation a sudden silence exposes the *composition* of the transcription, and also the dominant–tonic workings of tonality (a harmonic move on which tonality's subjectivities rely[28]). In *Aria for Edward John Eyre*, there is a sense that the music we have been hearing is a recording of something earlier. Its 'stylishness' itself risks reducibility to anecdote, as Boulez cautioned of any music driven by style,[29] but this style is also used productively, and it is employed deliberately, since the compound metre that the section under study uses is one of the principal characteristics of the 'horse topic', which is a nineteenth-century development of earlier 'hunting music'.[30] Lumsdaine stretches the topic by setting it at a slower tempo than one finds in Schubert or Brahms, for Eyre's horses are weary, noble perhaps, but hardly galloping triumphantly. The turbulence of this section is also not typical of the topic, but it does vividly suggest horses in the sea, and moves the topic away from its military associations; as one might expect from a composer who was also one of the Committee of 100,[31] these are not pompous, military horses, such as in Wagner's *Die Walküre*.[32] The horses here are closer to the horse of travel, such as found in Robert Franz's 'Wanderlied' 'where it is clear that the singer is a walker rather than a rider'.[33]

Lumsdaine's direction at the start of the section is:

From here [...] the effect of the bass clarinet and the brass should be a jagged and uneven *plod*.[34]

Again, the word 'plod' seems especially well chosen, given that its various meanings include: 'a laborious or tiring walk'; 'A sound of a heavy dull tread'; 'To plot, plan'; 'Of a hound when hunting: to linger behind the pack'; and perhaps most relevantly to this epic composition, 'A story, tale, or yarn' (this meaning comes from a dialect from the southwest of England, and it is also a usage found in Australia).[35]

This section is not, however, much about horses, the literal rendering of which – through the imitation of horses' hooves – would be too mimetic for Lumsdaine's music, much as his extensive recordings of birdsong are almost never recognizable in his notated scores. Instead, the use of a 'musical topic' raises the centuries-long transformation of a connection between the sound of travel and a musical idea. The connection is made musically, and is also audible in Lumsdaine's reconfiguration of Eyre's trochaic text – 'rambling in and out and in and out among the belts of scrub' – going with the music's compound metre. Working against this connection, the section's start interrupts the text's metre (sung by soprano): 'afflicted by swarms of sea horses'.

The distance from the usual musical expression of the horse topic is itself something that we ought to notice, since instead of Eyre's horses it is to the 'seahorses' that this allusion points. The connection is, again, not literally to the seahorses of the genus *Hippocampus*, but of the brain's hippocampus. This region was named after the sea creature by Aranzi (1587), and it is the area of the brain responsible for memory and spatial navigation. (This suggests a rather different reading of *Voss*, and its association of the desert with the mind.) In 1672, Diemerbroeck described its shape in terms of the mythical hippocampus, half-fish and half-horse; Poseidon's chariot, pulled by hippocampi, leads us not to *Voss*, but to White's *Riders in the Chariot*, which Lumsdaine hints at in his 'myth of the making of *Aria*' which begins with his suburban childhood experience:

> Mr. Hobson's Class, Tuesday afternoons, after playtime under the peppercorn trees: Australian Explorers wandered westwards across the large, yellowing, fly-spotted wall map in the stuffy classroom, died of hunger, thirst, exposure in its cracks, or were speared by Aborigines who ambushed them from behind the ink cupboard.[36]

Horse topics in music are exclusively masculine,[37] and in Lumsdaine's *Aria for Edward John Eyre* the multiple resonances of 'horse' alongside the soprano's musical transformation of Eyre's text is the musical asking of Lumsdaine's questions 'To what extent does Voss exist outside Laura's mind? Where would Ulysses be if Penelope forgot him?'

With Lumsdaine's *Aria for Edward John Eyre* we have the opportunity to take a long and broad consideration of sound, memory, recording and reproduction. The composition brings together long traditions of crafting sound, responding to practices of instrument and vocal technique, compositional technique, recording technique literature and myth. What makes the 'seahorses' moment so potent is that with Eyre abandoning the land, his journey's thread is lost; in Lumsdaine's setting the music, too, is without direction, since the 'seahorses' section plays no clear part in the work's longer-term trajectories, as indicated by the silence (a kind of forgetting?) with which it ends. Whatever the procedures for making the composition's pitch sequences, the impossibility of narration that this particular section embodies might well have pleased Porter, who in 1959 wrote a letter to Lumsdaine setting down his dislike of serialism: 'I've always thought that music existed in terms of what it cannot do as much as what it can. We all know it isn't literary: it cannot narrate.'[38]

This is music that is about landscape, if not about a particular landscape; it is propelled by a sense of place and occupied by the mediation of that sense though literature. With Lumsdaine living away from Australia, this is also music about remembering a place. Its poetics are finely honed, detailed and complex, bringing together literary and musical ideas through personal connections, such as with Porter, and with some of Australia's most significant writing of national myths, such as by White. In this it more closely resembles Banks's *String Quartet*, and his piece's relationship with other composers, than it does Meale's expressionist compositions, for example. It also resembles, formally, the relationship of Sculthorpe's music to visual art, which I will now explain.

Part II: Sculthorpe and Landscape Painting

This section of the chapter brings Sculthorpe's music into the light of two radically different artists, Russell Drysdale and Fred Williams, to address the idea of 'landscape music'. Sculthorpe's music is my focus, but to get there requires some explanation of the other artists, the context of how they were considered in the 1960s and what they might offer us for understanding Sculthorpe's music composed around the same time. Central to this chapter's argument is the idea that we need to understand 'landscape' in this period not through the depictions of particular places, but as an abstract topic that was shared between artists working in different media. By bringing together these artists and drawing out their common approaches to form – forms of nationalism, forms of argument – Sculthorpe's music can be reassessed. More specifically, through the relation between Williams's transformation of Frederick McCubbin, Drysdale's conception of drama, and two of Sculthorpe's compositions, we can see something of the changing politics of Australian nationalism.

Williams and McCubbin

The canonical reading of McCubbin's *The Pioneer* (1904) is that it paints the end of colonialism and the beginning of Australia, with the trees giving way to the city (Figure 7.2). It is, the National Gallery of Victoria writes, a 'monumental painting'[39] that 'reflects the self-conscious nationalism of the years immediately following Federation. Each panel [indeed, each *period*] is "read" to link the progress of toil on this land across time.' In the middle panel the bush is carved into a clearing for a cabin.

> In the final panel a bushman discovers a grave, and in the background a city begins to emerge. It is uncertain who has died and whether the male figure is the pioneer, his son or a stranger. By presenting his painting across three panels – the triptych format for traditional religious art – McCubbin elevated the status of the pioneer within Australian art history.[40]

What is not depicted directly is the exchange of the working body for the metropolis, in Jameson's sense.[41] Although this is not depicted – or, rather, *because* it is not depicted – its absence is one of the painting's strongest features. From this absence emerges its

Figure 7.2 Frederick McCubbin's *The Pioneer*.

clash of temporalities, for the city progresses at a rate that is apparently disconnected by the work of the individual. No sooner is there a clearing than the urban world arrives, and so the mechanism by which change takes place is raised as the relation with which the painting is concerned, but which it does not depict. *The Pioneer*'s futility is one of 'progress' in late modernity, and it is typical of the work of Australia's colonial art, painted in the high industrial era.

The particular painting by Williams that I want to consider is his 1966 work *Echuca Landscape II*, which is the final piece in a long series of etchings, and also of paintings (oil on canvas). Its strongest formal feature is the vertical line on the right, and the descending dark streak on the left that together divide it into three (Figure 7.3). Like *The Pioneer*, *Echuca Landscape II* is a triptych in which the lighter centre panel gives a sense of a new gap in the canopy, and the blue of the upper right is either some new landscape coming through, or the sky, or birds or a flowering eucalyptus. As in so much of Williams's work, the vertical lines are trees. Significantly, Williams 'eliminated the junction of trunks and ground as well as leafy branches as he proceeded on a formal exploration'.[42] So we have vertical lines that do not connect with the ground, and, in the engravings that come before the painting, these lines are more clearly the forest receding into the distance. The detail and colour that gives 'depth' to the engravings comes from the aquatint that is understood to be the light coming through the trees' foliage.[43] Distinct from the engravings, what the painting does is to invite us to mistake the wood for the trees. The middle distance's faint lines dissolve the background/

Landscapes in Painting and Literature 219

Figure 7.3 Fred Williams's *Echuca Landscape II*.

middleground distance that is so significant for *The Pioneer*'s transformation of temporality. As such, it transforms *The Pioneer*'s distance into the timber of domestic furniture.

The feature that complicates this is the 'x' in the right of *Echuca Landscape II*. This 'cross' suggests a campfire, though it is not a depiction of one (in the manner of McCubbin). And so if this is finished wood, the campfire that is not is transformed into a formal 'knot' (with the 'k' or without) to reinforce the rustic, patinated cabinetry that is actually depicted, at least in a sense. The wood is oiled, not engraved. Thinking more about the cabin in *The Pioneer*'s middle distance through *Echuca Landscape II*, it is as if the viewer's position is inside and outside the dwelling at the same time.

The Pioneer's narrative relies on the respatialization of the scene to connect the campfire and the gravesite's cross, left to right as progress, and right to left as loss, as the campfire and cross are transformed into each other. We ought to be open, too, to reading *Echuca Landscape II* both left to right and right to left, and, for that matter, upside down:

[James Gleeson:] Fred, just on a matter of technique, do you habitually work on a painting upside down?

[Williams:] Yes I do. [...] sometimes think that I'm absolutely bloody well blind looking at them straight on. But working on them upside down, I can forget what the subject is [...] And I sometimes do them sideways, but generally upside down. [...]

[Gleeson:] And you never touch it once you turn it up?

[Williams:] I try not to. [...] The ones I suppose that are less successful I probably do, because the implication being that if you alter it when you put it up the right way, you are sort of making a concession to reality or to the physical object.[44]

Of course, this effortless mirroring ought to come as little surprise given Williams's position as Australia's most significant engraver.

Returning to interiors and exteriors, *Echuca Landscape II* is both more and less domestic than *The Pioneer*, in that it presents simultaneously two spaces that *The Pioneer* keeps separate. The urban world that Williams does not show is this painting's setting, either a gallery or a domestic space. The respatialization that *Echuca Landscape II* accomplishes is both the new spatialization of global travel and international white boxes, and the art market itself. In both senses its specific relationship to *The Pioneer* also respatializes Australian Art, as the national gives way to the transnational. Williams's take on McCubbin transforms the painting's periodization and spatialization (both of which are already doubled to present the separation of colony and metropolis) as technique, through the iterative process of engraving, plates and painting. Progress and process. This transformation seems to be hopeful, since in its relation with McCubbin it undoes the obfuscation of the labour of production that modernist aesthetics so often works to hide.

In 1966, the same year that Williams painted *Echuca Landscape II*, Althusser wrote his influential essay on Cremonini, in which aesthetics is removed from production:

his whole strength as a figurative painter lies in the fact that he does not 'paint' 'objects' [...], nor 'places' [...], nor 'times' or 'moments'. Cremonini 'paints' the *relations* which bind the objects, places and times. Cremonini is a *painter of abstraction*. Not an abstract painter, 'painting' an absent, pure possibility in a new form and matter, but a painter of the real *abstract*, 'painting' in a sense we have to define, real relations (as relations they are necessarily *abstract*) between 'men' and their 'things', or rather, to give the term its stronger sense, between 'things' and their 'men'.[45]

We can think of something similar for Williams, as a painter whose landscapes seem to lack the subjects otherwise necessary for production or consumption. The cross, in relation to McCubbin, is the 'determinate absence' governing the social relations that are not possible to depict (the light in the centre of the painting is a transformation of Rembrandt's lit figures in the centre of a frame,[46] but without the subjects).

*

Subjects, and their absence, return in the chapter's next section, about Drysdale's painting, and in its third section, about Sculthorpe's music. By bringing these artists together we can understand them relationally, to support a new, abstract conception of Australian Music.

An old argument about Drysdale

The exhibition book for the major retrospective of Drysdale's painting, held in Sydney in 1960 at the Art Gallery of New South Wales, begins with a 'dialogue' between Drysdale and Paul Haefliger. Both sides of the imagined conversation were written by Haefliger, who was a painter, too, and who had been the art critic for the *Sydney Morning Herald*. In his conversation, he wrote:

> I want to speak of Drysdale, if you don't mind. Now you mentioned national and international. I think it is Drysdale's achievement that he has established an Australian national art-form. He is above all else an Australian artist.
> What is a national art-form?
> Surely an art-form which has developed in a country and is unique to that country.
> And what is at the basis of such a development?
> A tradition.
> And what shapes the tradition in this country?
> The life and work of our forebears.
> And who are those forebears? Where did they come from?
> Why, they are British, of course.
> So you might say that Australian art is a British art?
> With a difference.[47]

The thoroughly cosmopolitan Haefliger wrote this in Majorca, having left Sydney some years earlier (he was later to return). His criticism represented the modernist impulse in Australia (or, perhaps more accurately in this case, in Sydney), and also its frustration: the lack of dialogue, the difficulty of distance, the new nation. The year 1960 was close enough to the colonial era that 'the British element' might be imagined as having 'given way' – 'in a hundred years' time' – and near enough to the war in the Pacific that 'a great Australian tradition of Japanese art has been only narrowly averted'.[48]

Haefliger summarized the 'British element' easily: 'In the year 1960 one can still say that he who shows the most characteristic British trait, *power of narrative*, can be regarded as the most Australian artist.'[49] This has nothing to do with the subjects that Drysdale's art depicts, since they have no lasting significance. Nor are Drysdale's paintings 'topographical guides for unimaginative tourists'.[50] On one hand Haefliger sees Drysdale as a modernist at the foundation of Australian Art. On the other he sees him as a 'Romantic', for whom 'the interior' is his own, the continent's and the nation's: 'I meant to convey Drysdale's development of his subject, from the awkward beginning when he introduces his characters and scene, past the point where he directs their action, to the point where they possess him.'⁵¹

If the NSW Art Gallery's retrospective confirmed Drysdale's pre-eminence, the solo exhibitions of his work at the Leicester Galleries in London marked his international significance; two solo exhibitions (in 1950 and 1958) took place there before the NSW Art Gallery's retrospective. The catalogue to the third, in 1965, began with a disagreement: Alan Ross, who wrote the preface of that catalogue, took issue with Robert Hughes's description of Drysdale's art as 'parochial'.⁵² For Hughes, Drysdale's art is a stylized, indeed, an idealized version of the landscapes of the eighteenth century, 'a refuge of innocence', 'removed from history'.⁵³ Hughes's reading of the landscapes suggests Britishness (as Haefliger defines it), since they are composed of 'a long theatrical recession of red earth and rocks in which plane after plane is marked by the presence of a waterhole, a placed and posed figure, a telegraph pole or a stark tree'.⁵⁴ This makes Drysdale a Romantic, since the vision is Arcadian. Ross's counterargument is that Drysdale's landscapes are neither ideal, nor remote, since they are lived; he contrasts Drysdale with Sidney Nolan, writing that the latter, unlike the former, 'is moved by the variety of Australian myths and legends, by the heroic impulse at work'.⁵⁵ This is an unusually defensive way to begin an exhibition catalogue for an artist whose work is well known, and it attests to the significance of Hughes as a critic. The preface was written precisely because the idea of Australian Art had gathered through Hughes's criticism a guiding discourse that threatened to overwhelm Drysdale as its current leader, and so the preface worked to preserve the realism of experience that Drysdale's art could offer in the London market. Part of that experience is the 'toil' that Australia, in its colonial configuration, had always offered the British. And so:

> Drysdale's imagination *is*, up to a point, romantic, as [Graham] Sutherland's is; his manner dramatic, though he is concerned, as is Herman in another way, with functional activities, with the dignity of labour.⁵⁶

The Herman to whom Ross refers is, one assumes, Sali Herman – who arrived in Sydney in 1938, and who is known for his inner city streetscapes – rather than Josef – who arrived in Glasgow in 1940, and who is known for his red-hued paintings of men at work – though the ambiguity is productive. For Hughes, Drysdale's drama 'suggests no flow of events. Human figures are merely stage-props. They posture theatrically in the distance and give scale to the vista. But otherwise they contribute little to the painting; and, in *Landscape with Figures*, they distract from it.'⁵⁷ This is a very different kind of drama to the one outlined by Ross, aesthetic rather than ideological, with Hughes looking back to Drysdale as part of Sydney's bourgeois art scene, rather than to the political challenges of Drysdale's imagining.

The argument between Hughes and Ross that continued to play out did so as an argument over the aesthetic experience of the viewer in the guise of an argument about realism and taste. The connection between Sutherland, Herman(s) and Drysdale suggests an approach that might half agree with Haefliger's suggestion that 'reality is not to be illustrated', if not that '"reality" is to be intuited',[58] and to agree with his assessment of a nationalism in which 'one may dispense with the subject – no more swaggies, drovers or noble savages',[59] if not with his vague distinction between the intellect and emotion. In other words, to agree with Hughes that Drysdale 'made it possible for other painters to react freshly to their environment by showing them new relationships with it'.[60] This idea, of Drysdale as a painter of relationships, rather than a depicter of landscape, is the crucial aspect of Drysdale's art, since it understands him as a properly abstract painter, in Althusser's sense.

Thinking about labour provides a different take on Drysdale's *Red Landscape* paintings, of which there are three: the first painted in 1945, the second in 1958 and the third in 1965. The last of these was for Guilford Bell, who was the architect who designed Drysdale's house near the Boudi National Park. It shows the landscape around Kata Tjuta ('Mount Olga', in Australia's Northern Territory; it was painted in Double Bay, Sydney).[61] This painting gives its title to Sculthorpe's *Red Landscape* (1966). This composition is now known as String Quartet No. 7, having been also previously called *Teotihuacán*. Its connection with Australia is, as the changing titles suggest, problematic. Michael Hannan writes that '[t]he title was taken from a Drysdale painting, but for the composer it also refers to a large area of the painter's work which is characterised by desolate and drought-ridden land'.[62] Note that the reference is to Drysdale's work, rather than to a place, an idea to which I shall return below.

The score begins 'To Tass', referring to Sculthorpe's close friend, Drysdale. Drysdale explains the *Red Landscape* painting which gives the work its title as follows: 'One can look across a wide landscape which seems utterly devoid of life, or travel long distances without seeing a creature on the land.'[63] But titles are misleading, for Drysdale's *Red Landscapes* take their titles not immediately from the red earth that they depict, but from the Welsh landscapes painted by Graham Sutherland, and especially his *Red Landscape* from 1942.

Drysdale's work of the 1940s was strongly influenced by Sutherland's landscapes.[64] Simon Pierse argues that:

> By the late 1940s these influences had been digested and applied to an Australian subject matter. So it is hardly surprising that when quotations from Sutherland, Moore and Nash in Drysdale's landscapes boomeranged back to the UK from Australia, they met with ready approval from a British audience. The difference was that whilst the red-black hills of Sutherland's Welsh landscapes were an imaginative construction, influenced by currents in European art such as Surrealism, Drysdale's red-brown rocks and hills were the depiction of something actual, albeit painted at a distance.[65]

Of course, that 'painted at a distance' is no small qualification, but is the very mechanism that makes Drysdale's work modernist; indeed, which makes it a different but no less significant modernism than Sutherland's, just as Sutherland's modernism is a transformation of 'currents in European art'.

Writing about Sutherland in 1936, Peter Watson declared that he:

> aspired to a synthesis where the usual appearance of things is boldly eliminated and where there only remains a complex of relationships. These relationships are less symbols than the fusion of an image with reality; and it is with these that he has created this very personal poetry of forms, without ever making the least concession to the decorative composition of a motif. It is clear that Sutherland works outside all contemporary conventions, in a certain isolation[.][66]

Watson goes on to associate this isolation paradoxically with influence, since Sutherland is 'greater than any other English painter of our time.'[67] National distinctiveness is achieved through individual isolation, one standing in for the other (just as they did for Sculthorpe). Sutherland's work for the War Artists' Advisory Committee, alongside that of Moore and Nash, provides a context for Drysdale's paintings as battlegrounds, too. The 'horribly twisted lift shafts and girders created by bomb damage' that inform Sutherland's *Gorse on Sea Wall* (1939), and which 'evoke the skeletons of human or animal life forms that have been subject to destructive violence',[68] occur at the same time that Drysdale is being commissioned to depict Australia in drought.[69] The red sky in much of Sutherland's work, such as in *Gorse on Sea Wall*, speaks of the 'desolation as we scan the European horizon',[70] safe in distant Pembrokeshire, but thinking about German troops on the move. This horizon is rendered in fractured form. The composition is derived from Sutherland's previous work *Red Monolith*, which is also emphatically fractured, and the surface of which is coated in sand, as if to bring into material contact the paint and the landscape that the paint cannot depict. (On his cover for Sculthorpe's *Sun Music*, which shows a sun on 'white ground', Drysdale used soil from his land at Bouddi for the sun.[71]) For Hughes, Drysdale's 'forms', which were 'based on rocks, stumps, dead organisms, and burnt houses, took on an organic complexity reminiscent of, because derived from, Graham Sutherland and Henry Moore. [With the "drought drawings"] A new animistic view of nature had entered his work.'[72] In Drysdale's work the horizon itself takes on a new meaning distant from Sutherland – for whom the 'desolation as we scan the European horizon'[73] is not a literal horizon, but the political state of Europe in 1938. This horizon precedes *Gorse on Sea Wall*[74] and forms its red sky. Drysdale turns that sky into a motif that retains some of the anxiety of Sutherland's landscapes. Drysdale's landscapes, no less than Sutherland's, are not depictions.[75]

Sculthorpe's landscapes

In light of the arguments about Drysdale's art and drama, we need to be clearer about what 'non-developmental' music is for Sculthorpe. Typically the idea is attached to his interest in either Bali ('[a]n exotic soundworld of static perfection'[76]) or Australia (as a foil to 'developmental Western influences he was attempting to move away from'[77]). For example, in conversation with Sculthorpe, Hannan suggested that 'Another criticism has been that *Rites of Passage* doesn't contain any drama or passion.' Sculthorpe responded:

I'm not at all certain what is meant by this. The human cycle, which is what the work is about, is the greatest drama of all. [...] What may be meant in saying that *Passage* lacks drama and passion is that it's not like, say, Verdi, or Wagner, or Berg. This, of course, is true. Verdi's theme is betrayal. Wagner's theme is concerned with the search, the quest for the Holy Grail. Berg's theme, at least in his operas, is oppression and lust. My theme, in almost all my music, is man's alone-ness, the solitary figure in the landscape. I'm Australian; it's as simple as that.[78]

They then discuss works such as *Landscape* and note its symmetrical form as evidence for a non-developmental way of working. This suggests that music's relationships are, as in Williams's art, formal. Although the 'non-developmental' idea is broadly acknowledged in scholarship, the implications for understanding Sculthorpe's music have not been pursued, and its connections to painting have not been articulated.

The loneliness discourse in relation to Drysdale is exemplified in Geoffrey Dutton's 1964 book *Russell Drysdale*; the copy that Sculthorpe owned is inscribed 'For Peter, with all the best and old memories of Launceston and Lake Callabonna. Russell Drysdale 20.XI.64.' A leaf of paper slipped into his copy between pages 10 and 11 is annotated 'p 10 parag 2 and p 11 parag 1.' The first of these paragraphs explains that Drysdale 'is indeed a painter of great loneliness'.[79] Crucially, loneliness is also a discourse attached to Sculthorpe and described by Hannan: 'the composer's efforts to evoke the loneliness and the desolation of the Australian landscape'.[80] However, Drysdale's landscapes are full of figures – 'white or aboriginal', as Dutton puts it[81] – and Drysdale shows the landscape as populated. The second paragraph noted by Sculthorpe explains that the 'seamless unity with his landscape and its inhabitants once again disguises a divided world within'.[82] 'Once again' because Drysdale also lives the divide between city and country.

Sculthorpe's idea of drama comes from Drysdale, and it is either derived from or aligns with a reading of Drysdale such as offered by Hughes, of painting which 'suggests no flow of events' in dramatic, narrative terms. But what of other dramas? And, specifically, what of the drama that Ross finds in Drysdale, and which Haefliger finds in Sutherland and Herman, of 'functional activities' and 'with the dignity of labour'? Such drama is not absent from Drysdale, even in Hughes's analysis, in which the drama is stylized:

his volte-face from the 'international style' to regional images was abrupt; it happened after he went back to Australia in 1939 [...] Much of his work of the early forties could have passed for social realism. [...] Drysdale [...] saw [the war] obliquely reflected in home towns.[83]

Drysdale depicts the 'snoring soldiers' and 'loitering men', 'dragging their toes in the dust' to paint the relation between Australian and European towns; the latter, purposefully, are absent.[84]

There are some obvious connections between Drysdale's paintings and Sculthorpe's music. For example, in the 1969 book *In the Making*, Sculthorpe's living room is described as containing 'a typical Drysdale landscape which Drysdale has inscribed "To Peter Sculthorpe – 'Callabonna' – in admiration for String Quartette [sic] 6'".[85] The painting was a study for one of Drysdale's best-known pieces *The Ruins, Lake Callabonna*. In ochre, the painting shows dry ruins.[86] Sculthorpe is then quoted as saying:

> Callabonna's an inland lake, a very calm, remote, misty place where, as Tassie [Drysdale] described it, the birds suddenly rise up through the mist off the water. Well I'm using that idea in the string quartet I'm writing now, the *Eighth*. [...] I've got this calm, quiet thing going on here and suddenly, you see?' – pointing to the score – 'suddenly there's a flurry of sounds, like birds. It's a double-image thing working, in a way, because the *Sixth String Quartet* helped Tas through a rough time after his wife, Bonnie, died. It's dedicated to her.[87]

Graeme Skinner provides an explanation of this difference (between dry and wet) in terms of 'imaginary geography' in which the 'Bouddi lake [near where Drysdale lived, North of Sydney] and birdsong had fused in his imagination with Drysdale's Lake Callabonna.'[88] Drysdale's *Lake Callabonna* – in the painting on Sculthorpe's wall – is dry, dusty, red. Inhabited, but one wonders how its inhabitants remain. The lake is dry from a lack of rain, as is its usual state, and the wheel of a wagon is half buried in the earth. The figures stand by the bent, twisted and blackened remains of a tree, which is echoed in a ruined building in the middle ground. In contrast, the Lake Callabonna that Sculthorpe composes is wet and humid, quite unlike the painting immediately before him. The way that Sculthorpe explains this difference is through his relationship with Drysdale: 'as Tassie described it'. Sculthorpe's music is in this sense about his relationship with Drysdale, not Drysdale's painting, and certainly not Lake Callabonna.

The music's specific references are to *ketungan* and *arja*, Balinese music that forms part of Sculthorpe's imagination of Bali (which he had not visited), and so the lake that Sculthorpe composes is tropical. Australia's wet east coast meets the tropics, Bouddi meets Bali. In other words Lake Callabonna is transformed through Sculthorpe's relationship with Drysdale, and in so doing the conception of Australia in Drysdale-reds is transformed to reflect Australia as part of Asia. The formal structure of this transformation is similar to the one described above, in which the transformation of McCubbin by Williams speaks of a changing sense of nationalism.

To generalize the argument, Sculthorpe's music has nothing in particular to do with any specific place, which is something that his work shares with that of Williams:

> Although known as a landscape painter, he [Williams] is that only in a particular sense: his art draws more continuously on landscape motifs than on anything else. For he rarely paints a 'view' of the landscape, nor is the character or feature of a given place of particular interest to him. Thus, in the 1960s, a Lysterfield landscape could be virtually interchangeable with a You Yangs [in southern central Victoria] landscape. The same units of form, the same palette, even similar compositions, could encompass both.[89]

Sculthorpe did not share Williams's experience of daily working outdoors, and the rejuvenating force of 'landscape motifs' is not something that one finds in Sculthorpe's music, whose birdsong, for example, is generic. Sculthorpe's musical motifs are more varied than Williams's visual motifs, if only slightly, and they are less consistently drawn from physical forms, but such is indicative of the differences in their media. Patrick McCaughey argues that 'Of all his generation, Williams has understood most clearly, and acted most strenuously upon, the knowledge that paintings are made with paint, not with ideas or concepts, not with myths or legends, not from the imposing theme or the ambitious thought.'[90] Although Sculthorpe is not an artist with whom to begin an argument against McCaughey, the problems of the sonic depiction of a landscape are different to the problems of a depiction with paint.

The point is that in later years (long after *Red Landscape*) Sculthorpe's success would form a new naturalism. That shift would be in audience understanding more than a change in Sculthorpe's composition. The 'scorched earth' sounds of the 'Outback'[91] are always composed, not captured. Since Drysdale's reds look much like Sutherland's, and Drysdale's *Red Landscape* took its name from Sutherland's *Red Landscape*, Sculthorpe's *Red Landscape* (1966) cannot be assumed to be about Australia, so much as it is about a changing notion of landscape, colour and nationalism. Although Sculthorpe is sometimes considered as being outside modernist Australian Music, he is no less a modernist than Drysdale, Sutherland or Williams.

Bernard Smith considered that 'Williams seems to have taken up the problem of Australian landscape painting where Tom Roberts left off in the 1920.'[92] Roberts, rather than McCubbin, is the obvious connection because of the relationship that is exemplified in Williams's *My Garden* (1969), of which he said: 'I repaint other people's paintings. See that there? That's "Bailed up." You know, Tom Roberts. I've just taken the figures out [that is, removed the foreground] and repainted the background.'[93] McCaughey admits that 'Williams' landscapes do have an iconography, even if it remains implicit in much of his early art,'[94] though he finds differences in the attitudes of Williams and Roberts in terms of the ways in which the relationships of their figures are dramatized. Williams's paintings do not dramatize the landscape through the types of 'fictions' that figures bring in the work of the Heidelberg School, or at least that is McCaughey's argument. The NSW Art Gallery's note for *My Garden* reads in part:

> In a singularly profound homage from one artist to another, Williams transmuted the golden glare of a relatively gentle New England landscape into his own painterly expression of the hot red heart of the continent; acting out his long-held declaration that 'Bailed up' was the most important landscape painting in this country.[95]

At the very least this suggests that there was in the 1960s an easy transformation of one place for another, with the alteration of colour playing out a changing relation that *was* dramatic. It was dramatic in a similar way to Sculthorpe's transformation of Lake Callabonna.

What, then, of Sculthorpe's figures? The presence of people in McCubbin is key to his work, as it is to Drysdale's, and they are absent in Williams's landscape. For Sculthorpe's music the question is a complex one. In *Red Landscape* (1966), one easily overlooked set of figures are the string quartet's performers. The composition opens with a simple cluster – F, G♭, G, A♭ – which enters in pairs: the violins, and then the viola and cello. The chord is prolonged through an interlocking glissando in which the pairs of instruments swap notes; the voice exchange is between the instruments as individuals, performers on the stage, which bars 5 and 6 make clear with 'irregular changes of bow direction, each player to be independent' (see Example 7.2).[96] The (close) transformation of this material into *Sun Music IV* heightens the collective work with a stage full of musicians. In the eighth quartet (*String Quartet Music*) the contrast between a single player and a group is featured. The quartet begins with solo cello, which slowly and without metre unfolds a modal space on D. The second movement begins with *ketungan*, and the term was written into the version of the score from which the Austral Quartet worked (the Faber score published in 1974 omits this text), which also sets the tempo slightly slower (♩=108) than the published score (♩=120).[97] The interlocking rhythms are derived from, as Sculthorpe writes, 'rice-pounding music (Balinese)'.[98] The contrasting section 'calmo', which was originally marked '*Arja*', is described as a 'Balinese popular song-play', though Sculthorpe moves the music far from the examples of the genre given in *Music in Bali*;[99] its lyricism is retained, though not its theatricality, and Hannan notes that Sculthorpe's tempo in this section is approximately half the tempo of McPhee's examples.[100] The published score is less ornamental than the earlier version, with the Austral Quartet's recording following Sculthorpe's emendation: 'The melody, beginning 2 bars after figure 5 should be very simple and flowing, and all grace notes should now be omitted, except the B♭ in the 4th bar of the melody [six bars after figure 5].'[101] These adjustments explain one of the differences between sound and paint, which is that to hear the composition involves listening to performers. In concert, their gestural, coordinating communication is an intrinsic part of the music, and Sculthorpe's changes to the music show him responding to the performers in making his adjustments: '[t]he accompanying figure, 2 bars after figure 7[102] should be marked a little louder; it needs to be heard'.[103] That 'accompanying figure' is not dramatic, no matter how lyrical the melody that it accompanies, for it repeats four notes cyclically for four bars. Nevertheless, it has presence as 'a figure' that is balanced by the players in performance.

This sense of a 'figure' works against the existing narratives for Sculthorpe's music, in which the composer himself is the figure – the only figure, since he is 'alone' and 'solitary' – in the music. The scholarship for Williams does not place Williams in a similar configuration to his paintings. The scholarship for Drysdale sometimes configures him as the central figure in painting, but not 'in his paintings', and when that distinction is not firm it is highly contested, as the arguments (above) between Hughes, Ross and Haeflier demonstrate. It is, therefore, useful to read Sculthorpe's music in a way that does not centralize him as the only figure in it, so that his music can be understood in relation to the work of Drysdale and Williams. Through that relation comes better explanations of Sculthorpe's music in terms of changing ideas

Example 7.2 Sculthorpe, *Red Landscape*, bars 1–18.

of Australian distinctiveness. There is also an ethical dimension to this change in the existing scholarship, since it opens up a place for the performers, as the figures who are essential to making the music sound.

Landscape II (1978)

Sometimes the absence of Sculthorpe's figures can be more significant than their presence. *Landscape II* is an example of a composition where the question of the presence or absence of figures itself opens multiple possibilities attached in particular to the relationship between melody and motif. The mid–late 1970s were a difficult period for Sculthorpe, as they were for Meale, and where *Port Essington* (1977) is at the beginning of a new period, *Landscape II* is at the end of the previous period. It was premiered in April 1978 at the Queen Street Galleries, in the suburb of Woollahra, Sydney, nearby where Sculthorpe lived.

The quintessential reading of this composition has been given by Jeanell Carrigan in her Master of Music thesis in 1994,[104] in which she identified the motifs that play again and again in Sculthorpe's music: melodic material from *gagaku*; a *fuori passo* treatment of a melody; harmonic glissandi – 'seagulls'; symbolic pitches of G, D and C; references to *gamelan*; 'insect noises'; 'geological strata'; 'Aboriginal sounding melodies'; silence. She reads them in combination through short narrative arcs. These arcs fail to build a coherent scene, which is a failure that shifts the task of making meaning to the listener, who: 'by using his or her own imagination is expected to conjure an image of landscape once viewed or experienced'.[105] A listener's experience of nature therefore provides the continuity that the music cannot.

The collection of motifs returns us to the paintings of Fred Williams, whose experience of the landscape is painted as a long series of hardly changing motifs: the trunks of trees, a flock of birds, a flat of horizon, the arc of a hillock. The difference is that Williams's critics make no attempt to read these painting in overtly narrative terms, whereas Sculthorpe's commentators look to narrative to make sense of a similar sense of scattered motifs.[106] *Landscape II* is not an overtly dramatic composition, and we ought to take Sculthorpe's claims against drama seriously, and at least consider the possibility of conceiving the music as a series of disconnected motifs.

Landscape II's motifs are presented with the clarity necessary in order to hear them individually. Indeed, the first movement presents the 'Mushiroda' (a *saibara* melody) in the strings, as a series of hardly connected phrases, at a slow tempo, with 'seagull' sounds played by the cello in between some of the phrases (Example 7.3). The melody and the gulls do not interact. Nor does the piano, which plucks irregularly at widely spaced low pitches: C, A♭, D, as a continuous cycle. The composition ends with no meaningful transformation of the opening.

Nevertheless, the presence of the melody is significant. Sculthorpe's treatment of it is similar to that of the *Isé-no-Umi* melody in his *Mangrove* (1979) for orchestra, in which each instrument plays the melody *fuori di passo* – out of step. For Naomi Cumming, the technique's use in *Mangrove* explains the relationship between sonic and visual lines, as motifs and figures:

> Heard *fuori di passo*, the line at this moment seems to dissolve into an oscillation that is the sonic analogy to a visual line distorted by its reflection in moving water. At other points, when the melody has a leap of a fourth [...], its heterophonous

Landscapes in Painting and Literature   231

Example 7.3 Sculthorpe, *Landscape II*, bars 1–12.

repetition creates a vertical sonority that brings into question the identity of the part as a melodic 'line' at all. […] Something of the human voice is retained in its melodic structure, but at moments of 'blurring' the textural dissolution makes that voice become indistinct. When it becomes part of an harmonic sonority, rather than a distinct line, the place of the melody in the musical 'foreground' has been compromised. Its linear (or figural) identity has been merged into the harmonic background in such a way as to suggest a retreat into a sonorous 'environment'.[107]

A similar argument can be made for the start of *Landscape II*, in which the 'reverberation' of the melodic *fuori di passo* blurs its own melodic identity. This process is supported by the piano, which keeps the sustain pedal depressed, and this draws closer the piano's sparsely plucked strings, the resounding resonance of the melodic line(s) and the sound of gulls. Cumming reads *Mangrove* in narrative terms in connection with Sculthorpe's earlier thoughts about writing opera, and with Nolan's 'Mrs Fraser paintings'. The reading is enabled by *Mangrove*'s dramatic succession of motifs,[108] but *Landscape II* is more disconnected and less discursive. One of the challenges that *Landscape II* poses is to determine its 'linear (or figural)' identity. On one hand melody and motif are presented side by side, and on the other they are difficult to separate. In the fourth movement, the piano returns to its opening material, but now as a hocket with the 'Mushiroda' melody, with which it intersects. The strings play a twenty-four-bar section (of quasi-ostinati) four times, out of step with the piano. As such, the piano's part sounds less like a clarification of the motif/figure relationship than a frail, fragmented melody, which never securely relates to the strings: this means that there is no straightforward figural/background relationship, and no clear representation/repetition relationship either.

The second movement is made up of a series of ostinati that shift mechanistically at irregular time intervals. The change of pattern at bar 7 makes the first six bars a distinct section. From bars 7 to 10 the cello holds an A as a drone, against sparser string pizzicato and a faster piano ostinato. At bar 11 the ostinato repeats two notes in the cello to three in the violin and eight in the viola. A more radical relationship between piano and strings occurs at figure 4, where the strings play notes from an {F, F♯, G, A♭} cluster (the same pitches that begin *Red Landscape*) in free time, *poco misterioso*, against a stuttering rhythm (becoming regular) in the piano. At no point does the movement settle into a foreground/background or figure/motif relationship.

In the third movement a melody is conspicuously absent, as a figure that fails to appear. As Peterson argues, noting the absence of melody, 'the emphasis here is not on accompanying a melody derived from Aboriginal sources [as a simple ostinato was in *The Song of Tailitnama* (1974), for voice and piano], but on providing a central focus for the music'.[109] *The Song of Tailitnama* is a dramatic work, written for an ABC documentary, and also the first significant work written after Sculthorpe's theatrical (if not straightforwardly dramatic) composition *Rites of Passage*. The absence of the melody in *Landscape II* is crucial, not as a presence erased, but as a 'determinate absence', such as found in Williams's *Echuca Landscape II*, and such as Althusser finds in Cremonini. The 'determinate absence' in Sculthorpe's *Landscape II* is *drama itself* in the form of a decisive line/figure relationship. Just as Williams rejects sculpture and flattens the landscape into paint, Sculthorpe flattens his motifs into lines as a rejection of drama as a clarifying device.[110]

Landscape II's absent drama in its relation to *The Song of Tailitnama* has to do with the relation between figures in Drysdale's landscape paintings. Drysdale's landscapes are abstract, to open up new relations with place. Sculthorpe landscape is here an abstraction that similarly opens up new relations. That the music eschews a specific statement about those relations indicates that the specific relations are to come, rather than existing ones that can be defined. In the programme note for *Landscape II* Sculthorpe writes of the Japanese as a people who have embraced two, apparently contradictory systems of belief: 'I related this to my own situation, to the tearing inside me between Australia and Europe, and also between Australia and Asia.'[111] *Landscape II*, in its extension of musical ideas from the earlier quartets, further transforms the ideas of nationalism that these musical and visual landscapes are about.[112]

Music for Japan

With the ambiguous position of figures in Sculthorpe's music established, there remains something to be said about some of Sculthorpe's recurring motifs, which are sometimes also difficult to define. An example of productive inconsistency about motif can be found in Sculthorpe's earlier composition, *Music for Japan* (1970) (Example 7.4), and I will here focus on the example of one motif: the semitone. The composition is a good example of Sculthorpe working through modernist compositional practices, and the way in which he does this returns to ideas from his earlier composition *Irkanda IV*, composed in 1961.

Music for Japan is a work that is built from 'the semitone', which is one of Sculthorpe's most used motifs. Its opening gives the motif in general form, as a series of octatonic chords (Example 7.5). Not all the chords are strictly octatonic, since the F♮ in chord 1 is outside the octatonic pitch space, a chromaticism that is retained in the second chord. With the second chord containing fewer pitch classes, we can conceive of the F as less obviously chromatic; indeed, against the E drone it forms the only explicit semitone in the chord, the other pitches forming a dominant seventh chord on E (spelt with A♭). This opens up two possibilities: either the octatonic form has changed, beginning E-F rather than E-F♯; or the tonal implication of the dominant seventh chord deliberately and ambiguously contrasts an octatonic space. Chord 2 recurs as chords 5, 8 and 11. Chords 3, 4, 6, 7, 10 and 12 are all from the same octatonic scale as chord 1. Combined, these chords suggest an exploration of the semitone in its general form. This further suggests that even though this piece is in Sculthorpe's 'Sun Music' style[113] – in which lyrical melodies are avoided – the thinking is scalic rather than harmonic. The octatonic chords recur at figure 4, and with altered registral distribution at figure 22, and at figure 24. As for *Landscape II*, the sequence of these sections underlines no specific drama.

There are various aspects of the music that work against defining a semitone as a 'motif'. For Hannan 'the opening section [...] is organized entirely from a twelve-tone row,'[114] and he demonstrates that the semitones from figure 8 are derived from Nono's all-interval row, as used in *Il canto sospeso*.[115] The unfolding shape of this 'All-Interval Wedge'[116] is more significant in this composition than its other properties.[117] It is most clearly used in a section of dodecaphonic *liberamente* flourishes, where

234   *Australian Music and Modernism, 1960–1975*

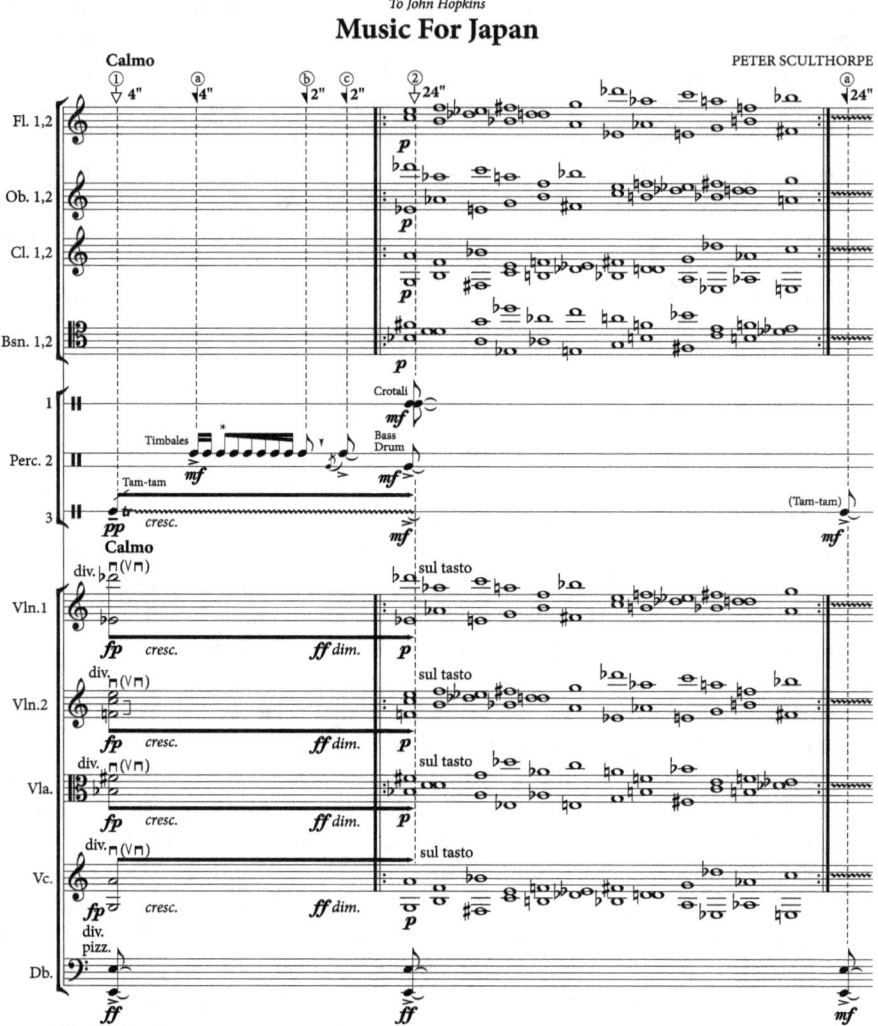

Example 7.4 Sculthorpe, *Music for Japan*, p. 1.

the wedge unfolds from a G (rather than Nono's A) at figure 8, expanding to E/ A♭ (Example 7.6). The same gesture repeats at figure 9, where it unfolds no further than E/B♭. Crotty, drawing on Blom's 1972 analysis,[118] also identifies the row in the second violins (and therefore in the flute, which doubles the second violin) at figure 2, though the homorhythmic and octatonic chords work against hearing the row linearly.

Landscapes in Painting and Literature 235

Example 7.5 The pitch content of the twelve chords from figure 2 of Sculthorpe's *Music for Japan*.

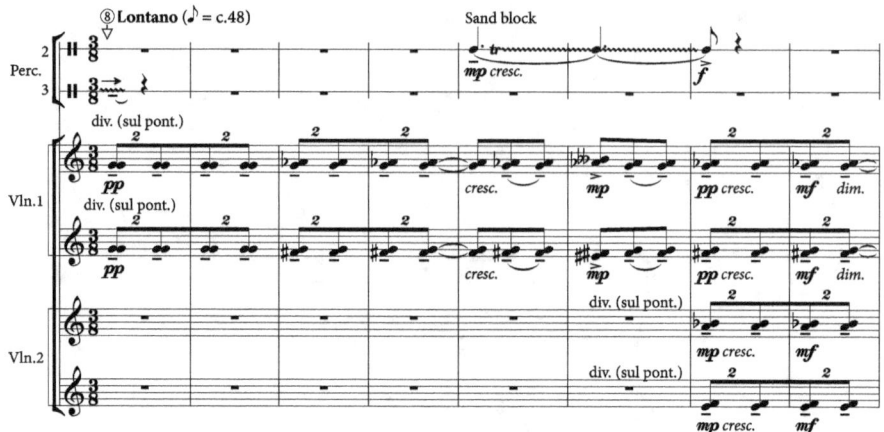

Example 7.6 *Music for Japan*, from figure 8, showing an instance of Sculthorpe's use of Nono's 'all-interval wedge'.

John Peterson, following Hannan, reads the ending of *Music for Japan* as a 'resolution to an E major chord with added major second (F♯)', and with the B♭ and E♭ as dissonant.[119] Peterson supports his reading as follows:

> *Music for Japan* was composed for performance at Expo '70, a festival whose theme was 'Progress and Harmony for Mankind', and whose pavilions and performances were specifically designed by the Japanese hosts to be innovative and unusual. Sculthorpe's score, with its unusual use of the orchestra and its instrumental timbres, is therefore placed in a more coherent perspective: Sculthorpe clearly intended to produce something new and unique for the premiere performances in Japan, while still evoking elements of his own composition style.[120]

Whatever Sculthorpe's intentions, the coherence of the final chord is not clear. The position of B♭ and E♭ in the upper registers, against the low E, suggests that they are part of the sonority, rather than to be heard against it, especially given that they are played as harmonics by Violin I. Peterson rightly suggests that they are 'reminiscent of similar chords found at the end of *Sun Music III*', but we ought to be careful not too quickly to read the ending as a straightforward resolution. The octatonicism of the opening (not a feature discussed by Peterson or Hannan) remains at the end, in its emphasis of the semitone. If we consider the F at the start as chromatic, then the same octatonic scale operates at the beginning and at the end. This configures G♯ and B as the chromatic pitches in the final chord – the very pitches on which a resolution to E major relies. Of course, the registration of the chord reinforces an E major chord as a more stable entity, but not without complication. The same tension present in the opening chords is present at the end, without apparent narrative, transformation or drama.

The final chord is very nearly the same chord that ends *Irkanda IV* (1961). The setting is very different, since *Irkanda IV* is more dissonant than other works from the time,[121] and its final chord therefore has no sense of resolution. In a work that deals so immediately with personal grief, the figure of the solo violinist is also significant, and the closing chord's harmonic E♭ is played by the solo violin. *Irkanda IV* is also notable for its clear melody, made from minor seconds, minor thirds and major thirds,[122] which give a different perspective to the later coincidence of an octatonic collection and a tonal chord. From this perspective the harmonic workings and the identity of the semitone is more about figuration than motif.

Skinner recounts an initial confusion about the title: 'He [Sculthorpe] called it *Music for Japan*, explaining that this meant "for" Japan, but "about" Australia.'[123] The composition's title suggests a stage for a consideration of national ideas and international practices. The kind of confusion that originally arose over *Music for Japan*'s title is also a confusion that exists for Williams. In conversation, Gleeson asked Williams about a You Yangs triptych from the mid-1960s in connection with Japanese screens, and they had a misunderstanding about which works might be being discussed.[124] Gleeson also saw a connection with Japanese screens in the earlier works involving saplings, such as inform *Echuca Landscape II*. Eventually Williams commented that the You Yangs work 'was most certainly influenced by a Japanese screen or a Chinese screen'. Anne Gray, writing in *Australia's Empire*, considers Williams's 1969 triptych *Australian Landscape I, II* and *III* in terms of McCubbin's *The Pioneer*, which Williams used as something of a model for these paintings.[125] The connection with McCubbin is less visible than it is for *Echuca Landscape II*, about which Williams expressed no such relationship. For Gray: 'whereas McCubbin depicts a foreground, middle ground, and distance, and showed the earth and the sky, Williams created an image that is more closely focused, more intense, more absorbed in the bush' and 'in creating a work in which the painterly gesture dominates, Williams shared an interest with both Monet in his later works and the painters of Japanese screens'.[126] With this in mind, Gray asserts that 'Williams replaced the ordinary pictorial concepts of up and down, back and front, depth and surface with spatial ambiguity' and this enables an 'international mode of expression – both contemporary and historical – [through which] Williams placed the Australian visual experience within a globalized world'.[127] This seems to have been Sculthorpe's aim, too. The Japanese motifs that others have identified in this music are often no more significant in their national meaning than the Japanese screen is for Williams.

Sculthorpe's contribution to the arguments about nationalism in the 1970s is more securely embedded in wider artistic practices than has often been articulated. The connections to Drysdale are specific and meaningful because they open up further relationships to other artists with their own histories of modernist practice, and with similar ways of using figures and motifs. From a modernist perspective Sculthorpe's musical landscapes operate meaningfully in relation to landscape painting, particularly in the way that they present a complex conception of nationalism during a time of new ideas about representation. *Landscape II*, like many of Sculthorpe's works, is both abstract, *resisting* connections to particular places, and tied to the wider artistic project of national distinctiveness.

Conclusion

The examples given here, which are a small number of short sections of music by Lumsdaine and Sculthorpe, demonstrate the rich possibilities of considering transnational perspectives that also cross different art forms. They demonstrate the value of being attentive to geographic specificity (be it national or otherwise) and personal connections. The musics of Sculthorpe and Lumsdaine relate very differently to Australia as a place and as an artistic conception, and they also differ in their relation to nationalism. Nevertheless, they are both composers for whom 'Australia' is an important idea, and who explored its possibilities in music. They both looked to other artists also working with similar ideas. The music that they wrote departs from stereotypical conceptions of Australian nationalism, and in this very departure their music questions those stereotypes. It is in this way that they both contribute to a modernist form of Australian Music. Although some of the works that I have discussed have been widely celebrated, those celebrations are out of step with the ideas that drive the music, which are idiosyncratic, political and artistic, and which seek to develop new, critical conceptions of Australia in relation to other places, people and artistic practices.

In the 1960s there were few national organizations for new music, and one of the paradoxes of their establishment in the early 1970s is that those organizations then pursued an agenda of celebration that was antithetical to the musical practices of many composers. The process of consolidating a movement therefore brought about its end, from which emerged a different form of Australian Music. Covell's position here is crucial: he was the most important critic in the country, and his 1967 book *Australia's Music* defined its field. By the 1980s he was even more influential, as the celebration of Australian Music dominated discussions of music in Australia, drawing directly on his writing. The change of emphasis from critical encouragement to uncritical celebration took place in the middle of the 1970s, and an early example of the two forms of Australian Music coexisting is present in a letter from 1972, in which Banks wrote to Porter about Covell to explain that Covell has both 'imagination' and 'energy', in planning for performances to take advantage of the new funding that was available.[128] Whilst Banks supported those applications, he was nevertheless sceptical of what he saw as Covell's 'empire building', which Banks understood as a way for Covell to strengthen his position at the University of New South Wales (at the time the university employed only Covell and one other lecturer in music). The problem, from Banks's perspective, was that Covell was 'very careful what he says about the local composers and is always encouraging to them'. Banks continued by arguing that 'I happen to think that this [uncritical encouragement] is a very bad thing'. The letter is one of the few articulations of the two models of Australian Music: Banks wanted a robust discussion of musical ideas, and Covell wanted to celebrate the composers who were local to him. This comes at the moment when Banks was at the centre of the most significant national organization for music, and when Covell was increasingly significant as a critic, working to build his position by aligning the composers near to him with the newly consolidated form of Australian Music that was centred on

Sculthorpe. The effects of this were far-reaching, since the momentum was with Covell and Sculthorpe, and Covell's view, alongside an increasing number of other like-minded critics and musicians, also aligned with the newly formed Australian Music Centre (based in Sydney), the function of which, after Banks's departure, was to promote Australian Music.

This all comes much later than similar discussions of musical modernism that had occurred in other places, and so Australian Music is late, difficult and self-conscious, and it is also aware of earlier modernist composition: hence the prevalence of serialism, and specifically of a form of serialism that is highly contingent, since the composers of Australian Music also understood that the heyday of serialism was over. Their work takes place in close connection with ideas from Europe, Britain and the USA, and so over the years from 1960 to 1975 the modernist discussions that dominated the start of the period quickly shifted to become the arguments of late modernity that would dominate the 1980s, and their music reflects and contributes to that change. Australian modernism is not, therefore, a late transplantation of earlier modernism. In Australian Music of the late 1970s one can see practices of technical exploration giving way to the celebration of individual composers, and to the rise of a form of nationalism that was to be expressed by those individual composers. Although their ambitions were not always in agreement, and their practices were diverse, nevertheless the arguments about nationalism that went with their music of the 1960s and early 1970s do define an era of modernist Australian Music.

If the idea of Australian Music is to be productive, it needs to be used to clarify the contestation of nationalist ideas, and its discourses need to be flexible enough to encompass different perspectives, whilst amplifying those differences continually to question the prevalence of nationalism. Australian Music in its early years meant something different to what it does today, and that difference itself should press scholars to find new and more critical ways of making distinctions between – to return to the quotation from Lumsdaine (Chapter 1) – "'music *in* Australia" and "music *of* Australia" and "music *about* or *for* or *from* Australia'".[129]

Notes

Introduction

1. Roger Smalley's contribution to a formal debate in Graeme Skinner (ed.), 'Debate: That Australian Composers Should Set Out to Develop a Distinctive Australian Music', in *The Composer Speaks*, ed. Graeme Skinner (Sydney: Sounds Australian, 1991).
2. The letter from Peter Sculthorpe to Barry Conyngham, dated 14 September 1988, and held in Conyngham's private archive, reads:

   > It occurs to me that you might like to have a few thoughts upon the idea of an Australian musical voice.
   >
   > I believe that the enduring music of every country has always spoken of its country, and grown from it. It continues to do so, and the better the music the more it speaks to all countries. Can one imagine Boulez, for instance, as German, or Stockhausen as French, or, say, Berio as either? I myself don't think that it's a matter worth discussing.
   >
   > On the other hand, in Australia it's always been a matter for discussion. I'm proposing, then, that those composers who reject the notion of an Australian musical voice could well have a grand vision. They just might achieve something that has never been achieved by any composers in the history of the human race: a truly global music, stateless, free from the shackles of Europe, betraying no particular place of origin. Given our isolation, even in the late twentieth century, if this could be achieved anywhere in the world, it could be achieved here.
   >
   > I do think that the matter is worth discussing in this light.

3. In 1968 James Murdoch described Meale as 'very much a modern man, a Marshall McLuhan man, closely involved in the world around him' (James Murdoch, 'Voyage of Discovery', *Sound*, February (1968): 6–9).
4. Conyngham in Skinner, 'Distinctive Australian Music', 12.
5. Roger Covell in Skinner, 'Distinctive Australian Music', 13. In her report of this debate in the *Sydney Morning Herald*, Gail Brennan argued that 'Covell's spoof of bureaucratic coercion was ironic. Covell's book – *Australia's Music: Themes of a New Society* – had itself functioned as a guideline for bestowing grants, whether that had been the author's intention or not' (Gail Brennan, 'They Said We'd Never Make It: The Music of Australia', *Sydney Morning Herald*, 24 September 1988, 81). Covell's contribution to the debate is not entirely satirical, and the debate as a whole was serious, though as in any staged debate the speakers tended to be less nuanced in their positions for the sake of winning the argument.
6. Brett Dean, Introduction to broadcast by the BBC Symphony Orchestra, *Hear and Now* [Radio broadcast] BBC Radio 3, 6 August 2016. Transcribed by the author. Unless otherwise noted, all written transcriptions of audio material in this book were made by the author.

7   *Sun Music I* is described by Peterson as 'sombre and intense'. John Peterson, *The Music of Peter Sculthorpe* (Kingsgrove: Wildbird Music, 2014).
8   'Extrovert Performance of Sydney Orchestra', *The Times*, 20 September 1965.
9   Richard Meale, Interview with Andrew Ford, *The Music Show* [Radio broadcast], ABC Radio National, 24 August 2002 www.abc.net.au/radionational/programs/musicshow/richard-meale/3515648.
10 Papers of Richard Meale, MS 10076, National Library of Australia, Box 39.
11 Fiona Richards, in the introduction to the book that she edited in 2007, also begins with Bryson on Australia: Fiona Richards (ed.), *The Soundscapes of Australia: Music, Place and Spirituality* (Aldershot: Ashgate, 2007), 1. Her book includes contributions from a wide range of writers, who are guided by the book's central aim, which is to understand Australian Music through 'a consideration of the complex connections between music, place and spirituality' (10). This describes one of the more recent forms of Australian Music, which is disconnected from the music of the 1960s and early 1970s, a cut produced through the stylistic change undertaken by many in the late 1970s. For example, in the book Anne Boyd argues that 'The droned character of the music [of the shakuhachi, of the didjeridu] has a special significance in Edwards's musical language: a stylistic crisis in the mid-70s led him to reject European modernism in favour of the development of a musical language based upon his acutely sensitive listening to Australian bush sounds – to frogs, insects and birds' (Boyd in ibid., 13). For Boyd this is part of a wider move towards the celebration of the earth itself. Although Boyd does discuss music from before the mid-1970s, by Australian-born David Lumsdaine, she positions him as an outsider: 'As a European modernist, working within an abstracted musical language, the product of advanced European consciousness, which nevertheless draws directly upon the sounds and rhythms of nature and of Australian landscape for its very essence, as a kind of higher order mathematics, his music is freed from the more conventional demands of the expression of the Ego and created a feeling of transcendence which is the essence of spirituality' (ibid., 33). Boyd's argument privileges a version of Australian Music built on 'crisis', from which emerges the celebrated work of Edwards and Sculthorpe; Lumsdaine did not have the same crisis, and continued to compose music that was 'modernist' long after Edwards had abandoned it. For Lumsdaine's music to be considered alongside the recent music by Sculthorpe and Edwards, Boyd needs 'spirituality' to transcend what for Edwards were irreconcilable ideas. Whether or not one agrees with Boyd, the argument has very little to do with how Australian Music was understood in the 1960s and early 1970s.
12 Roger Covell, 'Richard Meale: Intuitions of a Solitary Modernist', *Sounds Australian* 20 (1988/9): 5. The title of Covell's article itself is problematic, since the word 'solitary' belongs to the 'lonely' discourse centred on Sculthorpe, and which is historically the mechanism by which Sculthorpe – and Sculthorpe alone – represents Australian Music.
13 Covell, 'Intuitions of a Solitary Modernist', 5.
14 Ibid.
15 Between 1960 and 1975, The University of Sydney, The University of Western Australia, The University of Queensland, the University of New England, the Conservatorium at The University of Melbourne, the Tasmanian Conservatorium, the NSW State Conservatorium, La Trobe and the Canberra School of Music all appointed, for the first time, composers to academic positions (see Helen Gifford,

Zoe Sweett, Joel Crotty and Aline Scott-Maxwell, 'Composers in the Academy', in John Whiteoak and Aline Scott-Maxwell (eds), *Currency Companion to Music and Dance in Australia* (Sydney: Currency House, 2003), 170).

16 Barry Conyngham, '2nd Annual Peggy Glanville-Hicks Address', Sydney Opera House, 13 August 2000 www.newmusicnetwork.com.au/PGH/BC00.htm accessed 11 March 2016. Conyngham's music from this time is considerably less clear-cut than his comments about Australian Music might suggest, which shows a further aspect of the way that the discourse overwhelms musical nuance, and the need for scholarship that is musically detailed.

17 Ibid.; correction in the original transcription of the address.

18 Kay Dreyfus, 'In Search of New Waters: Australian Music Studies in the 1990s', in Frank Callaway (ed.), *Essays in Honour of David Evatt Tunley* (University of Western Australia: Callaway International Resource Centre for Music Education, 1995), 155–64.

19 Ibid., 155.

20 Joel Crotty (ed.), *Sounds Australian: Journal of the Australian Music Centre* 41, autumn (1994): cover.

21 Ibid., 6.

22 Ibid.

23 Bruce Johnson, *The Inaudible Music: Jazz, Gender and Australian Modernity* (Sydney: Currency Press, 2000), 48.

24 The principal exception to the disciplinary divide that Johnson describes is the scholarship of John Whiteoak, whose publications throughout the 1990s, for example, move between improvisation, sound art, electronic music, jazz, brass bands and the music of Keith Humble and Don Banks. His broad interests are brought together in the book he edited with Aline Scott-Maxwell, the *Currency Companion to Music and Dance in Australia*.

25 Johnson, *The Inaudible Music*, 49.

26 Ibid., 48–9.

27 This book is not a description of all music in Australia, but of Australian Music. It is also not a history of modernism in Australia, but of Australian Music in its modernist phase. For this reason the book excludes many composers before 1960 and many of the composers working since, both nationalists and modernists. It also excludes composers such as Keith Humble, whose work in Melbourne from 1966 (when he returned to Melbourne permanently) is not included here because his work was isolated to a significant degree from what came to be the central arguments of Australian Music; a different book would (and should) centre on his music. Similarly, this book includes no close examination of music by women. There were, of course, women writing music in Australia, and some Australian modernists were women, but Australian Music in its early phase did not include these composers. Such neglect was corrected from the late 1970s, particularly around the music of Anne Boyd, Moya Henderson, Alison Bauld, Jennifer Fowler and many others.

Chapter 1

1 Peter Porter and Don Banks, jointly drafted programme note for their collaboration *Tirade*, Papers of Don Banks, MS6830, National Library of Australia, Box 28. The reference made is to Smith's 1873 *Dictionary of Greek and Roman Biography and*

Mythology. Herostratus, having had his name 'condemned to oblivion' for burning the temple of Artemis, was named by the historian Theopompus. The reference suggests that 'naming Australia', which Banks and Porter's work *Tirade* does, with satirical Australiana, recovers the national at the same time it dismisses it. The 'lucky' surely refers to Donald Horne's just-published book *The Lucky Country* (Harmondsworth: Penguin, 1964).

2 http://www.australianmusiccentre.com.au/about accessed 3 November 2016.
3 http://www.australiacouncil.gov.au/funding/funding-index/arts-projects-for-individuals-and-groups accessed 28 March 2018.
4 http://www.australiacouncil.gov.au/workspace/uploads/files/australia_council_for_the_arts-55e50dcf21a28.pdf accessed 28 March 2018.
5 http://www.australiacouncil.gov.au/workspace/uploads/files/australia_council_for_the_arts-55e50dcf21a28.pdf accessed 28 March 2018.
6 https://www.legislation.gov.au/Details/C2013A00071 accessed 28 March 2018.
7 http://www.boardofstudies.nsw.edu.au/syllabus_hsc/pdf_doc/music-2-st6-syl-from2010.pdf accessed 31 March 2014.
8 http://www.vcaa.vic.edu.au/Documents/vce/music/musicSD2011-2015.pdf accessed 31 March 2014.
9 It is beyond the scope of this book to explain in detail what 'British Music' means, though the topic intersects with Australian Music in, for example, the exclusion of Malcolm Williamson and Don Banks from the book *British Music Now* 'on grounds of nationality' (Lewis Foreman (ed.), *British Music Now* (London: Elek Books Limited, 1975), 11), at a time when conceptions of 'British Music' and 'Australian Music' were similarly undergoing change.
10 In 1969 Wilfrid Mellers, Professor of Music at the University of York, wrote the Department of Music at Sydney University a letter, which in part reads: 'We are about to inaugurate the new Concert Hall and Music Department building in my British university of York. It is appropriate that on this (for us) momentous eve I should send a greeting to Donald Peart: whose department at Sydney University is the only one that has – as far as I'm consciously aware – influenced mine. When I visited the University of Sydney it seemed to me that Peart's department embodied more of the right ideas as to what a university music department ought to aim at than any I've come across; some features I have borrowed for, or adapted to, our English environment' (Mellers, Papers of Peter Sculthorpe, MS 9676, National Library of Australia, Box 27). The letter serves as a useful reminder that influence between Australia and Britain went both ways.
11 Gordon Spearritt, 'Musicology in Australia', *Australian Journal of Music Education* 15 (1974): 49–52.
12 Donald Peart, 'Editorial', *Music Now* 1, no. 1 (1969): 4.
13 Ibid., 4.
14 The author of this sentence, which introduces Peart before the start of his article, is not clear. The text was most likely written by one of the associate editors: Anne Boyd, Barry Conyngham, Meredith Oakes or Clem Dirago.
15 Mike Seabrook, *Max: The Life and Music of Peter Maxwell Davies* (London: Victor Gollancz, 1994), 98.
16 Davies wrote the Preface to James Murdoch's *Australia's Contemporary Composers* (Melbourne: Macmillan, 1972).
17 It therefore differs from, for example, Skinner's work on Sculthorpe, which relies on critical reception (Graeme Skinner, *Peter Sculthorpe: The Making of an Australian*

Composer (Sydney: University of New South Wales Press, 2007)). Although this chapter relies very little on newspapers for its argument, subsequent chapters do draw on articles and reviews published in the press to give a fuller context for Australian Music. This results in a change of emphasis: for example, the musicologist Rachel Campbell argues (in agreement with Sculthorpe himself) that the critical reception of Sculthorpe's music was key to his prominence (Rachel Campbell, 'Peter Sculthorpe's *Irkanda* Period, 1954–65: Nationalism, "Aboriginality," and Landscape', PhD diss. (The University of Sydney, 2014), chapter 5), and if that is the case then any study of critical reception of the period will tend to support a narrative centred on Sculthorpe. My book gives less weight to the criticism published in the daily newspapers (and which was written by a small handful of critics).

18 Matthew Riley (ed.), *British Music and Modernism, 1895–1960* (Aldershot: Ashgate, 2010).
19 J. P. E. Harper-Scott, *Edward Elgar, Modernist* (Cambridge: Cambridge University Press, 2006).
20 J. P. E. Harper-Scott, *The Quilting Points of Musical Modernism* (Cambridge: Cambridge University Press, 2012), xiii.
21 Ibid., xiv.
22 Ibid., 152.
23 Gordon Kerry, *New Classical Music: Composing Australia* (Sydney: University of New South Wales Press, 2009), 78.
24 In contrast, for Covell the 1960s was the time in which the 'reduction in time-lag between important developments in Australia' had been achieved (Covell, *Australia's Music: Themes of a New Society* (Melbourne: Sun Books, 1967), 269).
25 Natasha Silva-Jelly, 'Hyped Chains Accused of Dumping Stock Down Under', *Sydney Morning Herald*, 31 March 2013.
26 Kerry, *New Classical Music*, 82. Kerry collapses aesthetics and ideology, in explaining that 'aesthetically, the European avant-garde had a political program' (142). The 'lagging' problem is used by Hannan to describe Meale's experience of travelling to UCLA in 1960–1: 'Meale realised that his compositional development and that of most composers working in Australian [sic] lagged behind radical developments in European and American Music' (Michael Hannan, *The Music of Richard Meale* (Kingsgrove: Wildbird Music, 2014), 3).
27 Mark Carroll, 'Out of the Ordinary: The Quotidian in the Music of Graeme Koehne', *Music and Letters* 95, no. 3 (2014): 429.
28 Ibid., 435.
29 Victoria Rogers, *The Music of Peggy Glanville-Hicks* (Aldershot: Ashgate, 2009), 11. On p. 91, Rogers quotes from Glanville-Hicks on 'three stages' of modernism: neoclassicism, serialism and 'bringing together the assets of East and West'.
30 *Sounds Australian* was the house journal of the Australian Music Centre, and *Ossia* was a short-lived but lively alternative journal and CD label.
31 Rupprecht, 'Britten and the Avant-Garde in the 1950s', in Philip Rupprecht (ed.), *Rethinking Britten* (Oxford: Oxford University Press, 2013), 132ff.
32 Ibid., 141.
33 In Britain there was 'the popular tendency to treat the terms *serial* and *avant-garde* as virtual synonyms' (ibid., 141), but the discourse about new music such as existed in Australia in the 1960s rarely mentions either term. Indeed, there were few writers in a position to make judgements about the music from a technical perspective.

34 Donald Peart, 'The Australian Avant-Garde', *Proceedings of the Royal Musical Association* 93, no. 1 (1967): 1.
35 The question of the relationship of this notion with that of Aboriginal Australia is a complex one. Peart's vision for the Department of Music included the study of music throughout Asia (including Australia), and Sculthorpe, amongst others, lectured on Aboriginal music. However, the impact of this music is hard to discern in any of Meale's, Dreyfus's or Butterley's music. With that in mind, Peart's 'indigenous tradition' is synonymous with Australian Music, openly conceived.
36 Ibid., 1.
37 Covell, *Australia's Music*, xi.
38 See, for example, 'The Victorian Acclimatisation Society' http://museumvictoria.com.au/discoverycentre/infosheets/the-melbourne-story/the-victorian-acclimatisation-society-/ accessed 26 June 2014. The project was supported by government initiatives and private societies alike. Such societies existed in many countries, though for Australia the exchange took place only with Britain.
39 Thomas Dunlap, 'Remaking the Land: The Acclimatization Movement and Anglo Ideas of Nature', *Journal of World History* 8, no. 22 fall (1997): 303–19.
40 Covell, *Australia's Music*, 202.
41 Skinner, *Peter Sculthorpe*, 145.
42 Covell, *Australia's Music*, 290.
43 Sculthorpe, writing in *Hemisphere*, 1970, quoted in Skinner, *Peter Sculthorpe*, 561.
44 Covell's desire and the language with which it was articulated was still being referred to as late as 1983. See Reis Flora, Peter Sculthorpe, Margaret Kartomi and Cathy Falk, 'Music and Ethnomusicology in Australia', *Journal of the Asian Studies Association of Australia* 7, no. 2 (1983): 14–24.
45 Banks attended the London launch of this survey, which is a measure of its importance both in Australia and in the UK:

> I went to Australia House for the launching session of 'Music Survey'. It went very well indeed – the material was well displayed and Australia House did everyone proud with food and drink. A good start for a very important venture. (Banks to Callaway, 7 November 1969, Papers of Don Banks, Box 28)

46 Andrew McCredie, *Music by Australian Composers: Survey No. 1* (Canberra: Advisory Board, Commonwealth Assistance to Australian Composers, 1969), 1.
47 John Hirst, *Looking for Australia: Historical Essays* (Melbourne: Black Inc., 2010), 229.
48 Banks's CV, 1966, Papers of Don Banks, Folio 3 Pack 11.
49 McCredie, *Music by Australian Composers*, 7.
50 The classic text is Horne's *The Lucky Country*, in which an 'easy-going' attitude is linked directly to social stability.
51 Lorraine Hickman, 'Richard Meale: A Profile', *Walkabout*, June (1966): 22–5.
52 Ingrid Etter, 'The Man Who Turns Money into Music', *Women's Weekly*, 27 February 1974, 8–9.
53 Deborah Edwards and Denise Mimmocchi (eds), *Sydney Moderns: Art for a New World* (Sydney: Art Gallery NSW, 2013).
54 Mimmocchi, 'Making Sydney Modern: The Artistic Shaping of the Postwar City', in Edwards and Mimmocchi (eds), *Sydney Moderns*, 72.
55 Edwards, 'Ultra-*moderne*: *Implement blue* and *The Lacquer Room*', in Edwards and Mimmocchi (eds), *Sydney Moderns*, 148.

56 Peart, *Music Now*, 3.
57 Susan Stanford Friedman, 'Periodizing Modernism: Postcolonial Modernities and the Space/Time Borders of Modernist Studies', *Modernism/modernity* 13, no. 3 (2006): 425–43.
58 Meale, Interview with Andrew Ford, *The Music Show*, ABC Radio National, 24 August 2002 www.abc.net.au/radionational/programs/musicshow/richard-meale/3515648 accessed 12 May 2019.
59 Ibid. The transcription is the ABC's.
60 McCredie, *Music by Australian Composers*, 8.
61 Ibid., 16.
62 Ibid., 25.
63 Ibid.
64 Ibid., iii.
65 'Musica Australis Collection of Music Scores and Parts [music]' http://trove.nla.gov.au/work/156936121?q=+&versionId=171078547 accessed 1 July 2014. See also McCredie, 'The Preservation of Australian Music', in David Tunley and David Symons (eds), *The Contemporary Australian Composer and Society: Report of Seminar February 24–28, 1971* (University of Western Australia: Department of Music, 1971), 53.
66 Ibid., 55.
67 Ibid., 58–9.
68 Ibid., 60. McCredie left aside Covell's suggestion for including 'surviving European colonial materials in nearby Asia'. The plan also included 'Australian contributions to music theory and musicology and criticism' (60).
69 Ibid., 65.
70 Ibid., 66.
71 The 'Commonwealth Assistance to Australian Composers' scheme began in 1967, to 'encourage the publication and knowledge of Australian serious music composition'. Funding was available to publish music, copy parts for performance, record compositions and disseminate scores internationally. The board that advised the government about how to spend these funds comprised Bernard Heinze, Frank Callaway and John Hopkins ('Commonwealth Assistance to Australian Composers', *Australian Journal of Music Education* 1 (1967): 50).
72 Musical research was also boosted in 1973 with the establishment of the Humanities Research Centre at the Australian National University, which hosted seminars and visiting fellowships (McCredie, *Musicological Studies in Australia from the Beginning to the Present* (Sydney: Sydney University Press, 1979), 11–12).
73 David Tunley, 'Australian Composition in the Twentieth Century – A Background', in Frank Callaway and David Tunley (eds), *Australian Composition in the Twentieth Century* (Melbourne: Oxford University Press, 1978), 5.
74 Ibid.
75 Ibid.
76 Sculthorpe to Banks, Papers of Don Banks, Box 36. Banks was performed at ISCM festivals in 1952 (Salzburg), 1954 (Haifa) and 1959 (Rome) (Banks's CV, Papers of Don Banks, Folio 3 Pack 11).
77 http://www.fabermusic.com/repertoire/sonatina-4651 accessed 25 March 2014.
78 'More Australian Music Published', *Sydney Morning Herald*, 28 December 1964, 17.
79 http://conservatorium.unimelb.edu.au/pgh/workslist accessed 20 May 2014.
80 Skinner, *Peter Sculthorpe*, 350.

81 Covell, in ibid., 353.
82 Ibid.
83 Quoted in Skinner, *Peter Sculthorpe*, 399.
84 Callaway and Tunley, *Australian Composition*, 5.
85 Ibid., 5–6.
86 Quoted in ibid., 6.
87 Ibid.
88 McCallum's contribution to a panel discussion, in 'New Music Criticism in Australia', in Graeme Skinner (ed.), *The Composer Speaks* (Sydney: Sounds Australian, 1991), 45.
89 The move from serialism to tonality in 1970s Australia remains scantly theorized in the Australian context. See Andrew Robbie, 'Narrating the Early Music of Ross Edwards', *Resonate Magazine* (2008) www.australianmusiccentre.com.au/article/narrating-the-early-music-of-ross-edwards accessed 12 May 2019.
90 Meale, Interview with Andrew Ford.
91 McCredie, *Music by Australian Composers*, 21.
92 Lumsdaine, report to Banks, 25 September 1973, Papers of Don Banks, Box 35.
93 J. L. Sturman, 'The Status and Role of the Australian Composer', in programme booklet, National Conference of Australian Composers, Australian National University, 24–8 September 1973.
94 The date is a coincidence.
95 Lumsdaine to Banks, 26 January 1973, Papers of Don Banks, Box 35.

Chapter 2

1 Jenny Hocking, *Gough Whitlam: A Moment in History* (Melbourne: The Miegunyah Press, 2008), 343.
2 Covell, *Australia's Music: Themes of a New Society* (Melbourne: Sun Books, 1967), 269. Covell's 'new society' is an international one with 'a truly universal language' (290).
3 Murdoch, *Australia's Contemporary Composers* (Melbourne: Macmillan, 1972), cover note.
4 Davies, 'Foreword' to ibid., ix.
5 One may compare Banks and Humble here. The former returned to Australia less than a decade later than the latter; both returned with significant expertise in new music and formed centres for new music, Banks in London and Humble in Paris. Where the former was in a position to establish much essential Australian infrastructure, the latter was largely limited to a small sphere of colleagues and students around the Grainger Museum in Melbourne. This ought to suggest something of the cultural change that had occurred in those years, rather than any particular differences between the two composers in terms of organizational ability. For a short and enlightening introduction to Humble's work in terms of what he sought to establish, see John Whiteoak, 'Interview with Keith Humble', *NMA*, 7 (1989): 21–6 www.rainerlinz.net/NMA/repr/Humble_interview.html accessed 4 October 2014. For an introduction to Humble the modernist, see Graham Hair, 'Keith Humble's Modernism: From Homogenous Motivic-Thematic Organicism to

Heterogenous Gestural Constructivism' www.n-ism.org/Papers/graham_Humble.pdf accessed 4 October 2014.
6. Lumsdaine to Banks, 1972, Papers of Don Banks, MS6830, National Library of Australia, Box 35.
7. No date, Papers of Don Banks, Box 6.
8. 21 March 1969, Papers of Don Banks, Box 28.
9. Undated document, Papers of Don Banks, Box 36.
10. Banks to Murdoch, 13 July 1972, Papers of Don Banks, Box 36; see also Banks to Ahern, 20 June 1972, ibid., Box 4.
11. Written quickly, Banks's pun on the Association of Tennis Professionals ran into further letter jumbling.
12. Undated document, '1972 Quotes by Don Banks', Papers of Don Banks, Box 36.
13. Banks to Ahern, 20 March 1973, Papers of Don Banks, Box 4.
14. The name was later to change to the Australia Council for the Arts.
15. Banks to Alan Woolgar, 26 January 1973, Papers of Don Banks, Box 37. The previous government had appointed Banks a member of the Commonwealth Assistance to Composers' Board. 'Don Banks: Australian Activities for 6 Months Jan[uary] to Jul[y] 1972', ibid., Box 36.
16. The budget for music increased from $285,000 to ten times that figure. At the same time, Banks's remuneration as chairman was a modest $2,800 per year. Banks to Lumsdaine, 27 March 1973, Papers of Don Banks, Box 35.
17. Banks to Bill Colleran, 28 January 1973, Papers of Don Banks, Box 37.
18. 'Govt Reshapes Arts Program: Council Named', *Sydney Morning Herald*, 27 January 1973, 2; cutting in Papers of Don Banks, Box 20.
19. Banks to Lumsdaine, 27 March 1973, Papers of Don Banks, Box 35.
20. Banks to Lumsdaine, 27 March 1973, Papers of Don Banks, Box 35.
21. Banks to Murdoch, undated letter (early 1975), Papers of Don Banks, Box 36.
22. Banks to Furse, 9 December 1975, Papers of Don Banks, Box 35.
23. The letter from Lumsdaine responding to this is dated September.
24. Banks to Lumsdaine, undated letter, Papers of Don Banks, Box 35.
25. In an interview with Hazel de Berg, Banks explained that he was seeking to establish a reciprocal arrangement for young composers in Australia and Britain, by organizing concerts with the ISCM in Sydney and the SPNM in London (Don Banks, 'Donald Banks Interviewed by Hazel de Berg in the Hazel de Berg Collection' [Audio recording] (National Library of Australia, 1972), Oral TRC 1/626, Session 2, 44').
26. 'James Murdoch Management', Papers of James Murdoch, MS 8372, National Library of Australia, Box 34.
27. 'Rough Plan', 5 February 1973, Papers of Don Banks, Box 36.
28. Banks to Murdoch, 25 January 1973 (i.e., the day before the announcement of the Australia Council), Papers of Don Banks, Box 36.
29. Banks to Lumsdaine, 1973, Papers of Don Banks, Box 35.
30. Banks to John Wion, 9 September 1974, Papers of Don Banks, Box 36.
31. Professor Ian Turner, an historian at Monash University, was a member of the central committee of the Australia Council.
32. Banks to Murdoch, 2 December 1974, Papers of Don Banks, Box 36.
33. See Gwen Bennett, *More than Music: The Life and Work of Kenneth W Tribe AC* (Sydney: Australian Music Centre, 2011), 111–17. Bennett argues that: 'As far back

as Prime Minister Menzies's era, Dr H. C. (*Nugget*) Coombs had pushed for an Australian organization similar to the Arts Council of Great Britain' (111).
34 Banks to Colleran, 25 January 1975, Papers of Don Banks, Box 37.
35 Banks to Woolgar (Schott & Co), 25 February 1975, Papers of Don Banks, Box 37.
36 Banks to Lumsdaine, 21 January 1975, Papers of Don Banks, Box 35.
37 Banks to Murdoch, 1 September 1975, Papers of Don Banks, Box 36.
38 Murdoch to Banks, 12 December 1975, Papers of Don Banks, Box 36.
39 Lumsdaine's CV, Papers of Don Banks, Box 35. One can see a similar situation with the ISCM: 'The British Music Society briefly sponsored an Australian chapter of the ISCM in 1928, but the ISCM only began to be influential in Sydney musical circles after it was re-established by Donald Peart in November 1956' (Clinton Green, 'The International Society for Contemporary Music in Melbourne: Forerunners, Foundation, and Decline', *Musicology Australia* 32, no. 2 (2010): 247).
40 Banks's CV, Papers of Don Banks, Folio 3, Pack 11.
41 Banks's response to Murdoch, who on 8 April 1966 requested information for a book about 'Australian composers', Papers of Don Banks, Folio 3, Pack 11.
42 See www.khouri.co.nz/history.htm accessed 13 June 2014.
43 Gordon Kerry, *New Classical Music: Composing Australia* (Sydney: University of New South Wales Press, 2009), 7.
44 Lumsdaine, 'Memorandum and Proposals for an Australian Musicians Seminar', 1976, Papers of Don Banks, Box 35.
45 Banks to Tuckwell, 24 October 1976, Papers of Don Banks, Box 36.
46 Michael Vyner, 'The London Sinfonietta and Its World Tour', *Tempo* 119 (1976): 16–19.
47 Banks to Tuckwell, 24 October 1976, Papers of Don Banks, Box 36.
48 Ibid.
49 Ibid.
50 Banks to Salvatore Martirano, 8 October 1979, Papers of Don Banks, Box 36.
51 Banks to Martirano, 11 May 1978, Papers of Don Banks, Box 36.
52 Banks to Martirano, 20 October 1970, Papers of Don Banks, Box 36.
53 Lumsdaine, 'Memorandum and Proposals for an Australian Musicians Seminar', 1976, Papers of Don Banks, Box 35.
54 Ibid.
55 Banks to Lumsdaine, 21 January 1975, Papers of Don Banks, Box 35.
56 Banks to Martirano, 5 December 1974, Papers of Don Banks, Box 36. In a letter to Michael Vynar dated 11 May 1975, Banks also refers to the Music for Media Society and The Jazz Action Society (Papers of Don Banks, Box 37).
57 Banks to Martirano, 7 March 1975, Papers of Don Banks, Box 36.
58 Graham Hair, *Don Banks, Australian Composer: Eleven Sketches* (2008) www.n-ism.org/Papers/graham_DB-11.pdf accessed 4 October 2014. Also see Michael Hooper, 'Don Banks: Hammer Horror and Serial Composition', in James Wierzkicki (ed.), *Double Lives: Film Composers in the Concert Hall* (London: Routledge, 2019).
59 Banks to Colleran, 31 August 1975, Papers of Don Banks, Box 36. The emphasis is Banks's.
60 Vyner to Banks, 3 March 1975, Papers of Don Banks, Box 37.
61 Banks to Vyner, 11 May 1975, Papers of Don Banks, Box 37.
62 The relationship with Schott changed quickly when Vyner left and the state of that relationship in 1975 is in contrast to that in 1967, when Banks was receiving a retainer of £350 per year ('Agreement' between Banks and Schott & Co., 18 April 1967, Papers of Don Banks, Box 37). In comparison, Davies, in 1964, received a retainer of £1,200

a year from Boosey and Hawkes, up from £100 a year from Schott in 1963 (Mike Seabrook, *Max: The Life and Music of Peter Maxwell Davies* (London: Victor Gollancz, 1994), 76, 86).

63 Banks to Peter Makings, 14 October 1974, Papers of Don Banks, Box 37.
64 Following a meeting with Schott's representative Ken Bartlett in September 1973, Banks noted that talks were underway for Schott to establish an Australian operation, with local dye-line publishing facilities, and the intention that scores printed locally would enter their international distribution (Papers of Don Banks, Box 36).
65 Banks to Makings, 8 May 1975, Papers of Don Banks, Box 37.
66 Banks to Colleran, 15 December 1974 and 25 January 1975, ibid., Box 37. In a letter dated 3 February 1975, Colleran wrote to Barry Conyngham that Universal Edition was expecting $16,000 for their 'next publishing programme' (Banks to Conyngham, held in Conyngham's personal archive).
67 Banks to Lumsdaine, 27 March 1973, Papers of Don Banks, Box 35.
68 Banks to Murdoch, Papers of Don Banks, Box 36.
69 Banks to Murdoch, 21 August 1975, Papers of Don Banks, Box 36.
70 Gerhard, quoted by Banks in a lecture on 'Form', October 1977, NSW Conservatorium of Music, Papers of Don Banks, Box 34.
71 Banks to Martirano, 11 May 1978, Papers of Don Banks, Box 36.
72 Banks to Mátyás Seiber, 24 February 1953, Papers of Don Banks, Box 36.
73 That is, during Dallapiccola's 'second phase', in which his compositions' 'signal attribute is an increased sense of rigor and control' (Brian Alegant, *The Twelve-Tone Music of Luigi Dallapiccola* (Rochester: University of Rochester Press, 2010), 29).
74 The work was commissioned by Musica Viva for the Austral Quartet's 1975 world tour, which Musica Viva also organized.
75 Banks to Donald Hazelwood, Papers of Don Banks, Box 36.
76 Banks uses the term in opposition to Dr Reason in a lecture given on 30 September 1976. (Banks, 'Lecture on C20 Music', Papers of Don Banks, Box 34.) It is significant here that 'disciplined process' and 'musical intuition' never fully coincide.
77 The London Sinfonietta's performances received very good reviews. Indeed, so uniform were the reviews that Adrian Jack was compelled to write: 'Surely, the London Sinfonietta's Schoenberg–Gerhard series must have received as much critical attention as David Atherton, in his introduction to the programme book, hoped for.' And he concluded his review: 'The present cult of Gerhard is just a little absurd. I am not voting for this canonization' (Adrian Jack, 'Schoenberg and Gerhard', *Music and Musicians* 22, no. 5 (1974): 61). For Leslie East 'It is difficult to avoid a constant stream of superlatives in discussing the London Sinfonietta's series' (Leslie East, 'Schoenberg and Gerhard', *Music and Musicians* 22, no. 5 (1974): 39). Banks's quartet is written against this backdrop, and its connections with Gerhard came at the time of the greatest interest in the composer.
78 Banks to Vyner, 13 October 1973, Papers of Don Banks, Box 37.
79 'To my knowledge very few young composers in this country have sufficient technical foundations to guarantee their ability to continue (I'm glad to say that at this school [The NSW Conservatorium of Music] we have a couple of surprises in store for the musical world) but I do fear for certain of those who are achieving some kind of reputation now, as they could be in trouble in the near future having no support troops, as it were, to fall back upon' (Banks, 'Lecture on C20 Music', 30 September 1976, Papers of Don Banks, Box 34.)

80 In his 1960 article 'Is Modern Music Growing Old?', Gerhard writes of 'a healthy body of instincts [...] that can absorb and react positively to the inoculation of even a stiff dose of systematic or theoretical concepts' (Roberto Gerhard, *Gerhard on Music: Selected Writings*, ed. Meirion Bowen (Aldershot: Ashgate, 2000), 207). He argues that system and instinct 'need one another, not only for definition, not only for complementarity, but in order to *be*' (emphasis in original, 207).
81 Papers of Don Banks, Folio 2, Pack 7.
82 Papers of Don Banks, Folio 1, Pack 5.
83 Papers of Don Banks, Folio 2, Pack 7.
84 See Alegant, *Luigi Dallapiccola*, 123, for a discussion of polarity in Dallapiccola's *Ciaconna, intermezzo e allegro*.
85 Throughout the book square brackets, [ ], are used to indicate prime forms; curly brackets, { }, indicate unordered collections; angled brackets, < >, indicate ordered segments.
86 Papers of Don Banks, Folio 3, Pack 9; the same diagram is repeated in a different document, also located in Folio 3, Pack 9.
87 See Dmitri Tymoczko, 'Stravinsky and the Octatonic: A Reconsideration', *Music Theory Spectrum* 24, no. 1 (2002): 89.
88 Pieter Van den Toorn, *Music, Politics, and the Academy* (Berkeley: University of California Press, 1995), 129.
89 Ibid.
90 Papers of Don Banks, Box 30.
91 Ibid.
92 Ibid. The emphasis is Banks's.
93 Hair, *Don Banks*, 8.
94 Banks's *String Quartet* row is: <0, 11, 7, 8, 3, 4, 6, 5, 9, 10, 2, 1>. A manuscript (Papers of Don Banks, Folio 3) includes notes about deriving combinatorial rows from three-pitch sets ('Schoenberg and Webern were not aware of the fact that given any 3 notes you can *generate* a 12 tone set' (Banks's emphasis)) and the three pitches he uses to show this forms [014].
95 Papers of Don Banks, Folio 3, Pack 9.
96 Papers of Don Banks, Folio 1, Pack 5.
97 Papers of Don Banks, Folio 12.
98 See Gerhard, *Gerhard on Music*, 172. He uses the term in discussion of rhythmic schemes rather than about pitch, but the same principle applies.
99 {C♯, D, B♭, F♯, A}, assuming, as before, an error for the viola's G.
100 Henceforth $_0$I3 and similar.
101 A similar structure occurs at bar 239, where the cello plays $_0$I-1 from 1–8.
102 Banks uses the term in his 'Lecture on C20 Music' (30 September 1976, Papers of Don Banks, Box 34), and he uses it specifically in connection with the initial stages of writing a serial piece. He gives its history as 'a vogue phrase from the 1950s'.
103 The opening chord gathers together the first four pitches of P-0, which the cello continues in linear form. (Already a chord/melody opposition is in play.) The first chord of bar 3 is the first four pitches of P-8 (this designation is Banks's, from the sketches for the piece. He tends to use the matrix more widely than would strictly be necessary if making the most of the row's limited hexachordal transposition; R-6 is another possibility for this chord), but the second chord, which takes the next four pitches, crosses between hexachords and brings together four neighbouring

semitones. The final chord of that bar contains no [012] trichord, returning to the motivic pairs of semitones. (This chord is not clearly derived from the matrix, and whilst the vast majority of the first section of the composition (to bar 255) takes its pitches from the matrix, Banks does not follow his rows slavishly.) The violin then plays paired semitones solo (from I-4). The last pitch of the fifth bar joins with the first chord of bar 6 to complete the second hexachord of P-0 (say), and the following chord takes its pitches from the opposite hexachord. In this first phrase there is a transition from P-0 specifically (bars 1–3) with clearly conjunct motion, to less clearly derived pairs of 'semitones' (bar 5) in the leaping violin, to chords that can only be described in general, hexachordal, terms. And this shift from the particular to the general balances about the cross from one hexachord to the other, which produces a cluster [0123] in bar 4, second chord. (Block clusters that are not serially derived occur most perceptibly in the bars from 51 to 59, a sustained section that projects the composition's bombastic and assertive rhetoric.) Bar 19 flirts with the same cluster (also derived from P-0) as the opening, when the viola repeats 4, 5, 6, 7 at the same time as the violin 2 begins an 8, 9, 10, 11 ostinato. On this occasion the cluster is aborted before it is established, but it does introduce the possibility of the opposition between clusters and non-clusters as melodic as well as harmonic. This is fully realized from bar 76. The violin begins with P-1, the pitches played in order (1, 2, 3, 4), but then begins to loop (5, 6, 7, 8) an [0123] cluster. This looping initiates ostinato in violins and viola (the row now divided into tetrachords), the quick semiquavers forming a blur of all twelve pitch classes. The high cello now plays a melody beginning with I-0 and moving through R-1 and I-6. Crucially, the cello changes register at the hexachord boundaries, creating a break in the cluster at the centre of the row. Banks uses the lilting 'quasi 3' rhythm to contrast the saturation of the ostinato with the characteristic pitches that come from the hexachords of the row, the row divided into phrases that align with the hexachords in direct contrast to the tetrachords of the ostinato.

There is a great deal taking place here: the row's properties drive Banks's textures; the semitones are reconfigured as appoggiaturas in the cello's 'maestoso' melody; the instrumental roles of the quartet are divided between melody and accompaniment; the linear, serial working is phrased, and has the dynamics and articulations of tonal writing.

Bank's hexatonic seriality returns to his student days with Dallapiccola, a time when Dallapiccola was at the height of his octatonic serialism. Alegant's analysis of *Parole de San Paolo* reveals Dallapiccola's use of the [014589] hexachord, though there is no direct evidence that Banks knew that piece. (See Alegant, *Luigi Dallapiccola*, chapter 5, and especially pp. 252–3.)

104 To underline the nomenclature, P and R forms present no problem as they are the same in all version of Banks's material. I and RI forms are problematic.
105 Van den Toorn, *Music, Politics, and the Academy,* 129.
106 This example is not annotated with any serial designation. It could be that violin 1 plays: $_0$RI-10 from 1–8, or (as Banks indicates in the sketch) from P-3 from 7–12, then 5–6. Similar alternatives are possible for the other instruments, though Banks's label of the viola as moving through I-3 is a compelling case for Banks having switched schemes, especially since Banks labels the second violin as playing from the second hexachord of I-3 here. The point is that Banks is thinking about segmentation.

107 This is Banks's label, and it is another instance of him not using the orthodox form.
108 In this it differs from Schoenberg, for whom counterpoint could be used to make clear a row's combinatoriality. See Michiel Schuijer, *Analyzing Atonal Music* (Rochester: University of Rochester Press, 2008), 97.
109 Papers of Don Banks, Folio 2, Park 7.
110 See Rachel E. Mitchell, 'Roberto Gerhard's Serial Procedures and Formal Design in String Quartets Nos. 1 and 2', in Monty Adkins and Michael Russ (eds), *The Roberto Gerhard Companion* (Aldershot: Ashgate, 2013).
111 Gerhard, *Gerhard on Music*, 129–39.
112 Ibid., 136. This is Gerhard's version of 'Man proposes, but God disposes' ('Homo proponit, sed Deus disponit'), originally from Thomas à Kempis's *De Imitatione Christi*.
113 Ibid., 230.
114 See Mitchell, 'Roberto Gerhard's Serial Procedures' and Mitchell, '"Sonorous Possibilities" and Formal Continuity in Gerhard's String Quartet No. 2', unpublished paper presented at the Second International Roberto Gerhard Conference, Barcelona, 2012.
115 The orthodox form is not used.
116 The choice of P-0, I-6, RI-8 and R-6 for the first section is not arbitrary. Firstly, all are even transpositions. Secondly, one of each form is used. Thirdly, their initial pitches – C, F, D, G – form a partial circle of fifths. The next canon uses P-0, I-6, RI-4 and R-6, with the initial pitches being C, F, B♭, G: this is the mirror of the previous canon (Papers of Don Banks, Folio 12). The third canon does not use simultaneous rows, and instead the rows are used sequentially, distributed around the four instruments; the sketches make clear that the first two canons were planned together. None of these canons use the orthodox row forms. The sketches for these sections are on different paper stock; two are stapled together, and one has an $_0$I form, and one not.
117 Papers of Don Banks, Folio 12. A related sketch includes a section on circles of fifths in a tonal context (Folio 3, Pack 9).
118 Quoted in Schuijer, *Analyzing Atonal Music*, 94.
119 Ibid.
120 Papers of Don Banks, Folio 1, Pack 5.
121 Keith Potter, 'Gerhard's Second String Quartet: On Serial Identity and Identification', in David Atherton (ed.), *The London Sinfonietta: The Complete Instrumental and Chamber Music of Arnold Schoenberg and Roberto Gerhard* (London: Sinfonietta Productions Limited, 1973), 97.
122 Ibid., 96–7.
123 Banks to Murdoch, 21 August 1975, Papers of Don Banks, Box 36.
124 Darren Sproston, 'Roberto Gerhard: The Serial Symphonist', in Adkins and Russ (eds), *The Roberto Gerhard Companion*, 231.
125 Banks to Martirano, 7 March 1975, Papers of Don Banks, Box 36.

Chapter 3

1 'Richard Meale Interviewed by Hazel de Berg in the Hazel de Berg Collection' (National Library of Australia, 1965), Oral TRC 1/174, 3.

2 Michael Hannan, *The Music of Richard Meale* (Kingsgrove: Wildbird Music, 2014).
3 Peter McCallum, 'Meale's New Work Needs Weeding Out', *Sydney Morning Herald*, 10 June 2002, 16.
4 Roger Covell, *Australia's Music: Themes of a New Society* (Melbourne: Sun Books, 1967), 211.
5 The first String Quartet must count as one of the least understood works in Meale's catalogue, since it does in fact engage closely with the form's history, as traced through Ligeti and Lutosławski. In Meale's quartet the players have no score, and their parts contain only partial cueing information, which necessitates close playing.
6 Covell, 'Composer Winds Back the Clock', *Sydney Morning Herald*, 8 March 1994, 19.
7 Covell, 'A Meal for the Avant-Garde', *Sydney Morning Herald*, 3 April 1991, 14.
8 Meale, 'Interview with Andrew Ford', *The Music Show* [Radio broadcast], ABC Radio National, 24 August 2002 www.abc.net.au/radionational/programs/musicshow/richard-meale/3515648 accessed 10 May 2019.
9 Meale, 'Richard Meale Extended Interview from 2007', *Meale Not at 80*, ABC podcast, 30 August 2012 www.abc.net.au/classic/content/2012/08/30/3579339.htm accessed 30 August 2012.
10 Andreas Huyssen, 'The Search for Tradition: Avant-Garde and Postmodernism in the 1970s', *New German Critique* 22, winter (1981): 27–8.
11 Ibid., 29.
12 See also Evelyn Cobley, *Temptations of Faust: The Logic of Fascism and Postmodern Archaeologies of Modernity* (Toronto: University of Toronto Press, 2002), 158.
13 'Richard Meale Interview from 1965 on ABC Radio's "Away from It All"', *Meale Not at 80*, [ABC podcast], 30 August 2012, 16'00".
14 Ibid., 10'25".
15 Ibid., 24'40".
16 Ibid., 35'.
17 The general argument is made by Peter Bürger in *Theory of the Avant-Garde* (Manchester: Manchester University Press, 1984), 22–3.
18 James Murdoch, *Australia's Contemporary Composers* (Melbourne: Macmillan, 1972), 141.
19 Richard John Murphy, *Theorizing the Avant-Garde: Modernism, Expressionism, and the Problem of Postmodernity* (Cambridge: Cambridge University Press, 1999), 40.
20 Earlier in the interview he said 'I don't treat composition as a professional matter' (Meale, 'Away from It All', 16'55").
21 Ibid., 38'.
22 Ibid., 46'30".
23 Lecture about *Interiors/Exteriors*, c. 1976, Papers of James Murdoch, MS 8372, National Library of Australia, Box 24. Meale maintained that thinking about a composer and the events that led to a composition whilst listening to the piece would lead to 'anecdotal listening'. In the interviews from the 1960s and early 1970s, the details that he gives of his travels are directed towards his encounters with new music, and his personal life was not otherwise discussed.
24 Ibid.
25 Ibid.
26 Ibid.
27 Ibid.

28 For an introduction to the topic, see David Walker (ed.), 'The Cult of Practicality', *Australian Cultural History* 8 (1989).
29 Lecture about *Interiors/Exteriors*, c. 1976, Papers of James Murdoch, Box 24.
30 Ibid.
31 Herbert Marcuse, *Counter Revolution and Revolt* (Boston: Beacon Press, 1972), 129, quoted by Meale in Lecture about *Interiors/Exteriors*, c. 1976, Papers of James Murdoch, Box 24.
32 Papers of James Murdoch, Box 24.
33 Bürger, *Theory of the Avant-Garde*, 27.
34 Meale, 'Interview with Andrew Ford'.
35 Meale, 'Away from It All', 8'00".
36 Stephen Walsh, 'First Performances: Richard Meale's *Homage to Garcia Lorca*', *Tempo* 75, winter (1965/6): 18.
37 Meale, programme note for the first UK performance, Papers of James Murdoch, Box 24.
38 Ibid.
39 Deborah Beck, *Set in Stone: A History of the Cell Block Theatre* (Sydney: University of New South Wales Press, 2011), 108.
40 Covell, 'Concert at Cell Block', *Sydney Morning Herald*, 16 October 1964, 21.
41 It soon became clear that the work would be toured to London, its international premiere being the subject of some speculation: '[Dean] Dixon will obviously take every opportunity in the next month or two to prepare works intended for his London concert with the orchestra in September' ('Welcome Care in Concert Planning', *Sydney Morning Herald*, 26 May 1965, 12).
42 'He [Meale] will soon be as internationally recognized as Pierre Boulez' (Curt and Marea Prerauer, 'Tension to the Last Bar', *The Sun*, 28 July 1965). C. M. Prerauer stands for both Curt and Marea Prerauer, critics for the *Nation*. Their reviews are characterized by enthusiastic and uncritical support for any new music.
43 Covell, 'Dixon, Ferras, Berg and Meale', *Sydney Morning Herald*, 28 July 1965, 13.
44 Leonie Kramer, review of 'The London Magazine' and the *Times Literary Supplement*'s 'Sounding the "Sixties"'', *The Bulletin*, 9 October 1965, 54.
45 Peter Stadlen, 'Fine Brahms of Sydney Orchestra', *The Daily Telegraph*, 20 September 1965.
46 'Extrovert Performance of Sydney Orchestra', *The Times*, 20 September 1965.
47 Hugo Cole, 'Sydney Symphony Orchestra Concert', *The Guardian*, 20 September 1965.
48 David Brodbeck, *Brahms: Symphony No. 1* (Cambridge: Cambridge Music Handbooks, 1997), 31.
49 See ibid., chapter 5. See too John Eliot Gardiner in conversation with Hugh Wood: '[T]he bonus for us is the marvellous introduction – a musical prelude, inserted, as Ivor Keys says, as a mental postscript' (liner note to *Brahms: Symphony No. 1 & Schicksalslied* (SDG702, 2008), 7).
50 Walter Frisch, *Brahms: The Four Symphonies* (New Haven: Yale University Press, 2003), 52. Frisch devotes much of his argument to questions of coherence; see Chapter 1 in particular.
51 Arnold Whittall, *Schoenberg Chamber Music* (London: British Broadcasting Corporation, 1972), 9.

52 Meale had travelled to Europe earlier in 1965 to represent Australia at the international rostrum of composers in Paris. He was supported in his attendance by APRA and the ABC, and presented: *Homage to Garcia Lorca*, Butterley's *Laudes*, Dreyfus's *From within Looking Out* and Sculthorpe's *Sixth Quartet*, which is a fair overview of what was considered the best of the music of that time.
53 Both works are for either chamber ensemble or string orchestra.
54 Meale, programme note for the first UK performance, Papers of James Murdoch, Box 24.
55 Ibid.
56 Covell, 'Contemporary Concert', 1 June 1963, *Sydney Morning Herald*, 6.
57 Meale to Murdoch, 25 June 1965, Papers of James Murdoch, Box 24.
58 Robert Adlington, *The Music of Harrison Birtwistle* (Cambridge: Cambridge University Press, 2000), 159.
59 Covell, *Australia's Music*, 217.
60 Anne Boyd, 'Richard Meale's *Homage to Garcia Lorca*', *Music Now* 1, no. 1 (1969): 23.
61 Meale commented that the piece is 'freely chromatic (but not strictly serial)' in his programme note for the 1969 Festival of Perth, Papers of Richard Meale, MS 10076, National Library of Australia, Box 42.
62 Walsh, 'Richard Meale's *Homage to Garcia Lorca*', 20.
63 Ibid.
64 Richard Dehmel, in Arnold Schoenberg, *Verklärte Nacht and Pierrot Lunaire* (New York: Dover Publications, 1994), 2.
65 Respectively: 'Their breath kisses in the breeze'; 'and I remember the sad breeze through the olive trees'; 'bright night'; 'white death'. Translation of the Lorca quoted in Meale, programme note for the first UK performance, Papers of James Murdoch, Box 24 (translation of the Dehmel by Stanley Appelbaum, in Schoenberg, *Verklärte Nacht*, 2).
66 By 1971 the term 'plateau' was also associated with the theories of sexual response by Masters and Johnson.
67 Cole, 'Sydney Symphony Orchestra Concert'.
68 Walsh, 'Richard Meale's *Homage to Garcia Lorca*', 18.
69 Donald Kuspit, *The Dialectic of Decadence: Between Advance and Decline in Art* (New York: Allworth Press, 2000), 91.
70 Covell, *Australia's Music*, 218.
71 Philip Rupprecht, '"Something Slightly Indecent": British Composers, the European Avant-Garde and National Stereotypes in the 1950s', *The Musical Quarterly* 91, nos. 3–4 (2008): 289.
72 In 1966 Meale conducted a performance of Lutosławski's *Trois Poèmes d'Henri Michaux* (Papers of James Murdoch, Box 24).
73 Ben Earle, '"The Real Thing – at Last?" Historicizing Humphrey Searle', in Matthew Riley (ed.), *British Music and Modernism, 1895–1960* (Aldershot: Ashgate, 2010), 301.
74 Krystyna Tarnawska-Kaczorowska, 'The Musical Work as Sign: Significative Constituents, Layers, Structure', in Eero Tarasti (ed.), *Musical Signification* (Berlin: Walter de Gruyter & Co, 1995), 123–40 (135).
75 Caroline Rae, 'Beyond Boundaries: Dutilleux's *Foreign Leavening*', *Contemporary Music Review* 29, no. 5 (2010): n. 21.
76 Meale, *Homage to Garcia Lorca* (London: Boosey & Hawkes, 1966).

77 This was a series of programmes on the following topics: Schoenberg and Webern; Messiaen; Boulez; Stockhausen; Nono, Posseur, Maderna, Barraque; Berio (Papers of Richard Meale, Box 39).
78 Meale, 'Richard Meale Interviewed by Hazel de Berg', 7.
79 Ibid.
80 *Soon It Will Die* has also undergone a change of name, as Meale suggests in a note stuck to the manuscript in the Papers of Richard Meale, Folio 12:

> 'Soon it will die yet [/] no trace of this in [/] the cicada's shriek' – Bashō Haikū

> Foolish of me to title it by the first line. It made such an unpleasant impression that it was virtually never played. I like the piece so will retitle it as 'cicada'.
>
> R.M. 3/2/04.

81 It is unclear why it was not written. The score of *Cicada*, which dates from 1975, includes a reference to the third work in its preface.
82 Ann Bright, 'Pitch and Time Structure in *Clouds Now and Then*', *Miscellanea Musicologica* 10 (1979): 82–92. Ann Bright is now known as Ann Ghandar.
83 Ibid., 82.
84 The divisions listed here do not accurately fit the score, and Section C begins a bar earlier than this scheme suggests.
85 The score as first printed has the metronome marking '32–74', with an average of 48. Meale corrected this in 1978 (Papers of Richard Meale, Box 2). It is difficult to know exactly what Meale had in mind for the rubato; the Tasmanian Symphony Orchestra's recording (ABC Classics 4763221) includes very little.
86 *Clouds Now and Then* (Australia: Universal Edition, 1973), preface.
87 Papers of Richard Meale, Box 34.
88 Meale therefore contrasts smooth pitch space and diatonic pitch space.
89 From a 'Transcription of an interview between Richard Meale [...] and SSO Education Officer Brett Johnson [...] recorded in the studios of the ABC in Sydney on 21 February, 1990' (Papers of Richard Meale, Box 42).
90 Meale, 'Richard Meale Writes about Rimbaud, Australia and His Own Music', *The Listener*, 24 June 1971, 830.
91 Meale, Liner note, *Plateau for Wind Quintet* [Audio recording] (EMI Record No. OASD7565, 1972).
92 *Images (Nagauta)* is the work by Meale that is explicitly modelled on Japanese drama. Even so 'the music itself does not sounds like Nagauta music. If, at times, the sounds resembles any Japanese music, it is closer to Gagaku (Court Music)' (Meale, Liner note, *Australian Compositions* [Audio recording] (Record No. PRX 5585, c. 1975)).
93 The triptych is dedicated to Toru Takemitsu.
94 Richard Meale, Liner note for *Nocturnes/Soon It Will Die* [Audio recording] (World Record Club S/5656, c. 1975).
95 Bright, 'Pitch and Time Structures', 92.
96 The progression continues past bar 9 in a similar manner.
97 Meale, Liner note for *Nocturnes/Soon It Will Die*. It is easy enough to repeat the idea here about Meale's *Nocturnes* as an antithesis of Sculthorpe's *Sun Music*.
98 Meale, Liner note, *Plateau*.
99 Felix Werder, 'Felix Werder Interviewed by Hazel de Berg in the Hazel de Berg Collection' (National Library of Australia, 1969), Oral TRC 1/409–410.

Chapter 4

1. Ursula Vaughan Williams, *R. V. W.: A Biography of Ralph Vaughan Williams* (Oxford: Oxford Lives, 1968), 138.
2. Elliott Gyger's *The Music of Nigel Butterley* (Kingsgrove: Wildbird Music, 2015) is an excellent guide to these works.
3. Donald Mintz, 'Review of Records: Australian Music', *The Musical Quarterly* 53, no. 4 (1967): 596–603.
4. Butterley initially wanted to study with Michael Tippett, who suggested instead that he study with Rainier.
5. Butterley had been the pianist in the 1959 Australian premiere of *Pierrot Lunaire*, directed by Richard Meale, and so the instrumentation for *Laudes* is one that Butterley knew from the keyboard.
6. Deborah Beck, *Set in Stone: A History of the Cell Block Theatre* (Sydney: University of New South Wales Press, 2011), 42.
7. The forward by Sculthorpe to *Set in Stone* (ibid.) explains the importance of the space for his work, and to the formation of a musical movement of like-minded composers.
8. Butterley, 'Nigel Butterley Interviewed by Hazel de Berg in the Hazel de Berg Collection' (National Library of Australia, 1967), Oral TRC 1/303–305. Butterley's early life was in the evangelical tradition, and from his time in Adelaide in high Anglicanism. His father was an Anglican minister.
9. The premiere was conducted by Charles Mackerras, who some years earlier had attended the same school as Butterley. The Mackerras family was well known in the small Sydney world of the 1950s (ibid.).
10. '[I]t's a very intense experience still, one that I think I saw at the right time because I had the right sort of amount of belief and skepticism to appreciate it' (ibid.).
11. Ibid.
12. Ibid.
13. Ibid.
14. Ibid.
15. The other quotation in the preface is: 'The chief duty is praise because, when complete, it includes within itself all other duties', cited from Dewi Morgan's 1962 book *But God Comes First*, which was published when Butterley was in London. The subtitle to the book is 'A *Meditation on the Te Deum*'.
16. It also associates Butterley with Elizabeth Maconchy, whose 1978 work *Sun, Moon, and Stars* sets part of Traherne's meditations.
17. Quoted in David Jones, 'The Music of Nigel Butterley', PhD diss. (University of Newcastle, 2005), 174–5.
18. Josef Rufer, *Composition with Twelve Notes Related Only to One Another*, trans. Humphrey Searle (London: Barrie & Rockliff, 1954), 106–8.
19. Ibid.
20. Ibid.; the emphasis is Rufer's.
21. Gyger, *The Music of Nigel Butterley*, 44.
22. Roger Covell, *Australia's Music: Themes of a New Society* (Melbourne: Sun Books, 1967), 226–7.
23. David Swale, 'Nigel Butterley', in Frank Callaway and David Tunley (eds), *Australian Composition in the Twentieth Century* (Melbourne: Oxford University Press, 1978), 203.

24 This analysis, and the analysis of Meale in Chapter 6, owes a debt to the ic1/ic5 analyses of Shostakovich by Stephen Brown ('Ic1/Ic5 Interaction in the Music of Shostakovich', *Musical Analysis* 28, nos. 2–3 (2009): 185–220; 'Some Instances of Ic1/Ic5 Interaction in Post-Tonal Music (and Their Tonnetz Representations)', *Gamut: The Online Journal of the Music Theory Society* 6, no. 2 (2013), article 3 http://trace.tennessee.edu/gamut/vol6/iss2/3). See also Brown, 'Dual Interval Space in Twentieth-Century Music', *Music Theory Spectrum* 25, no. 1 (2003): 35–57.
25 Gyger, *The Music of Nigel Butterley*, 48.
26 Ibid.
27 The Te Deum as used in *Laudes* varies in its transposition, but in the third movement, where it is stated prominently, it begins: <C, E♭, F, E♭, F, G, A♭, G, F>. Dividing this sequence into three trichords yields [025], [024], [013]. The second trichord is a segment of the whole-tone scale. (Regarding the stopped horn-note in bar 5, the recording directed by Butterley does not change to an F when the stopped note is indicated.)
28 The process is similar to that used by Banks in his String Quartet.
29 Strictly, the 'a' tetrachord needs a D♮, which requires one of the pitches that is continuous, rather than newly sounded.
30 In his analysis of the String Quartet, Gyger finds Butterley frequently beginning with the last pitch of his row.
31 We might here repeat Rudolph Reti's questions: 'What is the explanation for this astounding process whereby "compositions with twelve tones" not only changes its character but even points to something which is almost opposite to its own nature? Whereby composers who actually do not practise this technique still like to call themselves twelve-tone composers?' (Rudolf Reti, *Tonality, Atonality, Pantonality* (Westport: Greenwood Press, 1958), 55).
32 I do not hear this as a single harmonic block, as Gyger implies that he does by labelling it 'chord x'.
33 The trumpet is often associated with praise (see Psalm 150:3), for example in Britten's *Te Deum in C* (1934).
34 Gyger, *The Music of Nigel Butterley*, 50.
35 The part was written specifically for Meale.
36 Nigel Butterley, *String Quartet* (Sydney: Albert Edition), ii.
37 Quoted in ibid.
38 Simon Standage, 'Historical Awareness in Quartet Performance', in Robin Stowell (ed.), *Cambridge Companion to the String Quartet* (Cambridge: Cambridge University Press, 2003), 128.
39 Nigel Butterley, *Words into Music: A Composer's Response to Poetry* (Armidale: University of New England, 1999), 7.
40 Butterley typically refers to 'English' when he might more properly mean 'British', which here is worth noting, given that he implies no distinction between, for example, English music and Welsh poetry.
41 Ibid., 8.
42 Like the quotation of Traherne in *Laudes*, the use of Vaughan's poetry further connects him to Finzi, who used Vaughan's poetry in his anthems ('Welcome Sweet and Sacred Feast', for example; see Diana McVeagh, *Gerald Finzi: His Life and Music* (Woodbridge: The Boydell Press, 2005), 27ff); Edmund Rubbra set 'The Revival' in a 1944 motet.

43 Butterley, 'Nigel Butterley Interviewed by Hazel de Berg'.
44 Richard Greene, *Edith Sitwell: Avant Garde Poet, English Genius* (London: Hachette Digital, 2011).
45 Butterley, 'Nigel Butterley Interviewed by Hazel de Berg'.
46 Butterley, *Words into Music*, 8.
47 Ibid.
48 Ibid., 10–11. Butterley more recently said that 'I must stress it's not just poetry which inspires me; poets must also' (Nigel Butterley, 'Turning Silence into Sound: Composers Talk about Inspiration', 2MBS FM, *HSC*. This website has been archived by the National Library of Australia: https://webarchive.nla.gov.au/awa/20140126065839/http://www.hsc.csu.edu.au/music/composition/tips/inspiration/comp_tips_inspiration.htm accessed 7 October 2014).
49 David Clarke, *The Music and Thought of Michael Tippett* (Cambridge: Cambridge University Press, 2009), 87.
50 In 1967 Butterley wrote to Banks about works by Birtwistle and Goehr at the Paris Rostrum, which 'made very little impression' (7 July 1967, Papers of Nigel Butterley, MS Acc09.081, National Library of Australia, Box 4).
51 http://petermaxwelldavies.com/?works_catalogue_entr=the-shepherds-calendar-30 accessed 18 August 2016.
52 Butterley, 'Nigel Butterley Interviewed by Hazel de Berg'.
53 This is found in the sketches (SQ1:04r), where it is crossed out. The nomenclature for referring to Butterley's sketches for this piece follows Peter Watters-Cowan, where the sketches are reproduced (Peter Watters-Cowan, 'Nigel Butterley's String Quartets: Compositional Process from Sketch to Score', PhD diss. (University of New South Wales, 2009)). The sketches for this piece are not in the National Library of Australia.
54 Ibid., 141.
55 This is shown in Ibid., SQ1:07r.
56 Gyger, *The Music of Nigel Butterley*, 52ff.
57 Watters-Cowan, 'Nigel Butterley's String Quartets', SQ1:01c.
58 N.B.: This graph shows relative changes in the distance between voice, not the melodic contour of any voices. Note also that voices are not tied to instruments here. The x-axis counts each harmonic entity.
59 Norton Dudeque, *Music Theory and Analysis in the Writings of Arnold Schoenberg (1874–1951)* (Aldershot: Ashgate, 2005), 198. See also Arnold Schoenberg, *The Musical Idea and the Logic, Technique and Art of Its Presentation* (Bloomington: Indiana University Press, 2006), 111.
60 Jonathan Harvey argues that the 'middle' can be positioned as the basis of harmony, rather than having the 'bass remain at the bottom', which is an idea that he derives from Schoenberg's 'unity of musical space'. This involves, and here he quotes Schoenberg, 'The connexion of serialism with heaven, or transcendental consciousness of some sort' (Harvey, 'Reflection after Composition', *Tempo* 140 (1982): 2–4).
61 Watters-Cowan, 'Nigel Butterley's String Quartets', SQ1:01c.
62 There are various potential elements in Butterley's quartet that suggest rigorous planning not carried out. For example, the unfolding motive's melodic line – <F♯, G♯, C♯, E> – is a set that contains a second, third, fourth, fifth, sixth and seventh, suggesting that it may possess the potential to operate as a modal resource, which has however not been implemented.

63 Timothy Baxter, 'Priaulx Rainier: A Study of Her Musical Style', *Composer* 60 (1977), quoted in Chris Van Rhyn, 'O Hidden Face! – An Analysis and Contextualisation of Priaulx Rainier's *Requiem*', MMus diss. (Stellenbosch University, 2010), 14.
64 The demisemiquavers in Tippett's quartet are played at ♪=100; the semiquavers in Butterley's quartet are played at ♩=100.
65 Ian Bent, *Music Analysis in the Nineteenth Century: Fugue, Form, and Style* (Cambridge: Cambridge University Press, 1994), 127.
66 Ibid., 128.
67 See Derrick Puffett, 'The Fugue from Tippett's Second String Quartet', *Music Analysis* 5, nos. 2–3 (1986): 233–64.
68 Christopher Chowrimootoo also finds 'ambivalence' useful for understanding Britten as a modernist, arguing that:

> Britten's ambivalent, peripheral, and diminutive relationship with the self-conscious 'greats' of musical modernism was central to his mainstream appeal as well as his position as a minor composer in the modernist canon. (Chowrimootoo, '"Britten Minor": Constructing the Modernist Canon', *Twentieth Century Music* 13, no. 2 (2016): 264.)

What is at stake here is the status of composers, considered in terms of a core modernist canon, and I agree with Chowrimootoo's argument that the hierarchies of significance are negotiated as the formation of a modernist canon, which construes 'minor' and 'major' modernist composers dialectically within a discourse of modernism.
69 Arnold Whitall, *The Music of Britten and Tippett: Studies in Themes and Techniques* (Cambridge: Cambridge University Press, 1990), 92.
70 Butterley, 'Nigel Butterley Interviewed by Hazel de Berg'.
71 The Butterley who composed *Laudes* and the String Quartet may well have agreed with David Matthews that 'To observe and enter into the spirit of wonder seems enough' ('Religious Art in the Twenty-First Century', *David Matthews: Composer* [website] www.david-matthews.co.uk/writings/article.asp?articleid=75 accessed 5 September 2014), and if Butterley's early work is any indication, he would also agree, to further quote Matthews, with 'A. N. Whitehead's definition of religion: "Religion is what the individual does with his own solitariness"' (ibid.).
72 Elliott Gyger, 'Nigel Butterley and the Problem That Wasn't', *Resonate Magazine* (2008) www.australianmusiccentre.com.au/article/nigel-butterley-and-the-problem-that-wasn-t. The suggestion that compositional approaches in this period are 'problem-free' raises the question of what kind of 'problem' is avoided. I am reminded of an interview that I undertook with Peter Maxwell Davies, in which he recounted his experience of meeting Stockhausen: 'I remember visiting Stockhausen, I think it was in 1960 together with Alexander Goehr. […] We went to see Stockhausen and he was rabbiting on about this, that and the other, and turned very politely to Sandy and me, and said "What do you make of these things in Britain", and Sandy said very quietly and very sarcastically: "These problems don't arise in Britain"' (Personal communication with Davies, 2010).
73 Gyger, 'The Problem That Wasn't'.
74 Nigel Butterley, programme note, quoted in Jones, 'The Music of Nigel Butterley', p. 206.
75 Matthew Riley, 'Introduction', in Matthew Riley (ed.), *British Music and Modernism, 1895–1960* (Aldershot: Ashgate, 2010), 9.

76 The dove's poetic migration of 'ten thousand miles' is, within a few hundred miles, the distance between Sydney and London.
77 David Clarke, 'Between Hermeneutics and Formalism: The Lento from Tippett's Concerto for Orchestra (or: Music Analysis after Lawrence Kramer)', *Music Analysis* 30, nos. 2–3 (2012): 315.
78 Jones, 'The Music of Nigel Butterley', 206.
79 Ibid. We might speculate that this idea of 'unfolding' is an evolution of Nadia Boulanger's *grande ligne*, given that Rainier had studied with Boulanger.
80 Or, perhaps, a Lutheran reference, given Butterley's Anglican upbringing.
81 Such is the weight of this idea that it overwhelms the possible reading of the 'unfolding' in connection with the end of night (Vaughan's 'day-star'), as in Milton: 'The star that bids the shepherd *fold* / Now the top of Heav'n doth hold' (my emphasis).
82 Butterley set Raine's text several times, in: *Sleep* (1992), *The Wind Stirs Gently* (1992), *The Woven Light* (1994), *Spell of Creation* (2000) and *Paradise Unseen* (2001).
83 Butterley, *Words into Music*.
84 W. B. Yeats, 'The Symbolism of Poetry', in Richard Finneran and George Bornstein (eds), *The Collected Works of W. B. Yeats: Volume IV* (New York: Scribner, 1900), 117–18. One thinks again of Rainier's distinctive pulse-driven music, such as in the early work Quartet for Strings, the last movement of which is the beginning of the style that reached its zenith in *Phala-phala* (which continues in Anthony Gilbert's *Groove, Perchants*) and which is relevant for her *Declamation*, written for Peter Pears, with texts by John Donne.
85 Andrew McCredie, *Music by Australian Composers: Survey No. 1* (Canberra: Advisory Board, Commonwealth Assistance to Australian Composers, 1969), 23.
86 Ibid.
87 Jones, 'The Music of Nigel Butterley', 206.
88 Despite the widespread significance of Alain Badiou's work throughout the humanities it has been slow to enter musical scholarship. For an introduction to Badiou's philosophy in its musical setting, see J. P. E. Harper-Scott, *The Quilting Points of Musical Modernism* (Cambridge: Cambridge University Press, 2012); his fourth chapter provides an overview of 'faithful', 'obscure', and 'reactive' subjects.
89 Daniel Albright, 'Yeats and Modernism', in Marjorie Howes and John Kelly (eds), *Cambridge Companion to W. B. Yeats* (Cambridge: Cambridge University Press, 2006), 62. There is no trace of the politics of the British Isles in Butterley's music.
90 Gyger, *The Music of Nigel Butterley*, 102; Jones, 'The Music of Nigel Butterley', 454.
91 The work was reviewed by Roger Covell with little enthusiasm: 'It was not entertaining music for the most part, but it was music that accumulated its own stature and dignity. It had those qualities of "keeping on-ness" that the late Percy Grainger diagnosed, for good or ill, as appropriate to the music of this continent. They were qualities also appropriate, though it is undoubtedly musically irrelevant to say so, to Cook himself' (Covell, 'A Success in Two Ways', *Sydney Morning Herald*, 4 May 1970, 14.).
92 Joanna Catherine Drimatis, 'A Hidden Treasure: Symphony No. 1 by Robert Hughes', PhD diss. (University of Adelaide, 2008), 27.
93 Quoted in Rhoderick McNeill, *The Australian Symphony from Federation to 1960* (Aldershot: Ashgate, 2014), 46.
94 The Beethoven bicentenary was also being celebrated.

95 Papers of Nigel Butterley, Box 6.
96 Ibid.
97 Ibid.
98 Farr later composed an *Explorations* of his own, premiered in 1972 in a concert that included Butterley at the piano (Covell, 'Mixed-Media Composition', *Sydney Morning Herald*, 24 August 1972, 31).
99 Gyger, *The Music of Nigel Butterley*, 103–4.
100 Lynne Bell, 'Composition for Oboe – and Transistor Radio', *Sydney Morning Herald*, 5 April 1970, 102.
101 Covell, 'Jazz Put Audience at Ease', *Sydney Morning Herald*, 22 September 1970, 11.
102 Butterley to Banks, 3 January 1970, Papers of Don Banks, MS6830, National Library of Australia, Box 6.
103 Banks, quoted in Jones, 'The Music of Nigel Butterley', 455.
104 In his sketches Butterley includes a note to himself about the programme note: 'At one stage I thought of linking this work to the magnificent closing section of Eliot's *Four Quartets*, but realized that the work would not be conscious [sic] evolved those words. If there is some unconscious affinity between the two I should be more than happy' (Papers of Nigel Butterley, Box 6). Eliot's closing section begins 'We shall not cease from exploration / And the end of all our exploring / Will be to arrive where we started. And know the place for the first time.' *Explorations* is therefore a further instance of an instrumental work that began with poetry.
105 Papers of Nigel Butterley, Box 6.
106 The committee itself was a state body, headed by E. A. Willis, who was the 'Minister in Charge of Celebrations'. The celebrations were for Cook's 'Discovery and Exploration of the East Coast of Australia', and so although theoretically restricted to that region, Cook's landing in 1970 functioned as an event for national celebration.
107 Newcastle is a short distance (c. 150 km) north of Sydney, New South Wales. It was close enough for Butterley to continue to live in Sydney.
108 'Cultural Collections, UON Library', https://uoncc.wordpress.com/2010/04/09/50con/ accessed 22 August 2016.
109 The range of specific jobs was large, and most positions at the ABC involved a mix of production and administration. For example, John Antill was employed by the ABC in 1936 as 'assistant editor to Howard Carr, the Music Editor', conductor and director of the 'Wireless Chorus' and as 'Balance and Control Officer for the live broadcasts' (Beth Dean and Victor Carell, *Gentle Genius: A Life of John Antill* (Sydney: Akron Press, 1987), 69).
110 Papers of Nigel Butterley, Series Orchestra.
111 John Hopkins to Butterley, 11 September 1972, Papers of Nigel Butterley, Series Orchestra.
112 Quoted in the programme for the premiere, 4 October 1973, Cleveland Orchestra, conducted by Lorin Mazel, Sydney Opera House. A copy of the programme is held in the Papers of Nigel Butterley, MS Acc.07.033, National Library of Australia.
113 Christopher J. Brennan, *Poems (1913)* (Sydney: Sydney University Press, 1972).
114 The capitalization is in the original.
115 Quoted in the programme for the premiere, 4 October 1973.
116 Personal communication with Butterley.
117 Ibid.

118 Papers of Nigel Butterley, Series Orchestra.
119 Ibid.
120 There is evidence that Butterley was thinking about resonance, and therefore about the space, in the sketches. 'After a short silence, the next event is in a different pitch [*sic*] – so that the resonance of the one before goes on unaffected' (Ibid.).
121 This is what Tymoczko might label a triadic tetrachord (D♭ major, with an added E♭), and it is a connection to Stravinsky (Dmitri Tymoczko, 'Stravinsky and the Octatonic: A Reconsideration', *Music Theory Spectrum* 24, no. 1 (2002): 68–102).
122 The texture here is comparable with b. 21ff of the last movement of Meale's *Homage to Garcia Lorca*.
123 Pieter Van den Toorn, *Stravinsky and the Russian Period: Sound and Legacy of a Musical Idiom* (Cambridge: Cambridge University Press, 2012), 228. My intention here is not to make any claims about the importance of Stravinsky and the octatonic scale, beyond arguing that Butterley needed a model for impressive orchestral writing and that in Stravinsky he found such a model.
124 Gyger, *The Music of Nigel Butterley*, 113–14. Although there is a discourse that considers the period to the mid-1970s as 'formative', it is more properly formative of the idea of Australian Music than of the development of particular composers, and we ought to be cautious about instances where one seems to stands for the other.
125 Papers of Nigel Butterley, Series Orchestra.
126 Ibid.
127 Ibid.
128 Ibid.
129 Ibid.
130 Gyger, *The Music of Nigel Butterley*, 111.

Chapter 5

1 David Carter, *Always Almost Modern: Australian Print Cultures and Modernity* (North Melbourne: Australian Scholarly, 2013), 127.
2 Roger Woodward, 'Roger Woodward on Richard Meale' [Radio broadcast], ABC 50th anniversary broadcast, recorded London, 3 August 1982, 11'00".
3 Personal correspondence with Lumsdaine.
4 Sculthorpe, 'Sculthorpe at 80 … in His Own Words'. *Peter Sculthorpe*. www.petersculthorpe.com.au/biography.htm accessed 6 January 2015.
5 See, for example: Graeme Skinner, *Peter Sculthorpe: The Making of an Australian Composer* (Sydney: University of New South Wales Press, 2007), 323; Michael Hannan, *Peter Sculthorpe: His Music and Ideas 1929–1979* (St Lucia: University of Queensland Press, 1982), 1.
6 Sculthorpe, 'Sculthorpe at 80'.
7 Michael Hannan, 'The Music of Peter Sculthorpe: An Analytical Study with Particular Reference to Those Social and Other Cultural Forces Which Have Shaped the Development of an Australian Vision', PhD diss. (The University of Sydney, 1979), 65; Skinner, *Peter Sculthorpe*, 256.
8 Sculthorpe, *Port Essington* (London: Faber Music, 1980), i.

9   Sculthorpe, quoted in Skinner, 'Booklet Essay', *The ABC Recordings* [Audio recording] (ABC Classics 481 1293, 2014), 42.
10 Ian McLean (drawing on Ross Gibson), *White Aborigines: Identity Politics in Australian Art* (Cambridge: Cambridge University Press, 1998), 26.
11 Although there are occasional uses of microtones in Sculthorpe's music, the work is not microtonal.
12 Wilfrid Mellers, 'Introduction to Sculthorpe's Compositions', *Peter Sculthorpe* www.petersculthorpe.com.au/biography.htm accessed 6 January 2015. For Mellers, 'solitariness' is also the distinguishing feature of Busoni, Satie and van Dieren (Mellers, 'The Problem of Busoni', *Music and Letters*, 18, no. 3 (1937): 240).
13 See, for example, Skinner, *Peter Sculthorpe*, 259–60.
14 Writing about melancholy in early Australian colonial art, McLean makes the point that '[w]hile the ahistorical metaphors of silence and stillness that constitute the sublime aesthetic are well suited to the art of exploration, they are inappropriate to the art of invasion and settlement' (McLean, *White Aborigines*, 24). McLean's general 'concern is the way that melancholy is used in their [artists' and writers'] texts as a tropic formulation or poetic closure for expressing social and ideological positions that exceed their own personal angst' (18). In Sculthorpe's *Irkanda IV* we see Sculthorpe's personal grief transformed through the grief of exile (of loneliness, distance, modernism) into Australian Music by way of 'the landscape' itself.
15 For full details of the chronology and the changes of designation of works in the Sun Music cycle, see www.petersculthorpe.com.au/worklist.htm.
16 In 1970 Sculthorpe was appointed a Member of the Order of the British Empire (MBE).
17 Andrew McCredie, *Music by Australian Composers: Survey No. 1* (Canberra: Advisory Board, Commonwealth Assistance to Australian Composers, 1969), 20–1.
18 Hannan, *Peter Sculthorpe*, 13.
19 Ibid.
20 Quoted in ibid., 15.
21 Quoted in ibid., 29. Hannan's footnote indicates that Sculthorpe denied having written this.
22 Preface to the score, quoted in Skinner, *Peter Sculthorpe*, 161.
23 See ibid., 162. For a more sceptical reading, see Rachel Campbell, 'Peter Sculthorpe's *Irkanda* Period, 1954–65: Nationalism, "Aboriginality", and Landscape', PhD diss. (The University of Sydney, 2014), 100–101ff.
24 Hannan, 'The Music of Peter Sculthorpe', 49.
25 Ibid., 22.
26 Hannan, *Peter Sculthorpe*, 62.
27 Ibid.
28 The piece was written just after the release of David Lewiston's recording in the Nonesuch Explorer series, *Bali: Music from the Morning of the World* (Elektra-Nonesuch (79714), 1967).
29 Preface to *String Quartet Music*.
30 Joel Crotty argues for *Sun Music III* as part of a geographical reconfiguration: '*Sun Music III* (1967) is a work of its time. It is an example of Sculthorpe's Asianist style, which was particularly influential in the 1960s as young composers tried to disengage (philosophically, at least), from European musical traditions and relocate Australian composition in its geographical region. In the score, the transplantation of the

melodies and gamelan rhythms of Balinese music is coupled with Sculthorpe's own individual voice to create a kaleidoscope of beautifully orchestrated sounds' (Crotty, 'Towards an Australian Art-Music Canon', *Quadrant* 55, no. 10 (2011): 97). The 'transplantation' was Sculthorpe's, rather than a passive event; indeed, the idea that 'Balinese music' needed to be transplanted reinforces the idea that 'transplantation' is necessary for Sculthorpe's music to realign Australia as a part of Asia.

31 Hannan, *Peter Sculthorpe*, 91–2.
32 Sculthorpe, *Sun Music: Journeys and Reflections from a Composer's Life* (Sydney: ABC Books, 1999), 139.
33 Malcolm Williamson, 'How Australian Can Australian Music Become?' *Music Now* 1, no. 4 (1971): 15.
34 Skinner, *Peter Sculthorpe*, 158.
35 In Sculthorpe's later works, politics, aesthetics and the aesthetics of politics are totally indistinct. One finds in Sculthorpe's *Quamby*, for example, the bluff at which 'Aborigines had the choice of being shot, or jumping', represented as an all-pervading 'falling tritone'. This is not to say that the sentiment is not heartfelt, but that a new representationalist paradigm incorporates Sculthorpe's pitch system, such as where the A♭–G semitone represents the Earth (via Kepler and Mahler), A represents Australia, D represents Death and so on ('Peter Sculthorpe Writes New Work in Aid of Climate Change', Faber Music http://www.fabermusic.com/news/peter-sculthorpe-writes-new-work-in-aid-of-climate-change-563 accessed 24 October 2014; Peter Sculthorpe interview, *The Music Show* [Radio broadcast] ABC, 28 February 2004 www.abc.net.au/radionational/programs/musicshow/peter-sculthorpe/3374698#transcript accessed 24 October 2014; John Peterson, 'Peter Sculthorpe: A Reflection on His Music and Its Context', *Australian Music Centre*, 19 August 2014 www.australianmusiccentre.com.au/article/peter-sculthorpe-a-reflection-on-his-music-and-its-context accessed 24 October 2014; also see Sculthorpe in McCredie, *Music by Australian Composers*, 17). This produces a potentially dangerously reductionist view of imperial war, something only tangentially acknowledged within Sculthorpe scholarship; for example, Skinner considers the massacre at Quamby Bluff to be 'a generic story, colonial atrocity dressed up for home consumption' (Skinner, *Peter Sculthorpe*, 49).
36 Roger Covell, *Australia's Music: Themes of a New Society* (Melbourne: Sun Books, 1967), xi–xii.
37 Ibid., 1.
38 For Covell, a musician from 'medieval or early renaissance Europe would have been much better equipped by musical predisposition and background to understand what was of value in the music of Australian Aborigines' (ibid., 2).
39 Ibid., 3. It was not until after Covell wrote this that the genetic study of songbirds demonstrated that the comparison ought to be written in the other direction. See Tim Low, *Where Song Began: Australia's Birds and How They Changed the World* (Melbourne: Viking, 2014).
40 Covell, *Australia's Music*, 6.
41 Ibid.
42 Sculthorpe, 'David Matthews in Australia – a Memoir', in Thomas Hyde (ed.), *David Matthews: Essays, Tributes and Criticism* (Woodbridge: Plumbago, 2014), 99.
43 Carter, *Always Almost Modern*, 2.
44 Ibid.
45 Covell, *Australia's Music*, 202.
46 Ibid.

47 Ibid., 202.
48 Ibid., 203.
49 To argue for Sculthorpe as exceptional Covell needs to contrast him against all the other composers who are working alongside him, and who therefore need either to be 'unexceptional', or to write music that is not at all part of Australian Music. For example, Cugley's *Pan, the Lake* is 'merely *Irkanda IV* gone to seed'. Not that this is necessarily 'unkind', since being second-rate Sculthorpe is still to be in some relation with Sculthorpe. The result is that *Pan, the Lake* can be recuperated through its connection with landscape: 'the metaphor [of the lake] could be captured in Cugley's defense. His music irrigates the parched loneliness of *Irkanda IV* with the moist sounds of flute, horn and Fillipino gongs and puts out its own green shoots of promise.' These are promising shoots because they support the wider interest in the music of Asia, of which Sculthorpe was the leading composer (ibid., 234).
50 Michael Hannan and Peter Sculthorpe, '*Rites of Passage*', *Music Now* 2, no. 2 (1974): 14. A draft is held in Archives of Donald Peart, University of Sydney, Box 19, P-171.
51 See Bill Ashcroft, *The Gimbals of Unease: The Poetry of Francis Webb* (Nedlands, Western Australia: Centre for the Study of Australian Literature, 1996).
52 In his 'Descriptive Note' to his 1965 solo exhibition at the Leicester Galleries, Russell Drysdale wrote that 'It is one of the delights of these lonely places to find so often that there is no loneliness. The constant and close company of birds in the central places of Australia is a charm and a reassurance to the gregarious nature of man' (Russell Drysdale, 'A Descriptive Note by Russell Drysdale', *Catalogue of an Exhibition of Paintings and Drawings by Russell Drysdale* (London: The Leicester Galleries, 1965)).
53 David Matthews, *Landscape into Sound* (St Albans: The Claridge Press, 1992), 38.
54 Sculthorpe, 'David Matthews in Australia', 95ff.
55 Roger Scruton, 'The Emancipation of Consonance', in Hyde (ed.), *David Matthews*, 105.
56 Matthews, *Landscape into Sound*, 100.
57 Ibid., 44.
58 Daniel Grimley, *Carl Nielsen and the Idea of Modernism* (Woodbridge: The Boydell Press, 2011), 139.
59 Ibid., 140.
60 Ibid., 141.
61 Criticism of Lumsdaine frequently makes the same claims about music and landscape as it has for Sculthorpe. For example, Max Lopert, writing in the *Financial Times*, remarked that 'Lumsdaine's best music leaves a mark: a quality of dry, uncluttered freshness, pervaded by sunburnt, sandswept perceptions of nature, deposits of potent sound-images' (Lopert, 'David Lumsdaine', *Financial Times*, 9 November 1981, 15). Nevertheless, the two composers had a fundamentally different attitude to Australian places.
62 Matthews, *Landscape into Sound*, 104–5.
63 'For violin alone' is the subtitle to the published score of *Irkanda I*. Sculthorpe wrote two works in 1955: *Sonata for Violin Alone*, and *Irkanda I*.
64 Sculthorpe, *Sun Music*. Also see: Skinner, *Sculthorpe*, 164 (quoting Deborah Hayes, *Peter Sculthorpe: A Bio-Bibliography* (Westport: Greenwood Press, 1993)). Amongst his papers at the National Library of Australia is an undated (c. 2002) 'reconstruction' of a trace from 1955 of the contour of Canberra (Papers of Peter Sculthorpe, MS 9676, National Library of Australia, Box 59):

65 Hannan, 'The Music of Peter Sculthorpe', 57–8.
66 Julian Johnson, *Mahler's Voices: Expression and Irony in the Songs and Symphonies* (Oxford: Oxford University Press, 2009), 61.
67 There is no sense, for example, of the dilemma that Adorno sees as central to Mahler's music. See Max Paddison, *Adorno's Aesthetics of Music* (Cambridge: Cambridge University Press, 1997), 259.
68 Ibid.
69 Skinner, *Peter Sculthorpe*, 243.
70 Karlheinz Stockhausen, *Stockhausen on Music: Lectures and Interviews*, ed. Robin Maconie (London: Marion Boyars, 1989), 44–5.
71 See Martin Iddon, *New Music at Darmstadt* (Cambridge: Cambridge University Press, 2013), 288.
72 According to Skinner, Sculthorpe's anecdote came well after the piece was written.
73 Skinner, *Peter Sculthorpe*, 165.
74 The 'bush' is nearly always populated, characterized by landscapes made by people, rather than 'wilderness'. (Based on our current knowledge about the extent of Aboriginal fire regimes, for example, all Australia's landscapes ought to be conceived of as shaped by people.)
75 Skinner, *Peter Sculthorpe*, 164.
76 McGregor faces similar contradictions in writing about Drysdale's painting. 'The *dérangement* of complicity also disturbs the relation between work and the world. One doesn't know how to "take" these paintings. Partly it has to do with the destabilization of the iconography. [...] One is also, however, struck by the ambivalence of both the subject *in* the painting [...] and the painting subject [...]. What this suggests is not identification but (in Derrida's sense) *différance*' (Gaile McGregor, *EcCentric Visions: Re Constructing Australia* (Waterloo: Wilfrid Laurier University Press, 1994)).
77 Carter, *Always Almost Modern*, 59 (quoting from *Art in Australia*'s editorial).
78 Jeanette Hoorn, *Australian Pastoral: The Making of a White Landscape* (Fremantle: Fremantle Press, 2007), 216.
79 Carter, *Always Almost Modern*, 5.
80 Ibid.
81 Similarly, *Sun Music III* is specifically about McPhee's book *Music in Bali*, which had just been published, and in a sense his 1968 piece *Tabuh Tabuhan* supersedes McPhee's piece of the same name (1934), of which Sculthorpe was critical (Skinner, *Peter Sculthorpe*, 495, 464).
82 Quoted in Bill Ashcroft and John Salter, 'Modernism's Empire: Australia and the Cultural Imperialism of Style', in Howard J. Booth and Nigel Rigby (eds), *Modernism and Empire: Writing and British Coloniality, 1890–1940* (Manchester: Manchester University Press, 2000), 306.
83 Ibid.
84 McGregor, *EcCentric Visions*, 169.
85 Ian McLean, 'Aboriginalism: White Aborigines and Australian Nationalism', *Australian Humanities Review*, May 1998 www.australianhumanitiesreview.org/archive/Issue-May-1998/mclean.html accessed 9 July 2015.
86 Ibid.
87 Ibid.

88 McLean, *White Aborigines*, 95. The 'white aborigine' is a figure who emerges from 'Aboriginalism': 'In a relatively quick reversal [in the 1940s], signs of Aboriginality became important insignias of a non-Aboriginal Australian identity' (87). In the years after the Second World War the new nationalism in combination with a move away from Eurocentricism produced a 'radical nativitism' (87). This move was 'to transform nativism into a distinctly anti-imperial indigenous consciousness' (88). For McLean, the modernists of the mid-twentieth century 'saw in Aborigines and the desert not a sublime ideology which might finally redeem Australia, but an emblem of the alienation and ugliness of Australia's colonialist history and identity' (91). This argument differs from that forwarded by Covell, for whom the hope is that a future Australian Music can overcome the colonial problem that left, as he sees it, Australia without a distinctive folk music; Covell's conception of redemption is racial in register, as the end of his book *Australia's Music* makes clear (Covell, *Australia's Music*, 290).
89 Skinner, *Peter Sculthorpe*, 570.
90 Ibid., 450.
91 Ibid., 282.
92 Ibid., 367.
93 Ibid., 242.
94 McLean, *White Aborigines*, 8. Sculthorpe, *Sun Music*, 59, 111.
95 Ibid.
96 Quoted in Sculthorpe, *Sun Music*, 59.
97 McLean, *White Aborigines*, 8.
98 Sculthorpe, *Sun Music*, 69.
99 See Skinner, *Peter Sculthorpe*, 305.
100 Ibid., 307.
101 Ibid., 311.
102 Quoted in ibid., 410.
103 Bernard Smith, quoted in McLean, *White Aborigines*, 81.
104 Quoted in Neil Roberts, '*Kangaroo* and the Narrative of Contingency', in Keith Cushman and Earl G. Ingersoll (eds), *D. H. Lawrence: New Worlds* (Cranbury, NJ: Associated University Presses, 2003), 192.
105 Ibid.
106 Jonathan Paget, 'Has Sculthorpe Misappropriated Indigenous Melodies?' *Musicology Australia* 35, no. 1 (2013): 103.
107 Ibid., 86–111.
108 Ibid., 90, 110 (citing Covell, *Australia's Music*, 64 and 65, respectively).
109 See John Peterson, *The Music of Peter Sculthorpe* (Kingsgrove: Wildbird Music, 2014).
110 Ellen Smith, 'Local Moderns: The Jindyworobak Movement and Australian Modernism', *Australian Literary Studies* 27, no. 1 (2012): 2.
111 Ibid.
112 Ibid., 3.
113 Ibid., 3–4.
114 Ibid., 4.
115 Quoted in ibid., 5.
116 Ibid.

117 Skinner, *Peter Sculthorpe*, 145.
118 David Symons, 'The Jindyworobak Connection in Australian Music, c.1940–1960', *Context: Journal of Music Research* 23, autumn (2002): 33–47.
119 Letter to Symons, quoted in ibid., 38.
120 Smith, 'Local Moderns', 11.
121 Covell, 'Richard Meale: Intuitions of a Solitary Modernist', *Sounds Australian* 20 (1988/9), 6.
122 Hannan and Sculthorpe, '*Rites of Passage*', 14–15. Hannan later wrote 'Since the composition of *Rites of Passage* Sculthorpe has changed his position on the subject [of "incorporating Aboriginal rituals" and "tribal music"] having, in his view, successfully integrated Aboriginal melodies into *The Song of Tailitnama* (1974), *Port Essington* (1977) and *Desert Places* (1978)' (Hannan, 'The Music of Peter Sculthorpe', 36). The transcription of the interview is annotated by Sculthorpe, who makes some minor modifications to some of what he said, mostly correcting typographic errors. There is no change of any substance to those of his comments quoted here.
123 Hannan and Sculthorpe, '*Rites of Passage*', 14.
124 Hannan, 'The Music of Peter Sculthorpe', 37 (quoting Manning Clark). Also see: Penelope Hanley, *Creative Lives: Personal Papers of Australian Writers and Artists* (Canberra: National Library of Australia, 2009), 106.
125 Hannan, 'The Music of Peter Sculthorpe', 37.
126 The spelling here reflects that used by Sculthorpe. Similarly the term 'Aboriginal music' or 'Aboriginal melody' are Sculthorpe's. The undifferentiated 'Aboriginal' goes with the undifferentiated 'Australian'.
127 Grainger, too, worked with Aranda songs. More generally, although I do not have space to explore the wider exploration of 'Aboriginality' in the 1960s, one finds pieces such as Earle Brown's *Corroboree* (1964), which serve as a reminder that music inspired by Aboriginal ideas (however superficial) is not the preserve of Australian composers.
128 Ann Stephen, 'Blackfellows and Modernists', in Mary Ann Gillies, Helen Sword and Steven Yeo (eds), *Pacific Rim Modernisms* (Toronto: University of Toronto Press, 2009), 157.
129 Ibid., 156.
130 Paget, 'Has Sculthorpe Appropriated Indigenous Melodies?' 99–101.
131 Skinner, *Peter Sculthorpe*, 636; Sculthorpe, *Sun Music*, 147.
132 Ibid., 205.
133 Skinner, *Peter Sculthorpe*, 635.
134 Paget, 'Has Sculthorpe Appropriated Indigenous Melodies?' 101.
135 Covell, *Australia's Music*, 326, 72.
136 Ibid., 72.
137 Ibid.
138 Paget, 'Has Sculthorpe Appropriated Indigenous Melodies?' 101.
139 Sculthorpe, *Sun Music*, 147.
140 Ibid., 205. Paget explains the precise relationships between the various scales and structures that Sculthorpe utilizes in 'Has Sculthorpe Appropriated Indigenous Melodies?' 98ff.
141 Sculthorpe, *Sun Music*, 96.
142 Ibid.

143 Joel Crotty, 'Onshore, Offshore, Unsure: Expo '70 and Peter Sculthorpe's Journey with Music from Japan', *Musicology Australia* 37, no. 2 (2015): 260.
144 Ibid., quoting Sculthorpe, *Sun Music*, 138.
145 Crotty, 'Onshore, Offshore, Unsure', 260.
146 For a reception history of Sculthorpe's early music, which also reveals some of the connections between Sculthorpe, Covell and the Prerauers, for example, see Campbell, 'Peter Sculthorpe's *Irkanda* Period'.
147 Paget, 'Has Sculthorpe Appropriated Indigenous Melodies?', 109.
148 Certainly there were none who saw music as their primary artistic form. Roy de Maistre's *Colour Music*, a painting from c. 1934, is a possible exception. The 'Sydney Moderns' were a group of artists working in Sydney in the 1920s and 1930s.
149 Meale, 'Richard Meale Writes about Rimbaud, Australia and His Own Music', *The Listener*, 24 June 1971, 830.
150 For Balaji and Worawongs, the film 'essentially framed the physical representation of Asian women as always being "beneath" that of White men' (Murali Balaji and Tina Worawongs, 'The New Suzie Wong: Normative Assumptions of White Male and Asian Female Relationships', *Communication, Culture and Critique* 3 (2010): 236). See also Minjeong Kim and Angie Y. Chung, 'Consuming Orientalism: Images of Asian/American Women in Multicultural Advertising', *Qualitative Sociology* 28, no. 1 (2005): 67–91. For a detailed account of the novel, and its adaptions in terms of orientalism, see Ho-ning Cloke Tsui, 'The World around Suzie Wong', MA diss. (University of Hong Kong, 2007), http://hub.hku.hk/handle/10722/51837.
151 The textural/structural division is itself problematic, though not straightforwardly so for Meale, since his music is more texturally driven and less structurally concerned than its programme notes sometimes suggest, and there is no oppositional mapping of either structure or texture onto any particular work, be it *Images* or *Evocations*.
152 Meale, 'Richard Meale Writes about Rimbaud', 830.
153 Ibid.
154 Belinda Webster, 'Peter Sculthorpe Interviewed by Belinda Webster in the Esso Performing Arts Collection' (National Library of Australia, 1989), Oral TRC 2466, Session 4, 6'30".
155 Crotty acknowledges the 'Suzie Wong' criticism, and remarks that *Sun Music III* 'is one of the best Australian examples of Western instruments translating and transfiguring musical sounds from beyond their traditional, Euro-centric frame of reference' (Crotty, 'Towards an Australian Art-Music Canon', 97).
156 Undated, anonymous interview. Papers of Richard Meale, MS 10076, National Library of Australia, Box 1.
157 Sculthorpe, 'Sculthorpe on Sculthorpe', *Music Now* 1, no. 1 (1969): 12.
158 Webster, 'Peter Sculthorpe Interviewed', 13'30".
159 In a letter to Anne Boyd, dated 10 February 2000, Sculthorpe quoted from Stephen FitzGerald, *Is Australia an Asian Country?* (St Leonards: Allen & Unwin, 1997), and agreed with FitzGerald's inclusion of Sculthorpe as an 'Australian Asian' (Papers of Peter Sculthorpe, Box 22).
160 The various obituaries written for Sculthorpe give a clear version of how such a slippage between terms operates. The following examples all demonstrate the way that his music and 'landscape' are brought together. His publisher Sally Cavender wrote: 'His most defining quality has been his ability to somehow create the feeling of the Australian landscape in his music' ('Peter Sculthorpe, 1929–2014',

> *Faber Music*, www.fabermusic.com/news/peter-sculthorpe-1929-201408082014-1, accessed 11 August 2014). Matthew Westwood, writing in *The Australian*, commented: 'From the 1960s he was a pioneer of music that sought an authentic expression of Australia, its landscape and people' (Westwood, 'Peter Sculthorpe, Composer of *Kakadu* and *Earth Cry*, Dies, Aged 85', *The Australian*, 8 August 2014). In the *New Yorker*, Teju Cole wrote:
>
>> It was music that perfectly evoked the landscape of southeastern Australia – its vernacular architecture, beautiful stands of eucalyptus, red hills, dry grass, and sudden screaming flocks of lorikeets. The mental process by which one matches an orchestral texture to a physical landscape is mysterious and, of course, highly subjective. But, just as the soaring horns and massed strings of Sibelius are inseparable from the idea of the Scandinavian wilds, Sculthorpe's pizzicati and percussive effects sounded to me precisely as the Australian landscape looked. (Teju Cole, 'Postscript: Peter Sculthorpe (1929–2014)', *New Yorker*, 8 August 2014.)
>
> Not all those writing at the time of Sculthorpe's death were ready to celebrate the connection between Sculthorpe's music and Australian landscape. Andrew Ford attributed the connection between music and landscape to a cultural understanding, rather than the musical presentation of landscape:
>
>> You can see how this [association of his music and Australian landscape] happened. First, there were Sculthorpe's titles, which often seemed to tie his music to a particular place. Then there was the character of his music, which generally unfolded slowly, like the eye travelling across a wide expanse of Outback. His melodic lines had rather narrow ranges, keeping close to the earth, resembling the undulating landscape itself. And those pedal points: were they not really drones, even didgeridoos? Perhaps, if Sculthorpe had been more of a Copland, he might have thought in such terms. But Sculthorpe did not draw on Australia so much as Australia drew on him. He gave us music that was *echt*-Sculthorpe, and we heard our land in its notes. (Andrew Ford, 'Peter Sculthorpe, a Composer in Australia', *Inside Story: Current Affairs and Culture from Australia and Beyond*, 11 August 2014 http://insidestory.org.au/peter-sculthorpe-a-composer-in-australia/.)

161 Joseph David Robin, 'A Philosophy of Change', MMus diss. (University of Melbourne, 1995), 2.

162 Crotty, 'Onshore, Offshore, Unsure', 260 (quoting Peter Sculthorpe, 'Japanese National Commission for Unesco', *Proceedings of the International Round Table on the Relations Between Japanese and Western Arts* (Japanese National Commission for Unesco, 1969)).

163 Papers of James Murdoch, MS 8372, National Library of Australia, Box 24. The document is heavily annotated and corrected, and appears as a rough draft. No edited version was published.

164 Andrew Ford, *Try Whistling This* (Collingwood: Black Inc., 2012), 232.

165 Papers of James Murdoch, Box 24. He mentions 'P[eter] M[axwell] D[avies]' in passing, in a way that suggests that this was an ongoing argument, to which Davies had contributed during his time in Australia.

166 Ibid.

167 The details of this chronology are from Skinner, *Peter Sculthorpe*, 447ff.

168 Quoted in ibid., 448.
169 Banks's *Tirade* (London: Schott, 1968), for example.
170 Tony Wood, 'At Tate Modern', *London Review of Books* 36, no. 16, 21 August 2014, 13.
171 Ibid.
172 Stephen Adams, 'Vale Peter Sculthorpe' [Radio broadcast], *ABC Classic FM*, 8 August 2014 www.abc.net.au/classic/content/2014/08/08/4056508.htm.
173 See Carter, *Always Almost Modern*, 33. Also see Michael Hooper, *The Music of David Lumsdaine* (Aldershot, UK: Ashgate, 2012) for a detailed analysis of the piece, and Chapter 7 of this book.
174 Hannan, 'The Music of Peter Sculthorpe', 159.
175 Ibid. The idea is familiar from Igor Stravinsky, *Poetics of Music* (Cambridge, MA: Harvard University Press, 1970), 28.
176 The Matisse cut-out plants of Coburn's *Curtain of the Sun* also resemble the tree in Malevich's *Shroud of Christ* which grows from the glowing body of Christ, set in a symmetrical landscape with two rising suns. This image is redemptive, but strangely so, and its date is early in Malevich's career, well before Suprematism. Butterley's *Canticle of the Sun* was named after one of Coburn's works.
177 Sculthorpe's characteristic birdsong, his 'seagulls', is also the sound of George Crumb's whales (1971). Sculthorpe learnt the technique for producing 'seagulls' from Aldo Parisot (David Matthews, 'Birdsong and Music', lecture at Gresham College, 2011 www.gresham.ac.uk/lectures-and-events/birdsong-and-music).
178 'Peter Sculthorpe: Obituary', *The Telegraph*, 10 August 2014 www.telegraph.co.uk/news/obituaries/11024382/Peter-Sculthorpe-obituary.html.
179 Skinner, *Peter Sculthorpe*, 628.
180 Brian Hood, quoted in ibid., 643.
181 See ibid., 411.
182 Whittall argues for a 'moderate mainstream' that is the 'coexisting […] complement' of a '"modernist mainstream"' of composers who were both distinctive and accessible to wide audiences. My argument here is slightly different, since Sculthorpe's nationalism is, from a transnational perspective, such as makes him a modernist, where Britten's Englishness makes him a conservative. Aesthetically Sculthorpe connects to the earlier artistic practices that work through the centre–periphery problem that makes it impossible to connect squarely England and Australia, or 'English' with 'Australian'. What my chapter demonstrates are some of the transformations that take place when one seeks to connect Australian and English nationalisms, or aesthetic modernisms, and, indeed, when one seeks not to (Whittall, 'Individualism and Accessibility: The Moderate Mainstream', in Nicholas Cook and Anthony Pople (eds), *Cambridge History of Twentieth Century Music* (Cambridge, UK: Cambridge University Press, 2004), 364–94).
183 Skinner, *Peter Sculthorpe*, 607.
184 Ibid., 600.
185 Ibid., 639–40.
186 Ibid., 640.
187 A. E. Haigh, *The Attic Theatre*, revised A. W. Pickard-Cambridge (Oxford: Clarendon Press, 1907), quoted in Anthony Sheppard, *Revealing Masks* (Berkeley, CA: University of California Press, 2001), 37.

188 See ibid., 142–3.
189 Webster, 'Peter Sculthorpe Interviewed', 11'34".
190 Philip Brett, 'Musicality, Essentialism and the Closet', and 'Eros and Orientalism in Britten's Operas', in Philip Brett, Elizabeth Wood and Gary C. Thomas (eds), *Queering the Pitch: The New Gay and Lesbian Musicology* (New York: Routledge, 1994), 251, quoted in Sheppard, *Revealing Masks*, 153.
191 Ibid., 154.
192 Papers of Roger Smalley, Acc.08.089, National Library of Australia, Box 1. This dates from either late 1965 or early 1966. See Smalley, 'Portrait of Debussy 8: Debussy and Messiaen', *The Musical Times* 109, no. 1500 (1968): 128–31.
193 Pierre Boulez, 'Frozen Perfection', *Music and Musicians* 16 (1968): 30.
194 Donald Mitchell groups Britten and Sculthorpe together in his article 'What Is Expressionism?' He hears in both composers a new interest in 'the glissando', and he argues that 'A study of the device means that we must take account of our century's exotic inclinations above all to Asia, since the glissando belongs, as it were, to East and West. In their very different ways both Britten and Sculthorpe owe their common glissandos not only to Expressionism but also to exotic influences from Asia' (Donald Mitchell, *Cradles of the New: Writings on Music 1951–1991* (London: Faber, 1995), 223).
195 Williamson, 'How Australian Can Australian Music Become?' 15.
196 It is worth noting that McCredie, in *Musicological Studies in Australia from the Beginning to the Present* (Sydney: Sydney University Press, 1979), is attentive to the problem of presuming uniformity at the national scale simply for the sake of convenience, and so within the progression of periods that make up 'Historical Musicology', he considers 'Australian Studies' in terms of both 'National and Regional Historiographies' (162).
197 Banks to Lumsdaine, 27 March 1973, Papers of Don Banks, MS6830, National Library of Australia, Box 35.
198 Hannan, 'The Music of Peter Sculthorpe', 25.
199 McCredie, *Music by Australian Composers*, 20.
200 Sculthorpe, *Sun Music*, 175.

Chapter 6

1 Derek Whitelock, *Festival! The Story of the Adelaide Festival of Arts* (Adelaide: D. Whitelock, 1980).
2 Lecture on *Interiors/Exteriors*, c. 1976, Papers of James Murdoch, MS 8372, National Library of Australia, Box 24.
3 Ibid.
4 Ibid.
5 Ibid.
6 Murdoch's archive includes material announcing Meale's appointment at the University of York (Papers of Don Banks, MS6830, National Library of Australia, Box 24), and later correspondence from Martin Wesley-Smith (writing from York) laments Meale's not coming to York (Wesley-Smith to Banks, 18 September 1972, Papers of Don Banks, Box 37).

7   Meale, 'Proposal for the Formation of Special Studies in Composition', Papers of James Murdoch, Box 24.
8   Ibid.
9   Ibid., my emphasis.
10 Don Dunstan to G. M. Badger, undated, Papers of James Murdoch., Box 24.
11 Don Dunstan to G. M. Badger, 5 November 1973, Papers of James Murdoch, Box 24.
12 See in particular Robert Delaunay's *Light*, 1912, in Mary Ann Caws, *Manifesto: A Century of Isms* (Lincoln: University of Nebraska Press, 2001), 156–7.
13 ANZAC Day.
14 Woodward's programme began with Takemitsu's *Undisturbed Rest*, then *Coruscations*, then Edwards's *Monos II* and Brouwer's *Sonata, Pian e Forte*; in the second half Woodward performed Barraqué's Piano Sonata.
15 Ross Edwards (1971), programme note for the première performance (Papers of Richard Meale, MS 10076, National Library of Australia, Box 69).
16 Aside from the sketches, there are two sources of information about the composition. One is a thesis written by Thomas Aitken (Aitken, 'Richard Meale: A Stylistic Survey', MMus diss. (University of Queensland, 1975)), the other a book chapter by Elizabeth Wood ('Richard Meale', in Frank Callaway and David Tunley (eds), *Australian Composition in the Twentieth Century* (Melbourne: Oxford University Press, 1978)). My explication of the pitch scheme owes a debt to both authors, who apparently had correspondence with Meale and access to some of the precompositional workings of the piece. My partial repetition of this material seeks to augment Aitken's thesis and to correct Wood's chapter. Wood's chapter is particularly confusing. She cites 'MS Papers' that are not in the NLA's current collection (and therefore were lost or destroyed), and even when these are cited from typeset examples, the annotation of procedures is not always correct. Either Wood misunderstood Meale's explanation of the work, the manuscript was misleading, or Wood was piecing together the procedures from a variety of sources without fully understanding the operations; perhaps some combination of all three. Aitken's thesis presents the scheme and annotates the score according to his tables; Meale's sketches are similarly annotated. Usefully, Aitken notes some of the differences between sketch and score.
17 Both Aitken and Wood follow Meale's nomenclature in labelling this a 'sonority'. A sonority refers to a chord in one transposition. This term is derived from Boulez's '*bloc sonore*'.
18 None of the chords are formed by multiplying by chord 2 (the note G) alone, since this yields simply a transposition of the starting chord.
19 The inversion about D implies that the five essential chords are actually a condensation of a row, the first pitch of which is D. The composition has no other sense of a row of pitches, and the chords generated by the multiplying procedure are in all other ways the work's basic building blocks. Wood does not detail this crucial step of the inversion about D, nor do the sketches contain any of the procedures before the final scheme.
20 Peter Weir's 1972 film *Incredible Floridas* shows Meale teaching chord multiplication. Peter Weir (dir.), *Incredible Floridas: Homage to Arthur Rimbaud* [DVD] (Pyrmont: Film Australia, 2011; first released 1972).
21 Pierre Boulez, *Boulez on Music Today*, trans. Susan Bradshaw and Richard Rodney Bennett (London: Faber & Faber, 1971), 39; the emphasis is Boulez's.

22 Ibid., 45; the emphasis is Boulez's.
23 Meale's sketches contain only one page of chord multiplications, which are not the same chords as used for the piece. The sketch shows four chords, each with three notes (all more similar to the harmony he favoured in works such as *Homage to Garcia Lorca*).
24 Richard Meale, *Coruscations* (Australia: Universal Edition, 1975).
25 Papers of Richard Meale, Series 3, Folder 139. His archive contains only a poor photocopy of this diagram.
26 Boulez, *Boulez on Music Today*, 46.
27 Strictly, the dynamic has not changed since the opening *ff*. Practically every performer I have heard privileges the obvious gestural need for something quieter before the *uguale*.
28 Ibid., example 6, p. 47. Boulez's example is from Webern's Op. 27/ii, bar 21.
29 At the end of the first stave, Meale uses J11 rather than J10. The sketch indicates J10, but the pitches are from J11. Such divergences from the scheme occur once or twice a page.
30 The pitch that is unaccounted for, though it ends the fourth cycle, is the G in bar 4. The scheme gives a G♯, and the fair copy gives G♯, as does Meale's final sketch of this section. The score's courtesy natural for the G in the fifth bar is unnecessary unless the lower pitch is G♯, which suggests that the lower G natural is an unfortunate engraving error.
31 Papers of Richard Meale, Series 3, Folder 139. His archive contains only a poor photocopy of this diagram.
32 *Roger Woodward* (EMI/His Master's Voice OASD-7567, 1972).
33 The piece allows considerable latitude in changing the accents: 'these accents may also be modified – or additional accents added – if considered appropriate' (Meale, *Coruscations* (Australia: Universal Edition, 1975), Preface).
34 Boulez, *Boulez on Music Today*, 44.
35 Ibid., 41.
36 Ibid., 45.
37 Ibid., 44.
38 Papers of Richard Meale, Series 3.
39 At the start, the primary level of rhythm is generated by the alternation of hands. Later (p. 5), Meale indicates an 'internal rhythmic grouping' which does not coincide with that alternation. The first of these rhythmic groupings comes with a long *uguale* passage, which is formed from six sonorities. The internal rhythmic grouping does not coincide systematically with the changes of sonority.
40 Boulez, *Boulez on Music Today*, 93.
41 The next time A1 is used the G is also used, and the third time – with the same registers and order of pitches as the opening – the G also appears. The fourth occurrence has no G, lacks an A and has a D instead, which does mean that Meale's chart of sonorities is unlikely to be the source of the G. The next A1 keeps the D, and lacks an F. The fifth A1 is as expected. The sixth A1 has a C and no F. This degree of instability is unusual in the piece. Since the composition relies on the flow of fields of pitch material and not motivic transformation, such changes are not particularly disruptive.
42 Ross Edwards (1971), programme note for the premiere performance (Papers of Richard Meale, Box 69).

43 Boulez, *Boulez on Music Today*, 30.
44 See John Croft, 'Fields of Rubble: On the Politics of Music after the Postmodern', in Björn Heile (ed.), *The Modernist Legacy: Essays on New Music* (Aldershot: Ashgate, 2009), 28.
45 Roger Woodward, undated programme note (Papers of Richard Meale, Box 68). An almost identical version of this note is contained in a different programme, whose authors are named as Brigette Schiffer and Meredith Oakes: programme notes to Australian Music in Lisbon, concert on 26 July 1978 (Papers of Richard Meale, Box 69).
46 Gilles Deleuze and Félix Guattari, *What Is Philosophy?*, trans. Graham Burchell and Hugh Tomlinson (London: Verso, 1994), 164–5.
47 Roger Woodward, *Roger Woodward on Richard Meale* [Radio broadcast], ABC 50th Anniversary Broadcast, recorded London, 3 August 1982.
48 Michel Leiris, *Aurora* (first published 1946), quoted in Christophe Bident, 'Blanchot, Leiris', *COLLOQUY text theory critique*, 10 (2005): 14.
49 Timothy J. Clark, *Farewell to an Idea* (New Haven, CT: Yale University Press, 2001), 8.
50 Curt Prerauer to Meale, 1 March 1965, Papers of Curt and Marea Prerauer 1930-2006, MS10040, National Library of Australia, Box 2.
51 Curt Prerauer to Wolfgang Fortner, 12 March 1965, Papers of Curt and Marea Prerauer, Box 2.
52 Meale to Murdoch, 25 June 1965, Papers of James Murdoch, Box 24. Boulez's *Pli Selon Pli* is surely the model for this plan, and, according to Aitken ('Richard Meale', 75) it was also the basis for Meale's *Nocturnes* (1967).
53 Murdoch to Meale, 7 January 1971, Papers of James Murdoch, Box 24.
54 The initial invitation for Meale to compose a work for the Pierrot Players came in 1970. There is a letter from Meale to Murdoch dated 30 July 1970 in which he says he will write something for the ensemble (Papers of James Murdoch, Box 24), and then a letter from Murdoch to Meale dated 11 August 1970 indicating that the Pierrot Players had been invited to give a concert of Australian music at the ISCM festival and that Peart, the major force behind Australia's contribution to the ISCM, was likely to suggest Meale. The letter comments on each of the players, and for clarinetist Alan Hacker, Murdoch writes 'tremendous player with all the Bartolozzi tricks', which accounts for *Incredible Floridas*' multiphonics, which Meale had already used in *Cicada* (1969).
55 Meale had recently been signed to Universal Edition by Bill Colleran.
56 Murdoch to Meale, undated letter, Papers of James Murdoch, Box 24. In a letter to Banks, dated 27 June 1971, Deborah Maguire, Peter Sculthorpe's assistant, wrote:

> We loved your letter and all the news, and Peter wants to thank you particularly for your thoughts on *Tabuh Tabuhan* [...] in fact, Peter didn't want that work performed at that concert; he felt it wasn't exactly a 'Fires of London scene' to quote him; whereas his *Dream* would have been just the thing. (Papers of Don Banks, Box 36)

In a letter sent to Sculthorpe, dated 29 April 1971, Banks wrote:

> The programme for Australia was announced by the ISCM here as Meale, Butterley and Maxwell Davies! I was prepared to flip about the last bit, as I know that Max had been vetoing works submitted by the Australia [*sic*] ISCM. (not good enough to be performed by *his* group 'The Fires of London'). Donald [Peart] asked me

to stand-by with alternate suggestions for a performing group as he couldn't straighten things out with Stephen Plaistow and Jamie [Murdoch]. I saw him briefly on Sunday and he said that Australia now had a programme of 90 minutes as your piece 'Tabu Tabuhan' [*sic*] had been agreed to. I should bloody well say so! (Papers of Peter Sculthorpe, Box 22)

57 Meale to Murdoch, 20 August 1966, Papers of James Murdoch, Box 24.
58 In Meale's programme note he writes: 'It [...] seemed to me that his four voyages of discovery could be used symbolically to describe the adventure of living' (Papers of Richard Meale, Box 34). For an account of the culture of the arts at the time, its association with drug use in Sydney's Kings Cross, and Richard Meale, see: Jim Sharman, *Blood and Tinsel: A Memoir* (Melbourne: The Miegunyah Press, 2008), 89–92; and especially John Stapleton, *Hunting the Famous* (Blackbutt, NSW: A Sense of Place Publishing, 2013).
59 Arthur Rimbaud, *Collected Poems*, trans. Oliver Bernard (Harmondsworth, UK: Penguin, 1962), 168.
60 Papers of Richard Meale, Box 34.
61 The use of an exposed piano flourish as a marker of structure is also found in *Clouds Now and Then*: bb. 7–8; bb. 23–4; bb. 38–9.
62 The beginning is reminiscent of the start of Berg's Violin Concerto, which brings together serial, dodecaphonic and tonal (triadic) arpeggios. See Anthony Pople, *Berg: Violin Concerto* (Cambridge: Cambridge University Press, 2012). Meale could have read about Berg's Violin Concerto in Josef Rufer, *Composition with Twelve Notes Related Only to One Another*, trans. Humphrey Searle (London: Barrie & Rockliff, 1954), 103ff.
63 'One day I'll tell your embryonic births' ('Vowels', in *Arthur Rimbaud: Collected Poems*, trans. Martin Sorrell (Oxford: Oxford University Press, 2001), 135).
64 Here, as is often the case for Meale's music, order is not important, and the pitches in the opening two phrases are considered as an unfolding structure. Indeed, a significant part of what hides the composition's triadic workings is the obfuscation that comes from a slowly evolving field.
65 See Jessie Fillerup, 'Eternity in Each Moment: Temporal Strategies in Ravel's "Le Gibet"', *Music Theory Online* 19, no. 1 (2013).
66 The movement's repetitive piano chords are evocative of the poem that gives the movement its title, and the poem's call to dinner. ('Hunger', *Arthur Rimbaud: Collected Poems*, 193).
67 Meale to Murdoch, 25 June 1965, Papers of James Murdoch, Box 24; Meale's emphasis.
68 See Osmond Smith, '*Temps perdu*: Aldo Clementi and the Eclipse of Music as Praxis', in Heile, *The Modernist Legacy*, 129. It seems likely that Meale had heard Davies's *Missa super l'homme armé* by this time, and responded by writing a piece that, like Davies's work, also gradually reveals its sources.
69 Meale would have known Cage's work well, since Butterley performed it frequently.
70 '[T]he sonata is a piece for instruments, especially the violin, of a serious and artful nature, in which adagios and allegros alternate' (Sandra Mangsen, 'Sonata: Baroque', *Grove Music Online*).
71 The fifth and rising motif is reminiscent of Debussy's 'Des pas sur la neige'.
72 The material in Meale's hand appears to be analytical, rather than precompositional, reconstructing his procedures.

73 'When the world has been reduced to a single dark wood for our four astonished eyes, – to a beach for two faithful children, – to a house of music for our manifest sympathy, – I shall find you.' ('Phrases', *Arthur Rimbaud: Collected Poems*, 272).
74 Debussy's Prelude Book 2, No. 6 is in the right key, and the earlier dance keeps it within the work's locus, even if it is faster than Meale's fourth movement, and the chords are not all major. Book 2, No. 10 and Book 1, No. 10, with their arches, are also relevant. An equally obvious precursor is Messiaen's piano music, especially the slow chordal sections of the *Vingt regards*.
75 Papers of Richard Meale, Folder 139.
76 Papers of Richard Meale, Series 3, Folder 139.
77 'The lightning comes back to the king-post. From the two ends of the room, scenes of some sort, harmonic risers join' (Rimbaud, *Collected Poems*, 265–6).
78 One of the problems encountered by Aitken ('Richard Meale') is in trying to pin 'Interludes' to alchemy. He writes that the movement 'refers to poems involved with alchemy from Rimbaud's *Les Illuminations*' (112). 'Interludes' responds to three poems: 'Phrases', 'Veillées', and 'Génie', none of which are explicitly alchemical.

In an early programme note for the piece, Meale mentions Enid Starkie (Papers of Richard Meale, Box 34). Cecil Hackett writes that: 'Enid Starkie, who tended to overstress the importance of alchemy, as others have drugs, in Rimbaud's poetry, saw in "Fleurs" imagery borrowed from books of magic and alchemy, the term "flower" being, for the alchemists, "the pure substance in the metal, the spirit of matter"' (Cecil Hackett, *Rimbaud: A Critical Introduction* (Cambridge: Cambridge University Press, 1981), 60–1). It is also possible that Meale read her work on André Gide, whose texts had been set by Milhaud. Meale met Milhaud in his early travels, and found the encounter disappointing: 'not [a] terribly important man today', 'a little passé' (Meale, 'Richard Meale Interview from 1965 on ABC Radio's "Away from It All"', *Meale Not at 80*, ABC podcast, 30 August 2012).

It may be that Aitken took the idea of alchemy from Vincent Plush, whose 1972 programme note explains the section as follows:

> The *Second Interlude* opens disarmingly with simple diatonic piano chords. This menacing superficiality gradually dissolves as it passes through three critical stages of alchemy symbolized by the 'magic' interweavings of a twelve-tone row. With the *Second Sonata* we are abruptly shaken from this hypnotic trance; our previous sensations are methodically repudiated. (Papers of Richard Meale, Box 1)

And Plush based this on Meale, whose article in *The Listener* ('Richard Meale Writes about Rimbaud, Australia and His Own Music', *The Listener*, 24 June 1971, 830) had described the Second Interlude in this way: 'passes through three critical stages of alchemy, symbolised by "magic" interweavings of a 12-note row'. (See the letter from Plush, 4 July 1972, Papers of Richard Meale, Box 1.)
79 See Heile, '*Weltmusik* and the Globalization of New Music', in Heile, *The Modernist Legacy*.
80 The tonal music in *Incredible Floridas* prompts the reverse of Keller's question about Schoenberg's work: 'Why, then, don't the *avant-couriers* who praise the piece as one of Schoenberg's greatest […] take note of the outbreak of tonality […]?' (Keller, quoted in Arnold Whittall, *Exploring Twentieth-Century Music: Tradition and Innovation* (Cambridge: Cambridge University Press, 2003). 76.)
81 Meale, 'Richard Meale Interviewed by Hazel de Berg in the Hazel de Berg Collection' (National Library of Australia, 1965), Oral TRC 1/174.

82 Meale, 'Away from It All', 14'45".
83 Bill Colleran to Meale, 17 February 1975, Papers of James Murdoch, Box 24.
84 Worrall to Murdoch, 11 February 1976, Papers of James Murdoch, Box 24.
85 Michael Hannan, *The Music of Richard Meale* (Kingsgrove: Wildbird Music, 2014), 71.
86 Papers of Richard Meale, Box 14.
87 Papers of Richard Meale, Box 14.
88 *Unfold* [Audio recording] (Move Records, MD3371, 2015).
89 Papers of Richard Meale, Box 14.
90 Arnold Whittall, *The Cambridge Introduction to Serialism* (Cambridge: Cambridge University Press, 2008), 277.
91 Stephen Downes, *Music and Decadence in European Modernism* (Cambridge: Cambridge University Press, 2010), 1.
92 Quoted in Karin Bauer, *Adorno's Nietzschean Narratives: Critiques of Ideology, Readings of Wagner* (Albany: State University of New York Press, 1999), 130.
93 Meale, 'Richard Meale Interviewed by Hazel de Berg', 6.
94 Preface to the score.
95 Meale, Liner note, *Plateau for Wind Quintet* [Audio recording] (EMI Record No. OASD7565, 1972).

Chapter 7

1 This part of the chapter is published in a slightly different form as 'Singing Seahorses', *Southerly* 75, no. 1 (2015): 114–32. It traces a different path through similar material to that published in chapter 4 of my *The Music of David Lumsdaine* (Aldershot: Ashgate, 2012) (a book implicitly about Australian Music and modernism). It is intended as a transformation of somewhat familiar territory, following a new, literary line, to explain a section of the composition not addressed in my earlier work.
2 Porter in Banks, 16 August 1968, Papers of Don Banks, MS6830, National Library of Australia, Folio 8. Elsewhere in the letter Porter writes: 'I am a total reactionary about Stockhausen. I've heard it [*Kontakte*, 1959–60] three times now and loathed it each time. But I know you and David [Lumsdaine] admire it. An American told me that Stockhausen was a true poet. Perhaps that's why he's not a musician.'
3 Michael Hall, *The Music of David Lumsdaine* (Todmorden: Arc Publications, 2004), 14.
4 Porter also wrote a poem for Lumsdaine's twenty-third birthday titled 'Exit, Pursued by a Bear' (a different poem from the one published later under the same title).
5 In this personal identification with discovery, and its use of Eyre's diaries, Lumsdaine's *Aria for Edward John* relates to Francis Webb's *Eyre All Alone*. Although Lumsdaine does not share Webb's spiritual journey, nor does the music embody Eyre's voice (since the music is sung by a soprano) nevertheless the work stands alongside Webb's poetry, and White's novels, as a significant work in postcolonial Australia. See: Bill Ashcroft, *The Gimbals of Unease: The Poetry of Francis Webb* (Nedlands, Western Australia: Centre for the Study of Australian Literature, 1996); Bill Ashcroft, Gareth Griffiths and Helen Tiffin, *The Empire Writes Back: Theory and Practice in Post-Colonial Literatures* (London: Routledge, 1989).
6 *Oxford English Dictionary*, 'air' n.1.

7   Lumsdaine's first return to Australia, following Australia's withdrawal from Vietnam, was in 1973. Porter was away from Australia for the same length of time, from 1954 to 1974.
8   Peter Porter quoted in Hall, *The Music of David Lumsdaine*, 26. The elongated speech in Seiber's *Three Fragments from 'A Portrait of the Artist as a Young Man'* (1956–7) could almost be describing Eyre: 'he raised his eyes toward the slow-drifting clouds, dappled and seaborne. They were voyaging across the deserts of the sky, a host of nomads on the march, voyaging high over Ireland, westward bound.' *Three Fragments* is for speaker, mixed chorus and instrumental ensemble; like Lumsdaine's *Aria for Edward John Eyre*, it, too, begins with humming rather than texted song.
9   For a more general discussion of temporality in this composition, see Andrew Schultz, 'Temporality in the Music of David Lumsdaine', *Studies in Music* 25 (1991): 95–101.
10 Ibid.
11 Still more correspondence that is not in a public collection surely exists between Porter and the music critic Roger Covell, with whom he also shared a flat in London in the early 1950s.
12 Don Banks, *Tirade* (London: Schott, 1968).
13 Ibid.
14 Porter to Banks, 8 December 1967, Papers of Don Banks, Box 28.
15 Ibid.
16 Vincent Plush, 'Roger Covell: The Go-Between', *Context* 41 (2016): 45–58.
17 Murdoch to John Winther (General Manager of the Australian Opera), 30 April 1976, Papers of James Murdoch, MS 8372, National Library of Australia, Box 24.
18 White's *Voss* (1957) is a novel based on the nineteenth-century explorer and naturalist Ludwig Leichardt, who explored Australia's north-east. In White's novel, Voss travels across the Australian continent, and for his adaption, Lumsdaine draws on the actual diaries of another nineteenth-century explorer, Edward John Eyre, who travelled from east to west across the continent. Of particular significance to Lumsdaine's work is the relationship between Voss and Laura Trevelyan, who remains in Sydney.
19 Patrick White 'The Prodigal Son', in *Patrick White Speaks* (London: Jonathan Cape Ltd, 1989), 15–16. See also White, *Flaws in the Glass* (London: Vintage, 1998), 83, 103.
20 Denise Levertov, *Relearning the Alphabet* (New York: New Directions Publishing, 1970). See David Lumsdaine, 'A Tree Telling of Orpheus', *David Lumsdaine* www.davidlumsdaine.org.uk/pn.php?pfile=A_tree_telling_of_Orpheus.html accessed 14 March 2015.
21 Edward John Eyre, *Journals of Expeditions of Discovery into Central Australia, and Overland from Adelaide to King George's Sound, in the years 1840–1* http://ebooks.adelaide.edu.au/e/eyre/edward_john/e98j/ accessed 20 March 2015.
22 Isa. xliii, 19.
23 White, *Riders in the Chariot* (London, Vintage Classics, 1996), 5.
24 Lumsdaine emphasizes multiplicity in a variety of ways in his treatment of 'alone'. If 'Wylie's non-existence, both on Eyre's journey and in the poem, is deeply indicative of the exclusion of the indigenous inhabitant' (Ashcroft, *The Gimbals of Unease*, 149), then Lumsdaine's speakers make that non-existence a topic, to criticize the colonial attitude of solitude. Firstly the soprano sings the text, rather than Eyre (since this is a work for solo soprano). Secondly the two speakers read texts that fragment each other's variation on Eyre's diaries. The first speaker reads: 'We, we were now alone,

myself, my overseer, and 3 native boys' and the second speaker reads 'We were now alone, my myself'. As I have argued (Hooper, *The Music of David Lumsdaine*), the treatment of this passage of text in its multiple forms, sung and variously spoken, is part of the composition's play of sense and nonsense, such that semantic failure of textual lines layers with the music's multiplicities.

25 Hall, *The Music of David Lumsdaine*, 44.
26 For the construction of this matrix, see Hooper, *The Music of David Lumsdaine*, 63–5.
27 Lumsdaine, 'Aria for Edward John Eyre: This Is My Myth of the Making of Aria' www.davidlumsdaine.org.uk/pn.php?pfile=Aria_Myth.html accessed 24 March 2015.
28 It is worth remembering that the term 'tonality' was in the nineteenth century an 'attempt to define contemporary European music in relation to the distinct tonal conceptions of early music on the one hand and non-Western music on the other – that is, in terms of its temporal and spatial others' (Nicholas Cook, 'Classical Music and the Politics of Space', in Georgina Born (ed.), *Music Sound and Space* (Cambridge: Cambridge University Press, 2013), 228).
29 See Jean-Jacques Nattiez, 'On Reading Boulez', in Nattiez (ed.), *Orientations* (London: Faber & Faber, 1986), 17–18.
30 See Raymond Monelle, *The Musical Topic: Hunt, Military, Pastoral* (Bloomington: Indiana University Press, 2006).
31 The Committee of 100 was a pacifist group founded in 1960, notable for its civil disobedience campaigns against nuclear weapons.
32 Raymond Monelle, *The Sense of Music* (Princeton: Princeton University Press, 2000) 46.
33 Ibid., 60.
34 Lumsdaine, *Aria for Edward John Eyre* (York: University of York Music Press, 1997), 91; the emphasis is Lumsdaine's.
35 All definitions quoted from the *Oxford English Dictionary*.
36 Lumsdaine, 'My Myth of the Making of Aria'.
37 Monelle, *The Musical Topic*, 24.
38 Porter to Lumsdaine, Papers of David Lumsdaine, MS Acc08/98, National Library of Australia. The problems of the deployment of serialism – which by this period hovers between being a technique of ongoing exploration and ossifying orthodoxy – is, in *Kelly Ground*, played out as a paradox of incorporation/disincorporation (Jacques Rancière, *The Politics of Aesthetics*, trans. Gabriel Rockhill (London: Continuum, 2004), 57) to express the social exclusion/inclusion of Kelly and his family, as well as to comment on the paradoxical deployment of the myth of Kelly for the formation of Australianness, a paradox that includes Lumsdaine's repetition of that myth. In these two compositions alone Lumsdaine demonstrates the viability of 'Australian History' for the formation of new work. The complexities of these two works, and the additional complications of their relation to Lumsdaine's own history, also goes to the aspect of Lumsdaine's music that is about the future. *Kelly Ground* is a work of political protest against capital punishment. Lumsdaine's delaying of his return to Australia until the end of its involvement in the Vietnam War comments on the idea of 'Australia' or being 'Australian' through compositional technique (and indeed, presents us with a narrative of compositional technique). Basing music on Kelly as a myth fragments 'Australia' as the myth itself does, being bound up with sectarianism and imperialism in Ireland/Australia. Similarly, Lumsdaine's transformation of

White's Voss/Ludwig Leichardt into Edward John Eyre presents a far from clear-cut transformation of Prussian/English/Australian identity. Eyre was born in 1815 in Whipsnade, a village two miles south of Dunstable (the composition is (like *Kelly Ground*) based on the metric 'grounds' that Lumsdaine developed from the composer named after the town) and died in 1901, the year of Australian Federation.

39 As we know, 'the monument is not something commemorating a past, it is a bloc of present sensations that owe their preservation only to themselves and that provide the event with the compound that celebrates it. The monument's action is not memory but fabulation.' And in this sense a monument can be 'contained in a few marks or a few lines', as I will argue for Fred Williams (Gilles Deleuze and Félix Guattari, *What Is Philosophy?*, trans. Graham Burchell and Hugh Tomlinson (London: Verso, 1994), 165).

40 'Frederick McCubbin *The Pioneer* 1904', *National Gallery of Victoria* www.ngv.vic.gov.au/frederick-mccubbin-the-pioneer-1904 accessed 7 July 2015.

41 Fredric Jameson, 'The End of Temporality', *Critical Inquiry* 29, no. 4 (2003): 700.

42 Irena Zdanowicz, *Fred Williams: An Australian Vision* (London: British Museum Press, 2003), 20. The quote continues 'interpreting the subject in purely pictorial terms', but the notion of the 'subject' in Williams's 'landscapes' is not straightforward, as I address later in the chapter. This formal exploration is 'distinctly Japanese in character'. Also see James Gleeson, 'James Gleeson Interviews: Fred Williams', 1978 http://nga.gov.au/Research/Gleeson/pdf/Williams.pdf accessed 7 July 2015.

43 Zdanowicz, *Fred Williams*, 20.

44 Gleeson, 'James Gleeson Interviews: Fred Williams.'

45 Louis Althusser, *Lenin and Philosophy and Other Essays*, trans. Ben Brewster (New York: Monthly Review Press, 1971), 230.

46 For Williams and Rembrandt, see Zdanowicz, *Fred Williams*, 17.

47 Paul Haefliger, 'Russell Drysdale: *a* Dialogue, Paul Haefliger', in *Drysdale* (Sydney: Ure Smith, 1960), 5.

48 Ibid., 6.

49 Ibid., 7; my emphasis.

50 Ibid., 9.

51 Ibid., 10.

52 Alan Ross, 'Preface', *Catalogue of an Exhibition of Paintings and Drawings by Russell Drysdale* (London: The Leicester Galleries, 1965).

53 Ibid. He misquotes Robert Hughes, *The Art of Australia* (Ringwood: Penguin Books, 1970; first published 1966), 191.

54 Ross, 'Preface'. Also see Hughes, *The Art of Australia*, 191.

55 Ross, 'Preface'.

56 Ibid.

57 Hughes, *The Art of Australia*, 195.

58 Haefliger, 'Russell Drysdale', 9.

59 Ibid., 7.

60 Hughes, *The Art of Australia*, 191.

61 'Red Landscape', *Russell Drysdale* www.abc.net.au/arts/drysdale/paintings/71.htm accessed 29 June 2015.

62 Michael Hannan, liner note, *Austral String Quartet* [Audio recording] (EMI: EMI OASD7563, 1975).

63 Drysdale, 'Descriptive Note', quoted in 'Red Landscape'.

64 Sutherland was nine years Drysdale's elder and Drysdale attended an exhibition of Sutherland's work in London in 1938.
65 Simon Pierse, *Australian Art and Artists in London, 1950–1965: An Antipodean Summer* (Farnham: Ashgate, 2012), 18. The argument is the same as that which Covell makes about *musique concrète* (Roger Covell, *Australia's Music: Themes of a New Society* (Melbourne: Sun Books, 1967), 6.)
66 Quoted in Martin Hammer, *Bacon and Sutherland: Patterns of Affinity in British Culture of the 1940s* (New Haven: Yale University Press, 2005), 13.
67 Quoted in ibid.
68 Ibid., 81–2.
69 Hughes, *The Art of Australia*, 194.
70 Hammer, *Bacon and Sutherland*, 68. In this painting the horizon is both horizontal and vertical.
71 Letters from Drysdale to Sculthorpe, 1 February 1966, 28 September 1966, Papers of Peter Sculthorpe, MS 9676, National Library of Australia, Box 22.
72 Hughes, *The Art of Australia*, 194.
73 Hammer, *Bacon and Sutherland*, 68.
74 Drysdale's *The Rabbiters* – which appears on the cover of the *Australian Festival of Music* (Volume 3), a collection of Australian music – is an inverted form of Sutherland's *Gorse on Sea Wall*.
75 'Abandon the question "What do they represent" and at once his pictures become moving lyrical Eric Newton (writing in 1940) quoted in Hammer, *Bacon and Sutherland*, 70.
76 Graeme Skinner, *Peter Sculthorpe: The Making of an Australian Composer* (Sydney: University of New South Wales Press, 2007), 465.
77 Ibid.
78 Michael Hannan and Peter Sculthorpe, 'Rites of Passage', *Music Now* 2, no. 2 (1974): 13–14.
79 Geoffrey Dutton, *Russell Drysdale* (London: Thames & Hudson, 1964), 10.
80 Michael Hannan, 'The Music of Peter Sculthorpe: An Analytical Study with Particular Reference to Those Social and Other Cultural Forces Which Have Shaped the Development of an Australian Vision', PhD diss. (The University of Sydney, 1979), 83.
81 Dutton, *Russell Drysdale*, 10.
82 Ibid., 11.
83 Hughes, *The Art of Australia*, 192.
84 As I have argued through Williams and McCubbin, Hannan's claim that 'With modern painters like Nolan and Drysdale the break with Europe appears to be complete' (Hannan, *Peter Sculthorpe: His Music and Ideas 1929–1979* (St Lucia: University of Queensland Press, 1982), 129) is fundamentally not correct.
85 Craig McGregor, David Beal, David Moore and Harry Williamson, *In the Making* (Melbourne: Thomas Nelson, 1969), 101.
86 Indeed, Drysdale's painting is strikingly similar in composition to a photograph of Dallas, South Dakota, taken in 1936, and which became one of the iconic images of the 'Dust Bowl' period. Generally, this suggests that Drysdale's vision of Australia was informed by the photographs of North America taken during the period in which he was honing his ideas about how to depict Australia. Specifically, the two images are so close as to suggest that Drysdale's painting of Lake Callabonna was modelled on the photograph of Dallas.

87 Ibid.
88 Skinner, *Peter Sculthorpe*, 477.
89 Patrick McCaughey, *Fred Williams* (Kensington: Bay Books, 1980), 15.
90 Ibid., 19.
91 'Peter Sculthorpe: Obituary', *The Telegraph*, 10 August 2014 www.telegraph.co.uk/news/obituaries/11024382/Peter-Sculthorpe-obituary.html. It is in the relation between Sculthorpe and Williams, sound and paint, that Sculthorpe's connection to Panderecki's music makes most sense, being about *sound*.
92 Quoted in McCaughey, *Fred Williams*, 138.
93 Fred Williams, 'My Garden, 1965–1967', Art Gallery of NSW (speaking in 1969) http://www.artgallery.nsw.gov.au/collection/works/165.1999/ accessed 19 June 2015.
94 McCaughey, *Fred Williams*, 23.
95 Williams, 'My Garden'.
96 Sculthorpe, *Red Landscape* (London: Faber Music, 1966), 1.
97 The Austral Quartet's 1971 recording (on EMI, OASD 7563) is slower than later recordings, such as by the Kronos Quartet in 1986 (*Kronos Quartet*, Nonesuch, 79111). It is likely that the Allegri Quartet, who premiered the work (in London), played from a similar score to that used by the Austral Quartet.
98 'Directions for Performance', from the performing score; private collection.
99 Skinner, *Peter Sculthorpe*, 481. See Colin McPhee, *Music in Bali: A Study of Form and Instrumental Organization in Balinese Orchestral Music* (New York: Da Capo Press, 1976; first published 1966), chapter 17.
100 Hannan, *Peter Sculthorpe*, 73 n9.
101 Sculthorpe's annotations to Hazelwood's part (Hazelwood was the first violinist of the Austral Quartet); private collection.
102 In the published score, this corresponds to two bars after Figure 6, in the second movement.
103 Manuscript, private collection.
104 Jeanell Carrigan, 'Towards an Australian Style: On the Relationship between the Australian Landscape and Natural Environment and the Music of Peter Sculthorpe and Ross Edwards', MMus diss. (University of Queensland, 1994).
105 Ibid., 31.
106 Some of Sculthorpe's pieces do invite such narratives, such as *Port Essington* (1977).
107 Naomi Cumming, 'Encountering *Mangrove*: An Essay in Signification', *Australasian Music Research* 1 (1996): 193–229.
108 Cumming quotes Sculthorpe in conversation with Jill Sykes ('Sculthorpe at Fifty', *The Sydney Morning Herald*, Saturday 28 April 1979, 'The Good Weekend', 15), saying: 'I think the Iain Fairweather painting called Mangrove in Adelaide is perhaps his greatest … Maybe mangroves are in the air – I heard Fred Williams is also painting them' (Williams painted *Mangrove Rootlings* in 1973).
109 John Peterson, *The Music of Peter Sculthorpe* (Kingsgrove: Wildbird Music, 2014), 59.
110 Sculthorpe's depiction of the horizon as a drone, like William's straight-line horizontal, is an aesthetically important motif.
111 Programme note for *Landscape II* www.fabermusic.com/repertoire/landscape-ii-1250 accessed 4 November 2016.
112 Such an analysis might return us to some of the ethical arguments around Sculthorpe's music. Jonathan Paget, for example, criticizes Sculthorpe's use of

Aboriginal melodies, and raises the importance of collaboration in negotiating the rights of ownership, which, inter alia, emphasizes the process of (co-)composing, in contrast to Sculthorpe finding his materials in 'books and recordings' (Jonathan Paget, 'Has Sculthorpe Misappropriated Indigenous Melodies?' *Musicology Australia* 35, no. 1 (2013): 90). The extent of that re-presentation, however, is difficult to discern in 'non-dramatic' music, and Cumming's conclusions for *Mangrove* are not directly applicable to *Landscape II*, even if they share similar sources. I agree with Paget when he writes that: 'the specific Indigenous melodic material adopted (and adapted) in Sculthorpe's music is often of the most abstract kind, and typically echoes motives already contained in his earlier pieces' (ibid., 109). The transformations, too, are often motivic/geometric, rather than figural/representational. And I also agree with Cumming that 'To hear *Mangrove* as aesthetically enclosed, ignoring the generic signification of the indigenous, is to remain unaware of the political values hidden in its "abstract" rhythmic forms' (Cumming, 'Encountering *Mangrove*', 228). When Paget writes that 'he [Sculthorpe] has striven to create a synthesis between diverse musical influences' (Paget, 'Has Sculthorpe Misappropriated Indigenous Melodies?' 109), Paget speaks of the output as a whole, forming a narrative that, again, stems from the paucity of drama in specific works (rather than its determinate absence), and this emphasis continues unnecessarily to reinforce the importance of Sculthorpe himself (the lonely discourse again), rather than Sculthorpe in relation to other artists. Similarly, I am less convinced that 'The way that Sculthorpe allows Indigenous music to shape and influence his style could be construed as a reversal of the colonial power structures', since that argument, too, relies on a narrative transformation that is difficult to generalize. This is hardly a criticism of Paget's article – which specifically seeks to compare multiple works, and to bring their similarities and differences together, with Sculthorpe as an 'icon' of Australian Music (ibid., 86) – so much as a reminder that neither 'Sculthorpe' nor 'the landscape' need be considered as uniform and coherent, since they need not be synonymous with a desire for a uniform and coherent nationalism. Much of the music is marked by stark difference and significant inconsistency.

113 See Skinner, *Peter Sculthorpe*, 553–4.
114 Hannan, 'The Music of Peter Sculthorpe', 98.
115 Ibid., and Diana Blom ('An Analysis of *Music for Japan* by Peter Sculthorpe', MMus diss. (University of Sydney, 1972), 56ff), which is thorough in its explication of Sculthorpe's use of the row.
116 See Jeannie Ma Guerrero, 'Serial Intervention in Nono's *Il canto sospeso*', *Music Theory Online* 12, no. 1 (2006).
117 The same shape is found in much of Roger Smalley's music, and Christopher Mark's footnote to Smalley's *The Song of the Highest Tower* connects the shape to Birtwistle's *Chorales* (1962–3) and *Nomos* (1968), which suggests at least the possibility of Sculthorpe encountering the idea through a British source (Mark, *The Music of Roger Smalley* (Aldershot: Ashgate, 2012), 211).
118 Joel Crotty, 'Onshore, Offshore, Unsure: Expo '70 and Peter Sculthorpe's Journey with Music from Japan', *Musicology Australia* 37, no. 2 (2015): 260. Blom, *An Analysis of Music for Japan*.
119 Peterson, *The Music of Peter Sculthorpe*, 142. See Hannan, 'The Music of Peter Sculthorpe', 121.
120 Peterson, *The Music of Peter Sculthorpe*, 142.

121 See Hannan, *Peter Sculthorpe*, 56–7; and also Rachel Campbell, 'Peter Sculthorpe's *Irkanda* Period, 1954–65: Nationalism, "Aboriginality," and Landscape', PhD diss. (The University of Sydney, 2014), 309ff.
122 Hannan, *Peter Sculthorpe*, 55; also see Ian Cudgley, quoted in Campbell, *Peter Sculthorpe's Irkanda Period*, 316.
123 Skinner, 'Booklet Essay', *The ABC Recordings* (ABC Classics 481 1293, 2014), 34.
124 Gleeson, 'James Gleeson Interviews: Fred Williams'.
125 She cites James Mollison, *A Singular Vision: The Art of Fred Williams* (Canberra: Australian National Gallery, 1989), 139–41.
126 Anne Gray, 'Art and Environment', in Deryck M. Schreuder and Stuart Ward (eds), *Australia's Empire* (Oxford: Oxford University Press, 2008), 131–2.
127 Ibid., 132.
128 Don Banks to Peter Porter, 22 June 1972, Peter Porter, Papers of Peter Porter, MS 6640, National Library of Australia, Box 62.
129 Lumsdaine, Report, 25 September 1973, Papers of Don Banks, Box 35.

Bibliography

Adams, Stephen, 'Vale Peter Sculthorpe [Radio broadcast], *ABC Classic FM*, 8 August 2014 www.abc.net.au/classic/content/2014/08/08/4056508.htm.
Adkins, Monty and Michael Russ (eds), *The Roberto Gerhard Companion* (Aldershot: Ashgate, 2013).
Adlington, Robert, *The Music of Harrison Birtwistle* (Cambridge: Cambridge University Press, 2000).
Aitken, Thomas, 'Richard Meale: A Stylistic Survey', MMus diss. (University of Queensland, 1975).
Albright, Daniel, 'Yeats and Modernism', in Marjorie Howes and John Kelly (eds), *Cambridge Companion to W. B. Yeats* (Cambridge: Cambridge University Press, 2006), 59–76.
Alegant, Brian, *The Twelve-Tone Music of Luigi Dallapiccola* (Rochester: University of Rochester Press, 2010).
Althusser, Louis, *Lenin and Philosophy and Other Essays*, trans. Ben Brewster (New York: Monthly Review Press, 1971).
Ashcroft, Bill, *The Gimbals of Unease: The Poetry of Francis Webb* (Nedlands, Western Australia: Centre for the Study of Australian Literature, 1996).
Ashcroft, Bill, Gareth Griffiths and Helen Tiffin, *The Empire Writes Back: Theory and Practice in Post-Colonial Literatures* (London: Routledge, 1989).
Ashcroft, Bill and John Salter, 'Modernism's Empire: Australia and the Cultural Imperialism of Style', in Howard J. Booth and Nigel Rigby (eds), *Modernism and Empire: Writing and British Coloniality, 1890–1940* (Manchester: Manchester University Press, 2000), 292–334.
Atherton, David (ed.), *The London Sinfonietta: The Complete Instrumental and Chamber Music of Arnold Schoenberg and Roberto Gerhard* (London: Sinfonietta Productions Limited, 1973).
Australian Festival of Music, Volume 3 [Audio recording] (Festival Records SFC80020, 1972).
Balaji, Murali and Tina Worawongs, 'The New Suzie Wong: Normative Assumptions of White Male and Asian Female Relationships', *Communication, Culture and Critique* 3 (2010): 224–41.
Banks, Don, 'Donald Banks Interviewed by Hazel de Berg in the Hazel de Berg Collection' (National Library of Australia, 1972), Oral TRC 1/626.
Banks, Don, Papers of Don Banks, MS6830, National Library of Australia.
Banks, Don, *Tirade* (London: Schott, 1968).
Bauer, Karin, *Adorno's Nietzschean Narratives: Critiques of Ideology, Readings of Wagner* (Albany: State University of New York Press, 1999).
Beck, Deborah, *Set in Stone: A History of the Cell Block Theatre* (Sydney: University of New South Wales Press, 2011).
Bell, Lynne, 'Composition for Oboe – and Transistor Radio', *Sydney Morning Herald*, 5 April 1970, 102.

Bennett, Gwen, *More than Music: The Life and Work of Kenneth W Tribe AC* (Sydney: Australian Music Centre, 2011).
Bent, Ian, *Music Analysis in the Nineteenth Century: Fugue, Form, and Style* (Cambridge: Cambridge University Press, 1994).
Bident, Christophe, 'Blanchot, Leiris', *COLLOQUY: Text, Theory, Critique* 10 (2005): 8–21.
Blom, Diana, 'An Analysis of *Music for Japan* by Peter Sculthorpe', MMus diss. (University of Sydney, 1972).
Boulez, Pierre, *Boulez on Music Today*, trans. Susan Bradshaw and Richard Rodney Bennett (London: Faber & Faber, 1971).
Boulez, Pierre, 'Frozen Perfection', *Music and Musicians* 16 (1968): 30–54.
Boyd, Anne, 'Richard Meale's *Homage to Garcia Lorca*', *Music Now* 1, no. 1 (1969): 16–24.
Brennan, Christopher J., *Poems (1913)* (Sydney: Sydney University Press, 1972).
Brennan, Gail, 'They Said We'd Never Make It: The Music of Australia', *Sydney Morning Herald*, 24 September 1988, 81.
Brett, Philip, 'Eros and Orientalism in Britten's Operas', in Philip Brett, Elizabeth Wood and Gary C. Thomas (eds), *Queering the Pitch: The New Gay and Lesbian Musicology* (New York: Routledge, 1994).
Brett, Philip, 'Musicality, Essentialism and the Closet', in Philip Brett, Elizabeth Wood and Gary C. Thomas (eds), *Queering the Pitch: The New Gay and Lesbian Musicology* (New York: Routledge, 1994).
Bright, Ann, 'Pitch and Time Structure in *Clouds Now and Then*', *Miscellanea Musicologica* 10 (1979): 82–92.
Brodbeck, David, *Brahms: Symphony No. 1* (Cambridge: Cambridge Music Handbooks, 1997).
Brown, Stephen, 'Dual Interval Space in Twentieth-Century Music', *Music Theory Spectrum*, 25, no. 1 (2003): 35–57.
Brown, Stephen, 'IC1/IC5 Interaction in the Music of Shostakovich', *Musical Analysis* 28, nos. 2–3 (2009): 185–220.
Brown, Stephen, 'Some Instances of Ic1/Ic5 Interaction in Post-Tonal Music (and Their Tonnetz Representations)', *Gamut: The Online Journal of the Music Theory Society* 6, no. 2 (2013): article 3. Available online: http://trace.tennessee.edu/gamut/vol6/iss2/3.
Bürger, Peter, *Theory of the Avant-Garde* (Manchester: Manchester University Press, 1984).
Butterley, Nigel, 'Nigel Butterley Interviewed by Hazel de Berg in the Hazel de Berg Collection' (National Library of Australia, 1967), Oral TRC 1/303–305.
Butterley, Nigel, *String Quartet* (Sydney: Albert Edition).
Butterley, Nigel, The Papers of Nigel Butterley, MS Acc07.033. National Library of Australia.
Butterley, Nigel, The Papers of Nigel Butterley, MS Acc09.081, National Library of Australia.
Butterley, Nigel, 'Turning Silence into Sound: Composers Talk about Inspiration', 2MBS FM, *HSC*. Available online: https://webarchive.nla.gov.au/awa/20140126065839/http://www.hsc.csu.edu.au/music/composition/tips/inspiration/comp_tips_inspiration.htm (accessed 7 October 2014).
Butterley, Nigel, *Words into Music: A Composer's Response to Poetry* (Armidale: University of New England, 1999).
Callaway, Frank and David Tunley (eds), *Australian Composition in the Twentieth Century* (Melbourne: Oxford University Press), 1978.

Campbell, Rachel, 'Peter Sculthorpe's *Irkanda* Period, 1954–65: Nationalism, "Aboriginality", and Landscape', PhD diss. (The University of Sydney, 2014).

Carrigan, Jeanell, 'Towards an Australian Style: On the Relationship between the Australian Landscape and Natural Environment and the Music of Peter Sculthorpe and Ross Edwards', MMus diss. (University of Queensland, 1994).

Carroll, Mark, 'Out of the Ordinary: The Quotidian in the Music of Graeme Koehne', *Music and Letters* 95, no. 3 (2014): 429–51.

Carter, David, *Always Almost Modern: Australian Print Cultures and Modernity* (North Melbourne: Australian Scholarly, 2013).

Caws, Mary Ann, *Manifesto: A Century of Isms* (Lincoln: University of Nebraska Press, 2001).

Chowrimootoo, Christopher, '"Britten Minor": Constructing the Modernist Canon', *Twentieth Century Music* 13, no. 2 (2016): 261–90.

Clark, Timothy J., *Farewell to an Idea* (New Haven: Yale University Press, 2001).

Clarke, David, 'Between Hermeneutics and Formalism: The Lento from Tippett's Concerto for Orchestra (or: Music Analysis after Lawrence Kramer)', *Music Analysis* 30, nos. 2–3 (2012): 309–59.

Clarke, David, *The Music and Thought of Michael Tippett* (Cambridge: Cambridge University Press, 2009).

Cloke Tsui, Ho-ning, 'The World around Suzie Wong', MA diss. (University of Hong Kong, 2007). Available online: http://hub.hku.hk/handle/10722/51837 (accessed 10 May 2019).

Cobley, Evelyn, *Temptations of Faust: The Logic of Fascism and Postmodern Archaeologies of Modernity* (Toronto: University of Toronto Press, 2002).

Cole, Hugo, 'Sydney Symphony Orchestra Concert', *The Guardian*, 20 September 1965.

Cole, Teju, 'Postscript: Peter Sculthorpe (1929–2014)', *New Yorker*, 8 August 2014.

'Commonwealth Assistance to Australian Composers', *Australian Journal of Music Education*, 1 (1967): 50.

Conyngham, Barry, '2nd Annual Peggy Glanville-Hicks Address', Sydney Opera House, 13 August 2000. Available online: www.newmusicnetwork.com.au/PGH/BC00.htm (accessed 11 March 2016).

Cook, Nicholas, 'Classical Music and the Politics of Space', in Georgina Born (ed.), *Music Sound and Space* (Cambridge: Cambridge University Press, 2013), 224–38.

Cook, Nicholas and Anthony Pople (eds), *Cambridge History of Twentieth Century Music* (Cambridge: Cambridge University Press, 2004).

Covell, Roger, 'A Meal for the Avant-Garde', *Sydney Morning Herald*, 3 April 1991, 14.

Covell, Roger, 'A Success in Two Ways', *Sydney Morning Herald*, 4 May 1970, 14.

Covell, Roger, *Australia's Music: Themes of a New Society* (Melbourne: Sun Books, 1967).

Covell, Roger, 'Composer Winds Back the Clock', *Sydney Morning Herald*, 8 March 1994, 19.

Covell, Roger, 'Concert at Cell Block', *Sydney Morning Herald*, 16 October 1964, 21.

Covell, Roger, 'Contemporary Concert', *Sydney Morning* Herald, 1 June 1963, 6.

Covell, Roger, 'Dixon, Ferras, Berg and Meale', *Sydney Morning Herald*, 28 July 1965, 13.

Covell, Roger, 'Jazz Put Audience at Ease', *Sydney Morning Herald*, 22 September 1970, 11.

Covell, Roger, 'Mixed-Media Composition', *Sydney Morning Herald*, 24 August 1972, 31.

Covell, Roger, 'Richard Meale: Intuitions of a Solitary Modernist', *Sounds Australian* 20 (1988/9): 5–9.

Croft, John, 'Fields of Rubble: On the Politics of Music after the Postmodern', in Björn Heile (ed.), *The Modernist Legacy: Essays on New Music* (Aldershot: Ashgate, 2009).

Crotty, Joel, 'Onshore, Offshore, Unsure: Expo '70 and Peter Sculthorpe's Journey with Music from Japan', *Musicology Australia* 37, no. 2 (2015): 260.
Crotty, Joel (ed.), *Sounds Australian: Journal of the Australian Music Centre* 41, autumn (1994).
Crotty, Joel, 'Towards an Australian Art-Music Canon', *Quadrant* 55, no. 10 (2011): 91–7.
Cultural Collections, UON Library. Available online: https://uoncc.wordpress.com/2010/04/09/50con/ (accessed 22 August 2016).
Cumming, Naomi, 'Encountering *Mangrove*: An Essay in Signification', *Australasian Music Research* 1 (1996): 193–229.
Dean, Beth and Victor Carell, *Gentle Genius: A Life of John Antill* (Sydney: Akron Press, 1987).
Dean, Brett, Introduction to broadcast by the BBC Symphony Orchestra, *Hear and Now* [Radio broadcast] BBC Radio 3, 6 August 2016.
Deleuze, Gilles and Félix Guattari, *What Is Philosophy?* trans. Graham Burchell and Hugh Tomlinson (London: Verso, 1994).
Downes, Stephen, *Music and Decadence in European Modernism* (Cambridge: Cambridge University Press, 2010).
Dreyfus, Kay, 'In Search of New Waters: Australian Music Studies in the 1990s', in Frank Callaway (ed.), *Essays in Honour of David Evatt Tunley* (University of Western Australia: Callaway International Resource Centre for Music Education, 1995), 155–64.
Drimatis, Joanna Catherine, 'A Hidden Treasure: Symphony No. 1 by Robert Hughes', PhD diss. (University of Adelaide, 2008).
Drysdale, Russell, 'A Descriptive Note by Russell Drysdale', *Catalogue of an Exhibition of Paintings and Drawings by Russell Drysdale* (London: The Leicester Galleries, 1965).
Dudeque, Norton, *Music Theory and Analysis in the Writings of Arnold Schoenberg (1874–1951)* (Aldershot: Ashgate, 2005).
Dunlap, Thomas, 'Remaking the Land: The Acclimatization Movement and Anglo Ideas of Nature', *Journal of World History* 8, no. 2, fall (1997): 303–19.
Dutton, Geoffrey, *Russell Drysdale* (London: Thames and Hudson, 1964).
Earle, Ben, '"The Real Thing – At Last?" Historicizing Humphrey Searle', in Matthew Riley (ed.), *British Music and Modernism, 1895–1960* (Aldershot: Ashgate, 2010), 293–326.
East, Leslie, 'Schoenberg and Gerhard', *Music and Musicians* 22, no. 6 (1974).
Edwards, Deborah, 'Ultra-*moderne*: *Implement blue* and *The Lacquer Room*', in Deborah Edwards and Denise Mimmocchi (eds), *Sydney Moderns: Art for a New World*, 148–53 (Sydney: Art Gallery NSW, 2013).
Edwards, Deborah and Denise Mimmocchi (eds), *Sydney Moderns: Art for a New World* (Sydney: Art Gallery NSW, 2013).
Etter, Ingrid, 'The Man Who Turns Money into Music', *Women's Weekly*, 27 February 1974, 8–9.
'Extrovert Performance of Sydney Orchestra', *The Times*, 20 September 1965.
Eyre, Edward John, *Journals of Expeditions of Discovery into Central Australia, and Overland from Adelaide to King George's Sound, in the Years 1840–1* (Adelaide: The University of Adelaide Library, 2014). Available online: http://ebooks.adelaide.edu.au/e/eyre/edward_john/e98j/ (accessed 20 March 2015).
Fillerup, Jessie, 'Eternity in Each Moment: Temporal Strategies in Ravel's "Le Gibet"', *Music Theory Online* 19, no. 1 (2013).
FitzGerald, Stephen, *Is Australia an Asian Country?* (St Leonards: Allen & Unwin, 1997).

Flora, Reis, Peter Sculthorpe, Margaret Kartomi and Cathy Falk, 'Music and Ethnomusicology in Australia', *Journal of the Asian Studies Association of Australia* 7, no. 2 (1983): 14–24.

Ford, Andrew, 'Peter Sculthorpe, a Composer in Australia', *Inside Story: Current Affairs and Culture from Australia and Beyond*, 11 August 2014 http://insidestory.org.au/peter-sculthorpe-a-composer-in-australia.

Ford, Andrew, *Try Whistling This* (Collingwood: Black Inc., 2012).

Foreman, Lewis (ed.), *British Music Now* (London: Elek Books Limited, 1975).

'Frederick McCubbin *The Pioneer* 1904', National Gallery of Victoria. Available online: https://www.ngv.vic.gov.au/frederick-mccubbin-the-pioneer-1904 (accessed 7 July 2015).

Friedman, Susan Stanford, 'Periodizing Modernism: Postcolonial Modernities and the Space/Time Borders of Modernist Studies', *Modernism/modernity* 13, no. 3 (2006): 425–43.

Frisch, Walter, *Brahms: The Four Symphonies* (New Haven: Yale University Press, 2003).

Gerhard, Roberto, *Gerhard on Music: Selected Writings*, ed. Meirion Bowen (Aldershot: Ashgate, 2000).

Gifford, Helen, Zoe Sweett, Joel Crotty and Aline Scott-Maxwell, 'Composers in the Academy', in John Whiteoak and Aline Scott-Maxwell (eds), *Currency Companion to Music and Dance in Australia* (Sydney: Currency House, 2003), 170.

Gleeson, James, 'James Gleeson Interviews: Fred Williams', 1978. Available online: http://nga.gov.au/Research/Gleeson/pdf/Williams.pdf (accessed 7 July 2015).

'Govt Reshapes Arts Program: Council Named', *Sydney Morning Herald*, 27 January 1973, 2.

Gray, Anne, 'Art and Environment', in Deryck M. Schreuder and Stuart Ward (eds), *Australia's Empire* (Oxford: Oxford University Press, 2008) 103–37.

Green, Clinton, 'The International Society for Contemporary Music in Melbourne: Forerunners, Foundation, and Decline', *Musicology Australia* 32, no. 2 (2010): 243–63.

Greene, Richard, *Edith Sitwell: Avant Garde Poet, English Genius* (London: Hachette Digital, 2011).

Grimley, Daniel, *Carl Nielsen and the Idea of Modernism* (Woodbridge: The Boydell Press, 2011).

Guerrero, Jeannie Ma, 'Serial Intervention in Nono's *Il canto sospeso*', *Music Theory Online*, 12, no. 1 (2006).

Gyger, Elliott, 'Nigel Butterley and the Problem That Wasn't', *Resonate Magazine* (2008). Available online: www.australianmusiccentre.com.au/article/nigel-butterley-and-the-problem-that-wasn-t.

Gyger, Elliott, *The Music of Nigel Butterley* (Kingsgrove: Wildbird Music, 2015).

Hackett, Cecil, *Rimbaud: A Critical Introduction* (Cambridge: Cambridge University Press, 1981).

Haefliger, Paul, 'Russell Drysdale: A Dialogue, Paul Haefliger', in *Drysdale* (Sydney: Ure Smith, 1960).

Haigh, A. E., *The Attic Theatre*, revised A. W. Pickard-Cambridge (Oxford: Clarendon Press, 1907).

Hair, Graham, *Don Banks, Australian Composer: Eleven Sketches* (2008). Available online: www.n-ism.org/Papers/graham_DB-11.pdf (accessed 4 October 2014).

Hair, Graham, 'Keith Humble's Modernism: From Homogenous Motivic-Thematic Organicism to Heterogenous Gestural Constructivism'. Available online: www.n-ism.org/Papers/graham_Humble.pdf (accessed 4 October 2014).

Hall, Michael, *The Music of David Lumsdaine* (Todmorden: Arc Publications, 2004).
Hammer, Martin, *Bacon and Sutherland: Patterns of Affinity in British Culture of the 1940s* (New Haven: Yale University Press, 2005).
Hanley, Penelope, *Creative Lives: Personal Papers of Australian Writers and Artists* (Canberra: National Library of Australia, 2009).
Hannan, Michael, *Peter Sculthorpe: His Music and Ideas 1929–1979* (St Lucia: University of Queensland Press, 1982).
Hannan, Michael, 'The Music of Peter Sculthorpe: An Analytical Study with Particular Reference to Those Social and Other Cultural Forces Which Have Shaped the Development of an Australian Vision', PhD diss. (The University of Sydney, 1979).
Hannan, Michael, *The Music of Richard Meale* (Kingsgrove: Wildbird Music, 2014).
Hannan, Michael, and Peter Sculthorpe, 'Rites of Passage', *Music Now* 2, no. 2 (1974): 11–19.
Harper-Scott, J. P. E., *Edward Elgar, Modernist* (Cambridge: Cambridge University Press, 2006).
Harper-Scott, J. P. E., *The Quilting Points of Musical Modernism* (Cambridge: Cambridge University Press, 2012).
Harvey, Jonathan, 'Reflection after Composition', *Tempo* 140 (1982): 2–4.
Hayes, Deborah, *Peter Sculthorpe: A Bio-Bibliography* (Westport: Greenwood Press, 1993).
Heile, Björn (ed.), *The Modernist Legacy: Essays on New Music* (Aldershot: Ashgate, 2009).
Hickman, Lorraine, 'Richard Meale: A Profile', *Walkabout*, June (1966): 22–5.
Heile, Björn, '*Weltmusik* and the Globalization of New Music', in Björn Heile (ed.), *The Modernist Legacy: Essays on New Music* (Aldershot: Ashgate, 2009).
Hirst, John, *Looking for Australia: Historical Essays* (Melbourne: Black Inc, 2010).
Hocking, Jenny, *Gough Whitlam: A Moment in History* (Melbourne: The Miegunyah Press, 2008).
Hooper, Michael, 'Don Banks: Hammer Horror and Serial Composition', in James Wierzkicki (ed.), *Double Lives: Film Composers in the Concert Hall* (London: Routledge, 2019), 95–105.
Hooper, Michael, 'Singing Seahorses', *Southerly* 75, no. 1 (2015): 114–32.
Hooper, Michael, *The Music of David Lumsdaine* (Aldershot: Ashgate, 2012).
Hoorn, Jeanette, *Australian Pastoral: The Making of a White Landscape* (Fremantle: Fremantle Press, 2007).
Horne, Donald, *The Lucky Country* (Harmondsworth: Penguin, 1964).
Hughes, Robert, *The Art of Australia* (Ringwood: Penguin Books, 1970; first published 1966).
Huyssen, Andreas, 'The Search for Tradition: Avant-Garde and Postmodernism in the 1970s', *New German Critique* 22, winter (1981): 23–40.
Hyde, Thomas (ed.), *David Matthews: Essays, Tributes and Criticism* (Woodbridge: Plumbago, 2014).
Iddon, Martin, *New Music at Darmstadt* (Cambridge: Cambridge University Press, 2013).
Jack, Adrian, 'Schoenberg and Gerhard', *Music and Musicians* 22, no. 5 (1974): 60–1.
Jameson, Fredric, 'The End of Temporality', *Critical Inquiry* 29, no. 4 (2003): 695–718.
Johnson, Bruce, *The Inaudible Music: Jazz, Gender and Australian Modernity* (Sydney: Currency Press, 2000).
Johnson, Julian, *Mahler's Voices: Expression and Irony in the Songs and Symphonies* (Oxford: Oxford University Press, 2009).
Jones, David, 'The Music of Nigel Butterley', PhD diss. (University of Newcastle, 2005).

Kerry, Gordon, *New Classical Music: Composing Australia* (Sydney: University of New South Wales Press, 2009).
Kim, Minjeong and Angie Y. Chung, 'Consuming Orientalism: Images of Asian/American Women in Multicultural Advertising', *Qualitative Sociology* 28, no. 1 (2005): 67–91.
Kramer, Leonie, 'Review of "The London Magazine" and the *Times Literary Supplement*'s 'Sounding the "Sixties"', *The Bulletin*, 9 October 1965, 54.
Kuspit, Donald, *The Dialectic of Decadence: Between Advance and Decline in Art* (New York: Allworth Press, 2000).
Levertov, Denise, *Relearning the Alphabet* (New York: New Directions Publishing, 1970).
Lopert, Max, 'David Lumsdaine', *Financial Times*, 9 November 1981, 15.
Low, Tim, *Where Song Began: Australia's Birds and How They Changed the World* (Melbourne: Viking, 2014).
Lumsdaine, David, 'Aria for Edward John Eyre: This Is My Myth of the Making of Aria', *David Lumsdaine*. Available online: www.davidlumsdaine.org.uk/pn.php?pfile=Aria_Myth.html (accessed 24 March 2015).
Lumsdaine, David, *Aria for Edward John Eyre* (York: University of York Music Press, 1997).
Lumsdaine, David, 'A Tree Telling of Orpheus', *David Lumsdaine*. Available online: www.davidlumsdaine.org.uk/pn.php?pfile=A_tree_telling_of_Orpheus.html (accessed 14 March 2015).
Lumsdaine, David, The Papers of David Lumsdaine, MS Acc08/98, National Library of Australia.
Mangsen, Sandra, 'Sonata: Baroque', *Grove Music Online*.
Marcuse, Herbert, *Counter Revolution and Revolt* (Boston: Beacon Press, 1972).
Mark, Christopher, *The Music of Roger Smalley* (Aldershot: Ashgate, 2012).
Matthews, David, 'Birdsong and Music', lecture at Gresham College, 2011, *Gresham College*. Available online: www.gresham.ac.uk/lectures-and-events/birdsong-and-music.
Matthews, David, *Landscape into Sound* (St Albans: The Claridge Press, 1992).
Matthews, David, 'Religious Art in the Twenty-First Century', *David Matthews*. Available online: www.david-matthews.co.uk/writings/article.asp?articleid=75 (accessed 5 September 2014).
McCallum, Peter, 'Meale's New Work Needs Weeding Out', *Sydney Morning Herald*, 10 June 2002, 16.
McCaughey, Patrick, *Fred Williams* (Kensington: Bay Books, 1980).
McCredie, Andrew, *Music by Australian Composers: Survey No. 1* (Canberra: Advisory Board, Commonwealth Assistance to Australian Composers, 1969).
McCredie, Andrew, *Musicological Studies in Australia from the Beginning to the Present* (Sydney: Sydney University Press, 1979).
McCredie, Andrew, 'The Preservation of Australian Music', in David Tunley and David Symons (eds), *The Contemporary Australian Composer and Society: Report of Seminar February 24–28, 1971* (University of Western Australia: Department of Music, 1971), 53–68.
McGregor, Craig, David Beal, David Moore and Harry Williamson, *In the Making* (Melbourne: Thomas Nelson, 1969).
McGregor, Gaile, *EcCentric Visions: Re Constructing Australia* (Waterloo: Wilfrid Laurier University Press, 1994).

McLean, Ian, 'Aboriginalism: White Aborigines and Australian Nationalism', *Australian Humanities Review*, May 1998. Available online: www.australianhumanitiesreview.org/archive/Issue-May-1998/mclean.html (accessed 9 July 2015).
McLean, Ian, *White Aborigines: Identity Politics in Australian Art* (Cambridge: Cambridge University Press, 1998).
McNeill, Rhoderick, *The Australian Symphony from Federation to 1960* (Aldershot: Ashgate, 2014).
McPhee, Colin, *Music in Bali: A Study of Form and Instrumental Organization in Balinese Orchestral Music* (New York: Da Capo Press, 1976; first published 1966).
McVeagh, Diana, *Gerald Finzi: His Life and Music* (Woodbridge: The Boydell Press, 2005).
Meale, Richard, *Clouds Now and Then* (Australia: Universal Edition, 1973).
Meale, Richard, *Homage to Garcia Lorca* (London: Boosey & Hawkes, 1966).
Meale, Richard, 'Interview with Andrew Ford', *The Music Show* [Radio broadcast], ABC Radio National, 24 August 2002. Available online: www.abc.net.au/radionational/programs/musicshow/richard-meale/3515648.
Meale, Richard, Liner note, *Australian Compositions* [Audio recording] (Record No. PRX 5585, c. 1975).
Meale, Richard, Liner note, *Nocturnes / Soon It Will Die* [Audio recording] (World Record Club S/5656, c. 1975).
Meale, Richard, Liner note, *Plateau for Wind Quintet* [Audio recording] (EMI Record No. OASD7565, 1972).
Meale, Richard, Papers of Richard Meale, MS 10076, National Library of Australia.
Meale, Richard, 'Richard Meale Extended Interview from 2007', *Meale Not at 80*, ABC Podcast, 30 August 2012 www.abc.net.au/classic/content/2012/08/30/3579339.htm.
Meale, Richard, 'Richard Meale Interviewed by Hazel de Berg in the Hazel de Berg Collection' (National Library of Australia, 1965), Oral TRC 1/174.
Meale, Richard, 'Richard Meale Interview from 1965 on ABC Radio's "Away from It All"', *Meale Not at 80*, ABC Podcast, 30 August 2012.
Meale, Richard, 'Richard Meale Writes about Rimbaud, Australia and His Own Music', *The Listener*, 24 June 1971, 830.
Mellers, Wilfrid, 'Introduction to Sculthorpe's Compositions', *Peter Sculthorpe* www.petersculthorpe.com.au/biography.htm accessed 6 January 2015.
Mellers, Wilfrid, 'The Problem of Busoni', *Music and Letters*, 18, no. 3 (1937): 240.
Mimmocchi, Denise, 'Making Sydney Modern: The Artistic Shaping of the Postwar City', in Deborah Edwards and Denise Mimmocchi (eds), *Sydney Moderns: Art for a New World* (Sydney: Art Gallery NSW, 2013), 66–85.
Mintz, Donald, 'Review of Records: Australian Music', *The Musical Quarterly* 53, no. 4 (1967): 596–603.
Mitchell, Donald, *Cradles of the New: Writings on Music 1951–1991* (London: Faber, 1995).
Mitchell, Rachel E., 'Roberto Gerhard's Serial Procedures and Formal Design in String Quartets Nos. 1 and 2', in Monty Adkins and Michael Russ (eds), *The Roberto Gerhard Companion* (Aldershot: Ashgate, 2013)
Mitchell, Rachel E., '"Sonorous Possibilities" and Formal Continuity in Gerhard's String Quartet No. 2', unpublished paper given in Barcelona at the Second International Roberto Gerhard Conference, Barcelona, 2012.
Mollison, James, *A Singular Vision: The Art of Fred Williams* (Canberra: Australian National Gallery, 1989).

Monelle, Raymond, *The Musical Topic: Hunt, Military, Pastoral* (Bloomington: Indiana University Press, 2006).
Monelle, Raymond, *The Sense of Music* (Princeton: Princeton University Press, 2000).
'More Australian Music Published', *Sydney Morning Herald*, 28 December 1964, 17.
Murdoch, James, *Australia's Contemporary Composers* (Melbourne: Macmillan, 1972).
Murdoch, James, Papers of James Murdoch, MS 8372, National Library of Australia.
Murdoch, James, 'Voyage of Discovery', *Sound*, February (1968): 6–9.
Murphy, Richard John, *Theorizing the Avant-Garde: Modernism, Expressionism, and the Problem of Postmodernity* (Cambridge: Cambridge University Press, 1999).
Nattiez, Jean-Jacques, 'On Reading Boulez', in Nattiez (ed.), *Orientations* (London: Faber & Faber, 1986), 11–30.
Paddison, Max, *Adorno's Aesthetics of Music* (Cambridge: Cambridge University Press, 1997).
Paget, Jonathan, 'Has Sculthorpe Misappropriated Indigenous Melodies?' *Musicology Australia* 35, no. 1 (2013): 86–111.
Peart, Donald, Archives of Donald Peart, University of Sydney.
Peart, Donald (ed.), 'Editorial', *Music Now* 1, no. 1 (1969): 4.
Peart, Donald, 'The Australian Avant-Garde', *Proceedings of the Royal Musical Association* 93, no. 1 (1967).
'Peter Sculthorpe: Obituary', *The Telegraph*, 10 August 2014. Available online: www.telegraph.co.uk/news/obituaries/11024382/Peter-Sculthorpe-obituary.html.
Peterson, John, 'Peter Sculthorpe: A Reflection on His Music and Its Context', *Australian Music Centre*, 19 August 2014. Available online: www.australianmusiccentre.com.au/article/peter-sculthorpe-a-reflection-on-his-music-and-its-context (accessed 24 October 2014).
Peterson, John, *The Music of Peter Sculthorpe* (Kingsgrove: Wildbird Music, 2014).
Pierse, Simon, *Australian Art and Artists in London, 1950–1965: An Antipodean Summer* (Farnham: Ashgate, 2012).
Plush, Vincent, 'Roger Covell: The Go-Between', *Context* 41 (2016): 45–58.
Pople, Anthony, *Berg: Violin Concerto* (Cambridge: Cambridge University Press, 2012).
Porter, Peter, Papers of Peter Porter, MS 6440, National Library of Australia.
Potter, Keith, 'Gerhard's Second String Quartet: On Serial Identity and Identification', in David Atherton (ed.), *The London Sinfonietta: The Complete Instrumental and Chamber Music of Arnold Schoenberg and Roberto Gerhard* (London: Sinfonietta Productions Limited, 1973), 95–7.
Prerauer, Curt, and Prerauer, Marea, Papers of Curt and Marea Prerauer 1930–2006, MS10040, National Library of Australia.
Prerauer, Curt, and Prerauer, Marea, 'Tension to the Last Bar', *The Sun*, 28 July 1965.
Puffett, Derrick, 'The Fugue from Tippett's Second String Quartet', *Music Analysis* 5, nos. 2–3 (1986): 233–64.
Rae, Caroline, 'Beyond Boundaries: Dutilleux's *Foreign Leavening*', *Contemporary Music Review*, 29, no. 5 (2010): 431–45.
Rancière, Jacques, *The Politics of Aesthetics*, trans. Gabriel Rockhill (London: Continuum, 2004).
'Red Landscape', *Russell Drysdale*. Available online: www.abc.net.au/arts/drysdale/paintings/71.htm (accessed 29 June 2015).
Reti, Rudolf, *Tonality, Atonality, Pantonality* (Westport: Greenwood Press, 1958).

Richards, Fiona (ed.), *The Soundscapes of Australia: Music, Place and Spirituality* (Aldershot: Ashgate, 2007).
Riley, Matthew (ed.), *British Music and Modernism, 1895–1960* (Aldershot: Ashgate, 2010).
Rimbaud, Arthur, *Arthur Rimbaud: Collected Poems*, trans. Martin Sorrell (Oxford: Oxford University Press, 2001).
Rimbaud, Arthur, *Collected Poems*, trans. Oliver Bernard (Hammondsworth: Penguin, 1962).
Robbie, Andrew, 'Narrating the Early Music of Ross Edwards', *Resonate Magazine* (2008). Available online: www.australianmusiccentre.com.au/article/narrating-the-early-music-of-ross-edwards (accessed 9 September 2016).
Roberts, Neil, '*Kangaroo* and the Narrative of Contingency', in Keith Cushman and Earl G. Ingersoll (eds), *D.H. Lawrence: New Worlds* (Cranbury: Associated University Presses, 2003), 183–94.
Robin, Joseph David, 'A Philosophy of Change', MMus diss. (University of Melbourne, 1995).
Rogers, Victoria, *The Music of Peggy Glanville-Hicks* (Aldershot: Ashgate, 2009).
Ross, Alan, 'Preface', *Catalogue of an Exhibition of Paintings and Drawings by Russell Drysdale* (London: The Leicester Galleries, 1965).
Rufer, Josef, *Composition with Twelve Notes Related Only to One Another*, trans. Humphrey Searle (London: Barrie & Rockliff, 1954).
Rupprecht, Philip (ed.), *Rethinking Britten* (Oxford: Oxford University Press, 2013).
Rupprecht, Philip, '"Something Slightly Indecent": British Composers, the European Avant-Garde and National Stereotypes in the 1950s', *The Musical Quarterly* 91, nos. 3–4 (2008): 275–326.
Schoenberg, Arnold, *The Musical Idea and the Logic, Technique and Art of Its Presentation* (Indiana University Press, 2006).
Schoenberg, Arnold, *Verklärte Nacht and Pierrot Lunaire* (New York: Dover Publications, 1994).
Schuijer, Michiel, *Analyzing Atonal Music* (Rochester: University of Rochester Press, 2008).
Schultz, Andrew, 'Temporality in the Music of David Lumsdaine', *Studies in Music*, 25 (1991): 95–101.
Scruton, Roger, 'The Emancipation of Consonance', in Thomas Hyde (ed.), *David Matthews: Essays, Tributes and Criticism* (Woodbridge: Plumbago, 2014).
Sculthorpe, Peter, 'David Matthews in Australia – a Memoir', in Thomas Hyde (ed.), *David Matthews: Essays, Tributes and Criticism* (Woodbridge: Plumbago, 2014).
Sculthorpe, Peter, 'Japanese National Commission for Unesco', *Proceedings of the International Round Table on the Relations Between Japanese and Western Arts* (Japanese National Commission for Unesco, 1969).
Sculthorpe, Peter, *Port Essington* (London: Faber Music, 1980).
Sculthorpe, Peter, 'Sculthorpe at 80 … in His Own Words' www.petersculthorpe.com.au/biography.htm accessed 6 January 2015.
Sculthorpe, Peter, 'Sculthorpe on Sculthorpe', *Music Now* 1, no. 1 (1969): 7–13.
Sculthorpe, Peter, *Sun Music: Journeys and Reflections from a Composer's Life* (Sydney: ABC Books, 1999).
Sculthorpe, Peter, The Papers of Peter Sculthorpe, MS 9676, National Library of Australia.

Seabrook, Mike, *Max: The Life and Music of Peter Maxwell Davies* (London: Victor Gollancz, 1994).
Sharman, Jim, *Blood and Tinsel: A Memoir* (Melbourne: The Miegunyah Press, 2008).
Sheppard, Anthony, *Revealing Masks* (Berkeley: University of California Press, 2001).
Silva-Jelly, Natasha, 'Hyped Chains Accused of Dumping Stock Down Under', *Sydney Morning Herald*, 31 March 2013.
Skinner, Graeme, 'Booklet Essay', *The ABC Recordings* [Audio recording] (ABC Classics 481 1293, 2014).
Skinner, Graeme (ed.), 'Debate: That Australian Composers Should Set Out to Develop a Distinctive Australian Music', *The Composer Speaks* (Sydney: Sounds Australian, 1991), 3–16.
Skinner, Graeme (ed.), 'New Music Criticism in Australia', in Skinner (ed.), *The Composer Speaks* (Sydney: Sounds Australian, 1991), 43–56.
Skinner, Graeme, *Peter Sculthorpe: The Making of an Australian Composer* (Sydney: University of New South Wales Press, 2007).
Smalley, Roger, Papers of Roger Smalley, Acc.08.089, National Library of Australia.
Smalley, Roger, 'Portrait of Debussy 8: Debussy and Messiaen', *The Musical Times* 109, no. 1500 (1968): 128–31.
Smith, Ellen, 'Local Moderns: The Jindyworobak Movement and Australian Modernism', *Australian Literary Studies* 27, no. 1 (2012): 1–17.
Smith, Osmond, '*Temps perdu*: Aldo Clementi and the Eclipse of Music as Praxis', in Björn Heile (ed.), *The Modernist Legacy: Essays on New Music* (Aldershot: Ashgate, 2009).
Spearritt, Gordon, 'Musicology in Australia', *Australian Journal of Music Education* 15 (1974): 49–52.
Sproston, Darren, 'Roberto Gerhard: The Serial Symphonist', in Monty Adkins and Michael Russ (eds), *The Roberto Gerhard Companion* (Aldershot: Ashgate, 2013).
Stadlen, Peter, 'Fine Brahms of Sydney Orchestra', *The Daily Telegraph*, 20 September 1965.
Standage, Simon, 'Historical Awareness in Quartet Performance', in Robin Stowell (ed.), *Cambridge Companion to the String Quartet* (Cambridge: Cambridge University Press, 2003), 127–48.
Stapleton, John, *Hunting the Famous* (Blackbutt, New South Wales: A Sense of Place Publishing, 2013).
Stephen, Ann, 'Blackfellows and Modernists', in Mary Ann Gillies, Helen Sword and Steven Yeo (eds), *Pacific Rim Modernisms* (Toronto: University of Toronto Press, 2009), 151–72.
Stockhausen, Karlheinz, *Stockhausen on Music: Lectures and Interviews*, ed. Robin Maconie (London: Marion Boyars, 1989).
Stravinsky, Igor, *Poetics of Music* (Cambridge: Harvard University Press, 1970).
Sturman, J. L., 'The Status and Role of the Australian Composer', in programme booklet, National Conference of Australian Composers, Australian National University, 24–28 September 1973.
Swale, David, 'Nigel Butterley', in Frank Callaway and David Tunley (eds), *Australian Composition in the Twentieth Century* (Melbourne: Oxford University Press, 1978), 203.
Sykes, Jill, 'Sculthorpe at Fifty', *The Sydney Morning Herald*, Saturday, 28 April 1979, 'The Good Weekend', 15.
Symons, David, 'The Jindyworobak Connection in Australian Music, c.1940–1960', *Context: Journal of Music Research* 23, autumn (2002): 33–47.

Tarnawska-Kaczorowska, Krystyna, 'The Musical Work as Sign: Significative Constituents, Layers, Structure', in Eero Tarasti (ed.), *Musical Signification* (Berlin: Walter de Gruyter & Co, 1995), 123–40.
Tymoczko, Dmitri, 'Stravinsky and the Octatonic: A Reconsideration', *Music Theory Spectrum* 24, no. 1 (2002): 68–102.
Van Den Toorn, Pieter, *Music, Politics, and the Academy* (Berkeley: University of California Press, 1995).
Van Den Toorn, Pieter, *Stravinsky and the Russian Period: Sound and Legacy of a Musical Idiom* (Cambridge: Cambridge University Press, 2012).
Van Rhyn, Chris, 'O Hidden Face! – An Analysis and Contextualisation of Priaulx Rainier's *Requiem*', MMus diss. (Stellenbosch University, 2010).
Vaughan Williams, Ursula, *R.V.W.: A Biography of Ralph Vaughan Williams* (Oxford: Oxford Lives, 1968).
Vyner, Michael, 'The London Sinfonietta and Its World Tour', *Tempo* 119 (1976): 16–19.
Walker, David (ed.), 'The Cult of Practicality', *Australian Cultural History* 8 (1989).
Walsh, Stephen, 'First Performances: Richard Meale's *Homage to Garcia Lorca*', *Tempo* 75 Winter (1965/6): 17–20.
Watters-Cowan, Peter, 'Nigel Butterley's String Quartets: Compositional Process from Sketch to Score', PhD diss. (University of New South Wales, 2009).
Webster, Belinda, 'Peter Sculthorpe Interviewed by Belinda Webster in the Esso Performing Arts Collection' (National Library of Australia, 1989), Oral TRC 2466.
Weir, Peter (dir.), *Incredible Floridas: Homage to Arthur Rimbaud* [DVD] (Pyrmont: Film Australia, 2011; first released 1972).
'Welcome Care in Concert Planning', *Sydney Morning Herald*, 26 May 1965, 12.
Werder, Felix, 'Felix Werder Interviewed by Hazel de Berg in the Hazel de Berg Collection' (National Library of Australia, 1969), Oral TRC 1/409–410.
Westwood, Matthew, 'Peter Sculthorpe, Composer of *Kakadu* and *Earth Cry*, Dies, Aged 85', *The Australian*, 8 August 2014.
White, Patrick, *Flaws in the Glass* (London: Vintage, 1998).
White, Patrick, *Riders in the Chariot* (London, Vintage Classics, 1996).
White, Patrick, 'The Prodigal Son', in *Patrick White Speaks* (London: Jonathan Cape Ltd, 1989).
Whitelock, Derek, *Festival! The Story of the Adelaide Festival of Arts* (Adelaide: D. Whitelock, 1980).
Whiteoak, John, 'Interview with Keith Humble', *NMA* 7 (1989): 21–6. Available online: www.rainerlinz.net/NMA/repr/Humble_interview.html (accessed 4 October 2014).
Whittall, Arnold, *Exploring Twentieth-Century Music: Tradition and Innovation* (Cambridge: Cambridge University Press, 2003).
Whittall, Arnold, 'Individualism and Accessibility: The Moderate Mainstream', in Nicholas Cook and Anthony Pople (eds), *Cambridge History of Twentieth Century Music* (Cambridge, UK: Cambridge University Press, 2004), 364–94.
Whittall, Arnold, *Schoenberg Chamber Music* (London: British Broadcasting Corporation, 1972).
Whittall, Arnold, *The Cambridge Introduction to Serialism* (Cambridge: Cambridge University Press, 2008).
Whittall, Arnold, *The Music of Britten and Tippett: Studies in Themes and Techniques* (Cambridge: Cambridge University Press, 1990).

Williams, Fred, 'My Garden, 1965–1967', Art Gallery of NSW (speaking in 1969). Available online: www.artgallery.nsw.gov.au/collection/works/165.1999/ (accessed 19 June 2015).

Williamson, Malcolm, 'How Australian Can Australian Music Become?' *Music Now* 1, no. 4 (1971): 15.

Wood, Elizabeth, 'Richard Meale', in Frank Callaway and David Tunley (eds), *Australian Composition in the Twentieth Century* (Melbourne: Oxford University Press), 1978.

Wood, Tony, 'At Tate Modern', *London Review of Books* 36, no. 16, 21 August 2014.

Woodward, Roger, 'Roger Woodward on Richard Meale' [Radio broadcast], ABC 50th Anniversary Broadcast, recorded London, 3 August 1982.

Yeats, W. B., 'The Symbolism of Poetry', in Richard Finneran and George Bornstein (eds), *The Collected Works of W. B. Yeats: Volume IV* (New York: Scribner, 1900), 113–21.

Zdanowicz, Irena, *Fred Williams: An Australian Vision* (London: British Museum Press, 2003).

Index

ABC *see* Australian Broadcasting Commission
academia *see* scholarship in Australian Music
acclimatization 17–18
Adams, Stephen 158
Adelaide
    Festival 24, 32, 40, 95, 106, 164
    Meale in 67–9, 163–4
Advisory Board funding 25
Ahern, David 34, 124, 182
alienation
    Meale 69, 163
    Sculthorpe 136, 142–3, 147–9
Allans Publishing 44
art *see* Australian art
art music, as a movement 7–8
Asian music
    Japanese musical ideas 153
    Orientalism 160–1
    representation and race 154–7
    in Sculthorpe's music 12, 137, 146–7, 152, 153, 154–7
Australian Composers Advisory Board 19, 25
Australia Council 25, 34–42, 43
Australian, meaning of 11, 28–30
Australian art
    Drysdale 221–4
    landscape painting 146–7, 217–37
    the sun 159, 224
Australian Broadcasting Commission (ABC) 12, 23–4, 42–3, 122–3, 125–6
Australian Contemporary Music Ensemble (ACME) 39–41
Australian Council for the Arts, *see* Australia Council
Australian idiom 20, 133, 150
Australian landscape *see* landscape
Australian Music
    celebratory model 3–6, 239
    emergence of term 18
    Meale 2, 3
    meaning of 1–3, 11, 238
    modernism 7
    nationalism 1, 27–8, 239
    relationship to Britain 6–7, 11–12
    representation 133–4
    Sculthorpe 1–2, 137, 142
Australian Music Centre (AMC) 36–42
Australian nationalism *see* nationalism
Australian Performing Right Association (APRA) 29
Australian self-government 23
avant-garde
    Australian Music 16–17
    Meale 21, 62, 65, 67, 68, 162
    modernism 21

Balinese music 138, 139, 159, 160, 224, 226, 228
Banks, Don
    1970s structural changes 12, 31, 34–42
    Australian idiom 20
    defining Australian Music 238–9
    English/Australian identity 25, 32–3, 41, 207–8
    international/local context 22
    output 42–6
    personal correspondence 60, 61
    programme notes for *Explorations* (Butterley) 124–5
    serialism 46–60
    String Quartet 43–60
Bashō, Matsuo 82
Bauld, Alison 12
Boulez, Pierre 16, 62, 161, 164, 165–73, 178–80, 207
Bourget, Paul 202
Boyd, Anne 12, 75, 82
Brennan, Christopher 126–8
Brett, Philip 160–1

Bright, Ann 82, 84, 90
Britain
    Australian modernism 17
    Butterley's links to 12, 94, 107, 108–9, 121–2
    colonization 19–20
    ecological imperialism 18
    imperialism 161–2
    Meale's comments 67
    modernism 15
    relationship to Australian Music 6–7, 11–12
Britten, Benjamin 95, 96, 108–9, 159–61
the bush 143–7, 148
Butterley, Nigel
    British links 12, 94, 107, 108–9, 121–2
    Explorations 122–5
    Fire in the heavens 125–32
    landscape 123–4
    Laudes 94–107, 108
    modernism 93–4
    serialism 97–106, 110–12
    First String Quartet 107–22
    style and critical reception 93, 98

Callaway, Frank 33
capitalism 15, 16, 20–1, 29, 68–9
Caroll, Mark 16
Carter, David 141, 146–7
celebratory model, Australian Music 3–6
centre/periphery 19, 22, 162, 273
chord multiplication 165–8, 179, 197
Clark, David 109, 120
Clark, T. J. 180
Coburn, John 159
Cole, Hugo 73, 80
Colleran, Bill 38, 43, 44
colonization
    cultural context 19–20
    distancing of Australia and England 121–2
    The Pioneer (McCubbin) 217–21
compositions
    1970s structural changes to support 32, 34–42
    incentives in Australia 44
    musicology 14
    survey of Musical Composition 19
    this volume 8

confidence 5–6, 31–2, 128
contemporary music festivals, 1970s 24
Conyngham, Barry 1–2, 5–6
cosmopolitanism 27, 138, 150
Covell, Roger
    celebratory model 4, 5
    defining Australian Music 18–19, 238–9
    landscape 18
    modernism 17–18
    reading Butterley 98
    reading Meale 63–4, 72, 74–5, 80–1
    reading Sculthorpe 26, 140–3
    world music 2
Crotty, Joel 4–5, 6, 153, 234
cultural context
    colonial history 19–20
    Japanese musical ideas 152–3
    Meale's influences 178, 182–3, 197
    modernity 7
    nationalism 20–1, 27–30
    in Sculthorpe's music 146–7

Dallapiccola, Luigi 45–6, 58, 60
Davies, Peter Maxwell 14, 32, 110, 160, 182
de Maistre, Roy 21
Dean, Brett 2
decadence, in composition 77, 80–1, 202
didjeridus 4, 5
distance
    scholarship in Australian Music 16–22
    Sydney and Perth 1
distinctiveness
    Australian idiom 1, 20, 133, 150
    isolation of Australia 15, 72, 94, 126, 136, 137–8, 141, 147, 154, 155, 224
    scholarship in Australian Music 13, 17–22
    Sculthorpe 141, 162, 237
diversity of music
    Meale 198
    Sculthorpe 138–9, 153
Downes, Stephen 202
Dreyfus, George 16–17
Dreyfus, Kay 6
Drysdale, Russell 147–9, 217, 221–4, 225–6, 233
Dylan, Bob 66

ecological imperialism 18
Edwards, Ross 26, 27, 165, 168, 173, 177–8
electronic music, infrastructure for 36
Ellis, Catherine 13
ethics, Sculthorpe's music 154–7
Europe
    acclimatization 18
    diversity in art 137
    representation and race 156–7
European modernism 15–16

Faber Music 26
Farr, Ian 123, 124
festivals, contemporary music 24
Fires of London 62, 181–2
Flier, Jaap 160
folk song 152
    see also Indigenous music
Friedman, Susan Stanford 22, 161
funding
    1970s structural changes 31, 32, 34–42
    incentives in Australia 44
    scholarship in Australian Music 25–6

gender 7
Gerhard, Roberto 40, 45, 46, 55–6, 58–60
Grimley, Daniel 144
Gyger, Elliott 118–19, 123, 131, 132

Haefliger, Paul 221–3, 225
Hall, Michael 213–15
Hannan, Michael
    reading Meale 62, 162, 199
    reading Sculthorpe 25, 134, 136–40, 151–2, 223, 233
Harper-Scott, J. P. E. 15, 23
Harris, Max 150
Herman, Sali 222
hexachords 47–50, 52–3, 75, 251
hirajoshi scale 152, 153
historical context, scholarship in Australian Music 6, 8–9
Hughes, Robert 122–3, 222–3, 225
Huyssen, Andreas 65

Ic1/Ic5 100, 103–6, 192–7
identity see nationalism; personal identity
imperialism 161–2
indigeneity 149, 151

Indigenous art 147–8
Indigenous music 12–13, 18
    in Sculthorpe's music 149–54
    see also Indigenous music
Indigenous art 147–8
Indigenous music
    landscape 18
    scholarship in Australian Music 12–13
    use by Sculthorpe 149–54
infrastructure for composition 34–42
international context
    modernism 179
    scholarship in Australian Music 22–4
International Society for Contemporary Music (ISCM) 25, 26, 75, 106, 181–2
'inward-looking' music 2–3
isolation of Australia
    distinctiveness 137–8, 141, 147, 224
    in Sculthorpe's music 141, 142–3, 147–9, 154–5

Japan
    hirajoshi scale 152, 153
    influence in Australia's music 153, 161
    influence in Meale's music 82, 88, 161
    Music for Japan (Sculthorpe) 138, 153, 233–7
    Orientalism 160–1
jazz, and modernity 7
Jindyworobak movement 149–51
Johnson, Bruce 7
Jubilee of Australian Federation 122–3

Kennedy, Victor 150
Kerry, Gordon 15–16
Koehne, Graeme 16

Labor election (1972) 31
landscape
    Aria for Edward John Eyre (Lumsdaine) 205–17
    the bush 143–6, 148
    Butterley 123–4
    ecological imperialism 18
    indigeneity 150–2
    isolation, alienation and rejection 141, 142–3, 147–9
    and place 161

in Sculthorpe's music 138–40, 143–7, 158, 224–37
and urban areas 158
landscape music 217–37
landscape painting 146–7, 217–37
lateness 16, 65, 81, 142, 146
Lawrence, D. H. 148, 149
local context, scholarship in Australian Music 22–4
London Sinfonietta 40–1, 43
loneliness, Australian landscape 137–8, 142, 225
Lumsdaine, David
    1970s structural changes 36
    Aria for Edward John Eyre 205–17
    Australian identity 32–3, 41, 207–8
    landscape 144, 205–17, 238
    national awareness 28–30
    in Sydney 134

'magic square' 213–15
Mahler, Gustav 135, 138, 144–5, 150
Malevich, Kazemir 157–8
Martirano, Salvatore 40–1, 43
Mason, Richard 154
    The World of Suzie Wong 154–5
Matthews, David 141, 143–4, 160, 261
McCallum, Peter 27, 63
McCredie, Andrew
    Butterley 121
    cultural context 20, 68
    modernism 22–4
    music journal 13
    Sculthorpe 28, 137, 162
    survey 13, 19, 23, 245
McCubbin, Frederick 217–21, 227, 228
    The Pioneer 217–21
McKinney, Tom 2
Meale, Richard
    Adelaide relocation 67–9, 163–4
    argument with Sculthorpe 154–7
    Australian Music 2, 3
    avant-garde 16–17, 19, 21, 62–3, 65, 67–8
    celebratory model 4
    Cicada 89–92
    Clouds Now and Then 2–3, 82–92
    Coruscations 164–80, 197

    first Australian performances 69
    Homage to Garcia Lorca 70–82, 87
    Incredible Floridas 63, 180–99, 204
    Interiors/Exteriors 91, 163, 180
    Japanese influence 82, 88, 161
    Las Alboradas 74, 106
    modernism 16, 22, 62–3, 179, 180–1, 197–8
    nationalism 27
    output 62–3
    personal correspondence 61
    popular music 65–6, 187–8
    return to tonality 64
    serialism 61–2, 75–7, 91–2, 189–97
    silent period 137, 181, 199, 204
    Sonata for Flute and Piano (1960) 17
    String Quartet 199–204
    style and critical reception 63–70, 77, 81–2, 181
    Viridian 62–3, 65
Mellers, Wilfrid and Peggy 134, 135, 148, 149, 243
modernism
    Australian Music 7
    Butterley 93–4, 121–2, 132
    celebratory model 4, 5
    distance, travel and distinctiveness 17–22
    gender 7
    indigeneity 150
    jazz 7
    Meale 16, 22, 62–3, 179, 180–1, 197–8
    meaning of 15
    progress concept 21
    scholarship in Australian Music 15–17
    Sculthorpe 140
    in Sculthorpe's music 141–2
    as transnational movement 179
Murdoch, James 31–2, 37, 38–9, 181, 182
Music Board
    1970s structural changes 34–42
    funding 25
    incentives in Australia 44
music festivals, 1970s 24
music journals 12–13
Music Now 13–14, 21–2
Musicology Australia 12

musicology in Australia 6–8, 12–15
  see also scholarship in Australian
    Music

national awareness, in Sculthorpe's music
  25–6, 28
national distinctiveness see distinctiveness
nationalism
  Australian Music 1, 27–8, 239
  Butterley 125
  cultural context 20–1
  and the individual 27–30
  international/local context 22
  Jubilee of Australian Federation 122–3
  Sculthorpe 133, 134, 140–1, 237
neoliberalism 4, 16
Nielsen, Carl 144
Nolan, Sidney 147, 222
non-developmental music 224–5

Orientalism 160–1
originality in Australian Music see
    distinctiveness

Paget, Jonathan 149–50, 152, 154, 285–6
Peart, Donald 12, 13–14, 16–17
periphery/centre 19, 22, 162, 273
personal identity
  for composers 32–3
  Meale 67, 72–3
Perth
  Australian Music 1
  contemporary music festival 24
Peterson, John 232, 236
Pierrot Players (Fires of London) 62,
    181–2, 277
pitch matrix 213–15
popular music, Meale 65–6, 187–8
Porter, Peter 205–8
  Tirade 208
progress concept 21
the public, music for 65–6

Raine, Kathleen 120
Rainier, Priaulx 95, 109, 110, 115, 118,
    120, 121
Red Landscape (landscape paintings) 223,
    227

religion
  Butterley 109–10, 121
  in *Laudes* (Butterley) 94–7, 107
representation
  Asian music 154–7
  of Australian Music 133–4
  in Sculthorpe's music 154–63
Roberts, Tom 227
Ross, Alan 222–3

Schoenberg, Arnold
  comparison to Meale 73–4, 80, 81
  serialism 49, 52, 55–8
  using two rows 97–8
scholarship in Australian Music
  contemporary context 8
  distance, travel and distinctiveness
    17–22
  establishment of musicology 12–15
  formation of 11–12
  funding 25–6
  history of 6
  international/local 22–4
  modernism 15–17
  nationalism and the individual 27–30
Schott (publisher) 34, 38–9, 44
Sculthorpe, Peter
  alone 18, 142, 143, 144, 147–8, 225,
    228, 241
  argument with Meale 154–7
  Australian Music 1–2, 137, 142
  as Australia's leading composer 8, 63, 137
  avant-garde 16–17
  British links 12, 143
  celebratory model 4–5
  compositions 2–3
  diversity of music 138–9, 153
  indigeneity 149–54
  Irkanda I 144–5, 146
  Irkanda IV 134–5, 136, 148, 237
  isolation, alienation and rejection 147–9
  and landscape 138–40, 143–7, 158,
    224–37
  Landscape II 230–3
  The Loneliness of Bunjil 137–8, 142
  move to Sydney 26
  Music for Japan 5, 138, 153, 233–7
  national awareness 25–6, 28

nationalism 133, 134, 140–1, 237
and place 161, 238
reading Sculthorpe through Covell 140–3
reading Sculthorpe through Hannan 136–40, 151–2
Red Landscape 157–8, 227, 228–9
representation 154–63
Rites of Passage 158, 159–61, 224–5
The Song of Tailitnama 152, 153, 232
String Quartet no. 8 138, 228
Sun Music 3, 135–6, 138, 159, 161, 224, 228
Searle, Humphrey 81
serialism
  Banks 44, 45–60
  Butterley 97–8, 100–6, 110–12
  Meale 61–2, 75–7, 90–2, 190–6
  modernism 16
  Porter's comments 207, 216
  Schoenberg 49, 52, 55–8
  Sculthorpe 137, 140
  using two rows 97–8
Sheppard, Anthony 160–1
Skinner, Graeme 137, 139–40, 148, 150, 153, 159, 160, 226
Smalley, Roger 1, 161
Smith, Grace Cossington 21
Smith, Ellen 150
Society for the Promotion of New Music (SPNM) 39–41
Stockhausen, Karlheinz 124, 145
Gruppen 145
Stravinsky, Igor 13–14, 129–30
Sturman, J. L. 29
the sun 159
Sutherland, Graham 222–4
Sutherland, Margaret 39
Swale, David 98
Sydney
  Australian Music 1
  intellectual cosmopolitanism 134
Symons, David 151

Taizé community, Burgundy 96
Thompson, Virgil 16
Tippett, Michael 108–9, 109, 115, 116–18
King Priam 109
transnational context, modernism 27, 107, 150, 161, 162, 179, 197, 238
travel
  Australia's relationship with Britain 207–8
  scholarship in Australian Music 17–22
Tunley, David 25, 27

Universal Edition 3–4, 44, 165, 179–80, 199
urban areas 3–4, 21, 134, 158, 218

Vaughan, Henry 107–8, 118–19
Vaughan Williams, Ralph
  Butterley comparison 97, 121, 123
  folk song 152
  'The Turtle Dove' 119–20
Vyner, Michael 44

Walsh, Stephen 70, 77, 80
Walton, William 15, 108
Watson, Peter 224
White, Patrick 158, 208–9, 213, 214, 216
'white Aborigines' 147–8
Whitlam Labor government 31
Whittall, Arnold 117–18, 119
Williams, Fred 217–21, 226–7, 230, 237
Echuca Landscape II 218–21
Williamson, Malcolm 139
'wombats and koalas' 2
Woodward, Roger 62, 165, 172, 179–80
Woolgar, Alan 34
'world music' 2
Wright, Judith 126–8, 131–2

Yeats, W. B. 120, 121

www.ingramcontent.com/pod-product-compliance
Lightning Source LLC
Chambersburg PA
CBHW072123290426
44111CB00012B/1752